SEEKING SAVANNAH

Peter Cookson Smith

SEEKING SAVANNAH

ORO

CONTENTS

PREFACE

The story of Savannah itself is positively intriguing, nurtured by philanthropic and idealist sentiments in eighteenth-century England, which echoed the utopian philosophies inherent in the European Enlightenment. While aspects of the bold original vision were not entirely realized, its design evolution in accordance with the organizational imperatives of the original plan form remains a quite remarkable achievement of exemplary urban design.

Savannah has always evoked a strong and admiring reaction from urbanists and those engaged with city planning. It represents a well-acknowledged and visionary plan, acclaimed for its many interwoven urban values, but it also embodies something else. Hidden within its rich history is a narrative that brings together and reflects the frenetic but frequently contested gestation of American urbanism itself, transformed by historic events that changed the development direction of both city and country. While Savannah remains as a virtual object lesson, open to both change and consolidation, the American city, like the nation, has undergone a colossal transition from ambitious colonial settlement to a twenty-first-century urbanism propelled by occasionally admirable but often troubled notions of opportunism rather than clear planning processes and development control.

This is not the entire story. Savannah was a place of both refuge and expectation on the part of its early settlers. Its antebellum history is cloaked with the atmospherics and historical representation of the South that can be sometimes disquieting, overlaid as it is with the stigma and ramifications of slavery. At the same time the city establishes an authentic and inescapable connection with the past. It is perhaps this elusive combination of circumstances that underscores our emotional engagement with the city and its evolution.

And then of course there is the plan itself: its strong but flexible form; its clear sense of organization and legibility; its embrace of social equity underscored by a clarity of intent; and its spatially coherent public realm, all essential parts of the now familiar "New Urbanism" agenda. We can similarly applaud its robustness in surviving revolution, civil war and natural disasters, leading to periods of decline but ultimate economic and physical resurrection in the later part of the twentieth century.

All of this, I felt was probably quite sufficient to satisfy an initial curiosity and research purpose. However, as exploration deepened and my sphere of discussion with academics and practitioners widened, I began to fathom wider and more connective possibilities. It is, I think, common in most areas of research to arrive at a certain point in our pursuit of knowledge, where we seem to be overwhelmed with questions rather than answers. In my case this seemed to raise several inter-related aspects that suggested equally related lines of enquiry.

First, as the city of Savannah approaches the 300th anniversary of its founding, a rather obvious question presented itself with regard to the historical influences and philosophical drivers behind the planned settlement, and its ingenious template for an articulate organisation of uses, reflective of a "model" society. The plan and resulting spatial form were not just bright ideas – they had to be derived from a potentially wide multiplicity of influences.

Second, I felt a need to bridge the gap between the planning ideology and the elusive crevices of the city that have much to do with indeterminacy, invention, growth and change associated with its context. In addition it seemed plausible to establish a clear link between these factors and much contemporary urban design theory that seeks to emulate the characteristics of traditional townships.

During discussions in Savannah and elsewhere I heard countless expressions of concern as to the state of American cities and the acceleration of urban sprawl, which then opened up a further line of research in seeking to identify the broad auspices under which American cities have charted a course of development, for better or worse, over the best part of two centuries. This initially reflected a largely confident and creative period of city building based on high civic qualities and responsive urban stewardship, which later fuelled the growth of metropolitan economies and the first commuter suburbs. However, in the early part of the twentieth century urban planning was thrown somewhat off course by increasing problems associated with both rapid growth and the accommodation of the automobile. Problems in achieving coherent urban expansion and inner city regeneration were also compounded by the increasing commodification of land coupled with a difficulty in instituting sufficiently strong land use controls. By the turn of the twenty-first century, this together with many other factors has compromised effective planning and led to a decentralised and unfocussed "Exurbia."

This, in effect, sets the scene for the final discussion on how we might best provide for liveable and sustainable urbanism to cater for projected population growth and demographic diversity, coupled with how to reconcile a multitude of challenges in reconfiguring the urban landscape as we head towards megalopolis. The central question here is what can we draw on in order to better control and shape production of the built environment in the face of the fragmented nature of new economic agglomerations and free-wheeling development imperatives. This suggests a shift in planning and urban design emphasis towards coordination and growth management to make capital investment efficient. The planning model must be shaped by what is smart and responsive to the social and economic health of communities. Cities must, in effect, be able to properly expand their boundaries in order to allow for more articulate regional planning, housing, energy, and environmental policies through an enhanced tax base.

This is where we come almost full circle. In reconciling the urban/suburban divide we need to place a greater emphasis on community planning, and pay heed to the form of "healthy" cities, such as Savannah, that regenerate and revitalize even as they preserve and reinforce their underlying attributes. The embryonic New Urbanism must extend to a more integral and cosmopolitan model if it is to redirect not merely its rationalised traditional emphasis on style, but transmit its underlying values to all contributors and participants at the larger scale through an extension of form-based codes. In the process this must resolve the elusive connection between plan form, architecture, neighbour-hood, and community.

And finally, we come to the means to bring all these things together in a respon-sive way, that emphasizes public gain just as it preserves natural resources, minimizes adverse impact and maximizes positive land use interactions. At the heart of what it takes to achieve good urbanism and environmental protection is the controversial issue of constitutional rights and how we resolve and interpret them. We cannot escape the fact that the US planning system is closely aligned with the legal process and the Fifth Amendment to the Constitution that protects the rights of private property owners. We need, in one form or another, to get beyond this level of imprecision and encourage and cater for a synthesis of interests.

My cast of characters who must respond to these challenges and debate their impli-cations, is entirely fictitious, as are their names and personalities, and even a remote resemblance to any person, alive or deceased, should therefore be taken as being entirely coincidental. They adopt certain roles, both informed and occasionally introspective that we can recognise being played out on a regular basis in all manner of meetings, forums, seminars, and conferences on this interrelated subject matter. Locating my gathering of urban commentators in Savannah I felt would help to underscore the experiential char-acteristics of the city in relation to the planning model itself, reinforcing its sense of egal-itarian and aesthetic qualities as well as its versatile dimensions. By and large it is best, as most conference organizers seem to acknowledge, to base such intense discussions in places where the participants can also appreciate liveable environment on a daily basis, and have a good time in the process.

Putting a coherent assembly of words into the mouths of others is not only a means to project different viewpoints other than a personal one, but offers the rather satisfying opportunity for an author to convey a refreshingly alternative view to him or herself under the guise of invented spokespersons. The various presentations, heroically orchestrated by the mythical Professor Maurice Hooguahay, attempt to explain and identify some of the fundamental issues and problems associated with contemporary urbanisation. However they are also intended to articulate some of the creative opportunities available to reshape urban America along genuinely sustainable lines.

The external events, all of them real, that run through the book and occasionally serve as a somewhat fraught background, supposedly take place during a single week in late 2016. These actually occurred over the course of perhaps two months, but I have condensed these in time to form an animated relationship between the suitably introverted world of academic debate and the somewhat more engaging opportunities and impositions of the real world.

The state of contemporary American urbanism, the real subject of the book, is both complex and problematic. Over the course of a century visionary urban design has become confounded by a combination of conflicting federal priorities and lax regulatory structures, together with an ideology that arguably prioritizes individual rights over those of the community at large and the private over the public realm. The built environment now represents a palimpsest of different policies and plans that embody urban ramifications ranging from the sometimes exhilarating to the occasionally uninhabitable. As Professor Hooguahay states in his final comments, the essential aim of our efforts must be to sensibly come up with the means, in short order, to meet the best interests of the community now and in the future.

Peter Cookson Smith

2018

10

OPPOSITE PAGE
The waterfront promenade along River Street serves as a gathering area for visitors, weekend artists, and craftsmen, and forms the mooring point for riverboats.

SAVANNAH AUTUMN 2016: DAY 1

My rendezvous is fixed for the comfortable early evening hour of 6 pm with Dr. Maurice Hooguahay ("call me Mo, and please be punctual"). I have for the past hour been contemplating the view of the Savannah River and the Talmadge Memorial Bridge from a comfortable bench on River Street, and have given myself ample time to proceed to the appointed place via a steep flight of stone stairs to Bay Street.

I turn to the south through a series of shaded squares, marked by Greek and Classical Revival architecture. My crumpled guidebook lets me know that both of these squares were associated with the history of black Savannah: the first accommodated the old Chatham County Courthouse where a slave market was held once a month; the second housed the largest slave yard in town that could hold up to 250 people at a time. This beautiful city has a haunted past. Aspects of loveliness and cruelty so often combine to form magnetic attractions.

We are to meet in Chippewa Square beneath the statue of James Oglethorpe, the erstwhile founder of Savannah in 1733, erected somewhat belatedly in 1910. This noble figure towers over the central part of the square, and is hard to miss as I approach from Bull Street, his domination assisted by a large pedestal on which is carved a portion of the colonial charter. The bronze visage, complete with tricorn hat and full military garb, is staring fixedly to the south to keep a watchful eye open for encroaching Spaniards, which evidently prompted a local wit at the time to suggest that he might have been better placed facing north towards City Hall in order to keep an eye on the politicians.

The Square is crowded, overhung with strands of Spanish moss dripping from the live oaks, and named to honor American soldiers killed in the battle of the same name. It has accumulated a great deal of history over 200 years. Cast-iron railings are adorned with the representations of celebrated statesmen and poets. I read from my guide that the first Baptist Church was constructed in 1833, but the square was seemingly better known as a

14

center of entertainment in the early nineteenth century, through William Jay's Savannah Theater, which formed a focus for touring theatricals, music performances, and evening lectures. In a seeming continuation of the tradition, a young boy with precocious talent is playing a violin.

And here is Mo, scampering across the square with his arms outstretched, graying hair long and combed back, with a flapping and extravagantly checked Brooks Brothers jacket over a yellow sweater, despite the warm sun. Here is a man who exalts in the guise of an aging preppie. He is being shadowed by a somewhat taller lady carrying a sun umbrella at his right shoulder. He stops and pushes up a large pair of orange glasses from his perspiring forehead, revealing a smile of singular intensity.

"I only use these bloody things for reading," he says, trying with one hand to extract his glasses from an obstinate lock of hair, while slapping me on the shoulder with the other, immediately dislodging the name tab I had been instructed to wear. Mo is a man of ideas, wide academic attainment, and extensive research credentials. I had heard him speak at a "green" symposium following his nomination for an American Institute of Architecture award and had read a selection of his many publications on cities. Currently an honorary professor at Columbia and distinguished visitor to innumerable Ivy League places of learning on the basis of his recent book on the Unconditional Urban Condition ... I hope I have this right as it is bound to come up later.

"Welcome, welcome to this gracious town on the Savannah River," he is saying loudly, "now when was it we last met? Yes, 2014 in Hong Kong. This is my wife Martha-Belinda Hooguahay, widely known as Martha B." A lady, perhaps thirty years younger than Mo, steps forward and looks me up and down before cautiously offering a hand and simultaneously raising an eyebrow. She stoops and picks up my name tab, Mo meanwhile recounting that she and he had been married for nine years, and that she had once been his student at Berkeley.

"I find your drawings interesting," she says by way of introduction. "My husband says that architects don't draw anymore, and anyway they have computers to do all that stuff." She puts an accommodating hand on Mo's arm, "and Mo really doesn't have time for it either."

Mo breaks into this discussion, possibly discerning that it might be heading in a questionable direction. "We thought you might like Chinese food, but Martha B. is rather allergic to monosodium glutamate, or whatever they put into it over in China." I notice that Martha B. is nodding determinedly.

En route to supper we walk across West Liberty Street and along Bull Street. Mo talks excitedly as we walk, arms flinging from side to side pointing out the geometry, the greenery, and the statuary. I am becoming increasingly aware that the latter appears to be singularly disposed to American soldiers and military followers killed in battle. As we approach Madison Square the central heroic figure is of Sergeant William Jasper. I read

OPPOSITE PAGE
Statue to Sergeant William Jasper holding the colors of the Second Regiment of South Carolina, where he died in 1889. Designed by Alexander Doyle in 1888, the statue stands in the center of Madison Square.

from the little explanatory sign alongside that he was mortally wounded at the Siege of Savannah by the British in 1779. I note the flinty sideways glance from Martha B. and wonder if, being British, my invitation is a kind of sacrificial retribution, but Mo pulls us forward like children, talking over our heads, "As you know, one of the secrets of a successful public square is the simplicity and consistency of its architectural elements, borne out by one of the earliest Renaissance Squares – the Piazza del Duomo. Leonardo da Vinci even drew up a plan to remodel Florence on a chessboard pattern, and the Baroque plan of Rome was planned along the spine of the Strada Felice, anchored by piazzas. So the Savannah planners had a lot to draw on."

Just at this point we come out of Madison Square and Martha B. Hooguahay who, encouraged by Mo and with an appropriate sense of decorum, I shall address in future simply as Martha B., suddenly brings us to a halt. Now we turn into this little corner restaurant Gryphon, in the shadow of an imposing and ornate temple building of the Scottish Rite Masons whose unspoken rituals go well back in Savannah's history. We enter into a pleasantly paneled and darkened space that Mo informs us has been recently converted from an old apothecary shop, with tables backed onto the remains of ancient medicine cabinets, silently rebuking any tendency to over-indulge.

We are seated in a quiet corner, but Mo is in full flow, his rich voice booming across the tables making it difficult to pinpoint its origins, but somewhere between the West Coast and a faint trace of Eastern Europe. He carries a certain authority, less by an assertion of seniority and more by a confident defiance of anyone who might like to question it.

"This is very special, yes?" says Martha B. "and very atmospheric," waving in the general direction of a waiter hovering near the bar.

"Very," I say guardedly, as tall glasses of Budweiser appear and are distributed around the table.

"So our gathering here, our Seeking Savannah, is not merely some inconsequential seminar where we present our preachy papers, congratulate each other, and disappear," Mo continues.

"I only have your outline program," I say. "Why Savannah in the first place?"

"The attraction of Savannah is its planning history, and of course its various points of past turbulence. In its modern sense it combines city and down-home small-town, as compared to the pattern of urban instability we have to confront elsewhere as we plan for our collective urban future," says Mo.

"Well there is certainly something wired into the Savannah configuration that provides its allure but I haven't quite figured out what it is," I say by way of a rejoinder.

"Do you think this is illusionary?" says Mo, "Or do we try to extract what makes its structure so resilient through its periodic remodeling. Something that provides so readily for a contemporary reconciliation of historical forces and events."

"From what I have seen," I venture, "the city seems to represent more historical reference rather than a revival that might suggest an urban model for the future. Am I being fair?"

"Now we order," says Martha before Mo can reply. "Three large Greek salads please waiter," and turning to me, "Mo and I are strict vegetarians since Mo found from some source or other that if we stopped raising beef cattle and all the required feedstock, we could resume around a billion or so acres of pasture, and save it from sprawl."

Mo smiles benevolently and murmurs. "My wife has an admirable sense of moral purpose, don't you my dear. We eat so much natural foods but we must remember that most people die of natural causes," he laughs.

"I can believe it," I say, pouring quantities of dressing over the fetta cheese.

"Tomorrow we will begin to explore our urban future by referencing Savannah, and we will, I hope, present a mix of urban possibilities."

"And who do we have offering their informed opinions," I ask, rather tentatively.

"You will find out tomorrow morning," says Mo. "In the meantime, Savannah remains an ecological city that still pays silent tribute to its original homesteaders, and yet allows for a contemporary urbanism of buildings and landscape that continues to reflect its underlying and timeless character."

Martha is preoccupied with bottles of vinegar and olive oil. I briefly entertain the clearly taboo subject of a possible side order of a hamburger or two, but catching Mo's eye I prudently reject this purely self-interested train of thought. I embark on another.

ME

This is my first visit to Savannah, and having arrived this morning I attempted to navigate it with a simple map.

MARTHA

Yes its wonderfully easy isn't it, just as long as you know where you're starting from.

ME

This can involve certain problems when it comes to identifying precisely what is where – at least in a Cartesian sense.

MO

I think I know what you mean. The statue of James Oglethorpe, the city's founder, stands not in Oglethorpe Square as one might expect, but in Chippewa Square; the monument to Casimir Pulaski one of the war heroes in our battles with the British (am I imagining a sideways glance from Martha B. again) is not in Pulaski Square but in Monterey Square; the statue to Nathaniel Greene is not in Greene Square but in Johnson Square; and John Wesley's statue is in Reynolds Square while Whitefield Square is named after his evangelical successor.

  ME

I did of course discover that but—

                                      MARTHA

—Yes, we can continue in this vein for some time. You just have to pick it up as you go
along.

                                        MO

Ellis Square is generally referred to as Market Square, Wright Square as Court House
Square, and Madison Square is known locally as Jasper Square after Sergeant William
Jasper, mortally wounded in 1779 defending the city.

                                      MARTHA

It therefore pays not to enquire assistance from normally obliging passers-by, as they are
probably visitors as well and know even less than you do.

                                        MO

Don't worry, I looked this up. In all, twelve squares were constructed in the eighteenth
century, and an additional twelve together with Forsyth Park added in the following century. Three squares are named after Georgia's royal governors, three after famous battles,
four for war heroes, and six for eminent statesmen.

                                      MARTHA

It is only superficially complicated. The system of streets, blocks, and squares works
admirably in practice, once the simple rules are understood.

                                        ME

Well, anyway, it's a pretty easy place to walk around. It's a veritable archetype of a walkable city in a connective sense.

                                      MARTHA

I have carried out my own research on this. There is a deceptively simple organizational
device. Wide sidewalks converge on squares at the center of each ward, and give you
a choice of eight potential directions. They should really translate it into a computer
game – it would be a best seller. We might even have planners playing it at E-Sport
conventions.

18

MO

Actually, it provides a natural traffic calming device where pedestrians are given priority by road vehicles without the necessity of traffic signals.

MARTHA

The simple rule with regard to vehicular perambulation is never make a left turn.

MO

To be fair, drivers seem to have a moral compass built into their satellite navigation systems – cars politely give precedence to horses and carriages, much as steam gives way to sail on the oceans.

ME

Have they tried this in Los Angeles? I can see certain advantages of creating as much discomfort to motorists as possible in that city.

MARTHA

We, that is Mo and myself, choose to cycle of course. That is apart from when we have to drive, or, I should say, when I have to drive Mo's 1998 Mercedes. Mo is an anxiety-challenged passenger.

MO

Well has everyone finished? Let's have our coffee in Poetter Hall just across the road. It's where we will all meet up tomorrow, 9 am sharp.

Martha, who is clearly in charge of group finances, pays, resisting my token protests. She leads us across Bull Street to a well-contoured, red-brick building on the corner on Madison Square. Mo tells me it was constructed as an armory for the Savannah Volunteer Guards and purchased by the Savannah College of Art and Design in 1979.

We move from the lobby to the first floor, furnished with representative artistic outputs from the college and arrive in a glass walled chamber. This houses a large conference table on which stand ten academic looking place settings. In the center is the yet-to-be-assembled PowerPoint apparatus, evidently the detritus of a recent management meeting.

Martha busies herself, distributing plastic wallets, name tags, note-pads, and pencils on all the place settings, ensuring adequate space for iPads, the personal accouterment of the contemporary thinker and doodler. Idly flicking through my plastic wallet I find invitation cards to receptions and vouchers for meals at the cafeteria. In addition, there is a ticket for a carriage tour around historic Savannah, and somewhat surprisingly, a voucher for a practice session on Segways, prior to a more ambiguous tour on foot of Savannah's celebrated ghostly places and celebrated spirits, in what I am alarmed to realize is the second most haunted city in America.

Martha tells me firmly to put everything back where I found it.

Mo reminds me to be punctual on the morrow, and Martha shouts her au revoir from across the room where she is arranging a large pot of bougainvillea.

"One final thing," shouts Mo from the other end of the room. "Don't forget to complete your paper for Seeking Savannah."

I decide to walk back to my guesthouse, thoughtfully and beautifully fitted out by the college, on Whitaker Street fronting Forsyth Park.

I retrace my steps in the lamplight glow of the early evening, across Bull Street, through Monterey Square and enter the park by way of a footpath around the cast iron fountain, where its aggressive-looking and bearded water nymphs blow cascades of water across the circular pool, which my guidebook tells me was installed in 1858.

We are all accommodated, that is to say my future colleagues and I, through the discreet machinations and hallowed friendships of Mo in a fine guesthouse belonging to the college – Magnolia Hall. Our group of participants have been arriving over the last two days although we have not yet formally met. The evident idea is to let us first absorb the atmosphere of the city, wandering at will to ensure that our new familiarity matches our background research and help us get up to date before committing to our presentations.

Our place of stay is normally occupied by visiting alumni and distinguished guests. It was built, I am reliably informed, in 1878 for a descendant of one Thomas Haywood, a South Carolinian who signed the Declaration of Independence. Rooms are meticulously fitted out with antiques, spotless fixtures, stylish fireplaces, ornate mirrors, and polished wood cabinets. All available wall surfaces are occupied by fine artworks from the college, and illuminated by intricate and ancient chandeliers and candelabras. Every coffee table and desk is piled high with books on art and design. On the mantelpiece in the Breakfast Room are set out a host of Royal Worcester porcelain figurines. My bedroom displays a fine painting of a reclining female nude, whether through chance allocation by the house-keeper or the mischievous whiles of Mo I can only speculate.

My mini-suite is on the top floor of the three-story mansion, reached by a wide and ornate staircase. After my crowded apartment in Hong Kong, it abounds with spacious comfort, and admirably soft furnishing from the duvet to the fluffy bathroom towels. Arriving back, I climb the stairs, and, although it is not my normal habit, turn on the CNN news. Barack Obama is saying he is ready to pass the baton to Hilary and holding the latter, who is wearing a tight blue trouser suit, in a tight embrace. Her husband Bill is standing a short distance away, waving to an exuberant crowd. I realize it is approaching termination point at the forthcoming Presidential Election. I switch channels and here

OPPOSITE PAGE
Bronze monument to James Oglethorpe on Chippewa Square, created by Daniel Chester French in 1910. The four lions guarding the base represent the seals of the State of Georgia, the Colony of Georgia, the City of Savannah, and Oglethorpe's coat of arms. The pedestal is carved with a portion of the Georgia Charter. Chippewa Square is named after the 1814 triumph by American forces over the British.

ERECTED BY
THE STATE OF GEORGIA,
THE CITY OF SAVANNAH
AND THE PATRIOTIC
SOCIETIES OF THE STATE
TO THE MEMORY OF
THE GREAT SOLDIER,
EMINENT STATESMAN AND
FAMOUS PHILANTHROPIST

is Donald mouthing less than pleasant comments on "Crooked Hilary" and promising a special relationship with Russia. Back to CNN where Mr. Obama is calling Mr. Trump "a tyrant in the making."

I go to my comfortably spacious bed early and vaguely troubled, but unsure whether this stems from the impending choice in the election or by Mo's parting words.

I drop into an uneasy sleep.

Utopian Intentions and Initial Challenges

24

OPPOSITE PAGE
The Oglethorpe monument faces
south, in order to keep a still
watchful eye open for possible
Spanish invaders.

A MODEL CITY

The new settlement of Savannah was the bold offspring of a rapidly modernizing society in eighteenth-century England. Its discreet beginnings were nurtured in London in the early part of the century by a group of reform minded and well-placed individuals. For Protestant Britain, new colonies in the Carolinas and Georgia were seen as a means to combat the Catholic Spanish and French who controlled much of the territory.

One of the most persuasive of the promoters was James Edward Oglethorpe, an aristocrat and social idealist who was to play such an energetic part in the first expedition and the colony's creation. Initial social and political influences on Oglethorpe were profound but also elusive. His family background embraced a royalist support role in the English Civil War and further patronage under the restored monarchy of Charles II. His father's political influence was strong but suffered a reversal when King James II was overthrown in the "Glorious Revolution" of 1688, the year of Oglethorpe's birth. The succeeding joint monarchy of William of Orange and his wife Mary, the daughter of James II, was to shape future events in 18th-century England, in particular the separation of civil and religious authority. However, it was the reign of Queen Anne, followed by George I that impelled Oglethorpe towards a utopian philosophy of reform, public service, and loyalty to the throne despite a predominantly Jacobite education at Corpus Christi College, Oxford.

Oglethorpe is known to have served in a diplomatic role to several Italian States including Sicily, and in 1714 was appointed Captain Lieutenant in the troop of the Queen's guards where he took part in active engagements against the Turks, and was in command at the Battle of Belgrade in 1717. During this period he acquired extensive knowledge of formalistic Roman settlement planning. Five years later he inherited the family estate at Godalming and secured a seat in Parliament, where he instigated an inquiry into the abysmal state of prison conditions in London, and chaired its committee. In particular he was concerned with the oppression of poor debtors and with political persecution. This was to foster a growing involvement in social reform at a time when vast numbers of people in England were moving from rural areas to cities where most lived in poverty amidst social disintegration and economic polarization.

The vision for the new colony was drafted by Benjamin Martyn in 1732.

"The Trustees intend to relieve such unfortunate persons as cannot subsist here, and establish them in an orderly manner, so as to form a well regulated town ... By such a Colony, many families, who would otherwise starve, will be provided for, and made masters of houses and lands; the people in Great Britain to whom these necessitous families were a burthen, will be relieved; numbers of manufacturers will be here employed, for supplying them with clothes, working tools, and other necessaries; and by giving refuge to the distressed Saltzburgers, and other persecuted Protestants, the power of Britain, as

a reward for its hospitality, will be encreased by the addition of so many religious and industrious subjects.

"The Colony of Georgia lying about the same latitude with part of China, Persia, Palestine, and the Madeiras, it is highly probable that when hereafter it shall be well-peopled and rightly cultivated, England may be supplied from thence with raw Silk, Wine, Oil, Dyes, Drugs, and many other materials for manufactures, which she is obliged to purchase from Southern countries ...

"All human affairs are so subject to chance, that there is no answering for events; yet from reason and the nature of things, it may be concluded, that the riches and also the number of the inhabitants in Great Britain will be increased, by importing at a cheap rate from this new Colony, the materials requisite for carrying on in Britain several manufactures. For our Manufacturers will be encouraged to marry and multiply ... and also many people will find employment here ..."

The charter for the colony of Georgia was signed by George II on April 21, 1732. Trustees were appointed for a period of twenty-one years and were granted powers to "prepare laws, statutes and ordinances" – the staple ingredients of effective planning. Colonists were to have "liberty and freedom of religion," which enabled a predominantly secular form of administration, although this caused some degree of disquiet among the well intentioned but pragmatic body which included the 4th Earl of Shaftsbury.

Clauses were inserted in the charter restraining all trustees from receiving any gain whatsoever from this undertaking. A seal was adopted for the authentication of official papers with two faces: one for legislative acts and commissions represented by the rivers of Savannah and Alalamaha; and one by a representation of silk-worms, indicating an underlying aim of the project to produce raw silk in the projected new settlement.

In order to promote this enterprise, the Trustees gave public notice that they were ready to receive applications from those who were disposed to emigrate, and also appointed a committee to visit prisons and make a list of insolvent debtors who might be discharged if they were willing to emigrate. To defray costs, they donated money themselves and solicited other contributions from Parliament and the Bank of England. It was stated that having been given assistance of passage, land, and necessary tools, "the fruits of every man's industry are to be his own. Every man who transports himself thither is to enjoy all the privileges of a free-born subject."

The group of advocates sold the idea so well that a screening committee had to be set up to review applications from among enthusiastic volunteers in London, which mainly included poor laborers and artisans. Their resettlement at the financial behest of wealthy trustees to a remote and isolated frontier was a far-reaching undertaking that was to evolve from an illusion of utopia to one of crisis and social ordering based on different sets of actors.

The name Savannah was derived from a Native American tribe who traded with

English merchant settlers in Charlestown.[1] In 1680 a trading post was built on the Carolina side of what was re-christened the Savannah River, which served as a busy entrepôt, primarily for trading with Charles Town, South Carolina, which shipped both goods and Native American slaves from other neighboring settlements.

The party of 114 emigrants, which included carpenters and bricklayers, sailed from Depford, England on the Ship Ann on the 16th of November 1732 accompanied by Oglethorpe, several Trustees, and a clergyman. The King's pilot assisted their arrival in Charlestown on 13th January 1733 and they proceeded with a naval escort to Tench's Island and thereafter to Beaufort at the mouth of the Coosawhatchie River. Oglethorpe, together with Colonel William Bull, who was sent to assist the new arrivals by the Governor of the Province, then continued up river and selected a new settlement site near Yamacraw where the remainder of the group arrived on the 1st of February. Oglethorpe, in a letter, describes the River as forming a half-moon with banks forty feet high but with a flat "bluff," that was close to the mouth of the River, and was sufficiently large to contain land for future villages and farms in addition to fortifications. Helpers were sent from South Carolina to assist with clearance of trees, to make enclosures, and build defenses.

The would-be colonists arrived only sixteen years after the end of the so-called Yamasee War – a conflict between early settlers in South Carolina, after the Cherokee tribe joined the colonists to defeat the Yamasee, Creek, Choctaw, and Catawba tribes that had been displaced from their lands. This had been the most serious challenge to European dominance in colonial America, and contributed to the formation of new Native American nations.

The early settlers nurtured an admirable commitment to the New World but with somewhat pre-industrial motives. These had to be met by a rapid adaptation to almost primeval conditions, and first entailed the creation of a new township, carved out of a prominent forty-foot-high plateau, originally covered with dense forests and surrounded by a threatening wilderness. It was fed by a river flowing from the west and across several hundred miles of coastal plain and swamps to the Atlantic Ocean, with an estuary divided by small islands and numerous channels. Georgia itself was crossed by three great rivers, namely the Altamaha, the Ogechee and the Savannah.

Walter J. Fraser describes a landscape of capillaries lined with dense groves of myrtle, cyprus, maple, gum trees, aquatic shrubs, and giant pine that towered above the thickets and marsh grasses. The hills were covered with oaks and hickory, wild walnuts, cedar, and the laurel tulip. Yamacraw Bluff, the last piece of high ground before the Savannah River joined the sea, was covered by pines and chosen as a site for a new defensible settlement perhaps because it reinforced the illusion of impregnability. This arguably ignored the legitimate territorial claims of its resident community of Yamacraw Natives, forged out

---

1   At the time of the early settlement the capital of South Carolina was written as Charles Town although after 1783 it became spelled as Charleston.

of two groups of Creek and Yamasee by its chief, Tomochichi, who offered protection from the menacing Spanish in the south. This in fact added to the multicultural mix, the complexity of use, and perhaps to the grand aspirations of the new settlers. One commentator in 1735 referred to the site in biblical terms as "a promised land," but in fact Savannah relates to a pre-modern era – the creation of something out of nothing.

Occupation and Consolidation

The occupation was demarcated virtually immediately in the form of four tents, but within a week Oglethorpe with the help of a surveyor, had marked out a two-dimensional simulacrum of wards, streets, and squares. However, this was a detached and separate world, which invited constant mix and change relating to the organization and immediate needs of an embryo community, supported by Charlestown but isolated from more universal relationships. The area covered some 24 square miles, and its carefully regulated planning was laid out by Oglethorpe and William Bull from Charlestown in the form of rectangular "wards," each of which housed forty lots in four blocks called "tithings," and containing five cottage lots – twenty to the north of each square and twenty to the south.

On the 7th of July 1733, all settlers gathered together for a ceremony to designate town wards and assign lots, helping to inject the spatial foundation of the remote Colony. Each household was issued with a Bible and a Book of Common Prayer, accompanied by a standard issue cooking pot.

Savannah's lot allocation was firmly controlled, with each settler receiving a one-acre town lot, a garden lot of five acres, and a country lot of forty-five acres. The City of Faith that characterized early Savannah was laid out with mathematical regularity along with building elements that gradually became more complex – for example the first public building, the courthouse, also served as a church. The new settlement was made entirely of wood to a uniform construction, built initially by skilled builders from Charlestown. This facilitated a unification of east-west street patterns along with the squares themselves. Settlers were required to ensure that all structures around the main public squares were uniform in relation to the overall urban design. Four "trust lots" were established for public uses in a geometric relationship to each of the central squares, and these played a significant role in establishing the long-term architectural landmark identity of the wards, some later becoming churches, museums, and government buildings, while others fell out of use.

The plan was in many ways intended to reflect the ideals of agrarian equality. Garden lots formed an outer layer of uses, with larger forty-five acre farmland plots on the outer fringe. Gardens were intended to provide food and to enable the instruction of new immigrant families in agricultural techniques. The ten-acre "Trustees' Garden" was the first public agricultural experimental garden in America, established within one month after the first arrivals. Botanists were sent by the Trustees to the West Indies and South America to procure plants, including vine cuttings, hemp, flax, olives, and medicinal herbs.

Silk Production

It was intended by the Trustees that a silk culture to compete with China, France, and Italy would form an economic focus for the new colony. Since the early part of the seventeenth century Virginia had made efforts to produce silk as an alternative to tobacco, and the coronation robe of Charles II in 1660 was made of silk from the Colony. In 1703 the silk culture was introduced into South Carolina.

By the early eighteenth century, England was importing a vast amount of silk from China and the Continent, and it was considered that there would be savings made from introducing its manufacture in a Colony where mulberry trees could grow in abundance, and where labor from new settlers would be both beneficial and cost-effective. Therefore, among the group of first arrivals in Savannah was a expert on silk-winding from Piedmont, engaged by the Trustees to introduce silk manufacture. Together with several Italian assistants, they planted white mulberry trees in agricultural land to the east of the city. Oglethorpe took some of the first samples of raw silk to England, which was later made into a court dress for Queen Caroline. The silkworm is, in effect, the larva of the moth Bombyx mori and to prevent the release of destructive enzymes, the harvesting of silk thread requires that the cocoons be sacrificed before this can be extracted – a painstaking process that might have reverberated with the relatively short and fitful lives of the early settlers themselves in an unaccustomed subtropical climate. While the silk was excellent in quality, it became increasingly unprofitable to produce in competition with other staple commodities such as rice and cotton.

Urban Organization

Oglethorpe's military experience, undoubtedly contributed to both the organizational and defensive elements of the plan. These were based on an equitable allocation of land, and the integration of physical and strategic protective devices, taking into account the need for cultivation, surveillance, and defense. Clear growth boundaries were established. The designated Village District beyond the large area allocated to farms, made up an outer defensive fringe, where militias could be formed, while the Town and Commons provided a protected refuge in the event of invasion. Villages within the planned grid were named after those on the outer edge of London, such as Hampstead, Acton, and Highgate. Other villages further afield were generally established either for strategic purposes or for their resources. Larger manors and estates were granted to self-supporting colonists who met the Trustee's requirements for production or cultivation activities, with many of these later converted into cotton plantations.

The first public squares of around one acre were given dimensions not dissimilar to those in London at the time, and were later planted with native tree species – a feature which was to distinguish the settlement throughout its future growth. Squares and streets were named after prominent Carolinians who had assisted the colonists. The first completed streets were Bull, Drayton, and Whitaker running north to south, with St.

Julian and Bryan Streets running east to west. North-south streets alternated in width, with the wider streets bisecting the wards and narrower ones representing the east and west boundaries. This created an easily replicable model, not necessarily unique to Savannah, but one which facilitated its remarkable character. Wards became regulated enclaves, named after Trustees of the charter which created the Colony: Derby Ward for the Earl of Derby; Percival Ward for Lord Viscount Percival, first President of the Trustees; Decker Ward for Sir Mathew Decker, governor of the East India Company; and Heathcote Ward for George Heathcote. Lower and Upper New Wards together with two new squares were added the following year.

Derby Ward was the first to be laid out around Johnson Square named after the Royal Governor of South Carolina, Robert Johnson, who had given great assistance to the first settlers. The other squares laid out in 1733 are now known as Wright, Ellis, and Telfair, followed by Reynolds Square in 1734.

On the 11th of March 1734, a group of 37 Protestant families from Salzburg who had suffered from persecution in Bavaria arrived in Savannah under the care of Baron von Reck, together with various pastors. Oglethorpe had earlier proposed to the Trustees that they should be given asylum. The Salzburgers later explored sites along the river and established a new community called Ebenezer, from which they relocated two years later to a site near the mouth of the river, New Ebenezer, with a plan very similar to that of Savannah itself. A monument carved from the green stone of Austria was sent to Savannah from Salzburg in 1996 to commemorate the early settlement.

In early 1734 Oglethorpe, together with a companion group set out explore the southern frontier area and sea islands of Ossabaw, St. Catherine, and Sapelo, together with the Vernon and Altamaha rivers. As a result of this visit it was decided to build a fort on St. Simons Island and a new military station at the mouth of the Altamaha River.

Within a year, ships from London disembarked increasing numbers of colonists under the trusteeship, mainly artisans and laborers, who were each granted fifty acres of land. Two hundred and twenty emigrants on two ships, led by Oglethorpe and at the expense of the Trustees, left for Savannah from Gravesend in 1735. The group included missionaries, Episcopalians, Lutherans, Moravians, and Methodists, and after a rough passage they arrived in Savannah on February 5, 1736. Many of the new Colonists were transported to St. Simons Island, and, directed by Oglethorpe, they began to erect simple cabins. Other ships brought Irish Protestants from Ulster, Scots from the Scottish Lowlands, Sephardic and Ashkenazi Jews from various parts of Europe, and Lutherans from Salzburg, possibly reflecting Georgia's charter, which encouraged a "liberty of conscience in the worship of God." However, the charter still managed to exclude Catholics, reflecting the prevailing sentiment in England at that time.

At this stage, around 200 houses had been built and trees planted alongside the streets and public squares. One of Oglethorpe's pet projects was a large market garden, intended to supply the settlers with fresh vegetables and as a nursery for fruit trees, olives, tropical and medicinal plants, together with white mulberry trees for the raising of silk worms.

A series of military installations were constructed around the settlement as a buffer against Spanish incursions from Florida, who with the French were desperate to counteract English expansion. The first defensive structures were Fort Argyle on the Ogeechee River, and other structures on Skidaway and Tybee Islands, and many of the new settlers were directed to these early military posts. The towns of Darien and Federica were established on the Altamaha River, with the latter becoming the site for a new fort to defend the southern frontier against the Spanish. Roads were constructed as rights-of-way to connect Savannah with Fort Argyle and Ebenezer, while the southern border area was linked to Savannah by road and waterway.

The town of Augusta was laid out, upriver from Savannah, by Roger Lacy. One of the first roads within the coastal area linked the two settlements, complementing the system of flatboats and sloops that traded along the Savannah River and the local waterways, establishing trading itineraries in skins and furs with Native American territories.

Relationship with the Native American Nation

The same year, Oglethorpe resumed his plans to visit England along with Tomochichi and his relatives who had established friendly relations with the English settlers, as well as five chiefs of the Creek Nation. They arrived on the 16th of June 1734 to wide acclaim, with Oglethorpe widely lauded for his patriotism and for sharing in "the fatigues and dangers" of the undertaking.

While in London the Native American chiefs were housed in the Georgia office. They were introduced to the King and Royal Family at Kensington Palace, were later entertained by the Archbishop of Canterbury, and visited Hampton Court, St. George's Chapel at Windsor, and Eton College. At their audience in the palace the King stated:

"I am glad of this opportunity of assuring you of my regard for the people from whom you came; and I am extremely well pleased with the assurance which you have brought me from them. I accept, very gratefully, this present, as an indication of their good dispositions towards me and my people; and shall always be ready to show them marks of favor, and purposes to promote their welfare."

Oglethorpe remained in England for a while to resolve further issues with regard to the settlement of Georgia, and was promised financial support for the defense of Savannah. He also assisted the preparation of a statute entitled "An act for rendering the Province of Georgia more defensible, by prohibiting the importation of black slaves." This was, at least in part, because the Trustees were insistent that the settlers should themselves be responsible for labor and personal application. However, although well intended this was to prove insufficient to counter the often self-indulgent nature of colonial development.

In the meantime Oglethorpe made preparations to help the Native nations in their request to speak the English language and receive instruction in the Christian religion,

32

A statue of John Wesley stands
in Reynold's Square.

overseeing the preparation of a book on "the ways of religion and civil government." It must be said that the relationship between Oglethorpe and the Native Americans was the exception rather than the rule. The first wave of settlers in Carolina traded and bartered with Natives for fur and animal hides, but there was little opportunity for this in Georgia. The Native communities did little farming but preserved the woods and prairies for a continual supply of animals and foul, while land around the new settlements was valuable for agriculture. Oglethorpe and Tomochichi had from the very beginning, evolved a mutual friendship, perhaps from their respective good nature, frugality and love of the outdoors. In a later account of Georgia, Oglethorpe recalled the generous nature of the Yamacraw, where the land or "homestead" belonged to the women together with what was grown on it, while the men hunted for buffalo, deer, wild turkeys and other game. The healthy lifestyle was sustained by many kinds of fruits, nuts, potatoes, pumpkins, and onions, while honey was obtained from combs in the hollow trees.

Disputes later arose between Georgia and South Carolina over boundaries relating to the regulation of trading rights with the Creek, Cherokee, Chickasaw, and Catawba Natives. Georgia's new laws on the prohibition of slavery and importation of alcohol, approved by the Trustees in 1835, also came into conflict with South Carolina merchants. This had to be resolved through a Committee of the General Assembly of South Carolina to the satisfaction of the local tribal nations, but also raised questions concerning the nature of guarantees that could be granted to native communities who had never owed any allegiance to the crown and had also traded with the French and Spanish.

Elsewhere in the American colonies a coexistence between both groups, above and beyond trading ties, was tense. Massacres were carried out by both sides that left a legacy of perpetual distrust but in the final event, in a similar way to the outcome of the Spanish invasion of South America, it was the infectious diseases the settlers brought with them rather than the destruction they wrought that was ultimately a cruel deciding factor. Settlers from across the world carried with them contagious germs such as smallpox, to which Native Americans had no immunity. It is estimated that the two million indigenous inhabitants of the United States in 1500 had been reduced to around fifteen percent of this figure by the beginning of the nineteenth century.

Religious Sentiments

Oglethorpe was accompanied on his return from England by two brothers, John and Charles Wesley. John Wesley was an Oxford educated Anglican clergyman, ordained as a priest in 1728. With his brother Charles, he founded the gentle evangelical Methodist movement as a breakaway from the Moravian Church. It would not be stretching a point to suggest that the experience of the brothers in accompanying James Oglethorpe to the embryo Savannah colony fanned their own philosophical ideal of self-improvement and accountability. This involved a lifetime of outreach based on religious instruction, pastoral care, and personal

34

OPPOSITE PAGE
Wesley Monumental United
Methodist Church on Calhoun
Square completed in 1890
containing busts of John and
Charles Wesley.

salvation. Methodists were possibly the first humanists, grounded in a tradition of sacramental theology but establishing practical outlets in social reform that necessitated a devout outlook tempered by a practical application of Christian ideas. One of these was to bring relief to jailed debtors, something that clearly struck a chord with Oglethorpe.

Oglethorpe had himself prevailed upon the thirty-two-year-old John Wesley to be minister of the new colony in part to replace Samuel Quincy, an Anglican minister who had been recalled by the Trustees for performing an "intermarriage" that was not permitted. In all likelihood the two years that Wesley spent in the settlement, itself based on a spiritual Christian ideology and self-sufficiency, re-directed Wesley's own religious direction away from the ancient ritual of the Church of England, which he chose to uphold to members of the Anglican community in Savannah.

While John Wesley was technically appointed by the Trustees as Minister at Savannah, Wesley himself claimed that his main work was as a missionary to the Native Americans who had opened the door to conversion through teaching and evidence of the true doctrine of Christianity. In discussions, Wesley had some initial difficulty in putting across the abstract concept of a "god who sits in heaven," in the face of Tomochichi's understandable difficulty in differentiating between different Christian belief systems and his observation of occasionally questionable Christian conduct at Savannah. However, it must be allowed that proper interpretation services were largely unavailable. Wesley continued to preach to the wider community, but reportedly gave sermons that were over-zealous, ignoring advice that with a more prudent respect for the unusual circumstances of the new settlers he should "become all things to all men, that he might save some." Primarily for these reasons the people of Savannah became disaffected with him, and he with them.

He was not assisted in his endeavors by a reputed attraction to a pupil, the step-niece of the Chief Magistrate, who was less than enchanted with Wesley and married another settler. Wesley prudently left for Charles Town and from there embarked to England in December 1737. However, a singular accomplishment of his consequent devotions before his return and a much-lauded life as a Methodist preacher in fields, halls, and chapels, was a publication of a collection of psalms and hymns partly written with his brother Charles – the first to be published in America.

While Wesley had been ordained as an Anglican priest, his deeply rooted social work among the needy that formed that spiritual basis of the Methodist doctrine, led him into occasional conflict with Church of England clergy. All this, however, was in the future, and Savannah simply remained as a rudimentary foundation to a lifetime of preaching through an amalgam of meetings and societies that later extended to frequent and ever larger gatherings. He would have likely been nonplussed at the worldwide number of around forty million Methodists some 200 years later. Twenty colleges in the US, starting with Wesleyan University in Connecticut, have been named after him.

Wesley was replaced first by William Norris who enjoyed an equally cool reception,

and then by George Whitefield, a travelling preacher, whose long-term achievement was to open a school for girls. The Trustees presented him with the living of Savannah, and granted him land to erect the Bethesda Orphanage that was run by Whitefield's colleague, James Habersham who was to have a long political association with the city including a role as acting governor in 1771.

The First Artistic Representation of Installations

Paul Fourdrinier's famous engraving of 1734 looking from the north across the Savannah River suggests an idealist representation of place and repetition, but also something else – the suggestion of a defensive structure staked out as a military cantonment, reflecting potential hostility from the quietly lurking Spanish and hostile Native tribes. Most of all, it records a conceptual relationship of ordered parts within an area defined by clearly articulated boundaries, and with a form that dematerializes into the surrounding landscape.

The date of March 29, 1734 on the engraving marked Oglethorpe's departure from Savannah. The engraving was carried out, at least partially, to satisfy the philanthropic aspirations and curiosity of the Trustees of the Colony, just one year after the city's foundation. This surprisingly detailed prospect was produced in London by Fourdrinier with material compiled by Peter Gordon, the First Bailiff of Savannah, during Oglethorpe's return visit to England – hence its stylized topographical and romantic overtones. Oglethorpe's tent can be seen to the left of the trees in the foreground, perhaps alluding to the preeminence of his organizational and military credentials. The view shows the chosen site for the yet unbuilt church, the public stores, mill, and the "house for strangers," built on a trustee lot, which served as a short-term shelter for new immigrants and passers-by. Bull Street formed the main north-south processional avenue through the central core of the town, which grew by incremental uniform stages according to the meticulously ordered modular framework.

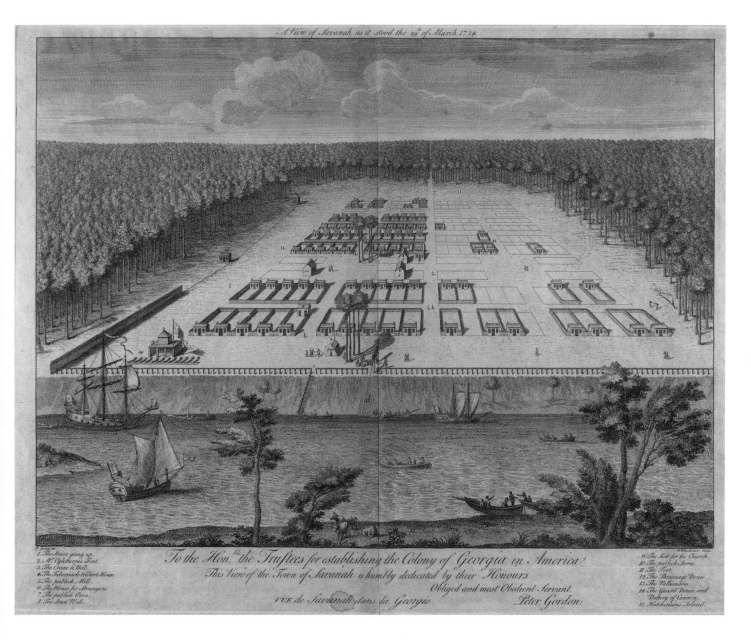

A View of Savanah as it stood the 29.th of March. 1734.

To the Hon.ble the Trustees for establishing the Colony of Georgia in America

This View of the Town of Savanah is humbly dedicated by their Honours

Obliged and most Obedient Servant.

VÜE de Savanah dans la Georgie.

Peter Gordon.

1. The Stairs going up.
2. M.r Oglethorpes Tent.
3. The Crane & Bell.
4. The Tabernacle & Court House.
5. The publick Mill.
6. The House for Strangers.
7. The publick Oven.
8. The draw Well.

9. The Sett for the Church.
10. The publick Stores.
11. The Fort.
12. The Parsonage House.
13. The Pallisadoes.
14. The Guard House and Battery of Cannon.
15. Hutchinsons Island.

37

A graphic view of Savannah
on March 29, 1734, by Peter
Gordon showing the town in its
environmental context. The
printer was P Fourdrinier.

Poetter Hall on Bull Street,
adjacent to Madison Square. It
was constructed in 1892, and
designed by William Gibbons
Preston as an armory, drill hall,
and guard club for the Savannah
Volunteer Guards, and used as a
social center for troops during
World War II. The building was
purchased and renovated by the
Savannah College of Art and
Design in 1979 as its flagship
administrative building.

SAVANNAH AUTUMN 2016: DAY 2

My travel alarm goes off at 7am, twenty seconds before the scheduled morning call. Where I have come from, Hong Kong, which is almost precisely on the other side of the world, we are exactly twelve hours in advance so no need to set clocks. The day over there is just closing and the evening news, such as it is, just commencing. My head feels dull – perhaps the beer, or maybe the salad. I plug in the neat little water heater and pour coffee powder from a small packet into a large cup. Shower, shave, and engage with the first serious decision of the day – what does one wear at this sort of impending assembly?

The dilemma is at least partly resolved by the limited capacity of my small suitcase. I generally travel light with a bright orange wheelie, which fits snugly into aircraft overhead compartments and facilitates a speedy exit from airports. It holds precisely four shirts, two jackets, newly pressed slacks, denims, socks, the usual knick-knacks, and a tie. Now whether to wear it? I think yes, then no, then yes again. I catch sight of collarless shirt on a hanger, which settles it. Scroll down messages on iPad, some calling for cursory responses, others for instant deletes.

I enter the drawing room, or breakfast room as it becomes in the morning, for coffee and remarkably good croissants, and spy a good looking lady in a tight pink skirt and long legs. She is studiously engaged with a copy of the *Wall Street Journal*, silently discouraging any frivolous attempt at an introduction. I leave Magnolia Hall by way of the terrace, and retrace my route across Forsyth Park, clutching a shoulder bag of papers and an assortment of things it is prudent to hand carry – my phone in case of emergencies, a far from complete draft of my supposed presentation, a guide to the city, and copies of correspondence with Mo, which only vaguely set out the envisaged procedures scheduled to extend over the best part of a week.

Through Monterey Square and along Bull Street. A positive tumult of people having to hastily avoid what must be the first meandering horse and carriage of the day, already full of pointing visitors with angled cameras. Students everywhere looking much too young, some with lycra backpacks, checkered shirts and jeans, and a few baseball jackets. Some of the males are huge bodied in bright sports shirts encrypted with logos of basketball or football teams representing visages of fearsome looking animals – wolves, rams, bulls, and other tribal references. The girls are resplendent in a rather wider repertoire of styles, with a distinct and rather fetching preponderance for shorts and flat sandals.

I see Mo and Martha B. in the distance heading doggedly to the entrance of Poetter Hall, the latter sporting a bright red jacket, and looking overburdened with heavy looking cardboard boxes of what might contain ominous amounts of reference material. Mo is in the same clothes as yesterday, although I note the red shoelaces have changed to a startling yellow. He looks preoccupied but waves across the crowded heads, and I follow him and Martha B., retracing our steps from yesterday, up to our first floor retreat.

Various relieved looking bodies begin to detach themselves from the crowd before a large handwritten sign that Martha is attaching to the wall outside the conference area. SEEKING SAVANNAH, it says, which seems at the same time adequately condensed and nicely ambiguous.

Mo seems reluctant to make introductions, but people are already picking up name cards and busily staring at the lapels of others, murmuring niceties, proffering hand-shakes, and emitting loud sounds of recognition. I walk around the table and encounter Miles Styles. A dark trimmed beard, somewhat follically challenged, with heavy eyebrows. He offers a jovial good morning, noting that he is from London like myself long ago, and is, he explains, a non-practicing and rather academic urban analyst specializing in the European City.

Apolonia Karawice of Polish ancestry with flaming red hair is seemingly out of the same class as Martha B. at Berkeley, large and thirty-fiveish with a Ph.D. obtained over five years. She seems fetchingly at home in academic circles, teaches urban history and theory at Cornell, and is wonderfully turned out in a purple kaftan.

And thank goodness the first All American, Daniel Schlomo in designer jeans, a base-ball cap, and black woollen t-shirt, on which is emblazoned a large white exclamation mark with something I cannot quite make out underneath, although it looks vaguely confrontational. He is an Assistant Professor of Urban Post-Modernism at UCLA but orig-inally from New York, and soaked in barely restrained adrenalin. Mo had evidently heard him talk for two hours at some conference in Colorado on Dialectic Materialism and the City as the celebrated author of several abbreviated publications around the challenging theme of deconstruction.

Brit Kris, a blonde American with Danish ancestry is wearing a braided pigtail and a quilted blue jacket ornamented with provocative slogans on badges associated with various unaligned movements. Originally from Copenhagen, which she tells me she left at the age of seventeen, she now runs a cooperative in Boston called "We Own the Streets,"

Mix of commercial and café uses
emphasize the historic role of
Bull Street as a historically
important public thoroughfare.

although I note later she has taught a course at MIT on Women and Protest. She has already struck up a friendly conversation with one Agnita van der Kampen, the preoccupied lady from breakfast, who is evidently attached to Wellesley College, Yale. She is flamboyantly sheathed in the same impossibly tight, pink two-piece suit I was destined to notice previously, and is evidently an academic authority on the role of artificial intelligence in geographic information systems.

Only two more late-comers now. Terry Fulbright from the University of Cardiff on a five-year exchange with Penn State University, looking slightly faded and defibrillated, having, he tells me, arrived at 4:30 am due to a delayed flight from London. "I'm actually on a Fulbright Scholarship," he says, "which is of course coincidental although it helps if people think you have relatives in high places." He further informs me, somewhat tentatively but immodestly, that he is one of the most quoted reference sources on suburbanization and its relationship with the diminishing availability of land supply.

And finally there is Jean-Paul Gournier, slim and coffee colored and with a face that suggests an exhausting schedule. He is in his fifties, clad discreetly in Armani, and senior partner in a successful New York architecture and urban design practice, which, as he whispers to me confidentially, occasionally employs Mo as a consultant. "I think one of my ancient ancestors was a plantation slave somewhere in these parts," he says, "and I'm not sure if my paternal great great grandfather wasn't the plantation owner."

"A miscellaneous but interesting assembly of the good, gracious, and potentially mischievous," I murmur to Schlomo who is looking thoughtfully across the table at Brit who is in turn looking thoughtfully at Jean-Paul, all presumably having come under the encircling embrace of Mo at some stage.

"You bet," he says, "but what are we doing here?" I had a computer failure that wiped out the entire program so I'm not sure what exactly we are seeking. "Fortunately the air ticket came courtesy of DHL."

"You have no idea?" says Apolonia Karawice who has crept up on us.

"I don't think its anything to do with geographic information systems," says Agnita van der Kampen.

Coffee is being served by an attractive girl in a black dress, and Martha is signaling us to sit down.

Mo, who has been toying with a plastic coffee cup, stands up.

He takes a deep breath and hands out photocopies headed SEEKING SAVANNAH in large print.

"Good morning everyone," he begins. "May I welcome you all to this lovely city? I selected the venue carefully. I hope you had a good night's sleep and have all obediently done your homework." He laughs to himself. "If you have not, then no matter." You will have your opportunity. You are all foot soldiers."

This draws a number of disconcerted glances around the table.

"Now we must start. We are here in part to discuss Savannah as a unique piece of urbanism. We will discuss how and why this intricately planned city came about. We will deconstruct the plan, that is verbally rather than literally." He laughs again. "I hope we will make a brave attempt at deciphering not only how America has reached the current point in its urban evolution but why, and what we can perhaps do about it as urban thinkers. Our cities and metropolitan areas are the future. If suburbia really represents the new metropolitan frontier then how can it be reshaped and consolidated in a responsive way. We have reached a stage when even our 'New Urbanism' turns back to the traditional small town for its inspiration. But of course in America we like our tradition to come with all the modern trappings and conveniences. So I am now going to kickstart our deliberations."

OPPOSITE PAGE
Savannah City Hall on the site of the old City Exchange built in 1799. The new City Hall was completed in 1906 as the fourth and final building in a sequence of civic constructions on the site.

PREAMBLE
PROFESSOR MAURICE REGINALD HOOGUAHAY

In the early twenty-first century, the make-up of cities is changing along with our evolving conceptions of territory. Much urban space has become residual following the disappearance or abandonment of what we deem to be obsolete. We have a grim residue of suburban sprawl, but cities are nothing if not resilient. They spring back into some form of shape, and transform themselves into new cityscapes although not necessarily with the same components. Smart City technology and new modes of mobility will most likely influence our approach to urban planning.

We are constantly subjected to more rather than less planning knowledge – most of it eminently sensible although some might be less than necessary. It is available everywhere and we are condemned to interpret this according to our own critical, perceptual, and even emotional priorities. This is why we are gathered here in Savannah: to examine the city as a means of understanding our heritage and nurturing our existence, and, perhaps, to enable us to point a finger towards the future. Eighteenth-century society, which marked the social idealism behind the colony of Savannah, was associated with an enlightened but restrictive political economy, ideological sentiment, and Romanticism, but we are now contemplating the city from almost 300 years of hindsight.

I'm not sure if there is any neat and tidy representation of urbanism anymore. We must of course respectfully acknowledge our fellow observers of the city who ably chronicle the ever-evolving urban situation, but who often cloak their analysis in an opaque way, perhaps being restrained by their own subjectivity. Critical analysis now seems submerged, or maybe a better term is "overloaded" with the outer limits of linguistic excess, so that we verbalize our problems and key issues rather than resolve them. We seem to have appropriated a complex new urbanistic vocabulary that often takes us into the realm of philosophy, clouding what we once considered transparent. As the splendid Joel Garreau, who enlightened us about the looming Edge Cities commented, our planning experts often tend to mistake incomprehensibility for profundity. So, from our participants here, we must expect some plain speaking.

(A ripple of suppressed amusement at this, with several participants looking somewhat reproachful.)

Paradoxically, some of our most prominent world cities are regaining their sometime former role as centers of contrast and culture, serendipity and stimulation. People are moving towards rather than away from metropolitan areas, which are being gradually absorbed within megapolitan conurbations. However, commuters are just as likely to travel daily from the city to employment on the urban edge or even beyond, rather than the other way around, although more suburbanites now work in the suburbs than the cities. And the city in an abstract sense continues to become an increasingly complex and multi-layered configuration, capable of self-organization and the promulgation of new life-worlds. This is important because material changes are challenging our post-industrial concept of the city and what it represents beyond the physical – the wider ethnicity, the exogenous entrails of new infrastructure, and a continuing social reconstitution of urban places.

This brings regional strategy into the picture, either in relation to an entirely new situation or as part of a city expansion program. While any such exercise requires clear objectives that reflect the ideas and aspirations of key stakeholders, we can in the process say goodbye to the central planner who imposes strategies from on high. Cities are much too complicated for that, and there are too many dimensions.

Plans and urban management are essential, but they need to establish a satisfactory equilibrium between fixed and flexible elements. The former must relate to the main armatures – the organizing elements of connectivity, transport, and infrastructure that establish an underlying functional order to the numerous city quarters that offer a wide range of design interpretations, each forming its own points of identity. This in no way needs to represent a deliberate collage of independent components but, instead, an organized framework that liberally interprets codes based on strict zoning, and accommodates different architectural interpretations geared to variety, diversity, and autonomy. This level of indeterminacy and complexity is largely dependent on the prerequisites for a form of planning that encourages new formats and juxtapositions but not predominant ones.

We must differentiate between the real and the simply aesthetic, the city as something fixed, but open to challenge and debate so that we can readily understand the dimensions of social reality and make it intelligible through all its processes of ordering and disordering. But we can also observe a simultaneous redefinition of urban territory – for example, the landmark rehabilitation of Savannah's Victorian District, its first street car suburb, the slumlord abandonment, and modestly gentrified resurrection. This is not a nostalgic nod of the head to an urban imaginary, but a reconstitution of the neglected—and something more—a model for affordable housing in historic districts that contains the drift to suburbia and a shift away from the notion of preservation as being an elitist process.

We have to beware of ideological standpoints – more often than not they are less than symmetrical, and somewhat incomplete in their hypothesis. We must keep a watchful eye on what might be hidden or repressed. The authentic interpretation of our cities only emerges through our understanding of many fragmented narratives – ethnicity, gender, demographic differences, the exploiters and the exploited, the conquerors and the conquered, and the successes and the tragedies. What is pertinent is not necessarily

Gibbon's Block - a nineteenth-
century building on West Congress
Street, adjacent to Ellis Square
which originally faced the old
central market.

the precise reality of the city, which is impossible to decipher accurately, but is rather how this seeps its way into a truthful representation. This is somewhat removed from the formal historical process, but rather reflects the allegorical picture which emerges through an interpretive dialogue such as this. I suppose it might be said to combine mediation, contemplation, and speculation.

Through our discussion we hope to discover an accumulation of left-over traces, references, and associations that add up to a fairly good reconstruction of our urban sense – the more vigorous and extensive the process, the nearer we get to authenticity. Our analysis and questioning always remain open, and so they should be. Savannah is a wonderful case study, firstly because it had a determined start point, and secondly, its development and social history is well documented. It is anchored in overlapping realms of instability reflected in social, cultural, and economic transitions, together with prolonged periods of political turmoil and revolution.

Savannah exalts rather than erases the past. It offers a duality of places laden with the baggage of past events, and sites of imagination seeking an equation with history. Its comfortable regularity, mellowed by time, challenges us to find differences and complexities, and we will, in all probability, discover that the city has multiple interpretations and artful realities. Its stately and contemporary representation of historical architectural materialism and tumultuous events might put one in mind of Jean Baudrillard's notion of the simulacrum – "an impression of an original that may never have actually existed." But there is also the practical sense in seeking the hidden reality through gaining insight of what lies behind the empirical setting. In Savannah, the experience of place, composition, and appearance are dominant elements in our perception even though past references have become eroded by time, obscuring the boundaries between the real and the imaginary. Savannah, of course, contrasts with its post-modern counterpart, which seeks a more immediate and controlled relationship with time and space, and yet it eerily displays, at a city level, virtually all the attributes set out in the Charter of the New Urbanism.

The established spatial composition induces a regularized pattern of "joined together" streets and squares, based on an articulate configuration of space, and maintained by a consistent scale of street sections and building edges. These represent a variable range of residential types that create the visual character and "weight" of building fabric. Setbacks and other threshold elements determine the more specific building interface with the street. This combination of vernacular tradition and regulatory tool has been succinctly described by Spiro Kostof as "the genetic code for urbanity" that shapes the urban framework but allows architects and builders to work within it with comparative freedom. A cognitive sense of rhythm tends to synthesize and organize disparate patterns into unifying sequences, thereby emphasizing patterns of correspondence but where there is also the sensory stimuli of both familiarity and novelty.

And we are enchanted by this city as both territorialized hyperreality and as a virtual

48

Much of the built fabric within the Historic Area embodies social and cultural importance as well as heritage significance. This allows cumulative benefits to accrue in terms of added asset values and the advantages associated with a vibrant and congenial visitor economy.

utopian plan form, somehow symbolic of our image of the Old South, charmed into a collective memory at a time when the Google version of cyberspace is recalibrating the way we look at ordinary space: dematerializing our established views of urban topographies, and recasting these around a more hallucinatory interpretation. The Savannah Square is a space of representation that impacts on memory, experience, and use. It speaks a language of both history and immediacy, shaping the substance and identity of the city while projecting a museum-like sequence of lived-in rooms.

Is Savannah caught in a time warp? Or put another way, is the confrontation between Old Savannah and the requirements of the modern city too abrupt, or can the two comfortably coexist and interact in a contemporary alliance? Certainly the plan remains to reinforce its cultural identity, but its postmodern success must reflect its democratic social and economic workings, including its historical references. The contemporary city must accommodate the requirements of a great variety of special interest groups. A diverse mix of users suggests a necessary degree of interaction and improvisation, which creates its own pluralist dynamic. This in turn requires participation by communities in neighborhood planning and decision making. It also implies a realigned role for the urban designer who must work with, rather than on behalf of a public clientele, customizing the process through advocacy. There is no longer any such thing as the celestial city or divine order.

50

We might start by posing several questions. Is the Savannah streetscape illusionary in its reassuring personification of a bridge between urban and suburban, as a pictorial and utopian assemblage? Is the image detached too far from its pioneering and ideological origins or does the city actually function in a not dissimilar way to the fabricated constructions of New Urbanism? Perhaps the answer is that constant recalibration and refinement has created a city with multiple possibilities of circulation, permeability, and representation. The regularity of streets and lanes establish a connective hierarchical pattern reflected in the rhythm of lots and the clear definition of frontages. This facilitates easy and directional pedestrian movement, but at the same time acts to slow down traffic to the extent that horses and carriages along streets and around squares are given an informal priority by motorists.

The necessary accommodation of change has been fundamental to the survival of Savannah, at least in a habitable sense. It has been subject to a long process of regeneration precisely to facilitate its building and environmental attractions, that has stimulated and provoked an energizing response from visitors. The combination of enclaves in the form of wards, and the shifting balance between them, has facilitated different architectural interpretations within a flexible but controlled framework of street blocks, and in the process provides an eminently adaptable mechanism for later conversion and connection. This reflects a civic consciousness that still evokes the discipline of the original plan, which astonishingly held together and consolidated into more or less its present coherent form during intermittent periods of growth, interspersed with disasters that ranged from disease, fire and revolution.

Urban management must be allied with the post-industrial city prerogatives in order to facilitate its livability. But is it only the application of regulatory or design codes and procedures that stabilizes a city's natural tendency towards messy disorganization? Anything more than this takes on a catalytic role, that is to say the transition of one urban state to another. There can be no optimum size or condition since the city is subject to perpetual change and economic shifts, now more than ever. This is something we see in the emerging global city, wired and gloriously technified for spirited competition in the information age, but unable to maintain and manage itself without human intervention.

The city is a forceful framework of different interests and trajectories, and a fragile container of aspirations. The three-dimensional spatial model can only arouse a sense of belonging and ownership through a fourth dimension – that of time. But intervention needs to tread a steady path. Contestation is a natural outcome of the intersections between competing systems, conflicting motives, and single-minded decision-making. The result can be an exultant entanglement of interactions, or a faltering descent into chaos.

It is generally acknowledged that cities have become increasingly difficult to manage, precisely because the ramification of the service economy has come to represent collections of relatively autonomous and frequently competing systems. As a result, urban

Tree planting between vehicular
streets and the townhouse terrace
creates an informal "green"
edge that visually frames the
private residential realm while
demarcating the public footpath.

design discourse tends to reflect a preoccupation with form rather than substance. It is a vanity of post-modernists to consider it possible to actually design an entire working city from scratch in the twenty-first century, mistaking the elegant language of architecture for the complex reality of urban operations. In many cities the prevailing silos of city policy and responsibility do not necessarily provide for the single-minded resolution of specific urban problems as much as a means of reconciliation to iron out the missteps and contradictions. There is therefore a natural tendency towards physical conformity and sameness.

So co-ordination calls for something more than mere urban management – it requires sensitive regulation, control of flows, and the installation of necessary safeguards. And top-down organizational structures need to be met through bottom-up participation by multiple local communities that shore up the livability agenda, reconcile multi-functional elements within enclaves, and influence the continuous process of sustainable revitalization. This includes the rehabilitation and adaptive reuse of functionally redundant older structures that add to the mix of heterogeneous neighborhoods within the city rather than subscribing to their eradication.

At the same time we must not mire cities in a cultural vacuum. A new urbanism must respond to a reinvigorated approach to community and sense of place, allowing for innovation, recycling and spontaneity. It must extend the notion of physical design to rejuvenating and redefining the city by preserving differences between places rather than obliterating them. I should remind you that the term "place-making" was in fact first used by the renowned English landscape architect Capability Brown as a form of creative horticultural engineering.

Savannah has bequeathed to us stunning built concoctions, but also a unique underlying organizational structure. Most of the narrative models were entirely rational for their time and signified a necessary response to patterns of trade, defense, and spiritual faith, tempered only by a need to accommodate a lot of people with their untidy habits, that quickly came to animate the urban stage and compete for attention. No one up to the 16th century thought of cities as urban models, but every city evolves its networks – social, economic, and cultural – so that parts coalesce, integrate, or subside giving rise to the poetics of creative space that now provide us with irreplaceable historic references.

The Savannah Plan of 1733 was composed of identifiable urban enclaves from the outset in the form of distinctive neighborhoods quarters while adjusting its primary armatures to best serve its evolving needs. While city wards have emerged and mutated during the course of growth and development, they continue to act as centering devices in relation to the evolving city structure. The present city is therefore made up of enduring elements that shaped the original settlement form, denoting an intrinsic respect for historical circumstance, heritage, and memory as distinguishing characteristics, set within the larger entity. The gridded and cellular nature of the plan provides a flexible and

Mix of mansion blocks on Oglethorpe Avenue synthesizing an underlying order from a variety of individual terraced buildings. Pattern recognition represents a means of detecting and synthesizing an underlying order from disconnected or fragmented forms so that urban design becomes responsive to the urban grain. On the right is the old house of Conrad Aiken, appointed Poet Laureate of Georgia in 1973.

additive framework whereby new wards gradually came into being while some have been transformed through special function and architectural manipulation. However, this has not fragmented the city – it has instead produced coordinated areas of special identity and the existence of distinguishing features situated within defined but generally permeable boundaries. This is best encapsulated in the historic preservation area where cultural heritage has been pristinely packaged and gentrified for visitor consumption, which establishes the type of symbolic image spaces that we associate with Savannah.

Under the Savannah Plan, the streets were essentially organizing rather than scenographic elements, albeit as containers for specific activities. The layout of avenues which initially took the form of unconstructed alignments accommodated the mobility of people on foot, wheeled horse-driven vehicles, and draft-animals but was easily adapted to accommodate the new age of motorized vehicles. An increased value of land as a result of this, opened up by continued planning initiatives, facilitated what we now appreciate as the Historic District's consistent pattern of architectural regularity. The present city armatures have a key role in establishing physical relationships within the city, acting to define movement channels, integrate public transport routes, and thereby accommodate a sequence of uses and spatial experiences, reflecting a need to reconcile private investment with public interest. As main connective devices they provide sets of formal, informal, experiential, or ceremonial characteristics that maximize their robustness in relation to the public realm, tying together a linked series of buildings, spaces, and other features within a coordinated design form, which establishes a direct relationship with its organizational capacity.

The axial arrangement of streets within the grid network, and the inherent capacity of these to develop into ordered sequences of different elements, create a framework for certain alignments to take on the characteristics of main streets. These became elongated according to stages of city growth and intensification of uses, reinforcing their public roles as both coordinators of disparate commercial, institutional, and cultural functions, and as signature elements. The image of the "main" street, as opposed to the more refined discipline of the square, is therefore one of mixed use, amenity, consumption, and competitive display - opposite but complementary.

The innate character of Historic Savannah can partly be attributed to the provisions made in the plan for accommodation of different building forms associated with squares and streets. Public buildings positioned on Trust blocks enjoy the most prominent sites, and this allows a singular form of expression that gives identity to the central spaces. These have traditionally facilitated forms of architectural expression that serve as prominent gateways on important corner sites, whilst ensuring consistency of building bulk, massing, height, and site coverage. Detached buildings are permitted if lots front onto east-west streets, providing that the lot is at least fifty feet in width with a garden fronting the square. Within Tything blocks, any type of dwelling is allowed, provided that design standards relating to height, massing, and street elevation are met.

The grid is logically made up of primary and secondary streets, working within the contours of the city and its occasional dynamic height differentials such as that between Bay Street and River Street. The one-way system assists flows of traffic to and from the downtown area and supports the overall connective structure, while certain alignments embody a transition between one-way and two-way traffic. This also preserves the sanctity of the squares themselves where traffic is not allowed to pass directly through. Axial service corridors form singular commercial armatures, linked back into the wider street grid and representing a dense and structured sequence of uses and flows.

The plan was both re-affirmed and reinvigorated in the late 1950s as a tight matrix of humanely scaled spaces that almost accidentally re-kindled a fond image of the Antebellum South and to a large extent its retained sense of historical grandeur rather than the more confounding association with segregation. It nevertheless brings with it the occasional but muted hints of friction, as Savannah in common with most rapidly urbanizing conurbations, stands in some danger of social and economic polarization, elevating job growth towards a professional technocracy on one level, contrasted with an underclass of low-paid service industry workers on the other.

According to the well-established city development narrative for Savannah, we can observe the early development profile, gradually growing in scale, density, and

54

The Telfair Academy of Arts and Sciences, designed by William Jay in 1819 for Alexander Telfair. It was later modified, and opened as a public museum in 1886. The building was declared a National Historic Landmark in 1986 and now forms part of a downtown arts complex that includes the Owens-Thomas Houses and the Jepson Center. The sculpted figures of Phidias, Michelangelo, Raphael, Rubens, and Rembrandt were reproduced by the Viennese sculptor V Tilgner in 1884.

organizational complexity. Between stable phases of growth and development are transitional phases that can set new or redirected courses of urbanization that brought with them more complicated systems of organization. Wards began to adapt and even compete in terms of their individual advantages, and in response to evolving technological, transport, and infrastructural changes, with a shifting relationship between the main urban elements. The transitional therefore becomes the transformational, as urban space becomes increasingly more intensified through use and appropriation.

Now I would like to talk specifically about preservation.

There are four different local historic districts in Savannah with different regulations and design standards that apply to each. These are the Historic District, the Victorian District, the Mid-City District, and the Cuyler-Brownsville District.

The preservation of Savannah's fragile fabric in the face of a long period of deterioration arguably goes back to 1875 when Mary Telfair bequeathed her mansion, designed by William Jay in 1819, to the Georgia Historical Society. Preservation was taken up again as a determined cause in 1934, after the demolition of several magnificent 19th-century houses. The recording of important buildings in the city was carried out under the auspices of the Historic American Buildings Survey, and was followed in 1935 by the establishment of the Savannah Commission for the Preservation of Landmarks. This led directly to the restoration and adaptive reuse of certain historical buildings, constructed in gray brick around

56

Delicate iron tracery and railings mark the double Rogers House designed by John Norris in 1858 on Monterey Square.

the older wooden structures. By this time the city of Charleston in the neighboring State of South Carolina had already passed America's first historic zoning laws and was reaping the tourist benefits of its architectural heritage preservation program.

In 1955 a Savannah Metropolitan Planning Commission was established, partly to meet the intentions of the 1954 Housing Act. The latter was beginning to have an enormous impact on American cities through large-scale urban redevelopment of overcrowded residential neighborhoods deemed to be "blighted," mainly reflecting their low-income residents rather than their actual building condition. In many cities the direction of comprehensive planning was deliberately transformative in its approach and ill-considered in its intention. In practice, federal assistance actually accelerated social and economic decay. Fortunately for Savannah, the potential ramifications of the Housing Act were considerably diluted through the efforts of the Historic Savannah Foundation – a turnaround that is sometimes referred to as the "Savannah Renaissance."

The Foundation was established in 1955 following the demolition of Savannah's City Market—an iconic and irreplaceable structure that had stood in Ellis Square since 1888—to make way for a parking structure. Savannah was in many ways ahead of its time in

The language of the urban square reflects both sensory and symbolic values, so that the community as well as the setting itself make a mutual contribution to place making, framed within the spirit and culture of the city.

reacting to the potential physical implications of wholesale redevelopment, and steering an altogether different course. The Foundation introduced a number of nationally recognized experts in historic preservation and inaugurated an annual citywide celebration of its founding. The successful initial tactic was not only to promote the importance of preservation but to persuade individuals to save threatened buildings. Funds were raised to purchase those that were under threat, and then held for purchase at a small markup by new owners who undertook to carry out restoration work. Preservation covenants were attached to all the deeds of sale to protect against future alterations.

The frequency of fires in the early nineteenth century created a need to turn from wood to brick construction, sometimes overlaid with stucco. Bricks, termed "Savannah grays," made partly from river sand, were of a beautiful appearance and texture, so that demolition companies a century later could sell the bricks for a considerable profit, thereby exacerbating destruction of older properties. Saving these therefore represented a good deal of negotiation, but marked a turning point in public understanding and appreciation of the historic environment and the fact that this was an underpriced and largely unrealized resource.

The Federal Historic Building Act was passed in 1966 and introduced guidelines for the preservation of buildings in designated historic districts. Equally important, a listing facilitated tax benefits to assist the process, which led directly to greater public concern for conservation. To avoid undue displacement of tenants through gentrification, preservation was broadly accompanied by affordable housing programs and assistance with self-help projects.

The largest restoration project in Savannah was undertaken for the area around Pulaski Square in 1965. A number of irreplaceable public buildings and mansions situated on the trust lots associated with the squares were also saved by the Foundation. As a result of some of the early restoration work in 1966, the US Department of the Interior designated the 2.2 square-mile Historic Area as America's largest historic district. The enabling legislation came in 1972 through Savannah's first historic zoning ordinance.

The introduction of tax credits for preservation led to 21,000 historic buildings being rehabilitated or converted through adaptive reuse. Many have been protected through the transfer of development rights to adjacent buildings. This has not only benefitted the process of urban revitalization, but has raised the value of properties and encourages heritage visitation to historic areas, boosting the local economy. In some cases this is extended to heritage corridors and trails that "trace the footprints of history" such as the Antebellum Trail in Georgia.

The Tricentennial Plan Assessment Report for Chatham County informs us that ninety-two percent of historic resources in the City of Savannah are residential structures, and the older housing stock provides both opportunities and advantages for rehabilitation in terms of maximizing use of the prevailing services and infrastructure. Also listing on the National Register of Historic Places qualifies older housing stock for grants and tax incentive programs. The Georgia Historic Preservation Act of 1980 provides minimum standards and guidelines for local preservation ordinances, and in addition the Certified Local Government Program facilitates eligibility for federal preservation grants and technical assistance.

Design and construction guidelines for development within the Historic District were approved by the City Council in 1997 as a local ordinance. In effect this has not only made demolition of existing buildings difficult, but it has led to the establishment of standards for repair and renovation in keeping with the wider historic character. As a positive byproduct it has also generated vigilance on the part of the local community.

Residential types vary but there are primarily four types: detached houses on a lot with a maximum width of forty feet; detached with a width greater than forty feet; row houses with party walls; and apartment blocks from three to eight stories, some of which date from the early twentieth century.

In order to maintain the unified spatial characteristics of the Historic District, different setback limits are set out. Most parts of the district permit a seventy-five percent site

Timber-frame houses in the
Victorian District create
an eclectic but distinctive
assortment of architectural
elements.

coverage for residential and 100 percent for commercial development to facilitate street containment. Residential buildings are commonly built up to the lot line, but a common characteristic is the protruding entrance stair that extends into the public right-of-way. Its design articulation animates the visual character of streets and squares, and establishes a consistent and tight relationship between the public and private realms.

Additions to historic buildings in order to accommodate changing needs are allowed but within tight control. Any additions are restricted to the most inconspicuous side of the building. They must be situated so as to emphasize the building's evolutionary character, but must be clearly distinguishable from the existing structure. Decorative details are in some cases integral to the overall design, in particular cast iron railings, downspouts, and corner quoining.

Exterior materials help to define both the overall character of the district, but also that of individual wards. Residential structures are typically of brick and stucco in the newer wards, and wood cladding in the older areas, in order to preserve the city's architectural and urban design integrity. Original windows are preserved wherever possible to reflect the design intent, and louvered shutters, which originally provided privacy and security to street buildings are still retained, partly to facilitate ventilation but also to allow for historical design continuity.

New residential developments are subject to mandatory covenants, governing what can be built within the community and acting to protect it from any future development that might have an adverse impact on its character. Neighborhoods with a historic zoning must allow for local design reviews of any alterations and new construction to ensure they meet established neighborhood design criteria. In 1990 the City entered into a Programmatic Agreement with the State Historic Preservation Office and the Advisory Council on Historic Preservation to conduct reviews for compliance with the Secretary of Interior's standards. This has enabled the City to assist in the rehabilitation of many affordable housing units.

The Historic District maintains a number of building forms comprising detached and semi-detached buildings and terraces that embody a degree of façade consistency. These forms contribute to the overall integrity and legibility of the cityscape, with a range of architectural styles that add a high level of design diversity. The Design Manual for the Historic District prepared by the Chatham County – Savannah Metropolitan Planning Commission cross-relates to the Historic Review Board. The Manual takes the stance that the city should be open to different architectural and urban design interpretations within the framework that has been set, and applies standards that are adopted by the Mayor and Aldermen as part of the Zoning Ordinance. It provides the entire development community with a full understanding of all design aspects so that both historical and contemporary buildings are addressed in the same way, with a consistent use of materials, compositional principles and use of architectural elements in the Savannah tradition. The Ordinance sets out procedures for granting variances providing that these comply with spatial and visual compatibility factors.

The regeneration process must contend with both expansion and inclusion. Under Savannah's Tricentennial Plan, further development in the Historic Landmark District is restricted, so that urban expansion requires planning parameters to be established in order to ensure an explicit continuity of streets, spaces, and places. Community Development Block Grants are managed by the city, and are intended to pro-actively address the problems of blight, in particular "brownfield sites which represent both vacant or underutilized sites, which occur to the east and west of downtown Savannah, and "grayfield" sites, which represent outer ring underperforming commercial developments surrounded by vacant parking areas.

So we come back to our gathering here. Under each subject area—and by the way these are all related, one to the other—the unruly logic of our deliberations can perhaps help unravel our collective view of contemporary urbanism within a combined narrative that extracts meaning and perhaps some object lessons from Savannah itself. This can be regarded as open-ended, to be reworked and re-examined, precisely because our analysis means dealing with many diversities and identities. A picture can hopefully emerge that might be shrouded in an ambiguity of isolated views until it is combined with other empirical material and elaborated with further knowledge, retrieved and possibly

dismantled by discussion, but hopefully opening a few doors on where we might be heading, or, rather, perhaps where we should be heading.

In this way we pry open the crevices of urbanism without the disbenefit of nostalgia. There is no such thing as a common experience just as there is no absolute truth – our individual perspectives differ according to interest, habit, customs, and culture, and maybe a lot more. What matters is how we choose to critically interpret the city for what it represents – the reality behind the appearance that emerges through the differences we encounter and the dialogues we generate. Our cities, as someone once said, represent a tapestry that is still on the loom. Our knowledge and discussion permits us to observe but the final picture is never completely visible.

And so we are assembled as a collection of voices – actors and commentators in a drama where we write our own parts, and where we must confront a continued subversion of the script.

We break in late morning for a self-service luncheon in a large and well-appointed canteen, shared by students and faculty, where almost every conceivable American dish is on offer. We are surrounded by fortunate classmates with startling appetites that one can only hope extends to the wider academic menus on offer. All is loud conversation and shrieks of merriment although some, of a more cerebral inclination, wander by in a silent trance, caught between ear-pieces and iPhones. One or two more in tracksuit bottoms and T-shirts have the still groggy look of the only recently awakened. I am seated at a long table, on one side of me, Apolonia Karawice and on the other Terry Fulbright. Apolonia tells me brightly that she had an American father but studied in Gdansk, supported the workers revolution, and worshipped the now deceased but perennially popular Polish Pope, John-Paul I. She then managed to make it to Cornell on the back of a paper on the medieval geography of Baltic cities.

Terry Fulbright to my right eats and says little, and his drooping head gives intermittent indications that it might suddenly drop on his sparsely covered plate. Dan Schlomo has his chair turned away from the table, in casual conversation with the volunteer waitress of the morning who turns out to be a college sophomore, still wearing the short black skirt that has clearly prioritized his attention. He has adroitly ascertained her name—Angel, short for Angelina—and that she comes from Paris, Texas. Schlomo is aimlessly recounting a summer spent in Paris, France. Angel looks amiably gratified but slightly confused.

On the other side of the table there is a discussion led by Mo on the forthcoming presidential election. Agnita is tempting fate by stating that in her opinion elections are about three foxes and one chicken voting on what to have for dinner. Brit replies that the trouble with most politicians is that they get elected in the first place. "And then get to know more and more about less and less," adds Agnita cheerfully. Brit retorts that it is about time a woman ran the country. Miles gazes at Agnita and nods vigorously.

Mo looks bemused, clears his throat and sits back in his chair. "You see," he exclaims authoritatively, "the basic process of selecting the president is set out neatly in the US Constitution, although this has been modified according to various amendments. Candidates must be at least thirty-five years of age, on the possibly questionable basis that they are sufficiently mature and have attained some degree of public recognition. Political parties hold conventions attended by delegates, many of whom are selected by state caucuses, and a majority of delegate votes effectively decides the party's nomination. Now here is where it gets tricky – the presidential election actually consists of separate elections in all fifty states and the District of Columbia, so voters are actually voting for electors who make up the Electoral College and have pledged to support a particular candidate. It is supposed to ensure popular support throughout the country. Of course some electors could violate their pledge and then, as far as I know, it is down to the House of Representatives.

"This does not mean that we are a country without problems," he continues. "Our actual freedoms are being compromised through an elusive insecurity. We are in retreat, not just from the fallacies of party politics, but from the real and uncompromising decisions that will get us back on track. Our politicians must stand up for the cause of equality and betterment. This should not reduce our freedoms – it should consolidate and direct them. We need to build communities that work in every sense, and that over time benefit everyone, not just a few. And of course how we are able to provide choices in the way we live through proper stewardship of our development process is quite fundamental to our future."

Mo who is proceeding in full flow suddenly pauses in receipt of a sharp glance from Martha B. who is tapping her watch, indicating a need to divert this irreverent conversational trajectory towards the matters in hand. He claps his hands for attention. "After a splendid lunch I hope we can reassemble in our equally resplendent headquarters in five minutes. Okay?" He claps his hands again to emphasize that this is an instruction, not a mere suggestion.

Apolonia has been identified by Mo to lead off on the first presentation of the afternoon, and is looking rather pale.

PROTECTION OF THE COLONY, ORGANIZATION AND TRADE

In 1737 Oglethorpe reported to a meeting of the Trustees in London, concerning the robust state of Savannah. During his absence the first magistrate Thomas Causton was replaced by Colonel William Stephens who arrived in November 1737 as Secretary of the Province, to safeguard the interests of the Trustees. Stephens later became acting Governor after the final departure of Oglethorpe. He was able to impart the news that the Spanish Governor-General and the Council of War of Florida had signed a treaty with the Colony, but that there was still fear of a Spanish invasion. The Trustees then petitioned the King to raise a regiment to protect the Colony. As a result Oglethorpe was appointed General and Commander-in-Chief of his Majesty's forces in Carolina and Georgia with a commission to raise a regiment to defend the two Colonies. This consisted of six companies of 100 men each, some accompanied by their wives. The regiment arrived at St. Simons on September 9, 1738 and set about reinforcing fortifications in the various settlements including Frederica.

On October 8th, Oglethorpe returned to Savannah to learn that the Colony had run into debt, and there was a general air of discontentment and factiousness, compounded by a group of self-interest "malcontents" who petitioned the Trustees about the lack of land titles and the need for slaves that they considered necessary to successfully emulate the South Carolina model.

For a number of years, British trade to America and the West Indies had been compromised by the seizure and confiscation of merchant ships by the Spanish who continually reasserted their claim to the South Carolina coast. War was declared in October 1739, and armed privateers were fitted out in Savannah. In April 1740 an Act of Assembly was passed to raise a regiment of 400 men plus various Native American tribes to begin an assault on St. Augustine in Florida. Oglethorpe marched south, taking small Spanish-manned forts as he went. The mission was unsuccessful, partly due to the necessary withdrawal of British ships off the coast because of hurricanes, but it succeeded in keeping the Spanish on the defensive and war at a distance.

During 1741 Oglethorpe had many difficulties to contend with: not only with Spanish incursions but with increasing French strength in the west where they had colonized the Mississippi River basin. In May 1742 the Spanish fitted out an armored fleet in Havana, including men-of-war and large privateers that set sail to St. Augustine. On June 21st the fleet, which included 5,000 men, appeared off the Georgia coast but were rebuffed by forces at Fort William. Five weeks later, a Spanish fleet of thirty-six ships appeared off the coast near St. Simons, entered the harbor and established a battery. The Georgian forces retreated to shore up the defense of Frederica, and the invading battalions were defeated by a combination of troops let by Oglethorpe, including the Highland Company and Native allies, and supported by British warships. The Spanish burned all the buildings on the south of St.

Simons and Jekyl Islands, having been defeated by a force only one tenth their size. For his leading role in the operation, Oglethorpe was appointed President of Frederica.

Having ensured the improvement of fortifications, Oglethorpe embarked on his final return to England on July 23, 1743, leaving William Stephens as the upholder of civil authority. He is remembered as the founder of Georgia and a father figure to the Colony. During his tenure he actively enlarged Britain's dominions, promoted its trade interests, and provided for the wants and necessities of its growing community. He was later raised to the rank of General of all his Majesty's forces and continued to reside at Cranham Hall in Essex, and in St. James, Westminster to attend his duties as a member of Parliament. He remained, however, a staunch advocate of the strong moral principles on which Savannah had been founded.

The Georgian Aera of 1834, Vol 11 states the following:

"As governor of the new Colony, he was exposed to numberless difficulties and vexations, but persevered with great ardour in the scheme, and expended large sums out of his private fortune with a view to ensure his success."

A contemporary was to write that he doubted "whether the histories of Greece or Rome can produce a greater instance of public spirit than this. To see a gentleman of his rank and fortune visiting a distant and uncultivated land, with no other society but the unfortunate whom he goes to assist, exposing himself freely to the same hardships to which they are subjected, in the prime of life, instead of pursuing his pleasures or ambition, on an improved and well-concerted plan from which his country must ... entitle him to the highest honor he can gain – the perpetual love and applause of mankind."

A New Slave Code

The lack of a steady labor supply led to a now notorious petition sent by 117 malcontent members of the Savannah community in 1738 requesting the right to own slaves – up until then prohibited under the Crown Charter. This touched off fierce opinions, for and against. Even evangelical movements allied themselves with supporters of African slave labor, who favored an alignment with Carolina on the issue. At the same time the continuing dispute with Spain, mainly over the boundary between Georgia and Florida, exacerbated an existing sense of frustration through ill-conceived land policies and a stagnant economy. A population surge in the aftermath of the Spanish defeat, played into the hands of a new realm of business people in Savannah with strong political connections and a motivation to expand the town. Slaves from neighboring South Carolina were smuggled into Georgia in increasing numbers, mainly to work on the irrigation of rice fields, which used a hydraulic system by which tidal flows of fresh water were regulated by a system of dikes and narrow canals.

William Stephens, the Deputy General of Georgia following Oglethorpe's departure, came under pressure to repeal the restrictive 1735 Slave Act as a stimulus to new settlement and investment. After the peace treaty with Spain, the Georgia Trustees finally acquiesced and began a process of withdrawal from twenty years of colonial administration. It had, however, succeeded in emphasizing secular authority and instigating a public debate on Enlightenment ideals. In 1750 the British Parliament legalized slavery of both Africans and Native Americans in Georgia, extending this to all thirteen British colonies in North America and the West Indies, in line with French and Spanish colonial policy. Somewhat incongruously, owners could be fined if their slaves were not allowed to attend Christian churches, setting the stage for future multi-denomination church building, evangelism, and missionary societies.

The Slave Code for Georgia, passed on March 7, 1755 by the Royal Legislature, was based on that for South Carolina enacted in 1712, which was itself based on a 1688 code employed by the British in Barbados. The intention was to facilitate "subjugation and obedience," permitting a sixteen-hour workday but attempting to prevent the exercise of excessive cruelty and, with a somewhat sanctimonious flourish, recognizing the Sabbath as a day of rest. Teaching slaves to read or write was forbidden, but the code stated that "owners may be restrained from exercising too great rigor over slaves, and that the public peace and order of the province must be preserved." Slave owners controlled the Georgian Assembly, and ensured that they were not prevented from renting out slaves as artisans. Legislation was later enacted to allow for the building of a workhouse for recaptured or recalcitrant slaves, who were confined until being claimed or sold.

Of more immediate significance, slave owners from other parts of the dominion began a rush to obtain land through purchase and crown grants that led the way to a new plantation economy. James Habersham who was appointed Secretary of the Colony in 1751 was himself a well-known slave trader.

The renewed sense of confidence was reflected in changes to the Georgia Assembly, with a new President, Patrick Graham, who effectively promoted greater development and trade while the trustees surrendered their own powers to the king in June 1752, making Georgia a province of the Crown. The release from relatively inflexible controls quickly encouraged an impetus towards agricultural cultivation of the coastal wetlands and tidal marshes for slave-dependent rice plantations. The wealth of experience, knowhow, and escalation in slavery encouraged further immigration from merchants, and as the export industry increased so did Savannah's prosperity.

English-owned ships continued to bring hundreds of slaves from the African Gold Coast, Gambia, and Angola to the slave market in Savannah. The number of runaway slaves also increased along with those enticed away, despite the threat of harsh punishment or death, so that the slave code was vigorously enforced. However, black slaves, poor whites, and free slaves fraternized nightly in drinking dens, developing lasting friendships and serving to mitigate, at least to some extent, the more overt racist policies.

Representative Government and Colony Organization

Representative Government and Colony Organization

John Reynolds, the first Governor representing the Crown, arrived in August 1754. As a naval captain he had coordinated coastal operations, and therefore represented both royal authority and the accompanying machinery of colonial government. Reynolds's first task was to set up a Legislative and an Advisory Council. To stand for election it was necessary to own 500 acres of land, although the Governor had supreme power and could both issue warrants for expenditure and grant land to favored parties. The Council House, which served as a court, was situated in Percival Square opposite the public jail, now known as Wright Square.

Later the same year, war was declared between England and France. Security suddenly became an issue, and the Militia Act in January 1755 required all adult males to enroll. Fortifications cost money, however, and this required tax increases. Plans were drawn up to build new forts and bastions along Georgia's borders and on Cockspur Island, and funds were requested from the Board of Trade in London without success. This put the embryo colony at great risk, and when the legislative bodies similarly balked at tax increases, Reynolds dissolved these bodies and was recalled to London in 1757, stating that it was impossible to deal with "lawless and anti-monarchical people."

At the time Spanish privateers prowled the coasts and frequently seized local craft. The new Lieutenant-Governor of Georgia, Henry Ellis, immediately understood the need for improved defenses and oversaw the construction of a palisade around three sides of the town, with bastions for mounted cannon, along with a series of new forts to the south. Two gates on each side controlled access in and out of the city. Troops were sent from Charlestown and an alliance was concluded with local Native tribes against the Spanish and French.

In March 1758 Ellis divided the colony of Georgia into eight parishes. Savannah was included in Christ Church Parish – the present Chatham County. Parishes could raise their own taxes, build churches and other public buildings, and a tax was levied on slave owners in order to fund public services. Savannah's cultural links with London led to two nearby villages being christened Hampstead and Highgate. Congregation leaders assumed civic roles, attempted to promote morality, and were permitted to arrest "negroes and other disorderly people" for refusing to attend church. While the Church of England remained the established religious body, other groups such as Lutherans and Presbyterians were allowed to build churches and meeting houses.

Immigrants continued to arrive, and debtors were given asylum with land available at little cost. Liberal polices were applied to granting and purchase of land, and women could apply for land grants in their own right under the royal government, some becoming successful in business. By 1759 it was estimated that around one-third of Georgia's population of 10,500 were black slaves. Some five years later forty-five percent of the population was of African origin, as more slaves came with their owners who arrived from Virginia and the Carolinas.

The following year, the Legislative Council voted funds to build a new Government House in St. James's Square, today's Telfair Square. However, Ellis was again frustrated with London's lack of cooperation in sending troops to protect the colony, and posted a request to return to England.

The new chief executive of Georgia, James Wright, arrived in time to celebrate the accession of George III in 1761 with a procession around the town. Wright was later promoted to Governor just as Spain entered the war against England.

Growth of Trade and Society

By the mid 1760s, more than 150 vessels a year were visiting the port, which continued to expand as a result of the surge in Savannah's import-export trade. A public wharf was constructed, and merchants began to build private wharfs. Beacons were placed in the river to facilitate navigation to and from the port, and as import-export business required increasing amounts of storage space, rice plantation owners constructed warehouses adjacent to the Savannah River. A bell signaled the daily opening of the central market in Ellis Square, which contained rental stalls for produce. Vendors included bond people from the countryside plantations, along with slaves who grew their own produce to raise money.

The growing diversity and volume of exports, in particular rice, lumber, and indigo, paved the way for the city's territorial expansion. An act of Parliament made the export of rice duty free, and it was shipped in barrels from storage areas along the waterfront. Unlimited land grants in Savannah together with slave labor made rice planting along the Satilla, Altamaha, Ogechee, and Savannah Rivers extremely profitable. Around fifty wealthy plantation owners held estates of between 5,000 and 27,000 acres, one of the largest being held by the Governor, James Wright. Hutchison Island became one of the most valuable areas of land holding.

The main lots along the Savannah wharf to the west of Bull Street comprised what was known as "commerce row," lined by large four-story warehouses, with stores and emporiums stretching along Broughton and Bull Streets. Shops sold a variety of goods, from silk clothing, perfumes, and jewelry, to liquors, chocolate, candles, and foodstuffs. Physicians, tailors, clothiers, hairdressers, and wig makers all offered their services. Commercial growth attracted investment in waterborne transportation, producing regular shipping runs to New York and the West Indies.

Increasing wealth led directly to investment in new town houses and country estates. Leading merchants built two-story timber-framed houses covered with shingles on brick foundations that often served as private accommodation as well as business premises. Houses had large living rooms, brick chimneys, several bedrooms, and cellars, with outbuildings that included a kitchen and stable. Larger houses had wide porches and balconies providing shaded outdoor exteriors. Main living rooms were on the first floor, with kitchens, storerooms, and lodging rooms adjoining the house.

Construction of new public and private buildings created a thriving industry for artisans – carpenters, contractors, and bricklayers. Cabinet makers used the red bay trees found in the swamps, together with cedar, cypress, and magnolia, to make tables, desks, and chairs. However, large quantities of mahogany were imported from the West Indies. Savannah also attracted watchmakers, jewelers, and gold- and silver-smiths, many of whom operated businesses on Broughton Street.

The first weekly newspaper was published on April 7, 1763 by an appointed public printer, James Johnston. The Georgia Gazette was required to publish all laws and official material as well as local news and advertisements.

A further reflection of growing affluence were the various clubs and societies, many of them following ethnic lines, but most contributing to social and charitable enterprises. Various social clubs met regularly at Machenry's Tavern. The St. Andrews Club, the Society of St. Patrick, the Masons, and Savannah Library Society were dedicated to both pleasure and learning. Music and dancing schools provided graduates for the many balls and masquerades, while teachers from European cities offered classes in a range of subjects, including languages. At the same time, church groups offered instruction in religious matters.

But there was another side to Savannah – the suburb of Yamacraw, named after the Native American tribe, was developed to house the poorest members of society, both black and white, who were employed to build the defensive structures of Fort Savannah, now Fort Wayne.

Unknown to Savannah's citizens, however, actions were afoot in the British Parliament to introduce a Stamp Act that was to ultimately bring about a cataclysmic change in Britain's relationship with North America.

*

We are now again assembled in the comfortable and strangely silent confines of the long conference room. Mo gets up to speak again.

"It was once stated, perhaps by a suitably modest historian, that the British Empire, which by the nineteenth century occupied a good proportion of the world's surface, was conceived through an absence of mind."

Low ripples of polite laughter echo around the table except, I noted, from Brit who bristled imperceptively.

"But in the twenty-first century we rarely build cities from scratch, even given our accommodation problems and our wealth of resources. This is interesting is it not? Have we lost our confidence or are all the political, economic, and social repercussions too complicated to handle?"

Mo gives a flamboyant wave of his arm. "It was not always so, but times were a little different a few centuries ago as we are going to find out from Dr. Apolonia Karawice." Mo waves a hand in her direction. "Cities have to start somehow and somewhere."

Apolonia stands and clears her throat.

FIRST READING DR. APOLONIA KARAWICE
WHY SAVANNAH

First I will try to explain the precise forces behind the colonization and city building process in North America. Then I will get a little more philosophical in setting out what lay behind it.

Yes, why Savannah? Or the rest of the North American colonies for that matter?

Certainly colonization began not as the grand "civilizing mission" that was later attributed to Britain's enthusiastic land acquisition program, but as something of a buccaneering exercise aimed at relieving Spain of its cargoes of gold and silver as their loaded galleons returned to Europe from Mexico and Peru via the Caribbean. Through the introverted channels of the Catholic World, a *Papal Bull* of 1493 generously allocated all land outside Europe into Spanish and Portuguese territorial hemispheres. Land to the west of the Azores was handed to Spain following the discoveries of Columbus. The Treaty of Tordesillas the following year appeared to ratify this, allocating most of the western part of South and Central America to the Spanish Crown. It was not until the early 17th century that the Portuguese effectively colonized various states on the eastern coast and eventually unified them under the state of Brazil in 1775. In terms of both timing and mineral wealth, Spain struck lucky.

Colonizing regimes led by the Spanish and Portuguese in the Americas, and closely associated with new European naval powers, were motivated not merely by financial gain but by religious conversions underscored by forms of social control. These involved the cultural assimilation of indigenous populations – an ideological excuse for overlaying older settlements with predominantly European "utopian" city forms, fashioned through the driving forces of maritime trade, the proselytizing forces of Catholicism, and the more benign itineraries of simple exploration. New cities came into being as ports, military concentrations, and centers of political or religious ideology. What they had in common were plans to construct or reconstruct cities to serve the best interests of colonizers, so this ultimately produced a significant shift from forms of production based on localized, sub-regional trading to an export market of resources and an import market for foreign goods.

Spanish voyages of discovery had, in large part, a Jesuit inspired agenda. The settlement of Santo Domingo in 1496 was the first European settlement in the Americas, although its meticulously ordered plan, dominated by a rectangular square and church, indicated imposition rather than respect for the spiritual beliefs of the indigenous population. The Aztec capital of Tenochtitlán was razed by the Spanish conquistadors under Hernán Cortés in 1521 and its new replacement became the symbolic capital of "New Spain" – today's Mexico City. Following this the Spanish overran much of what is now Latin America, destroying established native empires and constructing new Spanish cities on top of the ruins of large conquered settlements such as Lima, Bogotá, and Cartagena. These served as centers for new systems of administration and plunder. However, an interesting departure from the mercenary outlook of the conquistadores, was the appointment of Vasco de Quiroga to the governing assembly of conquered territories in 1531, who went on to become bishop of Michoacán, devoting himself to extending his utopian ideals to the needs of indigenous peoples, creating in the process what was perhaps the first humanitarian initiative in the New World.

The initial Spanish settlement in what became the United States was partly intended as a means to protect the treasure fleets, but later turned into a military protected base for Franciscan missionaries. In fact, the majority of colonizers in the American frontier regions of New Mexico, California, and Texas were soldiers and missionaries.

The first British authorized voyage to America was under Henry VII in 1497 and led by John Cabot, who landed on Cape Breton Island. However, it was almost a century later, in 1583, that Elizabeth I seized on the strategic possibilities associated with Cabot's original landing to stake a colonial claim on America north of Florida, and commissioned Sir Walter Raleigh to search for a suitable settlement site. Raleigh went on to lead the first colonization attempt at Roanoke in 1584 in what later became North Carolina. The real catalyst however was the English defeat of the Spanish Armada in 1588, clearing the way for a determined policy of colonization.

Following the Reformation, English frustration with Spanish hegemony turned to confrontation with the powerful forces of Catholicism through an aspiration towards a new Protestant empire. However, despite various expeditions to South America during the sixteenth century by such notable English explorers as Richard Grenville, Francis Drake, and Martin Frobisher, it was quickly deduced that the most direct means of securing *El Dorado* was the capture of either Spanish ships, or their Caribbean bases. From this emerged a new seafaring profession of privatized naval piracy or "privateering," quietly licensed and rewarded by the royal court. In turn, the self-justified plunder made from piracy could be even more profitably transformed by its protagonists into political power.

The term "plantation" that later became something of a symbol of the North American Antebellum South, can in its original form be best translated as a form of systematic acquisition through a process where land was purposely reallocated from its original status to new users through the auspices of a dominant power as a reward for loyalty. Robert Home points out that the predecessor of Britain's 18th-century Colonial Office was called the Board of Plantations as a means of settling or re-settling people, which underscored an ideological approach to colonial urbanization. Such a program was introduced by England as something of a political experiment in the early 17th century to "plant" new Protestant communities in Catholic Ireland under James I. The "Ulster" experiment in social organization that fomented political conflict for the next 300 years showed that colonization through migration and new trading settlements could be the Trojan Horse that effectively achieved the expansion of Empire, not merely by force but through new administrative and cultural institutions as part of a necessary "civilizing" campaign.

From the early seventeenth century, for all manner of reasons, there was an exodus of emigrants from the British Isles. For some the New World meant liberty and for others opportunity. It represented the beginning of an Empire, but also the means to fuel it. The notion of settlement in North America was, at least in part, a scheme to combat Spanish and Portuguese success in colonizing South and Central America, and to counter further French and Spanish penetration of virgin territories to the north.

The British were by no means the first to entertain colonial ambitions in this part of North America. Spanish explorers forcibly evicted the French from what was the first European colony at San Augustíne in 1565, and went on to construct a new capital, Santa Fé in 1610. The Spanish intention was to both trade and convert, and they went on to build a series of Catholic missions across what is now Georgia.

We can identify some crucial differences in these undertakings. The objective of Protestant England was, in theory if not in practice, of a different order from the ambitions of Catholic Spain and Portugal. While the conquistadors had set out to enrich the coffers of the mother country while converting their conquered peoples to Catholicism, often at the point of a sword, the colonization of virtually unoccupied lands was directed towards more private initiatives. This included the building of new agricultural settlements producing crops, which could be exported from the New World to the Old. In fact, what had become known as the "Columbian Exchange" dated from the voyages of Christopher Columbus, and involved an unprecedented transfer of edible foodstuffs and other produce. In most accounts at the time, including that of Sir Walter Raleigh, America was the garden of incredible abundance, delightedly embraced by arrivals with aspirations for a pastoral utopia. The potential for production and export of an enticing range of crops and commodities—tobacco in the case of Virginia, rice, cotton, and even silk from Georgia—was in fact often set out in sponsorship and investment arrangements. One of the later imports to Europe that is often overlooked is the exotic tree and plant species such as azaleas, hydrangea, and Virginia creeper that were sent to Britain to beautify the plethora of country house estates.

Migration from Britain over the course of the seventeenth century amounted to around 700,000 people, with one-third to North America, and the remainder to Ireland and the West Indies. The most fortunate of these were propelled by heroic motives of religious freedom and the opportunity of cheap or even free land holdings on which to work and prosper. The remainder left for the New World either through a system of indenture, or through enforced transportation as part of the brutal British penal system. This reflected a combination of poverty and religious intolerance including civil unrest in Britain as a result of the Protestant Reformation.

The British came to dominate other colonizing groups in the New World primarily through force of numbers and economic strength. The thirteen widespread colonies along the Atlantic coast were shaped by rapid growth and spatial change as they steadily evolved into towns and cities with the commercial expansion of key markets. An important incentive in attracting the more materially minded settlers was the offer of land, which was generally allocated to each settler and broadly according to either their connections in high places or the number of his or her dependents. To some groups, America also presented an opportunity to freely practice their spiritual faith, which was occasionally of the fundamentalist or even radical variety. Jamestown, Virginia, was settled in 1607 but in its early years was subject to harsh conditions and high death rates before its rapid transformation through plantation agriculture and tobacco cultivation in the Chesapeake. The puritanical group known as the Pilgrim Fathers arrived aboard the *Mayflower* in November 1620 to the somewhat remote shores of what had been christened New England.

In 1630 the Puritan English lawyer John Winthrop, the recipient of a charter from King Charles I, drew on the biblical metaphor of "City upon a Hill" in a sermon before disembarking from the *Arabella* at the head of a fleet of eleven ships, as it arrived in the New World, in what came to be named Boston after the Puritan settlement in Lincolnshire. It was to be a further 100 years before Winthrop's prophetic but literal sentiment became a physical reality on a solitary plateau to the south in Georgia, a land already settled over preceding centuries by Native Americans and other indigenous peoples who lived in both permanent and nomadic communities.

By the early eighteenth century large British colonial towns were already in existence in Virginia and Maryland, and other towns began to flourish, notably in New England. The importance of agriculture and lumber products to the Atlantic economy propelled the rapid development of port cities. Boston dominated early urban growth to the extent that it became the largest city in America until being overtaken by Philadelphia and New York City in the mid-eighteenth century. However, its rapid growth was less due to godly pursuits and more for the rich fishing waters in the North Atlantic, which, as the historian Niall Ferguson has succinctly commented, put cod on a not dissimilar basis to god.

The early Puritan towns in Massachusetts had an agreed optimum size beyond which no house lots were available. In 1684, some seventy-five years after its creation, the Crown revoked the charter of the Massachusetts Bay Company, thereby negating the independence of the early settlements and opening the door to more open-ended and flexible settlement plans. The new brand of colonizers were not predominantly male troops and priests, but young men and women who settled the land, married, and quickly produced offspring which perpetuated the conditions necessary to guarantee the colony's future.

In 1664 the British overcame the Dutch colony of New Amsterdam and renamed it New York, which thrived to become one of the most rapidly growing cities along with Boston, Philadelphia, Newport, and Charleston, all affiliated with Britain and focused on trans-Atlantic trade. These adopted a mercantile relationship with the mother country, and dispatched large quantities of raw materials such as grain, fish, firs, and lumber. In return they were the market recipients of much desired manufactured goods, which for a time served the interests of both sides. This allowed for the development of self-government in the British colonial cities, with administration carried out by elected representatives as part of a social and political hierarchy.

In a not dissimilar situation to today's economy the top ranks of urban society, comprising affluent merchants and government officials, controlled at least sixty percent of taxable wealth. Unskilled laborers, indentured servants, and slaves, the latter first brought to America under the auspices of the Dutch West India Company, formed an "underclass," permanently attached to the bottom tier of society.

Well before British settlers arrived in Georgia, Charles I had granted Maryland in what was then termed "British North America" to the heirs of Lord Baltimore, and his successor Charles II granted large estates in Carolina to his own powerful supporters. New York was handed to his brother, the Duke of York in 1664, while William Penn, who founded the city of Philadelphia, was granted a massive estate that was to become Pennsylvania.

While the rate of emigration to the American colonies was increasing at the time the first settlers arrived in Savannah, the most immediate choice for around two-thirds of all British emigrants in the eighteenth century was the West Indies. The Caribbean island group had gradually redirected its commercial priorities from a haven for privateers, to a key cultivator of sugar cane following William Penn's capture of Jamaica in 1665. Sugar dwarfed the total imports from the early colonies in terms of trade with Britain, and until the 1660s the superficially tranquil islands of the Indies formed a focus for indentured labor to service the increasing number of plantations. There was, however, a morbid downside to this – the tropical climate induced a range of diseases and a high mortality rate to the stoical but vulnerable workers from northern Europe. In contrast the more temperate climate of America's eastern seaboard, together with the more benign working conditions on tobacco plantations, provided a much healthier option.

In the American colonies, precisely because of the amount of agricultural, building, and production work, there was a heavy reliance on cheap labor. Far from the prospect of liberty and the pursuit of happiness that eventually came to be associated with the New World, the poorest migrants, which applied in particular to the Irish who made up forty percent of their ranks, entered into a tenure of indentured servitude and lived for the most part in poverty. Their services were advertised in the local gazettes, in a foretaste of the future slave markets that were to come in the South. Convicts, often given draconian sentences of transportation by British courts for minor offences, were employed in much the same way as indentured labor, and faired better in America than they would have done in Australia where redemption was equated with harsh conditions and forced labor. By the early eighteenth century more than 40,000 men and women had been transported to the thirteen American colonies, most living in predominantly rural areas, and largely engaged in agrarian pursuits.

The onset of the American slave trade was first established in 1662 under the auspices of the New Royal African Company. The prospect of high profits and the repeal of the Company's monopoly in 1698 encouraged later participation by private dealers. Initially slaves were purchased in West Africa and sent to Barbados, Jamaica, and Antigua. As the very first settlers were arriving in Savannah in 1733, Liverpool traders were sending thirty-three ships in a triangular operational chain of commercial deal-making between England, West Africa, and the Caribbean. The questionable preference of slaves to indentured immigrants was thought to be their strength and ability to withstand the back-breaking working conditions, the exhausting climate and debilitating disease.

The diverse group of settlers that arrived in Georgia on the *Ann* with James Oglethorpe in 1733, a little over 100 years after the Plymouth Brethren disembarked in Massachusetts, scarcely anticipated either a Promised Land or a Garden of Eden. However, compared to the original pilgrims, they stepped ashore in a relatively receptive state of mind, ready to confront and tame the prevailing wilderness. This optimism was assisted partly through the immediate and equitable allocation of land titles, coupled with a notable degree of self-determination and self-sufficiency. Oglethorpe's plan, however conceptual in its initial stages, contributed to the economic and social stability that had to quickly absorb all manner and backgrounds of new arrivals.

The burgeoning settlements along the northeastern seaboard were notable not just for their cosmopolitan population and economic development but for the driving ideals of their founders. The limited capacity of Spain's military presence had also opened up opportunities for French settlements in North America during the late seventeenth and early eighteenth centuries, prioritizing commercial trading routes along the Atlantic coast rather than military activities, and establishing a network of fortified trading posts throughout the eastern part of North America and Canada along the St. Lawrence River. Further areas of settlement were in the south in Louisiana around the Gulf Coast and the Mississippi Basin, centered on New Orleans, and contributing to a combination of French and African "Creole" culture that still survives.

It has been estimated that by the early eighteenth century only around five percent of the American population lived in urban areas. In the South only Charleston, founded in 1670 on the Ashley River, had emerged as an important economic entrepôt, with sufficient population to be considered a city. By the end of the eighteenth century one quarter of the largest American cities were in the South, including Savannah, which served as the colonial capital of Georgia.

But there is another question to be asked at this stage – would we still have had a Savannah without the new intellectual order that, by the time Oglethorpe and his group of Trustees were planning the new settlement, was beginning to sweep through Europe? Oglethorpe's philosophical commitment to the ordered and harmonious ideals of the Enlightenment with its strong moral overtones, took shape within a new age of reason, critical thinking and intellectual idealism. Viewed in this context the plan for Savannah, and the sense of moral purpose that encompassed it, can be seen as an articulation of humanist ideals that led to a clear vision for the Georgia colony that was transformative as well as progressive. It brought together, with heroic intent, many of the elusive philosophical precepts being widely discussed in the early eighteenth century, including achievements in science.

The utopian city is an elusive ideal, and has engaged both philosophers and city designers since Thomas More's scholarly publication in 1516, which claimed to reflect Plato's idealist vision in his *Republic*. *Utopia*, derived from the Greek *topos* or "place" was in many ways a humanist prescription for necessary social reform. Along with the Greek *polis* from which we derive our notion of political organization, we have a representation of the city-state. Its intuitive fascination even today, precisely 500 years later, is in the central question of how to reconcile idealized principles governing the notion of community equality and social convention. These of course must be equated with what is realizable in practice, given our seemingly eternal predisposition towards self-interest.

More's work coincided with the European "discovery" of the Americas, and their imaginative potential for a new society. The publication triggered controversy but also raised provocative questions about the nature of reform, which lay at the foundation of Protestantism. We might say that utopian theory poses a still relevant issue over the priorities of communal interest as opposed to self-interest, and how to navigate the awkward territory between them without stumbling into the chasm of dystopia.

This raises an interesting issue of how far we can exert control over a society, ostensibly for its own good. We know very well that society has an almost built-in tendency towards rebelliousness, inventiveness, and exploitation that in many ways drives it forward, even at the occasional expense of its own destruction. But there again, inertia can achieve much the same ends.

At any rate, More's fictional republic, situated in a conveniently vague mid-Atlantic location where residents shared available resources, inadvertently issued a serious challenge to well meaning philanthropists and overreaching members of the urban design profession. The latter, for several centuries thereafter, proved themselves willing to attempt a corresponding level of built perfection that matched this rarefied level of philosophical attainment. Occasionally an emergent social or religious order, coincided with the formulation of an "ideal" planning accommodation that induced an ambitious combination of political and physical harmony. This can be effectively summarized as the search for a better world, each attempt corresponding to a new urban ideal for the city.

We can perhaps be mindful of Thomas More's utopian theories on spatial organization which were suffused with ethical undertones and fixed societal references as an ideal and permanent setting for a static population, segregated by function and unsullied by any notion of impermanence. This must have struck an acute accord with the early settlers in Savannah, having exchanged the religious intolerance, inequalities and industrial squalor of London for what they hoped was freedom from religious bigotry and political persecution. Just as More imagined Utopia as a community surrounded by an agricultural hinterland for support and sustenance relatively free of external influences and protected by a stockade, so Savannah eventually became ringed by estates to further this partly imaginary and tentatively harmonious life-world that sharpened new attitudes to the emerging eighteenth-century pattern of urbanization.

Francis Bacon in 1627 extended the idealist scope of utopian literature in The New Atlantis to a more collaborative and scientific level, leading directly to the establishment of the Royal Society in 1660, which ushered in a new realm of utopian deliberation related to new discoveries at opposite ends of the world. Meanwhile, the European Enlightenment set new and radical realms of thought and debate – a freedom from religious oppression, together with tolerance and reason directed at the rights of man. It was both revolutionary and reformist, with influential philosophers and elite camp followers inspired by the possibility of achieving a better world, where scientific rationality was thought to facilitate and sustain progress. The American Revolution cannot be disassociated from the enlightened political and philosophical theories that preceded it. This was an age of reason, and the classical references of harmony and order were applied to architectural and aesthetic interpretation just as they were to scientific rationality and social progress.

Above all, the Enlightenment provoked a revolutionary philosophy in both the arts and sciences that came together in a pragmatic approach towards achieving a better world, and became the lens through which to liberate mankind by way of a transmission of ideas. Its essential characteristic, according to the musing of Immanuel Kant, was its emancipation of large sections of the population from superstition and ignorance. It kindled philanthropic ideas and set certain dominant European trading capitals on a new course of discovery and colonization in both the east and west hemispheres, although in practice this was often more exploitive than enlightening. It was also revolutionary in both a metaphorical and literal sense, and for all its contradictions its impact spread throughout the old and new worlds.

In England, John Locke's seventeenth-century philosophical theories on a contractual relationship between ruler and ruled, together with writings on moral values, became influential in disseminating ideas on reason, knowledge, and human understanding in tune with practical concerns for shaping society. Lord Ashley, the 1st Earl of Shaftsbury who was later appointed Lord High Chancellor of England, appointed Locke as secretary of a group dedicated to increasing trade with America, and almost immediately he was requested to draft a constitution for the new British colony of Carolina that allowed for civil liberty and freedom of worship. Later, the 3rd Earl of Shaftesbury, a pupil of Locke, pursued a practical school of thought based on the concept of Deism – a means of applying reason to religion, free from the high ceremonial affairs of the church, but with an obligation towards piety and virtue.

French writing on political, economic, and philosophical matters in the early eighteenth century had a similarly profound impact on European thought and the disbursement of knowledge. Montesquieu's publications on societal reform and social emancipation brought discussion on these issues to a public audience. The Meditations of Descartes constituted a means of bringing together philosophy and natural science, grounded in systematic principles and providing a context for discussion amongst eminent thinkers in terms of the conduct of life, health, and the arts. Voltaire elaborated his views on the new merchant class and its enlightened patronage towards the well being of society in his Letters on England published at precisely the same time as the first settlers arrived in Savannah.

This was also a period of ethics and aesthetics as subjects of philosophical inquiry and debate, with a resulting sensual discernment in the experience and validation of architecture and the unity of place. Artistic value was accordingly one of refinement, with a strong grounding in the imaginary, beauty, and the sublime. While Adam Smith did not complete *The Wealth of Nations*, the first explanation of political economy, division of labor and a laissez-faire system of economic growth, until 1776, the colonies being planned in the late 17th and early 18th centuries quickly learned that they had to operate as commercial enterprises. It was only possible to plan an entirely new one if its future citizenry could trade off the surplus food supply or offer some other potential means of self-maintenance.

This period coincided with a considerable expansion of trade, commerce and mercantile activity that followed the reconstruction of London after the Great Fire of 1666. Mercantilism essentially facilitated the means by which governments could regulate overseas trade to uphold and augment the interests of the state, and its concentration in London was a catalyst towards the city's evolution as a banking power. This in turn introduced a new political landscape. James Oglethorpe, who was an ardent student of political philosophy and an aspiring member of Parliament, was almost certainly open to the notion of mercantilism just as he was to the ideals of religious tolerance and reason. These were brought together in the Charter for Savannah in 1732. Oglethorpe was at the center of a group of young and reform-minded members of Parliament, and visionary proposals for the Georgia Colony were widely disseminated in intellectual circles at a time when changing political ideas emphasized humanism, social reform, and a strong sense of purpose.

Whether modernization, propelled through the Enlightenment, created just the right conditions for the social revolutions that were to come about in France and America, or whether it actually took these events to articulate the universal rights of man, is a moot point. A new age of ideology and *praxis* almost inevitably spawned another more material one in the form of the Industrial Revolution and its expanding narrative of urban-industrial capitalism. On one hand, this marked a new phase in the social production of cityspace, while on the other it re-fuelled the colonial process of empire building that had commenced in the 16th century.

Intentionally or otherwise, a lack of meaningful government reform and intervention forged a need for a reservoir of workers and led to a new urban underclass of extreme poverty and destitution. As Friedrich Engels noted, with reference to the later deluge of industrial urbanization, there was an almost complete disjunction between unbridled reliance on the workings of a free market regime of accumulation, and the lack of regulatory institutions to keep it in check and spread the benefits. This inevitably propelled certain groups with similar beliefs and courageous convictions to contemplate a largely unknown and somewhat perilous future in the New World under the auspices of religious and philanthropic organizations. Given the headstrong motivations for leaving Britain in the first place, fuelled by an exasperation with authoritarian regimes and the rational philosophy of the Enlightenment, there was an understandable backlash against imperial heavy-handedness. Some of the revolutionary figures involved appealed to a political consciousness that was later to evolve into a struggle for American independence.

By the early years of the 18th century, the political, economic, and cultural power of London as both an imperial and mercantile city extended well beyond England. In fact, it was on the brink of experiencing an unprecedented program of urbanization and societal change through divisions that re-orchestrated the earlier distinctions between urban and rural, into an elite urban bourgeoisie. This effectively controlled and managed the emerging industrial landscape, serviced by a proletariat of migrant workers. It also created a changed relationship between people and cities, which led to new ideologies and patterns of social and political reform. In the process it collectively shaped a new scale of spatiality that had to be sustained and regulated through a re-visioning of national ambition through overseas trade and colonization. The colonial settlements were viewed by the British government, at least in part, as suppliers of raw materials and as markets for home industries. In the first instance this introduced a new urban order, whereby the production of a social surplus was orchestrated within the city itself, developing dense urban cores and a vigorous reorganization of infrastructure and city space. In the second instance, colonial intervention in America was a colossal factor in the generation of city form, bringing with it both political and cultural transformations.

So by the beginning of the eighteenth century the stage was set for further colonial initiatives in America. The first idea for a new settlement—the "Margravate of Azilia"—was proposed by Sir Robert Montgomery in 1717 as a "buffer" between the Spanish colonies and Charleston, to be settled by civilian-soldiers partly for strategic purposes. It was to be situated between the Savannah and Altamaha rivers in "the most delightful country in the universe," and was made up of 160 one-mile-square plantations. This was endorsed by the British government, but failed to attract sufficient investment to ensure its viability. Shortly afterwards, the first Crown Governor of Carolina, Robert Johnson, after whom one of Savannah's squares is named, introduced a scheme for eleven new townships along with various inducements to attract settlers. Although these were largely unsuccessful, this initiative paved the way for the colonization of Georgia – the last of Britain's thirteen American colonies. The defensive and commercial potential of the area south of the Savannah River therefore formed part of the British government's long-term policy, and Fort King George was constructed in 1721.

While ostensibly promoting a new territory as a place of colonial settlement in North America for the "worthy poor" of England, the group of propagandists behind the last of the colonies in Georgia were also sufficiently shrewd and persuasive to accentuate the commercial as well as the strategic military advantages of a new colony. In particular they advocated the production of silk for domestic manufacture that had begun to spread in England through mechanization.

These aspects were brought together in a Charter for the establishment of a new settlement in Georgia. James Oglethorpe sought the cooperation of twenty-one associates who petitioned the throne for an act of incorporation and obtained letters – patent on the 9th of June 1732. The preamble to this stated that:

"many of his Majesty's poor subjects were, through misfortunes and want of employment, reduced to great necessities, and would be glad to be settled in any of his provinces in America,

where, by cultivating the waste and desolate lands, they might not only gain a comfortable subsistence, but also strengthen the colonies and increase trade, navigation and wealth of his Majesty's realms."

There was and remains a question over precisely how legitimate the ownership of land actually was. Virginia was home to the Algonquian and Powhatan Native American nations, the Yamasees and Cherokees occupied Carolina, and the Yamacraw and Creeks occupied the area along the Savannah River in Georgia. But that is an altogether different story.

We break for the day. Mo thanks Apolonia warmly, begins to pack his papers and, looking mildly relieved, sets off for what he pompously announces is an important meeting with the president. We are left to assume that this applies to the senior incumbent of our host college, rather than the resident of 1600 Pennsylvania Avenue, although one never quite knows with Mo.

Dan Schlomo catches my eye. "I think the local Sports Bar beckons," he says, indicating the general direction with an inclusive wave of his arm. This also happens to vaguely embrace a wider catchment of Brit, Agnita, Apolonia, Miles, and Terry Fulbright. The latter immediately excuses himself on the basis of sleep deprivation, while Agnita expresses some doubt about late evening commitments. Miles puts an encouraging hand on her shoulder as a presumptive indication of guaranteed companionship. Brit remains expressionless but follows Dan as he leads the way down the stairs, turns right across East Liberty towards the general direction of Yamacraw.

We stroll in the warm glow of the late afternoon sun, through Wright Square and Johnson Square, and west along West Bryan Street. Schlomo stops suddenly beside a darkened doorway under a sign, which advertises the vague promise of a strenuous happy hour activity called Stein Hoisting with the slightly less elusive addition of Hot Wings, Cold Beer, and Good Times. He pushes open the door, clearly intent on all three, and possibly more. I follow, then Brit and Apolonia, while Miles and Agnita look to be discreetly weighing up the evening's potential alternatives.

Passing on the stein hoisting, which looks a little too combative, I decide that this is the opportunity for a whiskey and soda. Schlomo frowns and orders a craft beer. Immediately, at his elbow appears Angel from Paris, Texas, now evidently putting in an evening shift as a cowgirl waitress. I glance across, trying to suppress the thought that our choice of destination might not necessarily be put down to coincidence.

Schlomo says, "Ask an American male where he would want to spend his last two hours on Earth and he would say in a sports bar. Present this profound information to an Englishman, ask the same question, and he would politely enquire the purpose of a sports bar."

Miles Styles is plying Agnita with what looks vaguely like a sprig of greenery floating in a tall glass of swamp water carried to our corner table by a beaming Angel. It is later revealed as a mint julep, supposedly originating as a late nineteenth-century prescription to counter sickness, and better known in these parts as a Georgia julep. The principal ingredient is bourbon – a potent concoction best diluted with an excess of ice cubes.

Schlomo addresses Apolonia, "Hey that was some talk. I mean all that cool stuff about scientific thought, Thomas More, and the Spanish plaza mayors. The only decent mayor we had in New York was Mr. Bloomberg. We don't do the history of things that much at UCLA these days. I don't know if the Dean is so keen on digging up things like colonization and domination – I think he studied under Lenin." He lets out a throaty laugh.

Miles looks nonplussed, takes a sip of Georgia julep and coughs politely. Dan continues, "By the way, Apolonia, I love the way you said plunder. Plunder – that's what it was all about hey?" He catches the eye of Angel who is hovering nearby, and indicates the need for another round of drinks.

Apolonia downs her julep in two gulps and looks mildly rejuvenated. "Actually its mostly from my dissertation," she says. "I confess to being kind of more absorbed with the past than the present. I took my class to Peru last fall to see Lima. They weren't all that interested in the Spanish cities but wanted to follow the Inca trail up Machu Picchu. Half of them got altitude sickness. The cleverer ones got flights online and then flooded Instagram with aerial photos of llamas."

She looks my way. "Actually, I've always wanted to explore the city of Intramourus in Manila – the only Spanish city in the East."

"It was," I say. "There isn't much left of it now. Your General McArthur returned there towards the end of the Pacific War, guns blazing to dislodge the Japanese, and just about blew it to pieces in the process."

Apolonia looks a little crestfallen but is unbowed. "They must have been wonderful—those seventeenth and eighteenth century days—the philosophy, the patronage, the ideological arguments over aesthetics ..."

Brit who has suddenly resurfaced interrupts, "... the unbridled capitalization, the debtors, the deportations, the slave trade, the plunder," she looks accusingly at Dan.

Apolonia is anxious to clarify. "Yes but everything was open to enquiry. Everything was radical. Without the age of learning could we really have arrived at the universal rights of man? Would we have had such a noble undertaking as the Charter for Georgia? It embodied so many honorable intentions."

Meanwhile a football game is going full blast on a big screen behind the bar, facing a highly vocal group of drinkers. The sportscast suddenly signals a break in play and here is Donald Trump explaining the precise height of a wall he intends to construct along the Mexican border. The football followers look mildly taken aback but appear quite supportive.

Trump is saying, "I would build a great wall. And nobody builds walls better than me, believe me. And I'll build it inexpensively and I'll have Mexico pay for it."

The channel switches to Hilary in a black pant suit, enthusiastically selling the idea that Donald is a fruit loop of the first order. A loud chorus of disapproval from the direction of the bar, and its back to football again.

"So who is performing tomorrow?" says Dan

"I am," says Miles Styles hesitating. "I have my notes somewhere." He delves into a bulging satchel as if to substantiate it. "I prepared it before I left," he says, "but when I got here I felt I had to more or less re-write it and I haven't quite finished yet. It's all about the grid and the square really. Tracking down the influence of the grid takes us all the way back to China. He looks around for sympathetic confirmation, one eyebrow raised. It's mainly to do with political order and behavior under the guise of social etiquette. All a bit removed from our comfortable civic elegance here in Savannah, with its friendly compositional geography. Mo has instructed me to kind of explore where this ingenuous plan actually came from. Was it just dreamed up in London, or did Oglethorpe put together all the pieces from his travels and military campaigns. There are so many possible sources it's difficult to be too exact."

Agnita who has been staring at the TV screen for several minutes has taken time off to obtain an explanation of the impenetrable rules governing American football. As a result she has already downed a sequence of juleps via a series of admirers at the bar to reward her obvious intellectual determination. She now weaves her way towards us with a face matching the color of her bright pink jacket. "Well, from my geographical side, it's all about capturing the readily available data. There are no boundaries." She looks up and smiles sweetly at Miles. "We can manipulate data to cover whatever analysis we want – it's much to do with space-time. Accuracy simply depends on how we encode our source material."

"Isn't it all to do with the representation?" says Miles innocently. "I don't want to confuse people with coordinate systems and satellite mapping. Renaissance designers used the grid more to conjure up the urban experience, while it suited the Spanish colonizers for its uniformity and ceremonial suitability. In Savannah it had a definite egalitarian role built around a search for social equality. You see we cannot really escape the political connotations of control whichever way we look at it. History seems to indicate that utopian notions of equity are generally short-lived."

"I can see that I'm going to have to sit down somewhere quiet and explain all this data conversion business," says Agnita meaningfully, leading a confused looking Miles to the door.

I turn to resume my discussion with Dan Schlomo, but he has refocused his attention to Angel from Paris, Texas, whose limited stint as a waitress appears to have lapsed. She is now seated demurely on a low couch, sipping a green drink through a long straw and listening with wide eyes as Schlomo expounds his views on Hilary Clinton accompanied by a wild flailing of arms. He is clearly saying something suitably tantalizing and not too damaging to patriotic instincts, as Angel leans across and plants a gentle kiss on his forehead.

Brit is now seated at one of the tables near the big screen with a perplexed expression, surrounded by several large bearded men wearing baseball caps, one or two with neck tattoos. They are drawing little diagrams on a large beer mat that might be either an indulgent means of explaining the role of a quarterback on football team formations, or a heroic attempt to clarify Republican election strategy. Brit, with genetic Scandinavian aplomb, is hoisting a stein, to the full-throated appreciation of the surrounding audience.

Feeling suddenly tired I leave and wander along Bay Street, past the old and silent cotton warehouses on Factors' Walk, now converted to other uses, including the River Street Inn, catching the lights and animated voices from the café terraces on River Street. It is a steep drop down to the river, and I wonder again at the sheer bravado of situating a new settlement on a plateau. It was only in the nineteenth century that its retaining walls were constructed, using stone ballast unloaded from the holds of visiting sailing ships, to make way for new cargoes of cotton. The walkways and bridges on Factors' Walk were named after the cotton graders who had to constantly move between different factory levels in order to inspect the cotton quality.

85

I continue down Abercorn Street, past the Colonial Park Cemetery and its scattered peaks and troughs of statues and memorials including those to Revolutionary War Soldiers, and Button Gwinnet, one of three signatories of the Declaration of Independence. Positioned in black profile against the almost full moon it looks like a mini-city, silent but not forbidding. Through Lafayette Square, past the impressive spires of the Catholic Cathedral of St. John the Baptist, and the Second Empire-styled Hamilton-Turner House, now a guesthouse known locally as the "Grand Victorian Lady." I remember being told it was the first in Savannah to be wired for electricity, and the lights are certainly burning tonight. I quicken my step through Calhoun Square and the familiar path across Forsyth Park.

In my little living room, after a shower, I turn on CBS News and inevitably encounter the aspiring candidates, dueling for majority support.

Trump asserts that Hilary's aggressive comments on Syria would lead to World War Three, and that the media are rigging the polls.

Hilary, in a long red jacket is in a warm embrace with Michelle Obama, who is being rapturously applauded and proceeds to inform us that Hilary is the best thing since sliced bread. She concludes on a triumphant note of discovery, "And she is a WOMAN." Thunderous cheers ring out.

I turn off the TV and go to bed.

Factors' Walk now houses an amalgam of commercial uses in nineteenth-century cotton warehouses. The retaining walls are constructed from ballast removed from old sailing ships.

A Vexed Policy of Taxation

THE FERMENT OF REVOLUTION

The Treaty of Paris in 1763, under which France and Spain relinquished their claim to North America, ended the Seven Year's War and effectively left Britain as the dominant colonial power in North America. The Spanish in particular had posed an almost permanent threat from the south, inhibiting the firm establishment of Georgia's southern boundary, which could now be aligned. This should technically have reduced Britain's financial burden, but a new colonial policy of taxation to help defray expenditure on protection of its colonies created an almost instant reaction from the colonists themselves. The Plantation Act and Currency Act of 1764, and most notably the Stamp Act of 1765 were all intended to raise revenue, but it was the latter that drew the most negative response and raised the famous adage "no taxation without representation." In practice, this simply involved the fact that everything that was printed had to use specially stamped paper, which was subject to tax. There was at first a difference of opinion between the Georgia Council and the Lower House of Assembly, which was largely composed of wealthy individuals with strong political ties. The Governor, James Wright, appointed by Parliament and charged with upholding and enforcing its legislation, was confronted by a radical group – the Sons of Liberty, who met in a local tavern.

The first demonstration began in November 1765, after the announcement of an appointed stamp agent. With armed resistance being planned, Wright called in soldiers to reinforce the local forces. When the stamps arrived one month later via HMS Speedwell, they were temporarily put under guard at Fort Halifax. As ships loaded with rice could not sail without stamped papers, export of goods quickly came to a halt, increasing the growing frustration.

The Georgia Assembly joined the twelve other American colonies in petitioning Parliament for a repeal of the Act, and following a public standoff, the stamps were removed to a guardhouse. After the arrival of the agent George Angus in January there was a temporary appeasement. Stamps were sold to the ship captains and more than sixty loaded ships left Savannah two weeks later with correct credentials. Georgia therefore had the questionable distinction of being the only American colony to comply with the Stamp Act.

This did little to cool down the situation, however. While white settlers, rich and poor, created a number of minor incidents and even burned an effigy of the unfortunate agent, some black slaves used the opportunity to flee to the north side of the Savannah River where they managed to elude the militia despite a price being put on their heads. The news in June 1766 that the Stamp Act had been repealed did little to ease tensions, as at the same time a Declaratory Act emphatically underscored the right of Parliament to impose laws and statutes to bind the colonies to parliamentary authority and tax them at any future time. This not only antagonized members of the Assembly, but also encouraged them to assert its powers.

One of the first emboldened acts of the Assembly was to argue against the terms of the Quartering Act that directed colonies to supply British troops with daily necessities. Although the situation was defused when troops were later withdrawn from Georgia, this was followed by further opposition to the Townshend Acts introduced by Charles Townshend, the English Chancellor of the Exchequer, which levied duties on various imported items such as tea, paper, paint, and glass. Jonathan Bryan, a member of the Governor's Council, publicly condemned the acts and was promptly suspended, making him a local hero. Bryan Street was later named after him, to honor "a friend of liberty."

An Escalating State of Confrontation

The political impasse between the Governor, Parliament's representative in Georgia, and the House of Assembly over "Rights and Privileges" continued to reverberate. The Governor could scarcely act against the instructions of the Crown, while the Assembly could refuse to pass essential bills and mischievously elect "Sons of Liberty" to prominent positions. In turn it remained the prerogative of the Governor to disallow the election or to dismiss the Assembly. This chartered a perilous course of confrontation. At stake was the issue of colonial rights, and the vulnerability of newly empowered communities to taxation through Acts of Parliament decided halfway across the world.

While Charlestown remained the busiest port and township in the South, by the mid-1770s river traffic in Savannah had increased several fold, over fifteen years, due to its expanding trade hinterland. Exports including rice, tobacco, skins, and timber had grown ten times, and as a result shipbuilding was carried out in nearby Yamacraw, and growth of the import-export trade led to more than fifty ocean-going vessels being engaged. Three roads linked the town with other parts of the Georgia colony, traversing old swamp and Native American trails along the sprawling network of rivers and creeks.

Things came to a sudden head in May 1773 with the Tea Act, which granted the East India Company a virtual monopoly on the tea trade with America, while making this subject to a revenue tax on legally imported goods. Known as the "Intolerable Act" this led to immediate resistance, the most common known response being the Boston Tea Party on December 16th when 342 boxes of English tea were unceremoniously dumped into the harbor. The British response was to close the port, alter the colonial charter, and replace the elective council by an appointed one.

The self-styled War of Independence was as enigmatic in its beginnings as it was confounding in its outcome. As the historian Niall Ferguson has pointed out, the New Englanders were quite prosperous by any standards, and were liable for only a minute level of tax. The Tea Act reduced the duty on tea rather than increased it. They had also wholeheartedly supported the British against the French in the Seven Year's War.

The issue represented something of an unfortunate conundrum – a collision between entirely separate ideologies within the bourgeoning British Empire. The East

India Company, which had a monopoly in the American tea trade, stockpiled around seventeen million pounds of the substance. It might also be said to have been landed with a surplus precisely because of the American boycott campaign against the Townshend Act, and therefore wished to unload part of its surplus stock to avoid a temporary financial crisis. There is little doubt that in practice the British Empire established a preferential market for American agricultural products, but it was really the constitutional principle over the right of parliament to levy taxes that was at the heart of the problem.

Benjamin Franklin, one of America's "Founding Fathers," played an interesting part in the ensuing situation. His intermittent but lengthy periods spent in England prior to 1775 as the colonial agent for several American States, including Georgia, coincided with the European Enlightenment, of which he was an enthusiastic adherent. In London he was acclaimed as a renowned author and philosopher who espoused the cause of colonial unity between the Crown and its American colonies. However, his mounting frustration over the obduracy of the Privy Council following the "Boston Tea Party" led him to leave England for France, where he became the first US Ambassador between 1778 and 1785. His excellent relations with the French Court did much to extract commitments of French military aid for the American independence struggle.

In retrospect the reasons for an inevitable clash had built up over a century between new representative assemblies in America and a despotic royal authority in Britain that appointed governors over each of the thirteen "crown" colonies. In this situation, any authoritarian intervention was going to be perceived as an act of hostility. Parliament's heavy-handed imposition of military force naively laid down an unnecessary challenge and brought things to a head. The famous rallying cry of "no taxation without representation" attributed to Samuel Adams was a legitimate assertion of the rights held by British subjects in America at the time.

In Georgia, a meeting was called, attended by representatives of all parishes. The majority were Whigs, conservatives or radical members of local elites, but who jointly opposed Crown policies. The two major parishes, Christ Church and St. John's both supported a redistribution of power rather than a revolution but could not settle their differences over what steps to take. However, the Continental Congress, which was convened in Philadelphia, brought together the most intransigent and rebellious representatives in September 1774. The assembly not only advocated a total boycott of British trade, it resolved to withhold all forthcoming imposed taxes. Thomas Jefferson drafted A Summary View of the Rights of British America setting out a basis of American rights, but politely addressed his remarks to George III on behalf of "your subjects in British America." Early the following year this was supported by a provincial congress meeting in Savannah. While this could be construed as the rashness of self-interested parties, it more than anything reflected an assured political maturity in response to the challenge of an imposing but imprudent parliamentary authority.

The first skirmishes between British and American troops occurred at Lexington in Massachusetts on April 19, 1775. It is famously believed that the colonial militia or "Minute Men" in Lexington were forewarned by Paul Revere, but their attempts to halt the British advance to Concord resulted in their death and future martyrdom. The following month, as the governor together with loyalist colleagues drank a toast to the birthday of King George III in Savannah, a crowd gathered to hoist a flag of liberty in front of his mansion, in what is today Telfair Square.

Royal authority began to be challenged in other parishes where loyalists were increasingly threatened, and in some cases had to flee by ship. On July 4th, a Provincial Congress was held that adopted a number of resolutions calling for the rights of Americans and for the King to recall all military forces. Several days later a large group of "Liberty Boys" who had commandeered an armed schooner—the Liberty—intercepted a British ship and unloaded its cargo of armaments, which were then used to supply colonial troops in Savannah and Charles Town.

While some, particularly the elder statesmen, viewed the traditional royal benevolence and protection as the very foundation of Georgia's prosperity, and gallantly believed that rebellion was an act of treachery, they were gradually outnumbered by those who instead felt threatened by that same jurisdiction, and became committed to independence. Savannah's revolutionary Council of Safety began to purge the Provincial Congress of loyalists, reaching out to the backcountry settlers in the face of plans to arm the Creek Native Americans. Meanwhile, the Council also authorized the closure of the port in order to enforce a boycott.

Declaration of Independence

The forceful idea of republicanism and its almost immediate impact was raised by Thomas Paine who came from an English Quaker background. Persuaded to seek a future in America by Benjamin Franklin who was in London to press the colonist's cause, Paine was a potent pamphleteer who arrived in Pennsylvania at the height of the colonist's confrontational battles over taxation. Writing for the Pennsylvania Magazine he denounced "African Slavery in America," but in January 1776 set out the then inflammatory case for independence in a pamphlet Common Sense, which sold half a million copies. As an aide-de-camp to Nathanial Greene, whose monument was later erected in Savannah's Johnston Square, he produced sixteen "Chrisis Papers," which heightened enthusiasm for the patriot cause. Paine arguably deserves equal or perhaps even greater credit than does Jefferson for articulating the republican cause, and for its public acceptance. A true revolutionary and fighter for individual rights, he travelled to France to raise money and equipment for the American troops, and refused to accept profits from his works in order to reduce costs and increase circulation. Many of Pain's words were echoed by Thomas Jefferson, and their implications aroused strong divisions among families, communities, and even staunch patriots. In addition, a large number of practicing Anglicans respected the position of the monarch as head of the Church of England, and there were in fact many loyalist forces, including those in Savannah.

In early 1776 the people of Savannah got news that four British warships were heading for the Georgia coast, and immediate steps were taken to defend the town. A Georgia Battalion was assembled and a vessel was sunk to prevent any incursion up the river. The armed vessels arrived on January 18th, and the Parochial Committee ordered the arrest of Governor Wright who later fled Savannah along with other loyalists. The civilian authorities believed that the British flotilla intended to capture the city, while the British insisted that the fleet simply required provisions, and attempted to seize the trading ships loaded with rice that were anchored off Hutchison Island. The standoff continued somewhat uneventfully until March 3rd when, after a day-long battle, the rice was transferred to naval transports and the British force sailed north. Wright briefly returned after the British resumption of power, and published a list of "rebels" who, not coincidentally, turned out to represent the elite merchant princes of the city.

Both sides then claimed victory although the colony, split between the Whigs and Loyalists, remained vulnerable to further attack. New recruitment and improved fortifications were still inadequate for defense, and Georgia appealed to Charlestown for help in outfitting additional vessels and equipping them with arms.

On July 4, 1776, in the Pennsylvania assembly chamber, the Declaration of Independence was adopted by the thirteen colonies, and famously stated:

"We hold these truths to be self-evident, that all men are created equal, that they are endowed by their Creator with certain inalienable Rights, that among these are Life, Liberty, and the Pursuit of Happiness. That, to secure these rights, Governments are instituted among Men, deriving their just powers from the consent of the governed."

Following this, a public reading of the Declaration of Independence was delivered, and an effigy of George III was burned in front of the courthouse.

In order to obtain ratification of the Declaration by the Southern "colonies" a compromise was reached whereby the foreign slave trade was allowed to continue until 1808.

In the same year Adam Smith's The Wealth of Nations was published in Britain, coincidentally during another form of revolution – the Scottish Agricultural Revolution. R. H. Coase, a Nobel Laureate in Economics, has stated that if one of Smith's earlier proposals for granting British colonies representation in Parliament proportional to their contributions to public revenue had been adopted, there would have been little real need for independence.

The Monument to Count Casimir
Pulaski on Monterey Square,
erected in 1853 on the anniversary
of his death while leading an
American and French cavalry charge
at the Siege of Savannah in 1779
during the War of Independence. It
is fifty feet in height surmounted
by a Statue of Liberty holding the
banner of the Stars and Stripes.

Occupation and Survival of the City

A temporary truce between the rival Whig factions failed to resolve their differences. The populist party won the Provincial Congress elections in November and formulated a new constitution that was adopted in early 1777. This created a powerful legislature, which was to annually elect the governor and council, replace parishes with counties, and also provide for freedom of the press and religions, along with trial by jury. While Savannah was offered four representatives to Congress this did little to stifle the differences between radicals and conservatives, and was followed by an abortive radical-led invasion of loyalist forces in St. Augustine, Florida.

The American forces were joined by France, Spain, and the Netherlands, but by November 1778 as a prelude to an invasion of the South, a force of 3,000 British, German, and Loyalist troops was assembled in New York and set sail for Georgia under the command of Sir Henry Clinton, while also attempting to orchestrate an invasion from Florida in a pincer attack. The land forces reached the Savannah River in December and anchored below the town, disembarking in flat boats at Giradeau's Landing. There was no coordinated defense and local forces were ill-equipped, but General Howe made a brave, if uncoordinated stand at what is now Wheaton Street, where he was outflanked by a force of British soldiers, guided by a former slave. The result was a rout, with many of Savannah's ill-equipped militia drowned in the swollen river and creeks around the town, and with the officers and many civilians fleeing to South Carolina. Most of Georgia's military supplies were surrendered, and captured forces transferred to a prison ship anchored in the river.

There was little damage to Savannah's 300 buildings, but most of Georgia came quickly, if temporarily, under British control. Protection was offered to those who swore loyalty to the king, and hundreds flocked to oblige. In Savannah, a temporary council and loyalist officials were sworn in, and appointed officials such as Governor Wright assumed their previous positions, while a Whig council in exile was held in Augusta controlled by low country conservatives.

Keeping control of the peace, proved to be a difficult matter. Food was scarce and had to be imported, and many artisans, merchants, and traders had left the town. However, the local newspaper was reconstituted as the Royal Georgia Gazette, and Charles Town provided a gathering point for the disaffected. The Augusta Congress devolved troop movements to Charles Town where they assembled under General Benjamin Lincoln. An invasion plan received the surprising assistance of a large French fleet and four thousand French, Irish, and Haitian forces under Count Charles-Henri d'Estaing. These were joined by troops from Augusta under General Lachlan McIntosh. The various forces made a rendezvous to the north of Savannah, while the French fleet disembarked troops at Beaulieu, south of the city. The British, who had brought hundreds of runaway slaves under their protection, used this new resource to reconstruct city entrenchments. Boats were sunk in the river to deter French vessels, and civilian volunteers were recruited to man the defenses.

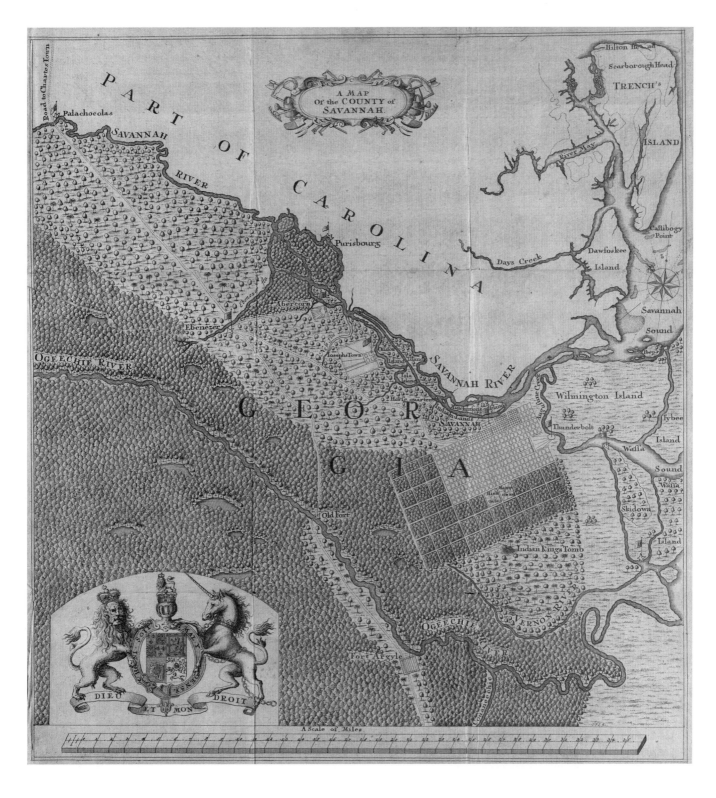

A MAP
Of the COUNTY of
SAVANNAH.

PART OF

CAROLINA

PART OF GEORGIA

Road to Charles Town

Palachocolas

SAVANNAH

RIVER

Purisbourg

Abercorn

Ebenezer

OGEECHIE RIVER

Iosephs Town

GEOR

GIA

Old Fort

Hilton Head
Scarborough Head
TRENCH'S
ISLAND

River May

Callibogy
Point

Dawfoskee
Island

Days Creek

SAVANNAH RIVER

Savannah
Sound

Wilmington Island

Tybee

Thunderbolt

Island

Wassa

Sound

Wassa

Skidown

Island

Indian Kings Tomb

VERNON RIVER

OGEECHIE RIVER

Fort Argyle

DIEU
ET MON
DROIT

A Scale of Miles

Bombardment of the city began on October 3, 1779, but resistance was fiercer than expected, and with heavy casualties from a battle centered on the Spring Hill fortification, the allied forces pulled back and the Polish General Casimir Pulaski was fatally wounded. Savannah not only remained in British hands but also became the staging point for the invasion of North and South Carolina. Charleston was placed under siege in early 1780 and later the same year an army under Lord Cornwallis inflicted a defeat on the American army at the Battle of Camden, and Georgia's capital of Augusta was captured by the British.

In Savannah, the impact was severe, with most buildings damaged by cannon fire. The British restored order, which discouraged insurrection, and troops were later withdrawn from the town to assist with further invasion forces. Runaway slaves had appealed for British protection, but it proved difficult to persuade them to reestablish the agricultural system in order to grow necessary produce, and many retained their weapons and fled the city. Meanwhile, the radical and conservative members of the Assembly in Augusta settled their differences, making frequent forays into Savannah and plundering the plantations.

Ultimately, Britain's position was fatally undermined, not merely by superior patriot forces, but by an aggressive Louis XVI anxious to gain revenge for the enforced loss of French colonial possessions in Canada. During 1781 the British surrendered many of their outposts, with Savannah being their last major stronghold. In October an army led by General Cornwallis was defeated by an army led by George Washington and a force led by the French Comte de Rochambeau at Yorktown, Virginia. In January 1782 Savannah was effectively sealed off by allied troops from the South, and as conditions deteriorated in the city the British government finally ordered the withdrawal of troops. Around 3,000 Loyalists and 3,500 slaves left for Florida and the West Indies, while many thousands of slaves had either escaped or died. On July 10th Lieutenant Colonel James Jackson accepted the keys to the city. Allied government was restored to Georgia with conservative Whigs in control of the State Assembly under the democratic Constitution of 1777, which remained as the foundation of government. The surrender effectively ended major conflict, and the British Parliament voted to end offensive operations in North America. The formal treaty ending the war was signed on November 30, 1782.

Under the new Constitution each state was given equal representation and three-fifths of all slaves were "counted" as population for purposes of representation as a concession to the southern states. While the states retained their civil jurisdictions the federal government was the ultimate center of political power. The "consent of the governed" helped to create a new liberal democracy, Thomas Jefferson asserting that "government is best that governs least."

The Historical Record of 18th Century Savannah states poetically that:

"The tents under the four pine trees on the bluff have grown into a city that looketh out over the sea and stretcheth its hands of trade to collect and transmit the wealth of the Empire State of the South. The Indians, who greeted and gave a home to those comers from a land over 'the great and wide sea,' have given place to the guests they welcomed with strange words and uncouth ceremonial. Their wigwams no longer crown the bluff, they no longer paddle the light canoe over the flashing waters of the river; warrior and maiden, with their brave deeds and simple loves, chief and brave, council-tent and home, have all disappeared."

While Savannah celebrated the treaty that ended the war on November 30, 1782, the city itself was left in a state of complete economic and social disorder.

SAVANNAH AUTUMN 2016: DAY 3

We are assembled again in our spacious meeting quarters at the head of the stairs in Poetter Hall ten minutes in advance of our appointed start time. Or rather, Apolonia, Jean-Paul Gournier, and I are seated, drinking coffee in silence, from a thoughtfully provided thermos.

Mo and Martha enter noisily, evidently in the middle of a heated discussion seemingly emanating from a breakfast news feature that followed campaign workers for candidates Hilary and Donald cruising the streets hoping to divert intrepid Pokémon hunters to their respective voting registers.

Martha is mortally offended at Donald's taunts of "Crooked Hilary," while Mo appears to be equally traumatized by Hilary's jibe at his supporters as a "basket of deplorables." Clearly the enthralling political agenda is escalating tensions in the closeted academic community. Mo is muttering something to the effect that Americans are brought up to believe that anyone can become president and now we are getting proof of it.

Dan Schlomo arrives looking not a little worse for wear but at least punctual. He chimes in on the political discussion. "Well, George Burns said the problem is that people who knew how to run the country are busy driving taxis and cutting hair."

Terry Fulbright enters with the vacant stare of the disembodied complaining that jetlag has further prevented anything approaching sleep. Miles Styles and Agnita van der Kampen silently enter together and sit demurely but separately. Brit Kris strides in briskly, dressed in denim, and full of sparkle having been informally offered, the previous evening, the position of principal cheerleader for the local football team.

It is 9 am. Mo perks up and springs an immediate test of our enthusiasm, inviting us to exercise our legs on this fine morning with a short stroll to Wright Square, and then perhaps a further short walk to one or two of the others.

Some of us, who independently consider we have already walked far enough for such an early hour, cast questioning looks at each other, but rise obediently. Miles Styles is excused to attend to his PowerPoint. Terry Fulbright has already laid his head on outstretched arms and is fast asleep. Schlomo lets out a low howl. Martha excuses herself as she has more handouts to print. Mo astutely recognizes a certain resistance hanging in the area and briskly produces a box of donuts as an inducement, after which he leads the way to the lobby. He is now in full flow.

"We are talking today about the plan for Savannah, so the best place to start is the square. Public space was always a determinant of the city plan – buildings simply define and furnish it. The module of the square recurs throughout the long gestation of the city, shaped by forward planning, community aspirations, and ready accommodation. It offers a central focus with its open opportunity for point references and a sense of repose. It represents a place of identity and distinction, but also one that defines and offsets its multi-cellular form and architectural set-pieces."

Mo pauses and looks around, assiduously counting our numbers as we enter Wright Square from York Street. He continues, "The Savannah square had a humble beginning as something of a heroic organizational tool, but its repetitive persistence came to personify the city's essential character. It articulates the layout just as it facilitates its regularized order and scale. And on top of this it is a 'container' for planting of native tree species, public activity, ceremony, and monument. And speaking of monuments, in the center of the square is one dedicated to William Washington Gordon, the pioneer of the Central of Georgia Railroad. You see, every square reflects an identification with its creative history.

Monuments and markers woven into the squares and city fabric act as expressions of durable city values, helping to create a landmark identity through their spatial emphasis and embedded memory. This shows a detail from the William Washington Gordon Monument on Wright Square dedicated in 1883 to the founder of the Central of Georgia Railroad.

The Lutheran Church of the Ascension in Wright Square dating back to the arrival in Savannah of the Lutheran Salzburgers in 1734. The church was granted a site in Wright Square in 1771, but the present stone building was completed in 1879 and stands next to the old Court House constructed in the late 19th century whose function was later replaced by a new court complex on Montgomery Street.

This ward is the largest under the plan. It was named after Viscount Percival, Oglethorpe's greatest friend and co-founder of the city. They served together on parliamentary reform committees and shaped the grand egalitarian strategy that formed the basis of the colony. Percival even came up with the name Georgia, although he might have been nudged in that direction by the incumbent monarch. Most of the royal nomenclature was removed after the revolution and the square was re-named in honor of James Wright, the third and last of Georgia's royal governors. In fairness, it must be added that he was probably the most able."

Jean-Paul murmurs that this might represent both the myth and the reality of the Old South, weaving the past into the present and preserving its memory. He adds, "Just look around the square – what we now call the Old Court House, built in 1889, simply replaced an older Greek Revival version built fifty-six years earlier. The US Federal Building has been periodically extended to accommodate necessary refinements in its operations. And what a collection of elaborate landmarks – the gothic tower on the courthouse, the tall marble bell-tower, and the elegant spire on the Church of the Ascension."

Mo breaks in, "What I wanted to impress on you was how the Square registers the passing of time, the shifting tempo marked by use, dappled sunlight, and shadow. Squares and parks can also be rented for special events. As Jean-Paul has told us, this emphasizes the simultaneous existence of complexity and pattern."

We walk along East President Street to Oglethorpe Square, originally Upper New Square, laid out in 1742, on land first granted to Moravian settlers. We pass a sign, which states "Stop Smoking and Start Vaping Today!"

Jean-Paul, an architect who knows his history, much to Mo's surprise, takes over. "The first Royal Governor made his home in the Square between 1754 and 1756 and granted sites to friends and supporters. It later became the setting for some of the oldest mansions. These included the Richardson-Owens-Thomas House designed by the English architect William Jay in 1819 at 124 Abercorn Street. It was purchased by a banker George Owens in 1830 and his granddaughter, Margaret Thomas, bequeathed it to the Telfair Academy of Arts and Sciences in 1951. The small Unitarian church originally located in the square was moved to Troup Square in 1860 where it serves as the Baptist Center. Some of the old houses have an indeterminate history. The McIntosh House is said to be the oldest brick house in Georgia, while the brick Georgian terrace is attributed to Charles Cluskey, the architect most associated with the Greek Revival style in Savannah."

Mo leads the way to a set of squares that make up the north-eastern sector of the Historic District, comprising Washington, Warren, Columbia, and Green, all added between 1790 and 1799. He explains that this involved a compromise to the original ward concept, so the appointed surveyor, one Lachlan McIntosh, while designating equal wards to the original six, adjusted the ward layouts by eliminating the tythings and trust lots in order to achieve the total of forty sale lots. The four new streets added in 1791 were named Lincoln, Habersham, Houston, and Price for leaders and revolutionaries. Green Square was

The Davenport House completed in 1820 in the Georgian style by Isaiah Davenport, a master builder and craftsman who also built a number of clapboard houses in the early 19th century. The house was one of the first to be saved from demolition and restored by the Historic Savannah Foundation in 1955, and gave rise to a number of other regeneration projects within and around Columbia Square.

developed mainly after the great fire of 1796, and because of its numerous small houses the area attracted many Irish emigrants including seamen, so that in the early nineteenth century it became a center for rooming houses and bars. It now provides a setting for a range of timber cottages on brick foundations with elegant ornamentation and entranceways.

Mo continues, "Many of the late nineteenth-century houses have been restored. Columbia Square contains two historical houses – the Kehoe House constructed in 1893 designed by DeWitt Bruyn for the iron magnate William Kehoe, and the Davenport House on East State Street built by Isaiah Davenport in 1820 and restored by the Historic Savannah Foundation in 1955. Davenport was a master builder and city alderman, and constructed a large number of early 19th-century clapboard cottages before completing his own Georgian-style house in 1821."

We move South along Houston Street to Crawford Square, constructed in 1841, named after William Harris Crawford, a native son of Savannah and Secretary of the Treasury under President James Madison.

The final stop is Lafayette Square whose residential popularity increased after the removal of the city jail in 1846. The better-known mansions are the Andrew Low House designed by John Norris in 1849, now a museum; the Greek Revival townhouse on East Charlton Street built in 1856, which formed the childhood home of Mary Flannery O'Connor; and the Hamilton-Turner House built in 1873. Dominating the square is the Roman Catholic Cathedral of St. John the Baptist, completed in 1896 in a commanding Gothic style.

Not possessing the stamina of Mo I sit down on a nearby bench, just within listening distance. It occurs to me that I have seen only horse-drawn carriages for the last ten minutes promenading around the square, and a welcome lack of motor vehicles. The noise of traffic seems far away, vaguely audible and strangely muted. Small swarms of tiny insects catch the morning light and infiltrate the Spanish moss hanging from the live oaks. I seem to remember it was known as Tree Hair by the Native Americans, and Spanish Beard by early explorers, and is actually a flowering plant, a distant member of the pineapple family, that has a pleasing fragrance during the spring and summer months. It can grow up to twenty-five feet in length, and can enterprisingly transfer itself to neighboring trees. I recall reading somewhere that beetles help to hold moisture that enables the moss to exist without ground roots. Perhaps because of its spooky similarity to hanging shrouds it forms an associated backcloth to local ghost stories, so it is perhaps invisibly bred by teams of long deceased gardeners.

I watch an old man throw down a cigarette butt and stamp on it. Mo looks on and frowns ominously. A squirrel bounds across, picks it up and scurries happily away.

A kindly looking lady approaches and sits down next to me. She asks where I am from. I say, "Hong Kong."

"Isn't that in Japan?" she replies.

"The People's Republic of China," I say.

"You don't look Chinese," she retorts suspiciously.

I confess that I am actually a colonial interloper from England.

"I thought we got rid of your lot about 200 years ago," she says looking bemused. She carries on, "I went to a Chinese restaurant once. I had something called dim sum. I took a dim view of it – it had no cheese topping. I must be candid – I was disappointed." She gets up and walks away without further comment.

On a bench some twenty feet away a young woman sits with one hand holding a cell phone, and the other wrapped around a leash, at the end of which is tethered a large and wary looking dog. She is engaged in a loud and somewhat one-sided conversation punctuated by urgent exhortations for doggy behavior that provokes periodic strangulated yelps in response.

" ... Yes, I know ... I know ... Sexually transmitted what? ... Oh that! ... MARLON PUT THAT DOWN ... Yes, I told him ... I know ... But that's Simon isn't it ... MARLON LEAVE THAT PIGEON ALONE ... Yes, I know ... She's from Atlanta so I suppose that's to be expected. I know ..."

After several minutes of this Mo looks at her with a fierce glance and holds up his hands, clearly deciding that the politest form of response is retreat. He leads his exhausted followers back to Poetter Hall only a short distance away, gesticulating and pointing to various features en route. We climb the stairs for the second time within the morning and seat ourselves.

*

It is still only 11 am, and Mo has another little surprise in store.

"In five minutes we have a small, private bus arriving to take us away from the land of the living to Bonaventure Cemetery, not far to the south. It is, of course, spiritually if not physically connected with the city. Its beguiling beauty comes from its boundary with the Wilmington River, and its serenity, enveloped by ancient oak trees and encroaching vegetation. Hanging clusters of Spanish Moss create an atmosphere not too far removed from the central squares themselves. It was once a plantation but became a private cemetery in 1846, and was purchased by the city in 1907. Since then residents and visitors are drawn to it, not merely to see the resting places of many prominent people from Savannah, but perhaps for something else – an elusive connection between life and death. The cemetery technically closes every day at 5 pm but some intrepid interlopers like to walk around its pathways and tree groves in the twilight, breathing in the smell of damp grass and fragrant earth, and communing, some say, with the more adventurous spirits. Just as it is said that Union soldiers stationed in Savannah rode out to picnic in its sheltered spaces that framed views across the river, we are all going to make a short visit to familiarize ourselves with this essential and contrasting part of the city.

Mo pauses and looks around to see if we are all alert and sufficiently enthusiastic. He is suitably reassured as we follow him down the stairs and clamber one-by-one, pushing and scrambling into a small bus, kindly provided by the college. Mo sits in front next to the driver.

We proceed east from Bay Street and south along the Harry S. Truman Parkway, engaging maximum speed as we pass malls, car showrooms, fast-food emporiums, and other run-down areas that we agree are best located on the urban fringe. We move along Skidaway Road and then turn onto Bonaventure Road.

Our little group walks respectfully and silently along the paths, voices lowered and hushed. Pieces of life-size statuary in repose, and sculpted, winged angels evoke a measure of tranquility that induces hushed voices in its visitors.

"I'm not quite sure what we are here for," whispers Apolonia. "Its all a bit spooky." Terry grabs her arm and pulls her along.

We pass the graves of the famous, those known and unknown: politicians and poets, comedians and commanders, songsters, actors, and lyricist Johnny Mercer who died in 2005. Mo tells us that the old house on the plantation that used to occupy the cemetery site was used as a hospital by the French during the Siege of Savannah in the early nineteenth century, and the house burned down in 1817. It was what probably gave Bonaventure its haunted reputation. It became a private cemetery in 1846 and the city bought it in 1907.

We reach a rather empty corner where the statue of the Bird Girl stood, before being relocated to a museum for her own safety in order to counteract the unhealthy tendency

OPPOSITE PAGE AND NEXT PAGE
Poignant statuary stand serenely over graves of many prominent people who rest in the Bonaventure Cemetery alongside the Wilmington River. Once a plantation, it became a private cemetery in 1846 and was purchased by the city in 1907.

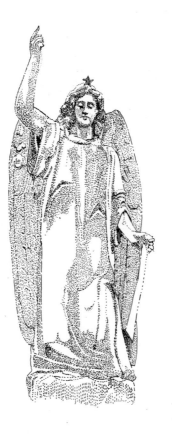

of visitors to chip off bits as souvenirs. The hauntingly beautiful figure, with arms out-stretched, was originally designed as both a statue and a birdseed holder, sculpted in 1936 by Syria Shaw Judon, and photographed for the cover of *Midnight* by Jack Leigh, himself now lying beneath a tombstone in Bonaventure. Then to the grave of little Grace Watson – a girl who charmed and captivated Savannah, and died at the age of six. Her ghost is said to be occasionally seen playing in Johnston Square where her father once managed the Pulaski Hotel.

We note the inscriptions. Edythe Chapman, one of the earliest screen actresses of more than fifty silent films; Conrad Telfair who unashamedly dealt in slaves, negotiated disputes between tribes of Creek and Cherokee Natives, and went on to become a three-term Governor of Georgia.

We walk a little farther and come to the grave of Conrad Potter Aiken, a United States writer and Poet Laureate, whose tombstone is thoughtfully fashioned to form a bench for weary visitors. Mo bids us to sit down, some of us on the flat stones. "I would like to tell you a story," he says, "which lays at the heart of all our endeavors. It is about an intrepid traveller by the name of John Muir – a Scottish-American naturalist. At some time in 1867

he arrived in Savannah as part of a long and arduous trek to Florida. Having virtually no money and sensibly scrimping on hotel accommodation, he decided to sleep under the stars on one of the gravestones in Bonaventure. He wrote a chapter on this in a book called *A Thousand Mile Walk to the Gulf*. The chapter was headed 'Camping in Tombs' – a clear candidate for the most discouraging non-fiction chapter title in the history of American publishing." He chuckles.

"Muir was one of the first of what one now might call an environmentalist-philosopher. He was obsessed with the complexity and beauty of the natural world and I would like to read you some of his words from all those years ago, because they summarize the Savannah of today so well. He notes that, 'nature is ever at work to reclaim the graves, and to make them look like the foot of man had never known them.' He relates that, 'the live oaks or *Quercus virginiana* were fifty feet high, with branches that reach out horizontally, while each branch is adorned like a garden with ferns, flowers, grasses and dwarf palmettos.' He wonders at, 'the calm undisturbable grandeur of the oaks, which make this place of graves one of the Lord's most favored abodes of life and light,' and goes on to note that, 'the long moss that drapes the branches, hang in long silvery-gray skeins of not less than eight or ten feet, and when slowly waving in the wind they produce a solemn funeral effect that is singularly impressive.'"

Mo continues. "He exalted in the natural environment and believed it came straight from the hand of God, uncorrupted by civilization. He describes, 'the bald eagles roosting among the trees in Bonaventure with their screams joined with the noise of crows, and songs of countless warblers and happy insects.' As he said, 'the dead do not reign here alone.' He opened our eyes to the complexity and beauty of the natural world. He was an advocate for the preservation of wilderness and co-founder of the Sierra Club."

Much later in life he persuaded Theodore Roosevelt to protect Yosemite through federal control and management, and was largely responsible for the establishment of the Sequoia and Yosemite National Parks.

California celebrates John Muir Day in April every year. He was a true American hero and what he would have made of the Edge City, I shudder to think.

Martha B. re-appears, having been taken in the bus to the local pizza parlor to collect our picnic lunch. She holds piles of sturdy brown boxes and a plastic bag containing plastic forks, plastic knives, and plastic plates. Another bag contains coffee, milk, sugar, and a mound of cardboard cups. I silently observe that John Muir would not have been amused. In deference to Conrad Aiken we decide to remove ourselves to a grassy knoll overlooking the river.

There are no bald eagles but plenty wildlife of both the flying and crawling variety, but Martha B., as if by magic, produces a large rug on which we compete for space to satisfy our selfish comfort.

Suddenly Apolonia, who has been gazing thoughtfully at the light illuminating the carved stone statues behind us, lets out a scream as three sub-human forms creep out of the cemetery, one a skeleton in a long cloak, another a zombie with frayed hair and popping eyes covered with whispery strands that looks like Spanish Moss, and the other a vampire in black with severe dental problems and a red, inky substance dripping from its mouth.

For the first time on record, Mo looks nonplussed. Martha B. grabs her umbrella to fend off the nearest ghoul who is making rapid strides towards the piazza boxes, while the other two howl encouragement. Jean-Paul stands up and adopts a confrontational stance. Terry is fumbling with his phone camera. Agnita and Brit look mildly concerned but keep on chewing. Miles stands behind Jean-Paul.

The deathly threesome dance towards us and duly unveil themselves as charity spooks on a trick or treat mission, holding out transparent collection boxes. Martha B. tries in vain to shoo them away. Mo offers them slices of pizza. They grin horribly through stage make-up and slide away after collecting fifteen dollars, happily consuming the remainder of our lunch.

Mo says, "I think its time to re-board our bus."

*

At 2:30 pm promptly we are re-assembled. Mo crouches over his notes and clutches his refreshed coffee cup. He stands, coughs.

"Let's cut to the chase here," Mo begins by way of introduction. "Every city must emanate from an ideal – essentially a need to separate urban and rural through a dynamic physical division. Savannah was intended as a specialized settlement for a new beginning. The settlers were escapees from debt and despair. It epitomized pre-modern America with its hidden and yet premature promise to meet the extravagant expectations of the huddled masses. Savannah was a European intervention, but was formed out of countryside and sat on a plateau. So at first glance, we have to admit that the context did not exactly suggest or even induce the ultimate solution. Now our friend Miles Styles, who specializes in the urban composition, is going to explain exactly how this plan might have been conceived, and what were the likely influences."

Miles fans himself with a purple handkerchief and stands up.

SECOND READING: MR. MILES H. STYLES
THE PATH TO THE PLAN

Well, Fernard Braudel said in a rather offhand way that a town or city only exists as such in relation to a lesser form of place. But Savannah appeared of its own volition – not conquered, castled, or commodified, but generously bestowed through a remarkable philanthropic colonial initiative with a more-or-less acknowledged pattern of use and ownership that best suited the collective experimental interests of a small and very optimistic community. Savannah, in fact, might be one of the few celebrated cities where the urban grid genuinely reflected a largely egalitarian situation, resonant with righteous conviction and rich with organizational potential.

What better way to initiate a city than with a sense of order that dignifies the ambition and makes the emerging city manageable. The settlers were not tied to the land – they negotiated for it, but clearly got a good deal. It was never a city of ceremony, and initially it had no walls and no gates. Ultimately, the only thing the unwary settlers needed to defend themselves from, apart from other colonial rivals and occasionally belligerent Native tribes, was the one they could not even imagine – cholera. The geometric subdivisions belied its subordination to the natural landscape. There was nothing overtly classical about it, but there was equally no pretention. The street-regulated layout with its clear circulation framework and articulation of space was a deceptively simple ordering device creating an equitable framework for an agrarian economy, later differentiated only by trade specialization and social hierarchies.

And the settlers quickly became land owners. Now, in general terms, the owners of land ultimately have the single biggest impact on urban form, encoding the memory of the city with fixed structures and symbolism, that is until they are progressively replaced or develop a hallowed identity through historical associations. I mean, in Britain a city isn't a city in official terms unless it manages to manufacture itself a cathedral.

So lets ask ourselves a fundamental question – where did the planning influences actually come from, and who conjured up the rules that circumscribed an entirely new and somewhat abnormal community. There was some logic and a large degree of precedent to the early gridded settlements in America. Philadelphia, laid out by Thomas Holme for William Penn in 1683, was the first American city to be designed with a gridiron plan form that might well have referenced the privately planned estates of 17th-century London as a model, although these in themselves were undoubtedly influenced by the earlier studies of notable Renaissance scholars as we will see.

The Philadelphia Plan followed a strong but diverse geometric order with a major central public square at the intersection of principal streets, balanced by four smaller squares that each occupied two of the elongated spaces defined by the grid. Montgomery's plan of 1717 for the "Margravate of Azilia" that eventually became the colony of Georgia was based on 640-acre squares, with the town itself surrounded by plantations. So the orthogonal grid and square plan form had, by the early eighteenth century, become almost a standard model for new planned communities.

Now what is the history of the grid, and is it all a matter of rational organization, composition, or a combination of both? The grid is often touted as a democratic device to ensure equitable land distribution but in the past has tended more to reflect centralized political and economic structures. In Savannah we have the example of land allocation both within the planned area for housing, commercial, and community uses, and outside it for agricultural production. Savannah was in fact part of a wider regional plan. Garden lots were situated just outside the city limits, with larger farm lots located even farther out. The city grid was envisaged as the core of a more extensive regional plan. Spiro Kostoff informs us that this was in fact the blueprint of a political system. The orientation of wards and free-holdings along east-west streets helped to visually unite the urban design, but probably also reflected the collective social equality of the early settlers, and their shared use of strategically placed public buildings to the east and west of each square, just as Philadelphia reflected Penn's Quaker principles of social equity.

In more recent times Edmund Bacon has commented on the ability of the cellular unit comprising the twelve-block enclave and the central square, to serve as a practical model for land organization and accretion, but also for extension through its linear connective model. In Savannah this provides for a designed interaction between the predominant street grid layout, and a regularized pattern of public squares, each with their own character. The orthogonal grid layout does not merely achieve organizational clarity

107

and convenience. It provides both a practical and design configuration for the planning of new conurbations, historically adopted through the inclination of kings, emperors, military governors, and pious church leaders serving an entire realm of democratic ideals, defensive formations and absolutist governments. Within the closed grid, forms of division can create their own patterns of hierarchy and rhythm.

Going well back in history, the grid structure governing city planning can be traced back to both Mesopotamia and to the Zhou Dynasty of 1,200 BC in ancient China, which represented an ordered and unified way of life. These were based on ideological relationships of ruling elites and their associated military and administrative bureaucracies. Intellectual ideas and philosophical precepts established a constant dialogue with physical layout patterns that both articulated and anchored the workings of society. The rulebook for Chinese urbanism that blended formal layout planning with an established social protocol was the *Zhou-li*. Chang'an, the ancient T'ang capital of China was laid out on a highly symbolic imperial grid, based in part on the elusive dictates of *feng shiu*, and with a spatial structure built around status and hierarchy. This comprised a standardization of ideological standardization of urban elements that regulated city layout through a metaphysical geometry of order and control with a hierarchical and regularized political diagram organized into urban quarters. It was sustained through the Confucian code of behavior and maintenance of social harmony, ceremonial rites, and patterns of etiquette. This was anything but egalitarian however. The rigid layout reinforced the symbolic power of the state, while urban perception was dominated by gates, main axial avenues, and ceremonial or religious spaces that acted to both segregate and embellish functionally specific enclaves.

The Greeks utilized the grid in their colonizing strategies around the Mediterranean, Aristotle in his *Politeia* crediting the practical and clear-cut planning of Hippodamus who invested the utopian division of the *polis* into squares. Land was devoted to sacred, public, and private space, and divided into three classes of use for artisans, farmers, and military. The Romans utilized the colonizing advantages of the grid for empire building further afield in Europe and North Africa. While few cities retained their initial rigid form, the grid was resurrected in the Middle Ages, notably in Italy, France, and Spain, motivated by the necessities of defense and rapid trading growth. During the Renaissance feudal and port cities were reconstructed or expanded using the same mechanism.

Leon Battista Alberti who famously produced a treatise *On the Art of Building* in 1452, established a set of rules for urban composition through referencing a combination of built elements extracted from the medieval city and cleverly drew on a set of precise conditions more or less inherited from the Roman scholar Vitruvius. These were utilized by Alberti in an organizational and visual sense as recognizable elements introduced through sets of urban relationships. This brought together both fixed elements that structured the overall urban matrix at whatever scale, along with a flexible use of design components that could be used in innovative ways to accommodate what might be loosely stated as material satisfaction and sensuality through pleasurable urban experiences. Almost 300 years before the formulation of the plan for Savannah this probably represented the first means of articulating urban design composition according to accepted rules and typologies, while allowing for an almost infinite number of permutations.

Alberti was the master magician of the Renaissance who claimed that conceiving a city was like designing a building, and that the palette of components was quite small. The new discovery of perspective encouraged the application of "ideal" symmetrically planned cities, which tended to follow the compositional forms of the High Renaissance, and accorded with certain acknowledged principles, for example the multi-centered grid with an ordered arrangement of a main central square with subsidiary squares arranged in relation to it. In fact the somewhat abstract plan for a theoretically "ideal city" by Pietro di Giacomo Cataneo published in 1567, based on the work of Alberti, has an eerie similarity to the later plan for Savannah.

Sebastiano Serlio, an Italian Mannerist architect and theoretician, expanded on these theories in a series of books that helped to convey specific settings in the Renaissance style, and is credited with canonizing the five classical Orders of Architecture. This practical application to urban design catered specifically to the needs of architects, builders,

and craftsmen in symbolic settings through geometric composition and the embodiment of ideal urban form through universal application of the Orders. In combination Alberti and Serlio brought together the worlds of architecture and planning, both ordered and diverse, dignified in a classical form but open to expressive interpretation, with multiple realms of organization.

The key architectural exponent of this was Andrea Palladio, whose work has had a lasting influence on urban design. His Villa Capra, built on a hillside in Vicenza later became the distant model for Thomas Jefferson's slightly more-quirky Monticello in Virginia. His *Four Books of Architecture*, published in 1570, generated an increasing use of the classical orders and proportions associated with the Georgian period, collectively termed "Colonial" in the American pre-independence period and "Neoclassical" thereafter.

As independent states shifted to a merchant economy with an emerging bourgeoisie, the urban hierarchy of church and fortress gave way to the market hall and council chamber. The ancient square established a multi-purpose tradition with church, administration, recreation, and commerce physically and socially intertwined in its form. As prosperity underscored civic identity, urban space was placed at the center of new urban compositions.

The French and British gridded cantonments and "civil stations" such as Pondicherry and Madras in India, with their gridiron layouts and rows of infantry lines defined by defensive walls, also served an ideologically inspired purpose around the same time as the first Savannah plan was conceived. In a similar way they contained a mix of administrative, military, and commercial uses, while accommodating the hierarchical organization of social groups that shaped the distinctive regularized colonial landscape.

The Giambattista Nolli Plan of Rome, produced at almost the precise time that Savannah was being laid out, proffered a new way of viewing the city through voids rather than three-dimensional forms, instigating a figure-ground revelation of the periodic shifts in urban fabric. This illustrates not merely a systematic replication of streets, squares, courtyards, and precincts framed and articulated by built forms and amenity spaces, but embraces the spontaneous and incremental insertions and adjustments that can be expected to occur over time and reduce negative cultural impact. The time dimension is important. It lets us understand the narrative of urban growth and change – the development spurts, the shifts, and declines; the significance of topography; and the consequence of interventions.

It is known that Oglethorpe, through his travels in Italy, was familiar with the work of Vitruvius set out in *De Architectura*. The dimensions of the civic squares in Savannah within the overall grid of wards, measured 315 feet by 270 feet, which accords with the Vitruvius ratio of 1.667 adopted by Renaissance designers. This allowed public buildings to be located on the east and west sides, with the other sides divided into town lots for houses, measuring 60 feet by 24 feet. Such a process generates formal "places" of its own volition in a way that an abundance of freestanding buildings and the competing but solitary functions of the contemporary city cannot.

There was, however, another reference source at hand that might have suggested certain planning parameters for Savannah. The Spanish honed their imperial ambitions through territorial expansion and economic exploitation in South and Central American cities such as Quito, Santiago, and Valparaiso. In the process they applied a distinctive approach to city building, which laid down the basis for governance, social, and economic functioning of their colonial settlements. By the end of the seventeenth century, around 500 new towns and cities had been created by the Spanish, the oldest in North America being St. Augustine in Florida to the south of Georgia.

The first authoritarian planning guidelines were issued by Ferdinand V of Spain in 1513, and were refined into an urban design code of 148 regulatory ordinances eight years later by Charles V. They were possibly first employed in the construction of the Inca City of Cusco, destroyed by Pizarro in 1533 and replaced by a new capital, Lima, based on a gridiron plan. This was laid out on the site of the obliterated Aztec ceremonial square, around which were built the viceroy's palace, military barracks, a cathedral, hospital, and a university – the first such facilities in the New World. In 1573, Phillip II issued a set of royal ordinances later known as the *Laws of the Indies*, which stipulated a structured uniformity with a hierarchy of uses and spaces, including presidios or military quarters and the Jesuit *reducciones*. The symmetrical ideal grids of 17th- and 18th-century colonial cities or *bastides* tended to follow the Spanish *Ordinanzas*, uniquely designed to guide the siting of buildings and spaces. Layouts were divided into equal blocks with a central *Plaza Mayor* as a setting for activities around which were grouped the governor's palace, the church, and town hall.

The royal order that emanated from Philip II might well have been derived from Alberti. It called for rigid grid layouts and the orderly arrangement of both public and private buildings. The Portuguese went further than the Spanish in stipulating uniform façades for their colonial cities in South America, to achieve even greater harmony. The relationship of uses in these situations reflected the prevailing link between Church and State, and acted as both dominating and defining elements around which the regularly spaced residential and merchant quarters were arranged. The street grid also integrated open plazas, which served as places of congregation, but also acted as central growth points and the basis for the formation of principal streets. The "ideal" form even directed that places chosen for settlement should be healthy, defensible, be near a river for unloading goods, and close to arable land.

Most of this could have constituted virtual guidelines for the siting and layout of Savannah. Oglethorpe could not have been ignorant of the Ordinanzas and might well have drawn ideas from the cities in the America *conquista* such as Mexico City founded by Hernando Cortés. The assignment of land parcels according to a social and spatial hierarchy was something that was also encapsulated in a 17th-century New England Ordinance – "The Ordering of Towns."

A further and more immediately available source of reference for the Savannah Plan was that of London. Sir John Evelyn, in fact, commented in his plan for London after the great fire of 1666 that "streets are not to pass through the city all in one tenor without varieties, useful breakings, and enlargements into Piazzas at competent distances which are to be built exactly uniform, strong and with beautiful fronts." The residents of certain eighteenth-century squares were allowed by Acts of Parliament to raise taxes to pay for planting and maintenance of trees.

Fourdrinier's famous engraving of Savannah in 1734 was not the first to be commissioned by James Oglethorpe. As a keen observer of Palladio's utopian planning and urban design theories set out in his 16th-century treatise on architecture, Oglethorpe had previously commissioned a folio by William Kent – *The Design of Inigo* Jones – in 1727. Jones had been heavily influenced by Palladio in his application of designs for parts of Georgian London, which in themselves emanated from well established agricultural divisions. These were transformed in the 17th and early 18th centuries through estate organization imposed by large landowners. Inigo Jones was appointed Surveyor to King James I in 1615 as a skilled exponent of the fashionable Italian Renaissance style. When Charles I came to the throne ten years later, Jones became a member of a new commission to control new development in London and to regulate its form.

The Covent Garden development laid out by Inigo Jones, and undertaken by the Earl of Bedford in 1632 as an integral urban design, was designed with a rectangular plan and uniform terraces. It was set around a central square, which formed a cellular structure for later development as a sequence of interrelated enclaves. A church was constructed at the request of George I and faced the piazza, which formalized the overall setting in a not dissimilar way to the trust lot in relation to the Savannah Square. Covent Garden was rooted in the neo-classical tradition but reflected a transition to the European Baroque – a period of resplendent design and technological advance, cultural exhibitionism, and urban transformation – at least at one end of the social spectrum. Its architectural language and compositional sense arose directly from the Renaissance, with streets that were "wide, straight and beautiful." This versatility in turn led to a more formal and regimented ordering of urban space through continuous building planes, regularized façade elements and monumental space markers. In addition, the Bedford Estate Office acted as an administrative mechanism to ensure overall design control and regulation – something that would have naturally appealed to Oglethorpe in his emulation of a natural order.

After the great fire of 1666, London's land owners imposed virtually independent architecturally composed squares, unobtrusive and relatively inconspicuous in terms of their defining role, with a central gardens of planted trees and lawns. Geometric configurations that stemmed from the notion of an urban grandeur with its comprehensive planning potential and use of neo-classical orders were introduced into Britain through privately orchestrated urban developments in the 17th and 18th centuries, where the design of public space was accentuated by appearance and architectural definition. These contributed an orderly mosaic of new places, streets, and terraces with a delicate balance between public and private space. The squares were designed to be lived in, and main thoroughfares were therefore excluded.

The designed combination of residential and civic elements cannot have escaped the notice of Oglethorpe and doubtless influenced and inspired his thinking in the layout of central squares and placement of public buildings in Savannah. In fact, it was not uncommon in British colonial city layouts to test and even embody a rationalized version of current planning ideas in far flung territories, including America where virgin land allowed for an unconstrained ideal layout, open to continued growth and expansion. It has to be stated however that in the long-term these often orchestrated rather than reconciled the societal divisions within new communities.

Savannah was by no means the first American settlement to allocate a public role for squares within a grid form. In 1638 New Haven was planned with nine regular sized squares. In 1680 Charleston contained a central square of two acres, and several years later Philadelphia was planned with a standardized and symmetrically orchestrated

113

A brick terrace with its long iron balustrade defines the edge of Oglethorpe Square and offsets the central passive space with its mature vegetation.

framework of lots with a 10-acre central square and a further four subsidiary ones. It was, however, a century later before the public role of the colonial square was protected from redevelopment.

In all, therefore, Savannah represents a reformist urban design that mirrored the new society, and some 200 years later would see some of its initiatives followed by proponents of the Garden City movement as idealist visions for new land settlement at the interstices of town and country.

To a degree Savannah was improvised, but it was also designed to fit within the constraints of its site. So too was the language of organization and integration of public buildings. Oglethorpe was undoubtedly assisted in preparing ideas for the Savannah plan by Benjamin Martyn who was Secretary to the Trustees and had written a book about the first Lord Shaftsbury, the founder of Charleston. Straight street alignments not only established practical opportunities to promote public order and policing, but advocates of uniformity equated this with socialist ideas of a new society and the elimination of social distinctions. By the early eighteenth century, city planning was loosening the tiers of excessive uniformity and encouraging more variety and diversity in the design of both streets and squares – something that the proponents of Savannah clearly took to heart.

With the settlement of Savannah, the stage was set for some of the great city plans, laid out as orthogonal grids following the enactment of the National Land Ordinance. In particular L'Enfant's 1792 grid plan for Washington with its intersecting axial diagonals established the ultimate in grand design. It was marked by two overlapping vistas towards the Potomac River from the Capitol and the White House, later compromised by the Lincoln and Jefferson memorials. The 1811 plan for Manhattan which came to be based on the market capitalization of land, allowed the grid to be extended according to development demand and to meet the expedient demands of private speculators, which later led to a building intensity that was stretched to support even minimal environmental standards.

In fact the grid is nothing if not egalitarian, at least in terms of intention, hence its association from the eighteenth century onwards with social reformers and early champions of the green city as a counter to prevailing urban conditions. The notion of uniformity through regularized block organization and sub-divisions of standard proportions formed an expedient response to squalid conditions introduced though successive periods of intense urban growth in rapidly industrializing cities.

Thus the urban grid as applied to large cities lost its chivalrous claim to a utopian ideology, although new typologies distinguished by uniform designs did introduce socially equitable building solutions, such as perimeter blocks that defined communal open space. On one important count, the gridiron plans were generally able to adapt quite successfully to those other later transitions – from carriage traffic to the automobile, and from relatively low to high density.

The grid personifies a quality of sameness charged with difference, but in practice history shows that social and economic equality is short lived, and changes with escalation in the cost of land. The grid can be overwhelmingly regular, endemic of artificial order and tedium, but with intelligent orchestration can evolve into a matrix of diverse enclaves, streets of contrasting scale and joined-together buildings, that produce places with a strong sense of identity. It is in fact difficult to conceive of a city plan developed over the past 200 years where coordination and connectivity are overwhelming requirements that could be anything other than a grid, however open-ended. This was something that Haussmann took to heart in his drastic recalibration of Medieval Paris in the 1850s through a system of wide *rue corridors*, and connecting public squares. The definitive gridded city prototype must surely be Ildefons Cerda's *Eixample* in Barcelona, also planned in the mid 19th century, which was said to be at least partially inspired by the Philadelphia grid. Barcelona's egalitarian planning framework effectively absorbed the irregular profile of the old walled city, but did not lead to an unvarying regularity of architectural forms that might be assumed from the plan – instead it ensured that changing and unpredictable events were able to co-exist with a stable sense of order and synergy.

So there is nothing abnormal about the regular street grid pattern. Aristotle noted that man, after all, generally walks in a straight line, and he was not necessarily the first to observe that an even distribution of land was as effective for marketing land parcels as it was for ensuring security. But the grid's superficial rigidity tends to carry the instinctive

The last of the historic squares was built in the 1850s. The square was dedicated to George Whitefield, the successor to John Wesley and founder of the Bethesda Orphanage. It now accommodates a Victorian gazebo.

whiff of exploitation and alienation that reflects the industrial revolution of mechanization, routine, and sameness from which later urban populations fled to the greener potential of the suburbs. In many 21st-century cities the primary frame has become a high-speed super-grid, which circumscribes enclaves rather than as a means of ordering and coordinating individual neighborhoods. The footprint of the superblock, frequently homogenous in its self-containment, becomes actively reductive in its relationship to the street corridor, which creates not so much a public interface as a district separator. This can only be overcome by the superimposition of pedestrian routes and sequences of streets and public spaces as part of permeable networks infused with local meaning.

Savannah is well situated in the historical lexicon of planned colonial settlements, which established a high degree of order and ensured their formal growth and development, with a strong urban identity that flourished over many years. The formality of the Savannah plan belies its inherent flexibility and variety of treatments through its long gestation. It attests to the role played by a continuous ordering system of civic space and its relationship with a gridded street pattern that formed the basis for subsequent phased expansion while still presenting an overall sense of coherence. Savannah's development cells have served mainly as an organizational model within which individuals, and later small scale development interests, were able to forge their own incremental inserts, while municipal and community bodies erected public buildings and monuments as and when

The Owens-Thomas House on Abercorn Street, Oglethorpe Square. Designed by William Jay in the English Regency style as his first commission in the city, it was completed in 1819 and bequeathed to the Telfair Academy in 1951.

they were required. The plan creates inherent conditions for spatial definition while traffic, whether horse and carriage or motor vehicle, is ingenuously accommodated and effectively routed rather than segregated.

The elegance of the Savannah square stems from its representation and ordered accommodation of diverse uses, while allowing these to be interpreted into an extensive urban design vocabulary. This creates a *locus* – a singular relationship between buildings and context. Savannah's entire composition therefore never loses its essential unity, and helps to establish an underlying and highly legible grain. It posits the individual, perhaps one of the twelve million who visit Savannah every year, as an observer and participant in the wider urban experience, arising from a combination of expressive textures, surfaces, landscape, and patterns of form. While the plan suggests a composed and repetitive totality, the trust lots have become positively charged with a verticality and invention of public uses that adds weight and visual equilibrium to the setting.

The grid survives in Savannah more or less in its nineteenth century form, refined and regenerated as an ordering system and a container of fine squares and street building that has generated an enervating urban experience to the modern city. As a compositional totality, the urban design provides for an articulate and even intimate grouping of spaces and movement arteries, while motorized traffic largely fails to distract from the sanctity of squares and pedestrian movement channels.

The greatest characteristic of the Savannah Plan is its inherent potential for meeting our urban expectations for both consistency and variety, and as a useful vehicle for adaptation and reuse. Its geometry stands for order and organization, whether compressed or extended. Beauty largely stems from imagination, preconception and control. It is all about interpretation, and successive realms of occupation, that create a dynamic balance between the plan form and its ability to absorb change. What cannot be changed is going to perish sooner or later.

With that I conclude my presentation.

Miles pulls a handkerchief out of his jacket pocket and mops his forehead, smiles modestly, and sits down next to Agnita, who supportively pats him on the back.

Mo thanks Miles and we all make appropriate gestures of appreciation.

Mo and Martha B. announce they are having an early supper and will retire at a sensible hour to recover from the considerable rigors of the day. The rest of us are left to our own devices.

Schlomo mutters that as he is performing tomorrow morning he is rejoining the football obsessed throng at the Sports Bar and is intent on testing the full range of craft beers in order to be appropriately prepared. Jean-Paul whispers that he has a half-cousin, about five-times removed, with a four-wheel SUV that can hold up to eight people. They are formulating a plan to drive to Tybee Island and fire up some crabs. Brit says count me in – if I go back to the bar they'll sign me on permanent terms as a cheerleader. "That's three," says Jean-Paul, "Anyone else?" Apolonia nods enthusiastically. Terry shakes his head, looks around, and then nods in the affirmative.

The car will be here in ten minutes says Jean-Paul, as we wander down the stairs, and sure enough right on the button comes a massive Chevrolet Yukon, the size of a small bus, with third-row seats. The driver jumps out, looking nothing like Jean-Paul, barrel chested with corn-row hair bound up at the back of the head, smiles and says, "My name is Rocksteady Williams. Nice to meet y'all." An older lady in the front seat is smiling and says her hellos quietly. "This is the aunt of my much removed cousin, Miss Anriette," says Jean-Paul, as the five of us slide into the rear seats.

We move off on Route 80 towards Tybee, about eighteen miles away, with Rocksteady Williams giving an almost continuous commentary. "You know, Tybee is the beach playground of Savannah," he begins. "Its name comes from a valuable old resource – salt. It was known as *tybee* by the Euchee native tribe and was settled by the Spanish some time in the sixteenth century as part of Spanish Florida. They were chased out by British forces under James Oglethorpe just around the time the British settled Savannah. Then they built a fort and a lighthouse to control access to the Savannah River."

Jean-Paul continues, "Tybee is part of Georgia's Sea Islands, full of marshland, tall grass, and some nice beaches. Tybee Creek flows along the south shore, through the wetlands to Lazaretto Marsh. It's the easternmost point in Georgia, but it played a big part in Savannah's history. It was the staging point for the French-led siege during the Revolution and was occupied by Confederate forces during the Civil War under Robert E Lee. They weren't so successful, as they were marshaled in Fort Pulaski to defend the city but were forced out by Union forces using new-fangled common batteries. After the war steamships began to carry visitors and folks with asthma and other allergies to breath in the clear salt air. Then the Central of Georgia Railroad built a line to the island and constructed the beautiful Tybrisa Pavilion in the 1890s. Boys and girls used to dance there on a big, open dance floor in the 1930, to the big bands. After it burned down they built a new pier with a pavilion at the end for the 1996 Olympic Games. It's a real nice piece of timber work."

Rocksteady Williams breaks in, "After that, the old Fort Screven formed part of America's coastal defense system until 1947. But the main thing was the completion of this Route 80 highway, completed in the 1920s, that connected the island with all its sweet, cool, saltwater breezes, to the mainland. Now all the old gun batteries and magazine stores are just a museum. Just one thing I should tell you about," he chortles loudly, "The US Air Force, during a military training exercise in 1958, managed to accidentally jettison an atomic bomb on the island. It didn't detonate, but they didn't find it either. They carried out a search in 2004 and the story was they found suspiciously high levels of radiation in Wassaw Sound – just off the coast. Don't worry through – the crabs haven't turned luminous green, at least not yet."

We are now entering the island, and after parking we walk down to the waterfront with its long wooden pier. In the distance is the lighthouse of brick and cast iron – one of the oldest in the country. We walk its full length and look back to the lights on the outside decks of restaurants and cafes, people flocking around the stores and bars. Others are streaming onto the beach as the moon rises in a clear night sky.

We wander back, Rocksteady Williams pointing to signs for deep-sea fishing, galleries, and tours to see the bottle nosed dolphins that enjoy the currents running through the barrier islands. The boardwalk is lined with signs that announce the price of crawfish, steamed oysters, baby clams, and a seductive offering called a shrimp and deviled crab plate. One entrance is defined by a gigantic orange crab. Other equally persuasive offerings from adjoining decks are the bubba gumbos, crab stew, and a rather tempting oyster roast.

We climb wooden stairs and sit on a broad deck surrounded by cockatoos in cages. Crab, shrimp, mussels, and crawfish are being dissected and placed delicately on plates with sweet potatoes and corn. We eat slowly and carefully, prodding shellfish with tweezers for their meat. I sit next to Miss Anriette, who speaks softly with an accent rooted in the Bayeux country. We talk about the barrier islands off the coast, where ancestry was rooted in West African customs, intertwined with Native inhabitants of the new world.

Isolated conditions magnified the culture and ritual, carried through the cotton fields and slave markets along America's southern contours, from French Louisiana to Georgia.

Miss Anriette continues to reminisce.

"My family goes back 200 years to Saint-Domingue – what we now call Haiti. Toussaint Louverture led a slave rebellion in 1802 to the threshold of independence against a brutal regime of slave-owners. But Mr. Louverture was torn between being a revolutionary and a reactionary. He identified with the French even though he was eventually jailed by Napoleonic forces, but he still managed to become the symbol of black emancipation. His constitution granted him almost total power, and he knew how to negotiate. He had a massive kinship network that went right back to his aristocratic forebears in Africa. This made him an oracle of knowledge, and he drew on the black veterans from the French units from the American Revolution. He might have been a Catholic, but he was a disillusioned one, and if anyone tells you he was not a voodoo practitioner, don't you believe them.

"Now, the interesting thing is that it was a much younger fellow, Henri Christopher, who fought at the Siege of Savannah during the American Revolution, and did much of the running, He was later promoted to the rank of General by Toussaint. Christopher is depicted as the drummer boy on the monument to Haitian soldiers in Franklin Square, but he was an unlikely patriot. After the French deported Toussaint to France and brought in troops to re-establish slavery, Jean Jacques Dessalines and Henri Christopher led the fight to defeat the French, and they christened Saint-Domingue with a new name – Haiti. French troops still occupied the eastern part of the island, and in 1805 Henri attacked the local towns of Moca, Azua, and Santiago, killing all male prisoners while the rest were taken captive before the towns were burned to the ground. He set up a separate government and was proclaimed King of Haiti in 1811 – an independent, black-led state. Henri I was a great city builder and his palaces included Sans-Souci – now a World Heritage Site. To subsidize this he reintroduced the plantation system of slaves through forced labor to increase agricultural production of sugar cane and signed profitable bilateral trade agreements with Britain. The coins of the realm showed the profile of Henri as a roman emperor, but he committed suicide in 1820 before the two parts of Haiti were reunited. I am one of his descendants.

"My great great grandfather escaped Saint-Domingue and went to Louisiana after the Purchase. He had to flee the island's revolutionary terrors, and he settled in New Orleans. My other distant relatives travelled farther up the Mississippi waterway. We were all mixed-up blood, a bit of French, Spanish, and black slaves, and we were all French speakers. Only the old speak it now. Us Louisiana Creoles kind of became part of the *Code Noir* – the black codes as they were called. They say they were passed by France's King Louis XIV; probably just to ensure French control and the future of the cane sugar plantations. It regulated the pattern of behavior not just for slaves but free people. It gave the black man certain rights – they worked and earned wages. The black codes allowed the Louisiana men and women of color to break the bondage of slavery and become free. We could live and build houses anywhere, run our own businesses, and educate our children. This was all set out in legal documents. We were not African American – just somewhere between French Creoles and slaves."

Miss Anriette takes my hand, and we walk behind the others who are all carrying bottles of beer down to the beach and sit on the long grass. The stillness and the starry sky seem to induce a sudden silence. I keep my voice low. "So," I ask, "how did you end up here – it's a long way from Bayou country."

"After the emancipation my folks came to the barrier islands in the Low Country," she says. "The Gullah Geechee part. The Geechee people came from Georgia, the Gullah from the Carolinas. They are all descendants of enslaved peoples from West Africa." She suddenly laughs. "So really, I'm a Gullah Geechee Creole. You see, when the Constitution banned slavery back in 1865, most of the slaves in the Low Country kept to an isolated life in small communities on the islands. Our language developed from more than thirty African dialects. If you're a black person born in the United States, chances are there is a bit of Savannah Georgia in your blood.

"My mammy taught me how to cook the Creole gumbo like we just ate. The essential thing is sassafras leaf – all these waterways are full of crayfish, crab, and shrimp, and we can spice them all up with seasoning. It's not like the Cajun country with its turtles, catfish, and alligators. Our lives were a ritual relationship between land and water – cultivation of rice on one hand, and medicinal plants on the other."

She gives a throaty chuckle. "Gumbo is really a stew – we use fat and flour to thicken it, scallions and special herbs, and then put everything in the broth with oysters or game; but you have to serve it on French bread."

We walk along the beach next to the waterline with the waves bubbling around our bare feet.

"You know Lafcadio Hearn's Gumbo Zhebes?" she asks. I tell her that I spent time in Japan, and have Hearn's book of Japanese legends and ghost stories, written after he became a naturalized Japanese.

"The Zhebes, they were Creole proverbs. They sum up our people. The one I like best is, 'Wait till the fish is in the pot before speaking,' and the old saying, if a man used to hang around the house not working, like Rocksteady here, they would call him un encadrement – a door frame. You know Creole music – jazz? Jelly Roll Morton was Creole, born in New Orleans. He grew up playing piano in the local brothels." She laughs.

Rocksteady, who has been listening to some of this, is grinning and says he is going for a swim before taking us back. Brit and Jean-Paul say they will join him, and they run down the beach, throwing off bits of clothing en route.

Miss Anriette pauses suddenly and says softly, "You know the Creoles were all Catholics – I don't know whether they got it from the Spanish or the French Christian

121

traditions. This was all mixed up with ingrained West Africa and Haitian beliefs, which turned into rituals. It was bound up in a spirit world they called *loa*, mixed with Louisiana Voodoo and maybe the Gulla Geechee too. The rituals are about serving these invisible spirits – *loa* means the law that we find in symbols. Some practitioners have a gift that allows them to interpret these in ceremonies that can invoke beneficial or less well-intentioned outcomes.

"Most *loa* come from Haitian voodoo and its spirits. *Legba* is the most important. *Kalfu* guards the cross forces for good or evil, and Guede—or Baron Samedi—is the keeper of the cemetery who controls the crossing from life to death. He is linked to the loa of sexuality, and enamored of eroticism and copulation. There are others who can take many forms, such as serpents. But down in these parts we don't call it voodoo. Its hoodoo – a spiritual link between Africa and America. You need the right herbs and roots, and the right incantation. Not many can manage that."

Her tone is now a whisper. "Ceremonies can direct fortunes or otherwise. Spells can extend life or terminate it, and can set out a chain reaction far removed from just sorcery. My mother, Miranda, had this sense. She lived near the Bonaventure Cemetery, and you would be surprised at the people who drove to her house at night – rich businessmen, politicians, and some in trouble from the law. I sometimes peeped out at them, all desperate to direct the future to serve their purposes. The money she made, I used to buy me a little cottage here on Tybee after she died. I wish I had her talents and spirit access, but I have only a little."

I ask her delicately what she sees in my future. She is, perhaps fortuitously, non-committal, but smiles gently. "I cannot say for certain she says, so I will be quiet." She continues to look thoughtfully, "I can say that your sets of companions have an interesting future together she says, enigmatically." I look at her, silently expecting further elaboration, but she continues to smile, and without making further comment she leaves to walk back to her cottage by the marshlands.

On the drive back we are largely silent. We arrive in Savannah, delivered right to the front door. Rocksteady gives Jean-Paul a bear hug. The rest of us shake his large hand. He shrugs and smiles.

We climb the dark stairs to Magnolia. It is late and we don't linger.

For once I avoid the late news on television.

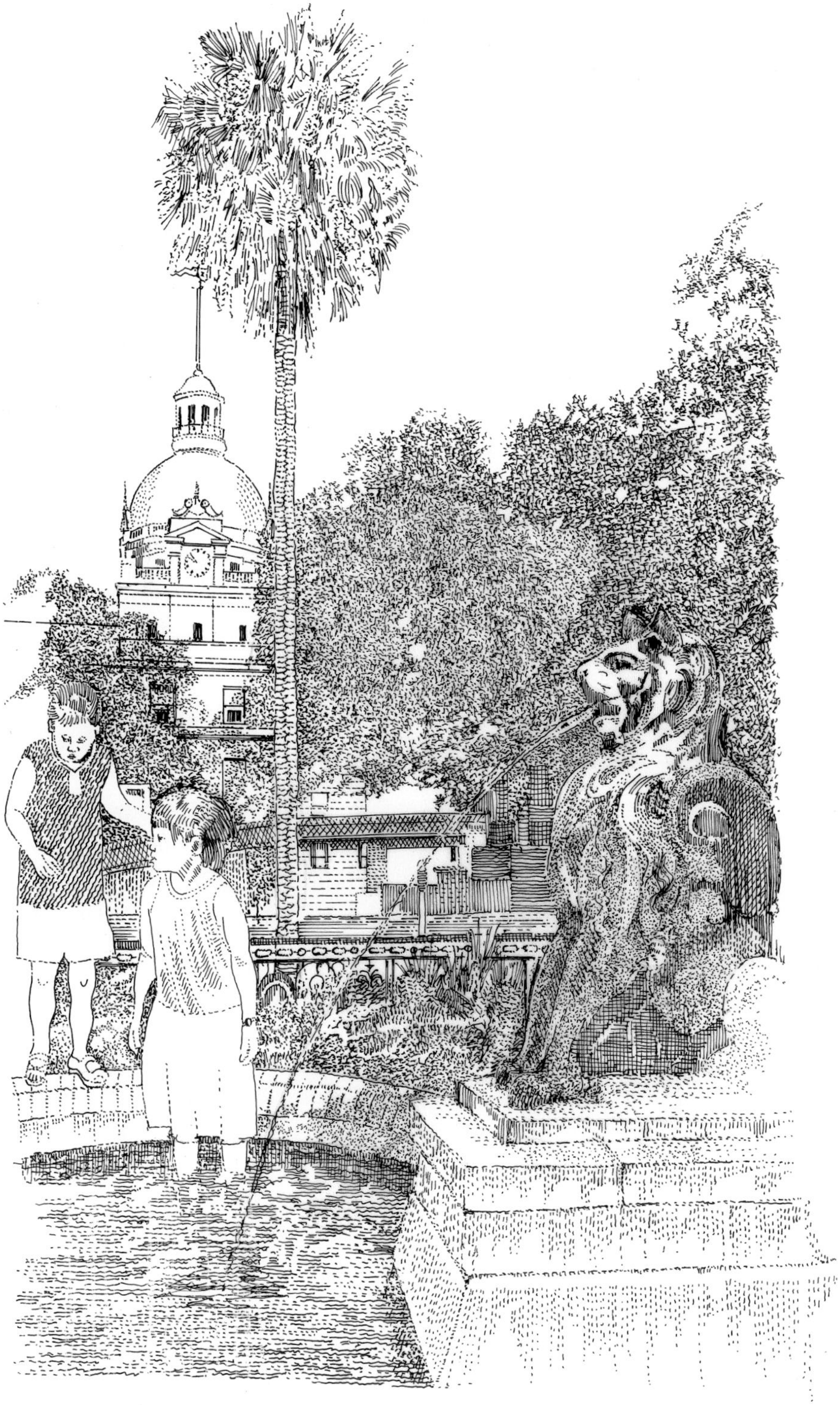

Reconstruction and Regeneration

RECOVERY, CONSOLIDATION, AND REVIVAL

The immediate aftermath of the Revolution was a reconciliation and reconstruction in the midst of physical destruction and social chaos. The delicate economic interdependency of cultivation and the commercial framework based on import and export business, had collapsed. A number of plantation owners had taken refuge elsewhere and crops had not been planted let alone harvested. Many slaves had used the maelstrom of events to escape to the countryside or to northern states. Both the remaining planters and merchants came to the questionable conclusion that a resumption of the slave trade was necessary to kickstart the recovery of the economic cycle and stimulate the production process that began with public auctions of plantations belonging to Loyalists who had fled the country. Credit was extended to planters, and merchants set up in business to receive new boatloads of slaves with import notices published in the local press. Owners were required to purchase a license in order to hire out slaves into the open employment market.

Planters had to contend with a low price for rice after the withdrawal of trade privileges by Britain, and some turned to planting sea-island cotton. To meet the costs of new public health measures, a new tax was introduced on property holders. A restoration of law and order became a primary concern of the State Assembly through careful rationing of foodstuffs, repair of both public and private buildings, and later by the regulation of slave labor.

In 1786 the state capital was relocated from Savannah to Augusta. At the Constitutional Convention in Philadelphia in 1787, representatives from Georgia and South Carolina persuaded the assembly to allow the trade in slaves to continue for a further twenty years. The following year the town was divided into seven wards, with wardens selected annually. In 1787 one of new wards was named after James Oglethorpe – the first time that the city limits had been extended since the original allocation, and included the old Native American settlement of Yamacraw. Streets were named after prominent property owners. In 1788 Georgia elected their representatives to the first Congress of the United States. In December 1789 Savannah was granted a city charter. Aldermen replaced the wardens, and promptly voted through an electorate of male property owners. The first official place of government in 1790 was the Silk Filature on Reynolds Square, and after each meeting the city marshal marched around the city to broadcast any newly enacted ordinances. Necessary health and safety activities were paid through taxes on slaves, property, and certain types of goods, including liquor, and by holding public lotteries.

Rice and tobacco production in the low country began to slowly regain its massive importance to the economy. City expansion and a booming economy called for skilled workers, and a prohibition against hiring slaves was lifted for artisan jobs such as ship's carpenters, painters, and navigators for boats that were necessary to transport goods to Savannah. While the owner's consent was necessary for slaves to live independently and sell produce, bond people and fugitive slaves who were hired out began to realize both social and economic independence, meeting in groups and building up more humanizing interracial relationships. There was similarly a need for unskilled workers for loading and unloading of ships, and as porters and carriers. In the city, greater income began to translate into a modicum of independence and self-respect. Flight was usually a means for slaves to escape cruelty but also a form of self-assertion, and the most likely destination from the surrounding plantations was the city, where they could often be harbored by friends and find menial employment in the flourishing port, or pass for bond persons. Some managed to stow away on vessels bound for northern cities or foreign parts. Others formed groups who avoided capture by evolving a self-sufficient lifestyle on the remote islands in the Savannah River.

By 1790 the slave population of Georgia, at around 13,000, was more than double that of the white population. However, there was also more employment for artisans, and an increasing number of plantation slaves were able to travel to Savannah to trade their wares and to socialize. Some managed to escape and in some cases formed armed rebellions, although bounties were offered for their capture. At the same time, the town acted as a magnet for fugitives because of its capacity to offer jobs and anonymity.

In 1792 the state legislature introduced a curfew on slaves, although the ideology of firm control became more benevolent and paternal, possibly reflecting not merely black resistance but the Christian ethic of new African American and biracial churches, such as the first African Baptist Church on Bryan Street, named after Andrew Bryan, its first minister, and the second Baptist Church on Greene Square. The black churches introduced a spiritual and a social identity, combining traditional beliefs with Christian values, while reaffirming the culture and identity of the black community. Other African Americans joined Catholic and Methodist multi-ethnic places of worship, while the Baptists and Jewish communities developed independent congregations.

Both religious and academic life quickly returned to normal, and the Presbyterian and Episcopalian Churches carried out much relief work. The Masonic Lodge provided charity, and the cosmopolitan reach of the town was extended by the return of the Georgia Gazette published in Savannah. This remained the only newspaper in the State, printing local news, international events, and educational and literary excerpts.

Municipal Resolve and Economic Expansion

The city had risen so much in stature by May, 1791, that it was visited by the United States President, George Washington. However, at the time of his visit there were no houses beyond South Broad Street – the eastern city limit was Lincoln Street and the western limit was Jefferson Street. The Georgia Gazette devoted its entire paper to the visit. The Historical Record of Savannah reveals that he was rowed down the river as a band played He comes, the Hero comes. He later dined at Brown's coffee house, and then attended a ball and a dinner tendered by the Cincinnati Society composed of officers of the American army. The Gazette reported that in his response he concluded: "That the city of Savannah may largely partake of every public benefit which our free and equal government can dispense, and that the happiness of its vicinity may reply to the best wishes of its inhabitants, is my sincere prayer."

Until 1790, cotton had been a labor intensive crop in Georgia, but Eli Whitney's invention of the hand-cranked cotton gin, which expediently removed the fiber from cotton seeds so that the process of cleaning cotton could be sped up, massively reduced production costs. Cotton could then be exported to Britain where steam-powered spinning jennies and mechanical looms transformed this into cloth. The result was an expansion of sea-island cotton across the southern states and in Savannah during the 1790s. Cotton joined rice and lumber as one of the three principal exports that fuelled the new economy.

This in turn led to a demand for all trades associated with export business, in particular the shipping industry. Both production and transport of goods had to be orchestrated through a web of accountants, wholesale merchants and commission agents, that once again led to an acceleration in demand for goods, construction, furnishings, and import of luxury items. Skilled workers arrived from Europe and other American cities, contributing to a more cosmopolitan outlook. Artisans took on the trappings of wealth, acquired properties, and employed increasing numbers of freed slaves as assistants or craftsmen. Wealth, at least to some extent, spread outwards and slowly generated a greater sense of independence in the midst of racial inequality and black subordination. In the process artisans gradually acquired voting power and became a latent political force.

With the outbreak of war between England and France, there was some polarization of political sympathies, and French privateers visited Savannah, bringing threats to law and order. Curfews were announced on top of those that prohibited gatherings of slaves and free blacks. A new fort was built on Cockspur Island some distance from the city, as part of a federal defense strategy along the southern Atlantic coast. Rumors of black insurrections led to a resolution by the City Council to block any slave bearing boat from the West Indies entering the Savannah River.

In November 1796 a fire raged throughout the city leaving only one-third of the 358 houses standing. While the conflagration left many residents with no shelter, it encouraged a surge of builders and craftsmen who helped to largely reconstruct the city in only two years. In a similar way to London after the Great Fire, much of the rebuilding was in brick and stone through private funding. Existing property rights were largely respected which created an opportunity for remodeling by skilled builders and craftsmen within the existing planning framework. A branch of the Bank of the United States was opened on Reynolds Square and supplied a source of funding for further economic growth. At the opposite end of the spectrum the new jail and workhouse was finally completed on Lafayette Square, and street patrols were increased in an attempt to maintain law and order.

Historical record reveals that a census of the city was taken in 1798, and it was ascertained that "there were 6,226 inhabitants, 618 dwelling houses, 415 kitchens, and 228 outhouses, stores and shops."

In the presidential election, Thomas Jefferson's victory was applauded by a large coalition of businessmen who were encouraged by the new republicanism, which dominated the City Council. The Council promptly set about changing the longstanding loyalist street names to better reflect the new political reality. The notion of political and social equality contradicted the constant reality of slavery, but reflected a growing concern about its political opposition at a national level. In 1799 the City Council required that all freed slaves had to register with the city. A continuing concern of the Council was the number of city taverns that encouraged fraternization between black and white residents after nightfall, which was said to threaten the maintenance of order and observance of the Sabbath. However, popular patronage of the city's brothels, and the clandestine pursuit of interracial relations, was perhaps the main reason that they were never entirely suppressed.

Vice President Aaron Burr visited the city for four days in May 1802 en route from Augusta, and was escorted into the city by the Volunteer Guards. By this time, Savannah had attained the position of the fourteenth largest city in America.

Threats to Health and Safety

By the turn of the nineteenth century Savannah was not a healthy city. City garbage was collected but then dumped on common land. Malaria was transmitted by mosquitoes during the hot summer months; typhoid, cholera, yellow fever, and dengue fever were also prevalent, in part due to pollution of drinking water and unhealthy conditions in the local marshes and swamps. Workers in the humid swamps and flooded rice fields fell pray to viruses, waterborne bacteria, dysentery, and tuberculosis. Epidemics of smallpox broke out in the city and led to constant toying with public health declarations, and invariably in the summer months reached epidemic proportions with a high mortality rate, although a successful vaccination initiative was later introduced. It was not until 1803 that a building in Yamacraw was converted for use as a hospital, and a quarantine station established on Tybee Island. Somewhat ironically given the debt-laden situation of some early settlers, a poor house was added for the city's debtors.

Hurricanes posed only an occasional threat, but their impact could be severe. Hundreds were drowned in the storm and ensuing high tides that struck in September 1804. The river rose above the wharves, inundating Cockspur Island and covering the whole of Hutchinson's Island along with the surrounding rice plantations, drowning both soldiers and slaves alike. Many storehouses together with all the boats on the river were destroyed. While the number of open squares mitigated its impact on residential buildings, part of the walls and the steeple of the Episcopal church were blown down, and many of the mature trees that had been planted years earlier were uprooted.

The Social Spectrum

While Thomas Jefferson piously proclaimed that all men were created equal, this scarcely applied to the 400,000 slaves that formed around twenty percent of the total population in the American colonies, and almost fifty percent in Virginia, Carolina, and Georgia. Jefferson was even a slave owner, although he managed to navigate around this problematic issue by cultivating an appropriately benevolent disposition towards it. The British abolished the slave trade in 1807, but in the southern states of America it continued to become a main point of contention between north and south that gathered momentum and created ever-deepening divisions over the next eighty years, finally propelling the country towards civil war.

One self-righteous way to combat slavery was introduced by the American Colonization Society in 1817, which actively sponsored the return of freed slaves to Monrovia in West Africa, modern Liberia, on the questionable basis that regardless of the principle of slavery, blacks and whites were not meant to live together. The first ship, the Horsa left with 202 emigrants. More than 1,000 had chosen this option by the mid-nineteenth century. Others such as black Baptists left of their own accord after the American Revolution and founded congregations in Africa and the West Indies.

Slavery and its disjointed implications continued to permeate the psychology of white society. A city watch was established in 1806, and the same year an ordinance required that all free blacks should be subject to the same restrictive conditions as slaves. In fact, few slaves committed capital crimes, and many inmates in the jail had been sent by their owners after being apprehended for attempting to escape.

Social life continued unabated, particularly during the energetic social season where wealth was exhibited in a cacophony of display that extended to influential political circles. Clubs for dining and recreation jostled with those for literature, poetry, and music, while private tutors offered lessons in all manner of subjects. The wealthy put on extravagant parties, dances, and dinners that perpetuated their political and economic ties. In 1809 a group of wealthy Jewish families founded the Savannah Library Society, which in due course merged with the Georgia Historical Society. The Literary Society encouraged intellectual contributions, while escalating membership of the New England Society provided evidence of how many businessmen from the north had come to take up residence in the city. At the other end of the social scale, it was estimated that there was one tavern or gambling den for every ninety-five members of the local population.

Perhaps the lingering memory of John Wesley, or news of his post-Savannah fame, enthused the Methodist congregation, who subscribed to a new church on what is now Oglethorpe Street, and ultimately attracted an attendance equally divided between black and white. The Hibernian Society was founded in 1812 and comprised Irish immigrants, both Protestant and Roman Catholic, who formed the core of a lively Irish-American community centered in the Bull Street area, and reinforced the colorful celebration of the annual St. Patrick's Day parade.

In October 1812 more than 1,000 people attended the funeral of Andrew Bryan, a freed slave who had become a widely respected Baptist minister.

A Half-Hearted Resumption of Hostilities

Since the preliminary treaty of 1782 British ships had preyed on American merchant ships, and in many cases had seized their crews and cargoes, to the extent that Congress passed an Embargo Act that for a time prevented ships leaving port. In Savannah, politicians lobbied for arms to protect the city, and the fear of invasion turned Savannah into what was described as a "Garrison Town."

On June 18, 1812 the American Congress, which had been put under great pressure, declared war on Britain. In Savannah, Fort Wayne was rebuilt and the new Fort Jackson completed. The Council required all freed slaves to work on the fortifications constructed to the west of Lafayette Square. The Governor of Georgia sent a force to help protect the city, and old ships were sunk in the river to inhibit a naval invasion. A British fleet finally appeared off the coast of Georgia two years later, but did not inhibit the July 4th parade in the city, which occurred only months before the Treaty of Ghent ended the war. In March 1815 the Savannah City Government, with a flourish of nationalist spirit, announced the naming of two squares after American victories—Chippewa and Orleans—and three streets after naval heroes – Hull, McDonough, and Perry.

Meanwhile, British forces had something of probably greater severity to contend with – war against France and the Battle of Waterloo on the June 18, 1815 which ended the formidable career of Napoleon Bonaparte, and set Britain on course to become the greatest power in the world during the remainder of the 19th century.

Civic Enterprise and Culture

The post-war situation called for accommodation of many new arrivals and the return of evacuated citizens amidst a recovering economy, but one that was plagued by poor public health, annual outbreaks of smallpox, and a high mortality rate. Charitable benevolence was directed mainly at creating educational facilities for the poorer white sector through the Chatham Academy and the Savannah Free School, while special societies were established to cater for the destitute, including the Dorcas Society and the Widow's Society, which catered for indigent white females of "good character."

On the back of cotton and lumber, exports increased in the post-war years – a growth of 600 percent in eighteen years. This was accelerated by the onset of steam navigation, following the launch of the Enterprise from the local John Watts shipyard. Steamboats drew only a small amount of water, and, although somewhat precarious, were ideal for the shallow Altamaha River between Savannah, Augusta, and Charleston. Within three years the Steamboat Company of Georgia was running eight steamers on the river.

In 1817 an ambitious and costly program was established to construct a canal system that helped to drain the swamps and marshes around the city and led to the establishment of a cordon sanitaire, which enabled the planting of crops other than rice. The city streets remained crowded with vendors, including plantation slaves who brought goods to sell such as fresh poultry, shellfish, and vegetables, ostensibly on behalf of their owners, but also their own home-grown produce. Poorer vendors also tended to collaborate with the more illicit trade in tobacco and liquor, which was said to account for "heavy drinking and violation of the Sabbath." Both slaves and free blacks were still subject to laws that forbid gambling, smoking, or the consumption of alcohol.

A theater designed in the Greek Revival style by a visiting English architect, William Jay, was completed in 1818 on Chippewa Square where plays by English playwrights were enjoyed by enthusiastic audiences, even though African Americans had to sit in a segregated section. The theater lasted for 130 years before being destroyed by fire. Jay went on to design the Savannah Bank at the intersection of Drayton and St. Julian Streets, and the City Hotel on Bay Street with a magnificent open view across the Savannah River that made it one of the most popular places for social gatherings. He also designed several mansions, all completed in 1819, including the Richardson House at 124 Abercorn Street, the Scarborough house at 41 Martin Luther King Jr. Boulevard, the Telfair house at 121 Bernard Street, and the Bulloch mansion on Orleans Square, all in the English Regency style. These refined designs had a significant impact on the urban design and overall cityscape, while the interior furnishings were largely constructed by craftsmen who had arrived from England, and were heavily influenced by the then fashionable furniture of Sheraton and Hepplewhite.

The United States President James Monroe visited Savannah in May 1819 primarily to inspect the coastal fortifications, and boarded a sailing packet named after the city that had been converted to a steamer by the Savannah Steamship Company. Later the same month the Savannah crossed the Atlantic to Liverpool in 22 days and, until it was destroyed in a gale three years later, continued to sail between Savannah and New York.

Conflagration and Epidemics

The successful completion of many grand properties unfortunately coincided with a sudden fall in the price of cotton due to oversupply and a commensurate plunge in bank shares and property values, the effects of which rippled through the Southern States. To compound the financial problems, a fire that began accidentally in a livery stable on January 11, 1820 quickly spread through the predominantly timber buildings, and turned into a conflagration. With the exception of the State and Planter's banks, the Episcopal Church and several brick buildings, virtually every house between Broughton and Bay streets, and from Jefferson to Abercorn Streets, were destroyed. Part of the problem was the prevalence of lumber yards and storage of flammable material. Flames engulfed virtually all the properties encompassing banks, mercantile houses, and the public market, and over 400 tenements were destroyed.

Many American cities contributed aid funds for reconstruction. The Mayor of New York City offered generous aid, but with a proviso that this should be distributed equally without regard for skin color – something that so angered the hot headed members of the Savannah City Council, that they returned the check. Aid was therefore withdrawn by New York and other northern cities, increasing the severity of the economic depression.

Eventually, the majority of houses were rebuilt in solid construction using brick or stone, changing the face of the old city, but adhering still to its overall planning framework. Property rights were broadly respected, which created an opportunity for remodeling with new styles of architecture using skilled builders and craftsmen. In 1824 the City Council allocated funds for the planting of sycamore, oak, elm, and laurel trees that grew to enhance the regenerated residential squares.

The combined effects of fire and epidemics created economic depression, with export revenue dropping by half and many businesses ending up in debt. This led to further concern over security, and although curfews were enforced, the city jail was badly maintained, and there were frequent breakouts of prisoners. To make matters worse, the empty building sites became filled with stagnant water during the summer of 1820 and led to an infestation of mosquitoes that carried yellow fever, creating a serious epidemic, which killed almost 900 people by December – around twelve percent of the city's population. More physicians were appointed, but the actual cause went unrecognized at the time. However, it acted to focus more attention on matters of public health and the importance of enforcing cleanliness in the city, together with the continued draining of nearby swamps. Outbreaks of yellow fever and typhoid continued to occur over the years and additional ordinances were enacted to reduce both health and fire risks.

In 1825 the first city firefighting force was established with all black units commanded by white officers, with a new fire station on Franklin Square. The annual firemen's parade of companies outfitted in distinctive uniforms later became one of the city's most colorful events.

The Plantation Economy

Savannah took some time to recover economically from the accumulation of disasters, and the eventual catalyst was an expansion of rice production, although plantations were frequently inundated by storms, particularly during the summer season. New plantations opened up while abandoned ones were restored, luring prominent personalities to participate in the boom including politicians and would-be planters from other parts of the South, such as Langdon Cheves, a former Speaker of the US House of Representatives. Other investors from Savannah included politicians, attorneys, physicians, and William Coffee Daniell, a future mayor of Savannah who gave up his practice to work a new plantation in St. Peter's Parish, only a short distance from Factor's Walk. Export potential was significantly improved in 1828 by the introduction of the first steam-powered rice-pounding mill, and by the 1830s planters were operating six such mills in the parish.

Many of the new and already wealthy rice planters built mansions in the city and only visited their holdings infrequently. This probably reflected the hectic social life that continued unabated despite the lingering recession, with parties, balls, weddings, and outings, competitively orchestrated by the wealthy and sophisticated doyens of Savannah society. While a Ladies Society was founded "to promote intelligent conservation," their husbands and sons were more likely to participate in military displays and hunting pursuits on St. Catherine's Island. The open hospitality of these exclusive sets remained as something of a contrast to life at the lower end of the social spectrum, where poor whites, free blacks, and slaves intermingled and fraternized in tippling houses and Saturday-night dances.

A short-lived Board of Public Works was established in the mid-1820s, which focused attention on necessary development to meet both physical and economic growth, with a particular emphasis on road, rail, and canal construction. The first such project was a canal to link the Savannah and Ogeechee Rivers across land owned by the city. This provided a 16.5-mile conduit that connected upland cotton plantation to the wharves of Savannah. It opened five years before the Erie Canal and until the 1890s carried cotton, lumber, rice, and fruit. Construction also began in 1829 on a chain of new fortifications along the Atlantic coast, including the new Fort Pulaski on Cockspur Island. One of the early supervisors was a new West Point graduate, Lieutenant Robert E Lee, who oversaw the complicated construction, which involved building a brick structure over mud, supported by wooden piles and oyster shells.

In March 1825, General Lafayette, a legendary figure in the American Revolution, visited Savannah and inaugurated monuments to two of its other heroes – General Nathanael Greene and Count Pulaski in Johnson Square, which were later completed through funds from a public lottery. His arrival marked one of the most imposing civic and military displays ever held in the city.

Fear of Insurrection

While there were a significant number of free African Americans in Savannah, over time this declined due to laws that acted to constrain and monitor their movements. By the 1820s freed slaves from within Georgia had to leave the state completely, while their incoming equivalent had to pay a large tax and were restricted as to their potential occupations – a prejudiced means of limiting competition with their skilled white counterparts, although they continued to be employed as carpenters, ironworkers, and masons. Some indentured slaves worked in construction and other industries but were obliged to pay a percentage of earnings to their owners. While some freed black women found it difficult to get legitimate work, others acquired independent wealth and property ownership, with a minority becoming slave owners themselves.

Most of the freed blacks and poor whites lived in Oglethorpe Ward in the Yamacraw area between the railways yards and the river. Here, a disordered amalgam of informal residences, shops, gambling dens, brothels, and taverns created an alternative biracial city heterotopia. This made the wide mix of residents vulnerable to disease, particularly to cholera, which erupted in 1832 and again the following year along the Savannah River plantations and coastal ports that operated around the fetid swamps and polluted water courses. Hundreds died, and inmates at the seriously underfunded hospital were transferred to the federal troop facilities at Oglethorpe Barracks.

The Baptist Church remained the most popular denominational congregation for African Americans, in particular the Bryan Street African Baptist Church ministered by a former slave, Andrew Marshall. They also attended other churches in large numbers, including the Methodist Andrew Chapel with its predominantly white congregation. The Independent Presbyterian Church conducted Sunday Schools for black children at the Baptist churches where they also learned to read and write – the Catechism used for moral instruction was said to induce obedience and docility in the slave population. A City Ordinance was passed in 1829 that forbade anyone to teach slaves, and educational pioneers were therefore forced to establish clandestine tactics, concealing educational areas behind other façades. The Unitarian church at the corner of Bull and York Streets was completed in 1834, and its leaders became associated with the anti-slavery movement gaining momentum in the North.

City Improvements and New Infrastructure

The "Nullification" crisis arose as a result of an Act of Congress that set high tariffs on imported manufactured goods, which prompted a standoff between North and South. This contributed to southern sectionalism, made more pertinent by the growth of cheap slave labor in the South, but was construed in the North as an economic threat. As the North continued to industrialize, European immigration to American cities contributed to growth. At the same time, doubts grew about the imbalance of interests in the House of Representatives.

In February 1833 a large assembly gathered to join the centennial celebrations in Savannah with a parade of troops. This coincided with the re-election of Andrew Jackson, a strong Unionist, as President of the United States. Unionists later won an easy majority of seats in the State elections of 1834.

The need for improved transport infrastructure became vital to cope with the city's expanding commercial practices, as the Savannah River itself was its only main link with other cities. The first iron-hulled steamboat in the United States was built in Savannah in 1834 with private funding from ambitious venture capitalists and parts imported from England. It was named the John Randolph and was followed by a second, the Chatham, two years later. By the mid-1830s more than twenty steamboats were running daily

134

between Savannah, Augusta, and Darien with merchandise, and returning laden with cotton and lumber.

As the new South Carolina railroad began to encroach on the hinterland of Savannah, a group of businessmen began to promote a new rail line that could compete with Charleston for passenger and freight traffic, given the growth in Georgia's upland cotton industry. The Central of Georgia Railroad, orchestrated by William W. Gordon, was inaugurated in 1835 to link Savannah with Macon, 191 miles away. In a short time this replaced water borne transport as the most effective and dependable means of transferring freight. The city provided a site for a depot and machine shops, part of which now serves as the Savannah Visitor's Center.

The demand for labor to build the railroad, shipyards, and buildings created a major migration of men to Savannah. This included 1,400 Irish laborers, the result of the potato famine in Ireland, which propelled countless desperate migrants to the United States. By 1850 this represented ten percent of the city's population. Immigration added substantially to the total white population of around 6,500 that had declined by more than 1,000 over the previous decade. While the Irish subscribed to the diversity of the city's slum population on its eastern and western edges, and to the St. Patrick's Day celebrations first staged in 1824, it also added to the economic polarization of its resident population, and for calls to curb the growing intemperance that led to frequent social disorder. With a rise in the immigrant Catholic population in 1845, sufficient funds became available to fund construction of the Cathedral of St. John the Baptist dedicated in 1876, which ultimately became the center of the Georgian diocese.

Towards the end of the decade, the economy again plunged due to a drop in the price of cotton and excessive private speculation on infrastructure projects. Shares in the Central and Georgia Railroad sank by eighty percent, but by 1839 around half the track had been completed, and the Company had to substantially increase both its passenger and freight cars to cope with the growing cotton harvest. The completion of the Savannah, Ogeechee, and Altamaha Canal also enabled the use of flatboats to transport heavy goods such as lumber, bricks, and rice.

By the end of the decade the city had been extended through three new wards to the south of Liberty Street – Lafayette, Pulaski, and Jackson. A painting in 1837 by a commercial artist, Firmin Cerveau, from the viewpoint of the City Exchange bell tower, shows a symmetrical plan but with considerable architectural diversity. At this time there were eighteen squares and the painting clearly depicts Christ Episcopal Church positioned on its trust lot in Johnston Square. On the surface, the city appeared tranquil, well laid out with handsome buildings and beautifully landscaped streets and squares, although the former remained unpaved.

A city guard was organized by the Mayor in response to rumors of black uprisings elsewhere, and the rise in anti-slavery pamphlets produced by northern abolitionists. Local

opinions were so extreme that Presbyterian and Quaker supporters of abolition, together with missionaries who arrived in the city, were forced to flee. In response to a rumor that free blacks planned to assist the escape of local slaves, an ordinance was passed for the arrest of any such persons arriving in Savannah. A further ordinance prohibited public gatherings of more than several black people unless there was a white person present.

The business and entrepreneurial community, however, continued to flourish, with the most prominent members serving on political, social, and benevolent bodies. On the back of new commercial enterprises came a fifty percent increase in population to 11,214, split almost equally between black and white. While there were more freed slaves than ever before, the total number of slaves and owners actually increased between 1830 and 1840. Half the white population owned no slaves, free blacks lived in all sections of the city and were well integrated, but with a widening gap between rich and poor, and a semi-permanent mix of uses in Yamacraw. This ambiguity had already been epitomized by John M. Harney in 1818 on his departure from the city:

> Farewell, oh Savannah, forever farewell,
> Thou hot bed of rogues, thou threshold of hell,
> Where Satan has fixed his headquarters on earth,
> And outlaws integrity, wisdom and worth.

In 1833, however, one observer painted a different picture:

> There is one immensely broad avenue, about halfway across the city called South Broad Street, and extending full length from east to west. This is magnificently shaded by rows of China trees full of odorous blossoms in the spring of every year. Then in laying out the city every other square has been left as an open one, enclosed with a railing laid out with walks and planted with shade trees and rustic seats arranged in them all about.

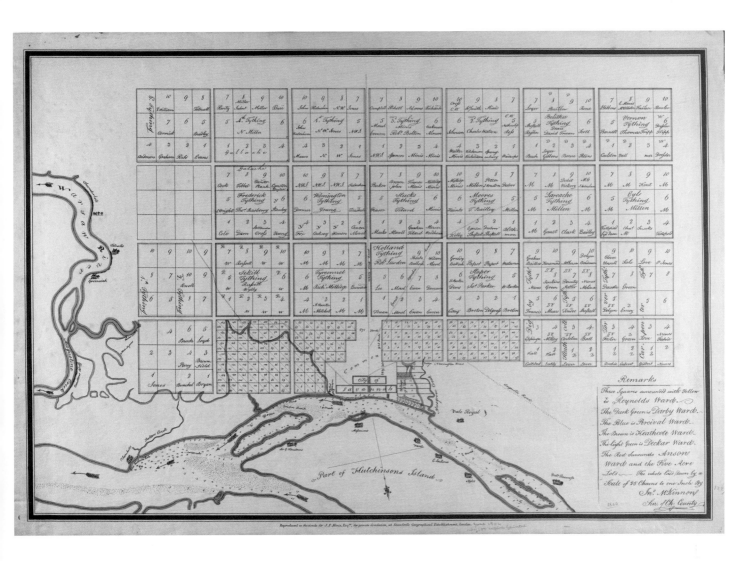

Survey Map compiled by the Savannah
Surveyor, John Mckinnon in 1798.

138

SAVANNAH AUTUMN 2016: DAY 4

Schlomo arrives late for breakfast the next morning, looking bleary eyed and nursing a hangover. The ever-accommodating housekeeper meets his request for a gallon of black coffee.

Mo looks up from his iPad briefly and shakes his head several times.

Agnita and Miles appear, appropriately apologetic about missing Tybee, but full of appreciation for an evening spent celebrating yesterday's presentations at a basement restaurant – The Wilkes House, followed by a couple of hours at a bar called the Baystreet Blues in Yamacraw.

We walk to Poetter Hall in twos and threes with Schlomo straggling behind with a bulging satchel. Jean-Paul tells us that Rocksteady Williams is in fact a fine banjo player. He makes a good living around the various watering holes between Savannah and New Orleans, looked after when he is on Tybee by his devoted aunt, Miss Anriette, and has the enviable habit of turning up occasionally in New York to play a few clubs.

Brit remarks that Rocksteady is rather dishy, and swims like a fish. Jean-Paul looks at her cryptically.

We pour ourselves a cup of coffee while waiting for Mo and Martha B. and arrange ourselves around the table.

Mo arrives, looks at his watch, nods his head and makes the introduction.

"Well, it has fallen on our friend Daniel Schlomo to discuss the notion of heterotopia. It seems to have taken on a new and slightly ambiguous life of its own within texts on deconstruction, where we delve into aspects of counter-culture or inversion of every-day societal norms. This might be interpreted in different ways to assist our communal diagnosis of the contours of urban space, so I hope you will interject with your own thoughts and interpretations as and when you wish. Let's get some interaction on this."

THIRD READING ASSISTANT PROFESSOR
DANIEL FILLIMORE SCHLOMO
THE HETEROTOPIA THAT INFILTRATES THE CITY

I would like to explain this enigmatic idea in terms of its necessary ability to bring about a dynamic urban balance and in the process help to maintain a stable process of urbanization. In practice it is one of those loaded but somewhat mystical terms, philosophically conjured up from the elaborate theories of Michel Foucoult and Henri Lefebvre to whom I owe much of what I am going to say. I think this can be directed towards an interesting interpretation of this fair city of Savannah. Its accepted order and delineation does most certainly include activity oriented "spaces of otherness" or counter-sites with unconventional identities that are somewhat "off-center" to the norm – or, perhaps, they actually are the norm. I hope these can propel our lines of enquiry a little way removed from the utopian representation for which Savannah is so well known. It might in the process raise questions that engage with the existing urban condition in a diverse and revealing way. Savannah is, after all, a place where our comprehension is situated somewhere between the real and imagined.

A contemporary examination of urbanism implies a need to examine the working condition of a city, which is often correlated with medical terminology, that is to say degrees of "health." The term *heterotopia* can perhaps be compared to the necessary accommodation of non-malignant but perhaps somewhat uncomfortable or occasionally irritant tissue that induces a certain tension without necessarily disturbing the overall functioning of the parent body. In the benign aspects of the relationship there is an effective tolerance, one to the other, which breaks down boundaries and creates balance, while possibly inverting normative criteria. This notion of "opposite and complementary" is in fact the very basis of the urban footprint. It is no coincidence that it has become resurrected through the introspective coming of age of Postmodernism and even New Urbanism – lines of thought that embrace heterogeneity, coexistence, and difference. This holds a special appeal to those brave urbanists who feel a need to delve into the workings of cities and to assimilate their spatial, social, and cultural health. Its hopeful significance is to assist our understanding of the city.

I sometimes think that we need a metaphysical abstraction of the past, present, and future so that we can simultaneously look forward by understanding what has gone before, where we are now, and where we might be going. To move beyond what is known to what we can speculate by recourse to new insights. This enables us to focus on the processes that have got us to the present and the forces of change involved, so that we can better articulate inventories for the future.

The notion of heterotopia in contemporary urban theory can be construed as the activity oriented realms that inject "difference" into the commonplace – a superimposition of interruptive elements on the utopian ideal that, as urbanists, we unconsciously strive for, although not necessarily the disjunction that might be involved. Its relevance is attached to the organization of space within the urban ideology of the modern age with its proliferation of networks and an elusive relationship between *place* and *non-place* – neither public nor private, but nevertheless collective, shared, and accessible. An early example in Savannah is the House for Visitors, built into the original plan as a temporary home for new arrivals and illustrated in the 1734 engraving as a distinct spatial entity, but also central to the everyday needs of the community along with the communal oven and refectory that regulated the motion of daily life.

We live in a heterogeneous world of diverse relationships, made more vivid through processes of instant communication, illusion, and fantasy that position and re-position our urban identities. The relationship to urban design depends on whether we can apply a consistent overview. Foucault points to heterotopias of crisis, with deviation depending on the way this synchronizes with the entropic tendency of societies to evolve towards disorder, however ordered the urban framework itself. In our evaluation of the modern city we can best equate "crisis" with problematic issues, and "deviation" with difference, but bearing in mind a contemporary interpretation of how such aspects as lifestyle choice, multiculturalism, and minority rights all contribute to the social and economic make-up of the contemporary urban environment. These are things that arguably cannot ever be entirely resolved to everyone's satisfaction. The heterotopia of crisis has periodically emerged in Savannah in response to disease, famine, and war, with various religious denominations administering charity and special houses for orphans and other victims of society, guarded in special buildings or compounds that orchestrated regimes of separation and categorization, open to the enforcement of social norms.

Planning the postmodern city is dominated by the need to reconcile the heterotopia of individual neighborhoods and their predominant characteristics – historic, business, residential, industrial, entertainment, themed, and mixed, all expressed as organizational patterns, some of them hybrid. These tend to stabilize but also generally satisfy city requirements according to dominant combinations. This situation might be said to proffer a wide range of sub-centers and service attractors within a dense urban conglomeration, but which possibly reflects continually changing urban values, and the equally challenging relationship between city users. This mix of influences through different interest groups shapes our perception of the contemporary city, and our interaction with it.

So we are presented with an ambiguous but important notion of "place" that falls outside the normative urban paradigm presented to us by engineers and highway builders. In effect, it represents functions that maintain a dynamic but varying balance within the urban system, and that are arguably important in ensuring its inclusive capacity. Urban heterotopias are sometimes unkindly referred to as being subversive in that they seem to challenge the generally accepted order and delineation of things, possibly leading to unstable or contested aspects over an extended period. However, this "alternative

141

ordering" also accommodates uses that, while not exactly fitting in, can comfortably co-exist and involve a multitude of relationships. Foucault notes that we are governed by strict delineations that sanctify "opposites" in a representational sense, such as public and private, work and leisure, presence and absence. In conceptualizing the notion of utopias he countenances an equal emphasis on counter-sites – "placeless" places.

Heterotopias of illusion act in certain situations to create deceptive images over an actual situation. We must accept that virtual reality and certain belief systems neutralize the predisposition to take things at face value, causing us to question what is real and what is unreal in relation to what we associate with ordered urbanism, made more pertinent by new modes of communication technology. To an extent this relates to aspects of change over time, and the ways that prevailing urban management systems, codes, and rules reflect constantly evolving cultural mores, resulting in unfolding patterns of form, function, and behavior. The result can be places of ritual, compensation, and transformation, or alternatively places of incompatibility, separation, isolation, and exclusion. We must recognize that Savannah represents a history of regulation, control, and surveillance – the relationship of space to both colonialism and slavery. But it also represents change, transition, and constant renewal. This is the predicament that lies at the boundary between the city's simultaneous identities, and the critical differences between the Historic, Victorian, Mid-City, and Cuyler-Brownville districts, and the 100 or so diverse neighborhoods.

Under the city model for early Savannah, the heterotopia perhaps represented a counter structure to the plan itself – something that implies a deviant or "reverse" situation that inverted the primary code of the urban model to ensure its workability or even its survival at the expense of exclusion. In the case of Savannah, this was slavery. Both socially and economically this became a self-justified system, intertwined with the disjunctive characteristics of the city, and fated to be forcibly associated with it through lingering pockets of poverty and separation.

The entire history of Savannah is caught up with the political DNA of race, which opens up pathways to the present via subjugation and marginalization, with a history of inequality only partly relieved by emancipation. The issue of slavery is a confounding but persistent presence in the city narrative. It intrudes like a constant thread, interjecting through the city's evolution – corrupting and corroding the otherwise refined antebellum representation, and touching it with an almost tangible sense of melancholy that permeates any attempt to define and elaborate the considerable cultural legacy of the Old South. This allows for a historical reconceptualization of African-American society, part peripheral part inclusive, but also a constant resistance pushing against oppressive demarcations and elusive, outer boundaries. The politics of difference and identity overlap with narratives of alienation sustained by power structures in society – some oppressive but others less so. Marginality was to many the space of contestation, resistance and survival in order to determine legitimacy and enable a necessary supportive culture.

MO

Is it not the case that in Savannah we have an ideal of frozen perfection that must of its own volition be held up against a mirror of conscience? Its very beauty and coherence mask the imperfections of the past, and perfection, as Foucoult pointed out, mirrors dystopia. What about the monuments to fallen southern heroes such as Robert E Lee? Are we commemorating our history, the growth of the nation, or effectively exalting our differences that extend into contemporary culture? Time is a healer but also a manipulator – it can be reversed through architectural set pieces that simply promote and glorify the sense of place that visitors expect. And expectations subscribe to this illusion if the city experience becomes merely one of elaborate representations.

BRIT

Well, the heterotopia can be associated with any culture or community; it can change its meaning and significance over time, and juxtapose different, temporary, and not necessarily compatible spaces including those of illusion or compensation. Foucault mentions the first Puritan societies in 17th- and 18th-century America that escaped the Old World to establish an effectively regulated utopian society in the new. Oh, and by the way, his notions on the heterotopias of deviance from a social norm included the prisons in eighteenth-century England where debtors were sent to pay off their debts under terrible conditions – a system that appalled reformers such as James Oglethorpe and other philanthropists, and indirectly led to the enlightened rationale for Savannah. Does this legitimize our discourse on the space of the city and help us to better dissect and deconstruct its possibilities, or are we too restricted by our conventional viewpoints?

MO

In fact, it was the historical situations that brought us to this lovely city of Savannah, so can we not just appreciate the urban aesthetic or do we have to use our urban spatial imagination? Space might not overwhelm the historical facts but does this have to blinker our critical interpretation or our residual consciousness? We cannot all be experts on historical materialism. We recognize the ontological process of settlement, independence, revolution, and emancipation. Do we need a geographical philosophy to explain the conceptual significance of city space? What we see are the containers of societal ambitions whatever the bruising realities of social relations.

AGNITA

But the relationship of servitude to the realms of displacement and plantation settlement cannot be separated from the heterotopic structure of slavery, which is about forms of control and crisis – a disenfranchised group of aliens from the other side of the world who, at least temporarily, were weak and disadvantaged within a fragmented organizational structure where the utopian dimension of morality and justice that underscored the original settlement mission were almost completely inverted. And what about the role of women – were they just about increasing the resident population? Where is the statue to Mary Musgrove who served as a cultural liaison between colonial Georgia and the Native American community, Fanny Kemble whose published descriptions of slave conditions shocked Britain, Nina Anderson Pape who was a pioneer in women's and poor children's education, Juliette Gordon Low or Mary Telfair?

MO

You make a good point. But Savannah was also a place of expectation, woven into its fabric at an early stage. We probably have to admit that it also employed a reversal of the early moral code – communal space became stratified, individual land ownership contrasted with the ownership of human beings, and freedom from persecution tainted with a regime of domination over others. This was gradually inflated in scale, where equality of one group was forged on the basis of inequality embedded within the overall system through independent sets of rules that regulated patterns of work and behavior. Slavery generated alternative and contrasting types of social order that were heavily resistant to change. When these circumstances eventually altered the heterotopia of slave conditions, its physical remnants were the first things to disappear, although I guess some have re-appeared via black history tours that take in slave burial grounds, the Civil Rights Museum, and the First African Baptist Church, not to mention the slave market sites.

SCHLOMO

Lefebvre has questioned the organization of space from a different perspective, adopting a strategy of centering knowledge on discourse rather than practice, positing a situationalist focus. Its relevance to the city is the injection of the spatial condition as being something that demands equal consideration with historical and social dynamics. If every event has a social or societal dimension this must necessarily be interwoven with historical and spatial values—a relationship between, as Lefebvre put it, the "representation of space" and "spaces of representation"—essentially between the "conceived" and the "lived" experience. The epistemology of space or urban condition therefore raises questions with regard to the citizen's right to react against a progression of events that tend to homogenize our conception of place without accommodating the shifting strands of difference. We need something that supplements and recombines the visual and the experiential, and expands its multiple possibilities.

145

MO

Well, an agreeable discourse on social processes notwithstanding, let's move on – this is about the city. We don't have to reconstitute the entire problematic history of urban space. We are trying to equate the postmodern with the historical, the social and the spatial, and to make sense of it – not to make us think differently about past events. Everything is open to other critical points of view. The city exists as a place of experience but also imagination. As someone said, I cannot remember whom now, "whether the city is real or imagined we have to make sense of it in exactly the same way."

SCHLOMO

We must seemingly concede that the complex physicality of buildings, places, and streets is paralleled by a hidden universe of procedures, expectations, aspirations, and memories that nurture the sense of belonging. Associations through time can be re-asserted or reoriented. In Savannah, precisely because it came to represent so many different faiths, the church acted as a bridge between forms of place association, positioned as they are on trust lots in the center of wards. This might link cultural geographies with spiritual heritage, but isn't it also a means of both recapturing and reinterpreting urban history? It certainly represents a persuasive argument for preservation as a basis for defining the present and contextualizing the collective future. As the city becomes progressively fragmented and re-formed, the power of place is recalibrated in both a physical and cognitive sense into new places of power. The ideological and cultural aspects of this are rooted in the Savannah plan itself – the social and political influences, the strategic military undertones, the organizational notion of tythings and trust lots, but also the incongruity. For example, owners could be fined if their slaves were not allowed to attend Christian churches, setting the stage for future multi-denomination church construction, evangelism, and missionary societies.

JEAN-PAUL

If we attempt to decipher spatial practice we must explore the routines, the places of work and leisure, the ensembles, the networks, the whole multitude of socially and economically produced empirical space. A heterotopic representation has to necessarily include all spaces of resistance to the dominant order, teeming with contradictions and symbolic references. Normal market operations, underpinned by the urban land economy in the contemporary city, influence, and to a large extent determine spatial outcomes, but of course the imprint and patterning of our geographic, cultural, and behavioral variables also come into play to explain our constructed configurations as well as the areas we choose to leave in their natural condition.

ME

We can only express what we see by describing fragments of urban material, which distill what exists but cannot give us real knowledge. My drawings can only reflect the conventional representation of space, not the sequential or the contradictory, and they don't aim to explain but merely represent character, mood, and identity. A drawing is not a narrative, and can only record an impression. It cannot express, as music does, the harmony, the rhapsody, or the repetition. It is fixed in the here and now, but it is also an illusion. This might also be what Lefebvre describes as an "encrypted reality."

SCHLOMO

Yes, but designed space is the interpretive realm of the architect and urban designer, reformulating a locale or enclave through imagination and the application of experience. In the utopian sense it therefore becomes symbolic. It is what we refer to when we examine the poetics and materiality of the Savannah Square. Its spatial cognition and significance appeals to us. It strikes a rational chord and provokes a mental image, quite separate from its social production and its relationship with history, while the discipline of planning establishes a distinguished setting that has doubtless prolonged the life of many older buildings.

MO

We must be sure that in our new historicism we do not merely describe the experience of urban space or make the new fit the past – but instead realize its significance, or as Edward Soja puts it, its "spatio-temporality." Space now reveals the real historical perspective rather than time, but it is the interplay between these aspects that helps us make sense of our contemporary situation in terms of representation.

SCHLOMO

Paul Virilio has surmised that as architecture's materiality is subverted by new and ever more clever ways of transmitting information, this is leading to a dematerialized environment of connecting spaces, screens, walls, and graphic mediums that seek to encourage and attract, with people interacting through integrated information networks and therefore leading to a breakdown in the orthodox values of urban space and street-scape. Under this scenario of grand illusion, the spatial distinctions between urban places and enclaves can only be defined by reference to old established and preserved environments – what supersedes this is the space of flows and intensified interaction with different activities now spread across an increasingly diffuse urban landscape.

MARTHA

The sometimes disquieting relationship between public and private space still tends to dominate our urban thinking and leads us to conjure up terms to explain and mediate its dimensions – alternating, virtual, and transitional, that create connections between the past, present, and future. It underscores the notion of *liminal* or marginal space – one of separation but also transgression, framed within the unstable framework of contemporary urbanism but nevertheless accumulating cultural and social capital.

AGNITA

Should we not include in this the imagineered mall design as an evocation of "Main Street," which decontextualizes its varied and versatile characteristics through cosmetic simulation, dedicated to the cult of exclusivity without the inconveniences of the genuine public realm?

SCHLOMO

Festival markets are in themselves heterotopias of illusion and hyper-reality, based on commoditized forms of leisure, and seductively themed and choreographed entertainment. This synthetic reproduction of such orthodox city spaces and movement channels as the plaza, precinct, courtyard, and boulevard, by the galleria, atrium, and arcade frames a counter place of compressed consumption and materialism – a "placeless place" of dissemblance and dispersal programmed around the beckoning proposition, neither wholly public or wholly private, but cloaked in the mantle of contrivance that stokes monstrous desire and offers seductive options of consummation. Its continual reinvention deliberately recasts the eclectic way in which the city has been traditionally experienced. There is of course nothing intrinsically wrong with this, unless we start to question the public's right to the city itself as a freely accessible and democratic space. The *Roma Interrotta* so painstakingly elaborated by Rowe and Koetter as the "city of rooms" illustrates the lessons we can learn in defining the public realm.

TERRY

SCAD itself has established specialist urban "rooms" converted from older buildings originally designed for altogether different purposes. The differentiation that preserves the city memory also becomes part of a connected assemblage of educational buildings – places of creative endeavor.

MILES

If I may interject, it seems an unfortunate paradox that by refurbishing dilapidated properties, the gentrification process perhaps reinforces exclusivity, but this is probably a price we have to pay. The Savannah squares fall well within the public realm as a living

OPPOSITE PAGE
The Savannah Cotton Exchange on East Bay Street completed in 1887 in the Romantic Revival style, at a time when Savannah was a leading exporter of cotton. It was originally known as King Cotton's Palace, and now houses Solomon's Lodge - one of the oldest Freemason's organizations in America. The original winged terracotta Griffon has stood as part of the fountain from 1889.

museum. The imagery of the square has bridged a somewhat unstable evolution by capitalizing on the cultural credentials of its antebellum history.

MO

Savannah is a city of split realities with ambiguous ideologies held by different camps. On one side, the presence of a carefully cultivated and indulgent urban design creates a timeless and immaculately choreographed presence, while on the other there exist counter-spaces that offer new programmable potential and invention? Do these sides act to separate and exclude, or is the design process one of continual coexistence and refinement motivated towards social condensement and homogeneity? Spatial and use differences themselves are not irreconcilable, and the fact that these are open to question and analysis means that they are tested on many levels, not merely social or ethnic ones. On top of that, different groups appropriate spaces for specific uses and discourses contributing to a constant process of change and multiplicity, instigating opportunities for both increased contact but also confrontation. This is the essence of a cosmopolitan city through which we can decipher a non-exclusive space of ritual, collective activity and certain common interests.

SCHLOMO

Savannah emphasizes its authentic link with history while exploiting its "brand-name" value. What might have been considered obsolete fabric in the 1950s has been successfully gentrified into culturally commodified attractions for visitors, tourists, and special interest groups. At the same time, the city is engaging with new symbolic references: for example, Gulfstream Aerospace and the Port of Savannah, which is the fourth largest container port in America. A new post-industrial economic order and evolving urban cultures have frequently brought with them a new social and spatial logic where postmodernism has come to reflect, in Sharon Zukin's words, "a landscape of contemporary economic transformation" and a new emblematic and tangible urban signature. In fact, corporate bodies and business conglomerates are defining a new type of restructuring where urban clusters are developing independently of the core city but contiguous with it, in association with new infrastructure systems. This has in turn allowed the older city to experience a gradual process of gentrification, establishing an economic inter-dependency, which advertises its attractiveness for business investment on both the national and international stage. The memory of the city might well be selective but the convergence of a largely preserved cityscape and the new consumption economy resonates with the visiting public.

150

OPPOSITE PAGE
The temple of the Scottish Rite Masons with its ornate golden vault rising above the adjoining row houses on Madison Square. The old Solomon's Drug Store on the ground floor has been converted to a restaurant.

MARTHA B.

What about the dead space – the *terra incognita* of dereliction, unplanned activities, and "unofficial" uses. Does this not offer a means to recalibrate the relationship of the spatial, social, and cultural based on the assumption that the heterotopic representation is diverse but also exists in a continual state of change? What are the transformative signifiers?

SCHLOMO

Maybe this introduces the notion of dynamic balance that holds the necessary key to urban accommodation and workability, but also in our cities it is where urban space and users resonate within networks of interaction to become part of everyday life and invention. The central issue is how these instruments and processes engage with the built environment and transform it, whether through illusion or empowerment, outside the bounds of normalization and design composition. For example, the galaxy dominates our perception of the heavens, but through advances in astronomy we no longer regard constellations as having mythical characteristics so we can now distinguish specific areas of space that are under their influence or domain.

152

MO

These "spaces of otherness" suggest a multiplicity of interpretations but also a need to understand those parts of a city bestowed with a special, unconventional, or even abnormal identity. Such a situation might represent aspects that challenge the tendency of planning and architecture towards a utopian representation. Its relevance is through an extension of the urban design process from abstract spatial composition to engagement with the practical realities of urbanization. Midnight walking tours of Savannah's renowned ghostly haunts, apparently vouchsafed by followers of the paranormal landscape, are discharged against the clip-clop of carriage horses and the descending entrails of Spanish Moss to create atmospheric stage sets.

TERRY

I have a passing interest in the paranormal. Savannah is ranked as the most haunted city in America by the Institute of Parapsychology. This is evidently due to the many unmarked mass graves from periodic outbreaks of cholera and yellow fever. Some say the plateau was the site of an ancient Native burial ground. Tree growth sometimes used to bring up old bones, leading to the old expression that "even the trees have teeth." Graves were uncovered during redevelopment and simply built over, so that the new properties, whether houses or inns, inherited the spirits. Various older houses are seemingly haunted by what went on there in the early days and the spirits of past occupants. These include the Sorrel Weed House on Madison Square, the Isaiah Davenport House, the Andrew Low House, the Juliette Gordon Low House, and the Owens-Thomas House.

MILES

Cemeteries as well as some of the old houses in Savannah now combine to offer tracts of passive visitation and contemplation, with a narrative of lives short and long, but also poignant and reflective memory. I have been reading up on this. The Colonial Park Cemetery, smack in the middle of the Historic District, served as the public burial ground from around 1750 and originally contained about 10,000 graves, including those of Revolutionary War soldiers. It used to lie, along with the Jewish Cemetery, outside the protective city wall, but was closed in 1853 following the many deaths from yellow fever, so there are probably mass graves below the surface. I have heard that Union soldiers vandalized some of the crypts when they occupied the city, decanted the bodies and used the vaults as a refuge from the freezing winter weather. The decaying old site was reopened as a public park in 1895, the government having acquired it from the Christ Church. It now marks the memorials to some of the better-known individuals all identified by the Georgia Historical Commission.

MILES

The point is that these things are connected with the overall morphology. They are integrated within the local street structure. The Daughters of the American Revolution commissioned the magnificent arched entrance to the cemetery in 1913, marking its more public role within Savannah.

153

MO

Yes, I enjoy this tribute to the past. It is surrounded by mature oak trees, the spires of the Cathedral of St. John the Baptist, and dome of the old city jail from where prisoners might ruminate on their misdeeds, real or contrived, while contemplating their possible ultimate destination.

TERRY

Ghosts tend not to like renovations, particularly if the buildings served as hospitals, asylums, or surgeries. For example the Savannah Poor House built in 1808 later became a hospital and asylum and they experienced many deaths. Bodies were often buried deep below the buildings to avoid the risk of contamination. The Marshall House—the oldest existing hotel in Savannah—was used as a surgery for badly injured servicemen during the civil war, and ghosts of soldiers and stretcher carriers are regularly claimed to be seen by guests.

AGNITA

Cemeteries tell their own story to geographers. Laurel Grove cemetery backs onto May Street Park. I visited it yesterday. It was originally a cotton plantation, it housed

Victorian monuments and statues with graves that include seven Confederate generals. The southern part of the cemetery was reserved for African-Americans, including some of the most prominent church leaders and civil rights workers.

TERRY

There is an interesting story about Jim Williams, the notorious central character of *Midnight in the Garden of Good and Evil*. In 1963 Williams bought an old property, previously built by a plantation owner, known as the Hampton-Lillibridge House, which had survived the great fire of 1820 but had a haunted reputation. He had the timber-framed structure physically moved to a site several blocks away. During the construction strange apparitions were seen in the house by workers and neighbors, and after Williams moved in the appearance of figures and strange happenings increased. Williams took up the clearly unfortunate habit of sleeping with a gun under his pillow but eventually moved out to what proved to be an even more eventful residency in the famous Mercer-Williams House on Monterey Square.

BRIT

Essentially, utopian spaces are inextricably linked to the prevailing system of power, through which regulatory and institutional control can be instigated. A question therefore is how disconnected "counter-spaces" are opened up and how they coexist and reverberate with utopian space through reinterpretation.

MO

Well the concept of heterotopia was explored by Foucault in a somewhat philosophical sense to describe metaphysical "places," which partly represent a human geography that contains a multitude of meanings, but also contradictions—that is to say they are open to different interpretations—real or imagined. But one can consider its relation to the city in so many ways – illusion, compensation, protection, identity, degree of fit, and so on.

SCHLOMO

These all imply a need for a diagnosis of the contours of urban space and the human condition. In a postmodernist sense this helps us to comprehend the role of urban identities as determinants of our city culture. Grahame Shane states that these reflect inevitable urban differences that cannot necessarily be reconciled purely through planning because they are about constant recombination of urban elements – cultural, educational, recreational, retail, etc., that act to stabilize the city model but also act as transitional forces as our urban enclaves shift from one state to another. Street blocks within the Landmark Historic District are tightly controlled, but the Downtown

OPPOSITE PAGE
The Colonial Cemetery next to the dome of the old city jail. The cemetery served as the public burial ground for Savannah from 1750 but was closed in 1853 to coincide with the opening of Laurel Grove.

Expansion Area to the West of Martin Luther King Boulevard and to the East of Broad
Street form places of contrast, housing low-income African-American communities in a
multiplicity of small enclaves with entrenched levels of poverty and unemployment, and
low levels of educational attainment. These spaces create a capacity to sustain particular
social codes and conforming behavior within a detached environment that might also
reflect an ideology of hegemony, however subtle. The communities in these areas do not
share the prosperity and visitation of the downtown area. Civic initiatives need to be
matched by strategies that diversify economic opportunities, establish affordable housing opportunities, and maximize mobility options to benefit long-term residents.

MO

I think we have explored this subject sufficiently for the time being. It is starting to put me in a mind-altering state. Now, after lunch I want to widen our scope of enquiry. We have examined Savannah as far as we are able, now we will turn our attention to the American city, from the post-Revolution period. We have seen how one of America's earliest cities evolved according to a firm plan, but what were the forces that prevailed over the wider and accelerating process of urbanization that has got us to where we are today for better or worse?

Now, off you all go, and hurry back by 2:30.

Dan Schlomo pulls me aside. "While Mo was thankfully rounding up for the morning, I've just been assessing the lunch joints on Google. These are the options. The Latin Chick's Restaurant on Waters Avenue with optional salsa dancing, some ancient Gastro Pub where they rather ominously serve "handcrafted cocktails" and, I know you'll like this, an authentic British pub where you can expand your waistband via comfort food – fish and chips or bangers and mash. What the hell is mash by the way – isn't that some sort of fermentation process they use in moonshine? Anyway I suggest we flip a coin – Heads it's Latin Chick's, Tails it's the pub."

Schlomo tosses a coin. It lands tails. He looks stricken. "Okay," he says. "It's on West Bay Street nearby. But next time lets take the salsa."

We are on the street, joined by a refreshed looking Terry Fulbright. Miles Styles and Agnita wander into Madison Square, while Jean-Paul Gournier and Brit Kris are still locked in a deep discussion on whether Lefebvre should be read in French or English. Apolonia and Martha announce they are on diet plans and cross to the canteen which has a salad bar. Mo is taking a sandwich and completing a book review.

Schlomo flags down a cab. "Its around ten minutes walk," he says, "but I have done walking for today. Angel from Paris, Texas insisted on going on to something called the Square Bar last night, which they say is good for communal grazing. They served something called a Savannah Fizz. I can't remember much after that – I think it kind of injects a bubble into your blood stream and you black out."

We arrive and sit in a line at the carved wooden bar, and order three craft beers. I order onion soup and shepherds pie, Schlomo orders pretzels and meat loaf, and Terry Fulbright macaroni and cheese. There is a pungent smell of warm expectations and stale beer. A notice above the bar reads, "We Support Local Farms."

"Well, what's your take on Heterotopia," demands Schlomo.

"I like the idea of the unknown," retorts Terry.

I say that the notion of contrasting utopias and heterotopias together with ideas of "space" related to power and knowledge raises a fundamental question about urban representation. Therefore Terry's comments on parapsychological diagnosis are quite relevant.

"True," says Schlomo, "but what makes Savannah interesting is that it is an ideal city in one sense, but in another it has also grown in an opportunistic market-led way. How else could it survive?"

Terry intercedes, "Koestler used to say that stability is maintained by an equilibrium of forces pulling in opposite directions, one asserting independence, autonomy, and individuality, the other keeping everything in place as a dependent unit of the whole. Don't you think there is something in that?"

"Well," Schlomo retorts, "even discordant forms generally arise from other economic or social processes, but these can always be challenged. I have always liked the idea of organized complexity. It reminds me of this meat loaf. Look how many processes it went through before being served in a slab with a craft beer. Anyway, who is presenting this afternoon?"

"Agnita," I say. "She has disappeared into one of the squares to commune with nature and hone her verbal delivery on Miles Styles under the ancient oaks." Schlomo contemplates this information with an uncommitted look but says nothing.

Just then the TV, situated on a wall opposite the bar, lights up and heads turn. Hilary Clinton, this time wearing a black trouser suit and a wide-eyed electric smile, is pointing, arm outstretched, in mock recognition towards some anonymous person in the audience. She begins the short news clip by revealing new leaks about Trump's taxes and questionable charitable foundation, and asks her captive but wildly supportive audience, "What kind of genius loses a billion dollars in a single year?" Trump in turn states that the unfairness of the tax laws is unbelievable and that avoidance reflects a brilliant use of them. Hilary says that entrusting Trump with overhauling the country's tax-laws would be like letting the fox into the henhouse. Trump says he has a fiduciary responsibility to pay as little tax as legally possible. Hilary states that Trump has taken corporate excess and made a business model out of it. Trump retorts that as a savvy business survivor he is poised to save the nation.

Schlomo says, "Some guy at U.C. around ten years ago analyzed all America's past presidents on the basis of their I.Q. derived from speeches, writings, and biographies, and came up with a ranking of the least intelligent. It wasn't all that bad – George Washington came in 23rd, Dwight D. Eisenhower 21st, Ronald Reagan 15th, and Gerald Ford 10th. George W Bush was well among the leaders, mainly for his unusually eloquent statement – 'I have opinions of my own, but I don't always agree with them.' Ulysses S. Grant, who actually played a main role in bringing the Civil War to an end was in first place. The interesting thing is that intelligence had virtually nothing to do with how effective or popular they were."

I reply that I always had a soft spot for Ronald Reagan – one of the most popular presidents. He said something along the lines of, "Hard work never killed anyone, but I figure why take the chance."

We leave the bar in thoughtful mood. Terry and I overrule Schlomo's intention to take a cab and we all walk slowly back along Bull Street. Schlomo says, "I'm not sure about craft beers. I heard that some place called The Distillery on West Liberty serves Left Hand Milk Stout and Moon River Apparitions. You have to hand it to these brew houses – they might get you too drunk to comprehend election tactics, but you go down reading poetry."

Back in Poetter Hall the other members are already standing around the table holding coffee cups and enjoined in sporadic conversation, except for Brit Kris and Jean-Paul Gournier who are still animatedly debating what might be either the multi-facetted aspects of Savannah's heterotopia, or the forthcoming evening's entertainment. Agnita van der Kampen has managed to change into a blue and extremely tight two-piece outfit and spiky high heels from which she is able to gaze down at Mo who is wearing a black jacket and a red polo neck sweater. Mo claps his hands for silence. He speaks.

"From the early eighteenth century, cities became the generators of the American economy and the epicenters of social and cultural change. In the process they formed the focus of mass immigration from all corners of the world, and created opportunities for unprecedented numbers of migrants from rural parts of the country. Industrialization created employment but also exacerbated competition for housing and other basic needs. We really have to look at the history of urbanization in America, however briefly, to draw something of a parallel. If we know how we got to our present urban situation we can hopefully then contemplate how we might be able to better it. Agnita van der Kampen is going to enlighten us."

Agnita commences with a modest protest that this is not the enlightenment but a brief run-through of the salient factors—of course, open to interpretation—that have led to the confusing and ever evolving state we term American urbanism. She begins.

FOURTH READING
AGNITA VAN DER KAMPEN

One of the most immediate repercussions of the post-Revolution period in America was a recalibration of land tenure in the eastern states up to the Mississippi, and in the Midwest through the Louisiana purchase, which just about doubled the size of the United States. Substantial tracts were purchased through trading companies, with a crucially important aspect being the right to buy and sell land, free of the previous Crown prerogatives. It is arguably at this point in history that American land law became somewhat detached from its long-standing association with responsive and sustainable stewardship, and land itself became a commodity, open to speculation and capital gain. In the long term this has become a fundamental concern of land use planning.

In effect, the Fifth and Fourteenth Amendments to the Constitution significantly restricted the ability of government to regulate the use of land for the public good if by doing so this would deprive an owner from enhancing its economic value. This simple fact, intricately tied into "freedom of the individual," has been at the heart of the American planning dilemma for the best part of 200 years and has arguably constrained the role of planning as a force for urban betterment and environmental protection. This emphasizes a fundamental contrast to that inherent in the modified Savannah grid plan that was focused from the outset around public space.

Cheap and exceptionally fertile land in the "frontier" Midwest states attracted massive migration with the going price of land in 1800 at only $1.50 an acre. The National Grid imposed a standardized division, rationalizing land into square blocks of 640 acres, and this was sold mainly in sections regardless of topographic constraints, to accord with a more or less standard farm size. New townships were largely slotted into the grid system conveniently sub-dividing the urbanized landscape into private lots bereft of any compelling need to evolve an articulate public realm. William Penn's initial Philadelphia plan for example divided the initial grid into 10,000 one-acre lots for single dwellings, and it was only when new owners began to sell off lot sub-divisions that the street based plan form evolved.

Plan making at a city scale was arguably at its most confident when it was at its most creative and imaginative, for example, following Charles L'Enfant's plan for Washington in 1791. Older European cities at this time had acquired the accumulated civic trappings of ceremonial, cultural, and political identity incorporated within a framework of grand avenues, esplanades, and squares, while the American city was largely aligned around the more restricted repertoire of processes that maximized development potential. The situation that brought both of these aspects together was industrialization, unleashed in the early nineteenth century. As Leo Marx has stated in *The Machine in the Garden*, it enabled America to pursue a myth of the rural ideal while devoting itself to the more serious matter of acquiring wealth and power, and imposing progressive ideas on the world. The

industrial revolution reinforced concentrations of economic activity around areas where raw materials were available and sources of power could be exploited. It also fuelled the first suburban developments, led largely by the service requirements of growing metropolitan economies. Plans for a national highway and transportation system began under Thomas Jefferson in 1806, and many of the initial projects were constructed during the course of the nineteenth century. The majority of preindustrial cities in the United States were located on navigable rivers or harbor fronts, and those along the Atlantic seaboard began to slowly evolve from trading settlements to manufacturing, leading to greater investment in construction and transport. The Erie Canal was completed in 1825 entirely without federal assistance. This connected New York with the Great Lakes and fertile farmlands beyond the Appalachians. It brought about an immediate growth in export trade together with the fortunes of New York, and effectively secured the economic primacy of the United States for years to come. However, the nineteenth-century city for the most part remained dense and compact, concentrated around waterfronts with a tight agglomeration of housing and workplaces, where public health conditions were often dreadful.

Large merchant-trading cities along the eastern seaboard including Boston, Philadelphia, and New York expanded rapidly in the early nineteenth century, following new realms of manufacturing. Cities became the centers for capital investment, organized labor, trade associations, and massive immigration. By the end of the nineteenth century the majority of urban populations were foreign-born, the domains of the poor in the emerging metropolitan communities being largely dominated by those of the wealthy.

Industrialization created a new level of urban intensification exacerbated by a lack of zoning, which in many cases produced a degraded environment of overcrowded tenements along with an arbitrary congregation of mills and factories, made worse by a lack of proper infrastructure and public health legislation. Louis Mumford has described the scale of tenement squalor and congestion that occurred in industrial New York as generating a pent up desire on the part of many of its long suffering inhabitants to abandon the city altogether.

The means to at least partially accomplish this were surprisingly near at hand. Central Park, designed by Frederick Law Olmsted and Calvert Vaux, opened in 1858, successfully introducing a natural form of landscape on 840 hectares of scrubland two miles to the north of Manhattan. This was a massive engineering as well as a landscape project comprising gardens, playing fields, lakes, and quiet trails. It was also an opportunity to urbanize the health-giving attributes of its unspoiled scenic surroundings. Olmsted is said to have been inspired in his vision for Central Park by seeing the first publicly funded park in the world at Birkenhead near Liverpool designed by Joseph Paxton in 1847. Olmsted proceeded to build over 100 municipal parks, while Vaux, who was an architect, went on to design the American Museum of Natural History.

The mechanism to translate an even broader idealistic vision of a rural arcadia into romantic reality, at least for the rising affluent class, came about through the advent of the railroad. This initially facilitated the capacity of wealthy families to move well away from the urban pollution and production lines to newly fashionable neighborhoods such as Washington Square in New York or Beacon Hill in Boston, or to build mansion estates in new Main Line suburbs. While the poor lived primarily within walking distances of factories, suburbs began to reflect the new social profiles of an emerging middle class.

At the same time, civic qualities began to reflect the Baroque conception of plan making emanating from European city remodeling, which glorified the potential of urbanization through a combination of visual composition, harmonious order, and convenience. Civic buildings were cloaked in a Beaux Arts neo-classicism, and were focused in formal conjunction with axial alignments and prominent nodal points to create a regularized urban realm, symbolic of new social mores and conventions, and intended to induce a high code of public behavior. Not coincidentally, this also reflected the onset of new transit systems and movement corridors. City building programs picked up on the bravado and public appeal of World Fair expositions, the first in London in 1851 designed by Joseph Paxton, which exploited the invention of sheet glass to remarkable effect in the Crystal Palace. This was followed by the Barcelona Exposition in 1888, and then the Paris Universal Exposition in 1889. These showcased both culture and industry as celebrations of art and design. While they intentionally broadcast national achievements they also sought to project a better future through advanced technological and architectural devices.

The Columbian Exposition in 1893, held in Chicago to celebrate the 400th anniversary of the "discovery" of America by Christopher Columbus, represented an extravagant means of closing the nineteenth century with positive aspirations for the ideology of the new in terms of a highly articulated civic design, determined largely by the aesthetically focused City Beautiful movement. It heroically attempted to bridge the gap between the looming industrialized reality of the city and a rather more idealized state, but more significantly it reflected strong moral undertones that attempted to reconcile civic improvement with social reform. Daniel Burnham, who, with Frederick Law Olmsted, designed the Exposition on the existing Jackson Park as a "Palace on the Prairie," went on to complete a comprehensive plan for Chicago in 1909 along much the same lines that brought together the idealized theme of civic grandeur and classical order as a social imperative.

The Municipal Arts Society of New York and the American League for Civic Improvement sought to instigate collective responsibility for the city along with progressive agendas, which called for more social mix and diversity. Other volunteer groups were involved with issues of poverty, overcrowding, and public health, as part of a new environmental determinism.

Local transport around the time of the first commuter suburbs was initially supplied by steam ferries, street cars propelled on rails, and canals for transport of heavy goods and freight. This facilitated low-density development along linear corridors, with the grandest developments facing the main streets. For a limited time the suburban prototype created an acceptable balance between the urban and rural setting, bridged in the 1880s by electric trolley cars, which were both cheap and non-polluting. It made commuting between the suburbs and city, and even weekend visits to the countryside, cost effective. Below ground, the nation's first subway was initiated in Boston in 1897 followed by what was then the world's fastest mass transit system seven years later in New York, knitting together the city's five boroughs. In the process, nodes of dense building disposition created a significant impact on land values.

By the turn of the twentieth century, the residential suburb had become a fully-fledged part of the expanding American city. Transport franchises were granted by local municipalities, and by 1903 there was more than 30,000 miles of electric track. Roads were largely unpaved, and in cities only cobblestones were used, but street-car subdivisions gradually created an outer series of urban settlements. The pastoral ideal that many were searching for was largely sacrificed to compact lot layouts necessitated by easy street car access.

During the first decade America admitted almost nine million new immigrants, a ten-year total that was not exceeded until the final decade of the century. An inevitable result of the mushrooming in the urban population was the incorporation of municipalities and boroughs in a wide radius around the central city. Their primary purpose was to orchestrate necessary public infrastructure improvements, and in some of the larger cities suburban municipalities were merged into a more consolidated form to better serve that purpose. The introduction of land use zoning ordinances, first in Los Angeles in 1908, and eight years later in New York, was however primarily concerned with public health issues. At the same time, federal support for citywide zoning and building controls helped change the spatial landscape of private buildings, while discreetly safeguarding communities from forms of development that might have a negative impact on property values.

The American Vitruvius, sub-titled *The Architect's Handbook of Civic Art*, was published in 1922. Its authors largely skirted around the genuinely innovative eighteenth-century designs associated with early colonial American townships that fostered a form of social and economic equality. Instead, city building principles were formulated at a large scale with both design conviction and social confidence. The components of this were architecturally defined boulevards, which maintained a continuity of form and prominent alignments, civic set pieces, and parkland. This might be described as a watershed in American urban design. As city planning turned from the Arcadian to the simply arcane, and as design gave way to urban management and enablement, the urbanist turned into a technician. Aesthetic refinement gave way to the rationality embraced by an accelerating process of urbanization and industrialization, encapsulated by the city-building and organizational possibilities of the skyscraper and a commensurate momentum towards urban expansion for newly fashionable garden suburbs.

This was a confident and optimistic era, marked by urban growth and expressive of the New Republic, founded in 1914 as a progressive force for moral authority and humanitarian ideals. High-rise construction met the immediate demands of urban real estate markets, characterized by the rapid spatial transformation of America's largest cities. Several inventions made the technological transition to tall structures possible, namely the invention of steel by Henry Bessemer in 1856, and the introduction of curtain wall construction by Gustave Eiffel who honed his inventive capabilities on the internal skeleton of Bartholdi's Statue of Liberty, France's gift to the American people in 1886. However, in the process, towers created new and problematic issues such as street shadow and wind effects that had to be countered by new sets of planning and building codes together with zoning that regulated site coverage, built footprints and setbacks. Such controls, coupled with a tall building boom, materially affected urban form but also created unprecedented architectural opportunities through use of new materials and construction processes that created a succession of styles.

By the 1920s, the number of cities had multiplied to more than 5,000 mainly through the granting of charters to individual municipalities with over 2,500 people, but also through annexation via the recalibration of municipal borders, and the merging of neighboring communities for mutual advantage. Between 1914 and 1930 around one and a half million workers left the South for better paying jobs in northern cities, but faced both direct and subtle forms of discrimination and de facto segregation through such things as restrictive covenants. Certain city neighborhoods such as Harlem in New York became magnets for poor migrants and also fuelled political movements to support social and economic improvement. This set the stage for more progressive planning and urban design of metropolitan regions under agendas set out by the American City Planning Institute and the Regional Planning Association, but there was one overriding catalyst to urban change – the introduction of the automobile, which rapidly realigned the delicate equilibrium between cities and suburbs.

It was possibly the formality associated with early twentieth-century cities, coupled with their inflexibility in dealing with unprecedented population growth that directed planning trajectories towards more intensely practicable and utilitarian measures that dealt with functional order over aesthetic concerns, urban management and social organization. Progressive planning was now seen as part of a new rational urban consciousness aimed in particular at the regulation of housing development. Much city building was in the hands of engineers, through a pragmatic approach to the mounting need for urban infrastructure and utilities, while publicly-orchestrated planning was aimed mainly at regulatory zoning and land use coordination under the jurisdiction of City Hall. After the adoption of standard zoning in 1926, there was an acceleration of zoning ordinances by cities and local municipalities. It was perhaps at this point that planning began to falter in its empathy with the City Beautiful and began to consolidate around the practical orchestration of urban efficiency and mobility.

If good urbanization is about heterogeneity at various scales, then a recurrent theme in urban discussion is the lingering impacts of the Congrès d' Architecture Moderne – CIAM, founded in 1928, which broke with a historically referenced urbanism based on street and urban place formation. At the time, this provided just what commercially competitive American cities were deemed to need – a conveniently standardized means to rationalize city planning. Modernism, outside the rarified ateliers of the modern masters who exploited the opportunity to create a number of long-lasting city landmarks, was unfortunately galvanized by less than inspired imitators. In the process it ushered in a new urban doctrine of functionalism and efficiency, applied to the city itself as an emerging engine of commerce.

The city's new physicality was characterized by realms of separation rather than cohesion – something that Colin Rowe has described as, "cities of conspicuously disparate objects." The planning process dealt with acknowledged urban ailments not by resolving their causes, which had much to do with health and safety, but by wholesale redevelopment to maximize land value. Downtown renewal strategies led to an expedient penchant for situating buildings on independent sites, devoid of street context, reflecting an ideology that stand-alone buildings fringed by primary roads were of greater importance than urban fabric and the defining qualities of urban space. It was to be another fifty years before the false idealism of the Athens Charter was symbolically refuted by the demolition of the incongruous Pruitt-Igoe housing complex in St. Louis in 1975, only twenty years after its first occupation, as being largely unfit for human habitation.

There were, however, some inspired responses. Ebenezer Howard's ideas for combining both urban and rural characteristics through "garden cities" were taken up in America by Clarence Perry in response to the squalid conditions to be found in industrialized cities, and the increase in motorized traffic in the 1920s as car ownership reached twenty million. Interestingly, as pointed out by Lewis Mumford, Howard's proposals for a minimum lot size—around 6m by 32m—was exactly the same as the typical New York City lot before overbuilding took place.

The application of Perry's work in the 1929 Regional Plan for New York set out both physical parameters and guidelines for relatively self-contained residential, business, and community uses within urban enclaves or city "cells." His diagram of a neighborhood unit and core principles to eliminate through traffic, street design, and walking distances published by the Regional Plan Association of New York in 1929 could in fact be easily mistaken for a modern "new urbanism" layout, but at a somewhat lower density of only ten detached houses per acre. Perry's ideas were further developed in the plan for Radburn in New Jersey by Clarence Stein and Henry Wright. Variety and diversity of residential types within a connective structure of greenways influenced a number of township planners at a time when accommodation of the automobile was becoming an overriding design concern. Like its contemporary equivalent, the walkable neighborhood was not without its critics, although the notion of sustainable communities was not high on the agenda.

What became known as "cluster zoning" involved condensed areas of development with significant amounts of the site used for recreation and amenity uses. Now we might ask, why neighborhood design did not evolve naturally from this into sets of refined criteria for livable communities? The brief answer is the introduction of strict zoning designations for reasons that might have seemed both necessary and logical at the time. The application of zoning brought about a rigid planning demarcation between different uses, discouraging social equity that might be served by a mix of housing types, and significantly compromising opportunities for physical cohesion around streets and places. The result was the growth of residential enclaves in both cities and suburbs that instead of creating neighborhood communities, orchestrated states of exclusion. This led indirectly to the wide adoption of the gridiron plan, which, after all, had significant predecessors from previous eras. This not only met the rigid organizational prerogatives of the land ordinances, but proved to be a convenient tool for land speculation. Around the same time, Frank Lloyd Wright conceived "Broadacre City," based on an alternative to the city with a gridded distribution of four-acre agricultural plots as a means of facilitating self-contained communities.

Many facets of the auto business, including new assembly line production and cheap petroleum, created a deluge of new jobs, spiraling wages, and corporate behemoths. However, within ten years, the cracks in this hitherto robust model became apparent. Mechanization of agricultural production led directly to a downsizing of farm populations as workers migrated to cities and jobs in industry. In the late 1920s, manufacturing, highway building, and property development reached their natural limit. Much urban wealth had been funneled into the stock market and something had to give.

The Great Depression that followed the stock market crash in 1929, at least in part reflected the lack of diversification in the economy, declining industrial trends, and low levels of exports to Europe following World War I. In combination, this led to a massive economic downturn and consequent large-scale unemployment, but ultimately acted to reconfigure economic directions. The Chicago World's Fair of 1933 and that of New York in 1939 with the theme "World of Tomorrow" tellingly pointed towards what was to come over the next decades – a predominantly suburban landscape supported by federally subsidized highways. The political response had a significant impact on large cities that accommodated around nineteen percent of America's population. While President Herbert Hoover established a Reconstruction Finance Corporation to assist key banks, business houses, and city governments, Franklin Roosevelt's "New Deal" policies went much further in terms of liberal economic intervention in social welfare. These effectively created a sympathetic context for the establishment of the Federal Housing Administration in 1934, and the Social Security Act of 1935. Arguably their greatest impact on cities was the mortgage insurance policy, which had an immediate impact through a large-scale program of house building and public works. On the plus side one percent of public building construction funds were allocated to artistic embellishments, which made a credible contribution to the urban realm.

A new US Conference of Mayors provided for an effective relationship between cities and federal government, and marked a turning point in the ability to provide funds directly to cities. This was timely, as America's participation in World War II brought a flow of migrants into the industrial cities, attracted by new employment opportunities. The burgeoning urban population included large numbers of immigrants from Latin America together with migrants from the South and Puerto Rico that began to change the cultural complexion of urban neighborhoods, and shaded the older and more distinct racial categories. The Urban Renewal Act of 1948 ushered in a period of intense tenement clearance, road construction, and urban redevelopment. The urban design process thereafter became one of separation in both two and three dimensions – pedestrians from traffic, and in some cases from streets themselves through large ground level areas of parking; internalization of shopping complexes; and vertical stratification of connective elements. The Machine City underscored the prominence of the urban highway as the key armature of movement and connectivity between points of production and transfer. The high-speed highway marked the predominance of private surface transport, putting urban rationalization and expediency before regeneration of tightly packed inner city neighborhoods.

The Housing Act of 1949 technically represented a breakthrough in terms of providing a vehicle for effective urban planning and regeneration, as it facilitated the purchase of land by government under the concept of eminent domain, which essentially involved the legal resumption of land for public purposes. In addition cities could be reimbursed for up to two-thirds of their urban renewal costs. Technically, government could clear purchased land and build public housing, but perversely it could also sell the cleared land to private developers. In practice, however, large and vibrant ethnic and working class neighborhoods were blighted through this process, and countless households displaced with little community gain. Around 5,300 miles of expressways were driven through American cities despite the massive costs of land assembly and neighborhood destruction. Radial urban expressways were promoted as a means of increasing accessibility to the commercial districts. This led to the clearing of more than 600,000 housing units paid for mainly by the federal government. It was followed by a further Housing Act five years later which had the effect of removing four, older, low-rent units for each new one as part of redevelopment programs, intended to preserve property values in downtown areas and to provide parking areas for new commercial development. The biggest impact however was visited on the urban poor.

Many facets of the rapid growth in manufacturing, including assembly line production and cheap petroleum, created a deluge of new jobs, spiraling wages, and corporate behemoths. However within ten years the cracks in this hitherto robust model became apparent. The indefatigable Robert Moses in New York seized the Roosevelt administration's measures to realign the embattled economy by single-mindedly promoting a highway, bridge, and tunnel building program, putting himself at the head of a new Authority that was dedicated to this process.

In its negative impact on all forms of public transport this had massive consequences. The federal highway-building program effectively saw the triumph of the urban expressway and the complete ascendancy of the motor vehicle over mass transit, which imposed quite unnecessary physical and social upheaval. In certain cities it destroyed entire urban quarters and paved the remnants both literally and figuratively. Unsubsidized streetcars were gradually put out of business, and new bus companies led to the dismantling of electric trolley systems. In effect, public transport systems became almost entirely replaced by private modes.

Urban renewal essentially focused on contested policies, which served to incentivize redevelopment in order to generate more tax-generating commercial interests. The federal highway system provided access to new manufacturing industries that became the focus of new low-density communities beyond the urban fringe. This in turn induced further anti-urban movements and civic unraveling as separate municipalities competed for revenue-generating forms of development. Suburbia therefore blossomed not entirely on the back of its mythical bucolic attractiveness, but on a spiraling combination of new employment opportunities on one hand, and alienation from the core city on the other – each one reinforcing the policies and prejudices of separation. Superhighways literally pried open the previously outer hinterlands around the nation's largest cities, reshaping the Metropolitan landscape and facilitating a new age of commuting. In the process it formatted a new urban frontier based on an elusive but significant covenant between the government and the up and coming middle class – the advent of a suburban dreamscape based on cheap land, personalized transport, and detached homes made possible through the generosity of the Federal Housing Administration, with expansive mortgage arrangements.

A point to ponder is that at this precise time in the euphoric post-war period, on the other side of the Atlantic, a Metropolitan Green Belt was being established encircling London and several other English cities under the 1947 Town and Country Planning Act. This has not only prevented large-scale sprawl in the ensuing period but has successfully preserved large tracts of land for farmland, ancient woodland, sites of special scientific interest, and rural recreation.

Planning in America became slowly marginalized and driven by discord. At an educational level, many universities curtailed their planning programs, signaling a breach with urban design and a tendency to move towards theory over practice. Decentralized urban policy making became effectively surrendered to City Hall. At the same time, the almost parallel "Great Society" programs under the Lyndon Johnson administration that attempted to stem the precipitous decline of cities often made bad situations even worse, destroying older communities and incentivizing an even greater exodus to suburbia.

Large-scale suburban development opened up opportunities for privately framed and financed shopping malls and commercial cores beyond the beltways, enthusiastically advocated by exponents at the time as the contemporary equivalent of medieval market places and town squares. Roads, endless parking areas, and flyovers became both a means of access but also the agents of separation, in effect creating non-places in terms of overall comprehension and community, even in the central city. Joni Mitchel's 1960s lament that "they pulled down paradise and put up a parking lot" articulated a realization that the sins against the city were becoming irreversible. A synthetic urbanization had outflanked genuine urbanity, and pure functionalism had overturned a longstanding appreciation of good city attributes. Urban violence and civil rights created a raft of initiatives from the "War on Poverty" to "Community Action" and the "Model Cities" programs that slowly brought into focus new thinking on planning and urban design.

What transpired was an almost total emphasis on the private at the expense of the public realm – a process that Jane Jacobs made abundantly clear in *Death and Life of Great American Cities* published in 1961. Jacobs's famous dictum that "a city cannot be a work of art" was not intended as a condemnation of the City Beautiful but rather a challenge to reflect on the many other social and economic factors that intensify contrast, diversity, and exchange rather than merely monumental order. In passing, perhaps her admonition against artistry might have excluded Jackson Pollock whose drip painting was once described as the "unorganized explosion of random energy" an equally forceful metaphor for the city.

Industrial cities continued to experience decentralization and a shift to sprawling urbanization within the wider metropolitan region well into the 1970s. The administration of public housing was redirected in 1976 in response to a Supreme Court ruling that

169

prohibited high concentrations of public housing in single neighborhoods in order to avoid the extension of poor ghettos.

By the 1980s it was estimated that around sixty percent of metropolitan populations, or 100 million people, lived in suburbs. This broadly reflected continuing prosperity and promotion of greater levels of infrastructure, while mortgage programs and federal tax regulations favored the development of single-family homes. The HOPE program of home ownership launched in 1989 attempted to incentivize home ownership for low-income families within multi-family projects, and provided tax incentives for businesses to locate within reach of poor communities.

It was not until the 1998 Transportation Equity Act for the 21st century that inter-modal surface transport was properly linked with environmental legislation and energy policy, focused on new planning directions. Meanwhile almost ninety percent of all federal funds handed to states for transit went on road construction – a percentage that still exists today.

In New York City the Tenant Interim Leasing Program helped to rehabilitate run-down apartment buildings that had been abandoned by landlords, in part because poor residents found it impossible to get loans for repairs and maintenance. Over a ten-year period it empowered low-income residents to buy their houses as co-ops, and in the process re-established a sense of community, orchestrated under management and tenant interim leasing programs.

The National Register of Historic Places, set up in the aftermath of New York's Penn Station demolition, now acts to protect historic buildings and districts, supported by state preservation offices and historic landmark commissions. Perhaps in the nick of time, these have brought about successful restorations of older urban environments, and in many cases have introduced economic resurgence through cultural tourism. The Clean Water Act of 1972 was the catalyst to regeneration of harbor and river frontages, facilitating the waterfronts of many older cities to be upgraded into accessible mixed-use visitor attractions so that the back door of cities suddenly became the front door.

A combination of cultural and creative initiatives has in recent years gradually begun to transform entire urban districts through conversion and recycling of older industrial buildings, and the regeneration of downtown areas through various local bodies, civic organizations, and business groups, utilizing the established advantages of mellow, older neighborhoods and existing urban places. Related to this is a new architectural respect for contextualism that establishes a level of fit with the complex urban character, seeking inspirational references and reinterpretation from past styles, rich in expressive detail and novelty.

In the wake of the mortgage securities implosion in 2007 there has been a soul searching response to many concerns, stemming partly from a historic inability to reign in private landowners and speculators, but also the need to counter negative land use trends. It is, however, necessary to adopt an interventionist rather than a purely prag-matic approach, and to examine a proactive and refocused reshaping of metropolitan geography. A resistance to change is to be expected, but while at this particular time energy costs are low, it is likely that this, together with new forms of autonomous vehicles, will be the key to urban transformation, whether we choose to call it a new suburban or a metropolitan future.

All of this is propelling necessary and arguably inevitable changes to the central city, generated through simple democratic principles, open to choice and lifestyle. This requires a combination of incremental development and economic regeneration, each subscribing to a process that acknowledges the necessity of accrued investment in the quality of the city itself and its elusive patterns of livability. But gentrification in isolation is clearly insufficient if it simply equates to displacement of low-income residents. The initial objective must be to resolve the issue of vacant lots and abandoned buildings that create blight and inhibit rather than encourage investment. Tax credits for preservation and refurbishment of old properties and urban quarters must equally equate with meas-ures that combat economic disparity and discrimination.

The "creative class," astutely described by Richard Florida, are the New Urbanists, repre-sentative of the twenty-first-century urban economy and perhaps even the ultimate saviors of the city in its evolving form. This has the capacity to promote an effective connection between new high-end urban industries and a revitalized urban fabric that draws on the embodiment of the new city dynamic together with the changing pattern of society. Since the turn of the twenty-first century, the growth of population in central cities has gradually outpaced that of the suburbs for the first time in a century as the creative generation, and in particular its younger demographic components, begin to re-engage with the full potential for new urban lifestyle opportunities, focusing on the role of the "urban village," with its mix of uses and private investment in the rehabilitation of older building fabric for a range of new creative visitor attractions. This perhaps relates positively to Louis Mumford's notion of the city as a symbol of collective unity, and brings into focus the need for the consolida-tion of community programs for a social urbanism and a change in city image and identity.

Regenerating the central city as part of metropolitan area planning rather than a completely separate program requires some parallel thinking. We have got to work on the assumption that America's love affair with free market capitalism will not simply come down to the survival of the fittest by whatever means. Policies therefore need to be accompanied by economic stimulation at a federal level with a clear differential between downtown invigoration at prescribed physical densities, inner urban enclaves, and sub-urban neighborhoods. This must form part of a visionary transformation strategy, and needs to be properly examined in spatial, social, and market-attractive terms.

The allure of the city has not disappeared and we need to acknowledge and utilize its social and cultural power to create more livable communities. Christine Boyer has referred to the "contemporary merchandising of history," in particular along urban waterfronts that combine with amenities laden with historical allusions to old city quarters and traditions. Collections of historic buildings, whatever their primary functions, serve to create distinctive and atmospheric destination that provide strong foci such as Ghirardelli Square in San Francisco, Pioneer Square in Seattle, Quincy Market in Boston, Fulton Market in New York, or the Vieux Carré in New Orleans. And we must not exclude River Street in our beloved Savannah. The festival marketplace manipulates the intimate scale of rehabilitated streets and places, and although there is a line of reasoning that such urban landscapes of consumption can tend to be overly stage-managed, they offer both a strong identity and visual spectacle. They personify fun, often reflect maritime history, and can be connected with other urban attractions and cultural venues via landscaped promenades, precincts, and well-defined urban spaces.

This perhaps brings us back to Savannah and the art of urban place-making. The public realm is essentially what urban design is all about but its central relationship with other disciplines is an uneasy one, often fudging its essential modus operandi. City planning is arguably a coordinating activity set around an overall vision. It must therefore fit neatly into a framework based mainly on administrative procedures but can all too easily devolve into bureaucratic channels with little overall responsibility other than land use control and coordination. While zoning and design codes have their place, they require a good deal of consideration to the needs of separate localities, and must be applied with a degree of flexibility. Designers all too often perceive urban solutions as "architecture writ large" and conduct a dialogue on the serious business of urbanism as an opportunity to air their personalized design credentials and spatial theories – something for which there is a not unreceptive developer clientele. Traffic engineering is by contrast an overwhelming force in its own right, in response to unequivocal and often uncompromising objectives that often run counter to the fundamental goals of community betterment and livability.

Urban design must draw on a range of contexts and critiques, bringing them together with a common focus that straddles diverse practices and disciplines and of course a central one – the political economy. How this focus is determined is reliant on many factors, notably the political will to evolve a responsive urbanism. This infers that we use the smart city linked to the sustainability agenda to connect and reconcile our reservoir of knowledge in focusing on the urban challenges, drawing on philosophical ideas, and, in part, relating these to best practice. While the urban design approach must occasionally counter questions as to its precise and legitimate role in shaping the physical and social public realm, it is as much a force for urban enquiry as it is for informing practice and prioritizing sustainability.

But the difficulties are loud and clear. Opportunities for effective urban design,

Renovated and remodeled warehouses on River Street up to six-stories in height, with buildings and monuments that bear testimony to the history of the city. The street was reconstructed in the 1970s owing to the decay of its old wooden supports, but retains its cobbles and railroad track. It now functions as a mixed use area of restaurants, shops, and apartments, linked to Upper Factor's Walk by steep stone staircases.

regeneration, and sustainable human habitats have, over the past century, been squandered on the back of the machine age and the priority given to the automobile. The essential problem is what has been termed the "sprawl paradigm," whereby the various living components – housing, shopping, working, institutional, and civic uses have been approved and implemented with little or no consideration given to coherent urban design or community aspects, and are often only accessible from interstate highway interchanges. This is not to downplay the positive aspects of new suburban communities, developed on a separate design trajectory from the city itself, that offer something between "escape" and "exclusiveness." However, it would seem logical to concentrate on ways to make both urban and suburban environments walkable and people friendly – to suitably resolve aspects of scale, density, building relationships, and connections at a metropolitan level, and to ensure landscaped comfort to streets and other public spaces; in other words, a logical prioritization of the public over the private realm that we see in Savannah.

To complement such initiatives there is a need for measures that can bring about long-term benefit, such as removal of the causes of urban blight, infrastructure improvement, realignment of urban expressways, and greater levels of pedestrian connectivity. All of these, and I dare say there are a lot more, provide important measures for stitching together parts of the urban fabric.

Cities can only ultimately thrive by attracting private investment to bring about public gain, thereby creating a catalyst to which public agencies can subscribe through appropriate initiatives and controls. As opposed to a one-off privately developed neighborhood, the city building process must reflect a multitude of continuous recalibrations and represent countless interests and values. These must aim at ensuring livability, connectivity, versatility, and diversity in every sense.

Design objectives rightly represent a moveable feast that respects the fluidity of change across the economic, social, cultural, and political spectrum. This might suggest that we are caught on the horns of a dilemma in meeting the requirements of the new urban political economy. We appear to be stranded between the perceived need to maximize economic competitiveness in the global age and the undeniable need for government intervention to achieve urban environments that are safe, equitable, workable, and self sustaining, and that cannot simply be left to evolve of their own accord.

That is all I have to say for now.

Mo jumps up to his full height and finds himself on a horizontal alignment with Agnita's chest, now elevated on stilettos. "Well done, well done," he says. "You covered all the bases, as we say over here, and you left us with something of a question – how do we bring things together?" Agnita looks bemused. Mo continues obliviously, "I hope we have some answers to this, but tomorrow Mr. Terence Fulbright is going to relate another side of this story – precisely how and why our cities are now surrounded by sprawl and why eighty percent of the population have chosen to live there.

"Tonight you are all free to wander at will, and please do not let Dan lead you into the jaws of evil and temptation."

Dan rises with an exaggerated, "Who me?" expression. Agnita says, "Well after all that I can resist anything except temptation."

We all leave together but separate on Bull Street, Mo and Martha heading north, and the rest of us south past the bearded water nymphs cavorting and blowing plumes of water across the Forsyth Park Fountain, which Terry assures me is dyed green every year to celebrate St. Patrick's Day. We head towards Magnolia Hall past the Confederate Monument, which honors those from the city who lost their lives fighting for the Confederacy. As a clear hint that a degree of prejudice and persecution still lingered, the Ladies Memorial Association insisted that at the time of its construction in 1879 no Northern materials should be used, nor Northern craftsmen employed.

We reach our resplendent quarters via a set of approach steps flanked by two solid Corinthian columns and several of us immediately seat ourselves on the front porch on prim, little, wrought iron chairs. These are set around a circular table which overlooks a tiny,

planted garden and across Whitaker Street to the park. Agnita wants to cool off. Schlomo says he needs a shower. Terry is preoccupied shuffling piles of notes. The rest of us are offered tea or coffee by an accommodating housemaid. Apolonia, who has ordered a glass of Prosecco, mutters that there is a lot to be said for the Antebellum south and its languid ways.

Schlomo suddenly reappears, damp hair dripping onto the porch floor. He pauses solemnly, "The Lady Chablis is dead." We stare blankly at him. "Oh," says Apolonia. "Really – who is she? Sorry, who was she?" says Miles. "I'm sad to hear that," says Jean-Paul. "I read the book and saw the movie." Terry simply looks baffled.

Heads turn again to Schlomo. He puts a hand through his hair and expands. "The lovely posturing Ms. Chablis was a Savannah modern legend. A transsexual whose unlikely birth name was Benjamin. She was hurled into the spotlight by John Berendt in *Midnight in the Garden of Good and Evil* – sometimes referred to in Savannah, rather nervously, as 'The Book.' She even played herself in the movie adaptation, heroically cast by Clint Eastwood. After that, as a noted local celebrity, she wrote an autobiography *Hiding My Candy* – it's almost essential reading at UCLA. Anyway, she was a black doyen of Savannah's LGTBQ community and Club One's first female impersonator, variously known as the Doll, or the Grand Empress of Savannah."

"Actually," interrupts Jean-Paul, "I think she used to present herself as 'incog-negro.' She would always say, 'This isn't a Disney show so you better strap in.' She gave two shows a month at Club One, and visitors programmed their trips to the city around her appearance dates."

"I am now going to seek consolation in this sad demise with Angel from Paris, Texas, at somewhere called The Jinx on Congress Street," confesses Schlomo. "Angel says it's a bit Gothic, but that they play rock, metal, country, and hip hop. I think I might stop by Club One en route to see if there is a wake going on. Do I have any takers?"

Brit and Jean-Paul put their hands up. Terry shuffles some papers. Agnita reappears and announces that as this might be one of the last remaining sunlit evenings, she would like a stroll around the Victorian District, and if she has the stamina and correct walking shoes, she might extend this to Mid-City. "Who wants to come and interrupt my solitude," she asks. Miles and Apolonia stick up their hands. Terry looks doubtful but joins them. "Now, which way do I go? The walk perhaps?" Bluegrass sounds interesting, but I don't want to break up the foursome. I put my hand up.

We plot a determinedly southern course along Whitaker Street at the edge of the park, take a left at West Gwinnett Street, regain Bull Street, and crisscross the area between Gwinnett Street and Anderson Street, and Montgomery and Abercorn Streets. The tight street matrix of small blocks makes for a walkable neighborhood. Some streets have been narrowed to provide bike lanes, orchestrated by the Savannah Bicycle Campaign. The district framework resulted from the first horse-drawn street-cars followed by the extension of railway alignments in the nineteenth century. Large multi-family homes are interspersed with small wood-frame cottages. Apolonia, who is well versed on her local geography, guides us along past the restored wood frame gingerbread houses dating from the 1870s that are embellished with ornate brackets and cornices, extravagantly detailed porches, verandahs, and pointed turrets. Eccentricity abounds. We pass one house with a post-box on the front lawn in pink and yellow. On the yellow side, there is a hand-painted quote from Mary Flannery O'Connor, a local writer – *Some old lady said that my book left a bad taste in her mouth. I wrote back to her and said you weren't supposed to eat it.*

Miles, who has evidently been delving into the city's planning credentials, tells us that the Victorian District began life as Savannah's first streetcar suburb in the 1870s on public land which forms the established National Historic Landmark District, in close proximity to the downtown area and Forsyth Park. Its focal point was Thomas Square. The district was originally laid out on a simple grid pattern with no inclusion of residential squares that would have reduced tax revenues to the city. Houses were of wooden construction, reflecting its status as a low-income suburb. Over time, however, the physical condition of the predominantly freestanding properties deteriorated, and many poorer families moved to outer suburbs. As low-income areas on the east and west sides of the city such as Yamacraw became subject to federal clearance and urban renewal programs

OPPOSITE PAGE
Timber-frame houses in the Victorian District create an eclectic but distinctive assortment of architectural elements.

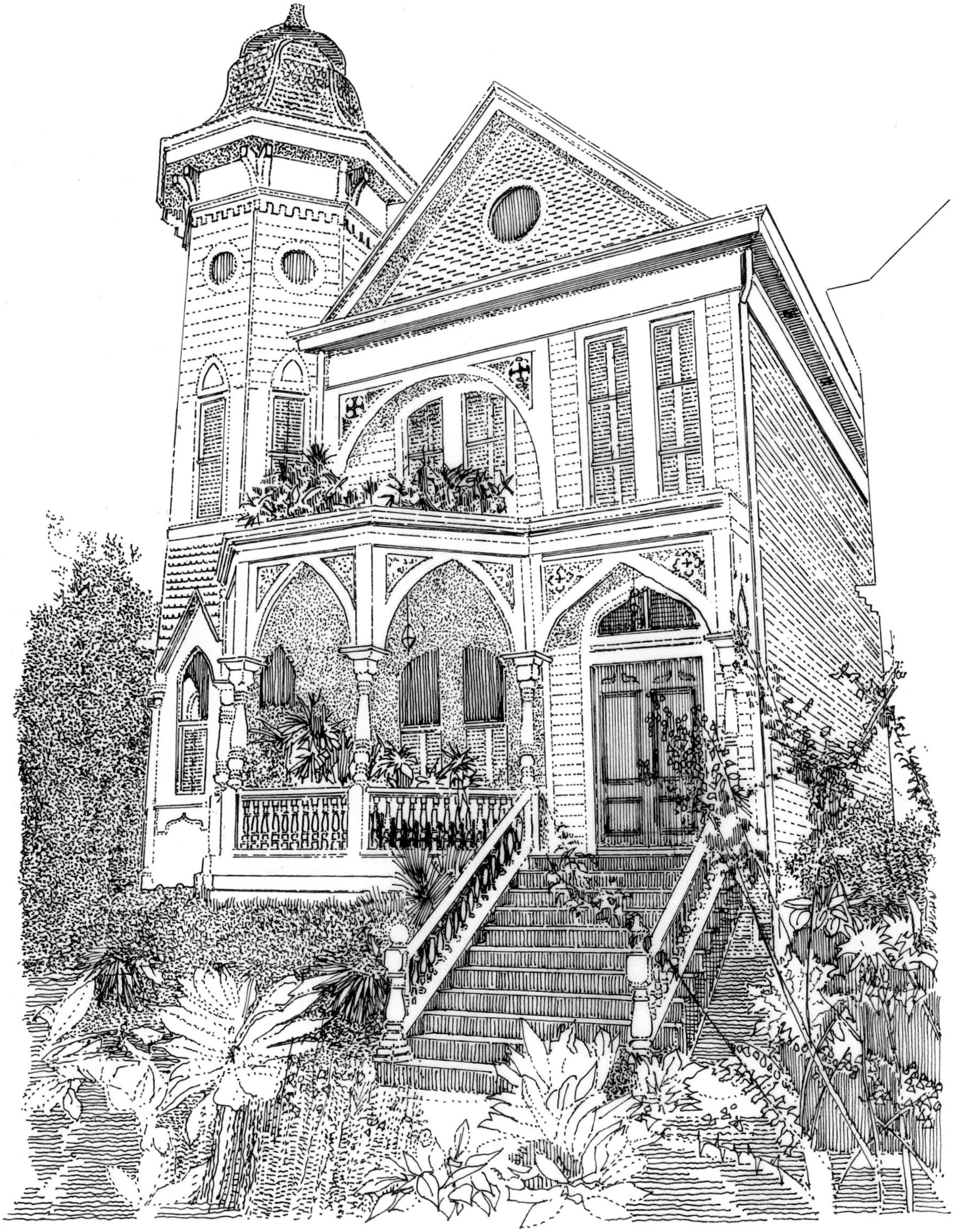

in the 1960s, many residents re-located to the Victorian District and rented substandard properties from slum landlords. At the time a number of deteriorating buildings were abandoned altogether or were pulled down.

The rehabilitation project, founded by one of the eminent leaders of Historic Savannah, Lee Adler, covered around 1,200 housing units and effectively complemented the work of the Historic Savannah Foundation in restoring available properties. The project was incorporated in 1974, aimed at refurbishing properties for rental by responsible residents, and securing options for the Foundation to purchase buildings cost-effectively. Properties were controlled and maintained by Savannah Landmark, commencing with a pilot project through an initial grant from the National Endowment for the Arts. Federal funding was directed through the Housing Authority, with an appointed contractor who instructed young people from the neighborhood in building, carpentry, and maintenance skills. Grants from HUD and the National Trust for Historic Preservation facilitated expansion of the program, while the Ford Foundations contributed the acquisition loan for the purchase of 261 dilapidated units. In 1982 the City of Savannah was awarded HUD's National Recognition Award, for both national excellence and for using the Community Development Block Grant Program to achieve an exemplary public-private partnership. The City Preservation Office is responsible for the spatial coordination of development to ensure visual compatibility within each of Savannah's four districts, administered by the Metropolitan Planning Commission, and subject to an architectural review process.

OPPOSITE PAGE
The Victorian District is situated between Forsyth Park and Ardsley Park to the south - one of the first automobile suburbs in America.

We are appropriately impressed, nodding our heads, and walk farther to the Mid-City District which appears to be experiencing a mix of redevelopment, rehabilitation, and preservation around Thomas Square and the Baldwin Park Neighborhood with a proposed density of 100 units an acre. SCAD has now extended its portfolio of historic buildings to the south of the Historic District by taking over the statuesque St. Paul's Academic building on 38th Street for classrooms, hastening revitalization initiatives and attracting investment.

Apolonia and Agnita announce they are hungry, and Terry volunteers a suggestion – something called *The Pirate's House* on East Broad Street. It is too far to walk, but as if on a sudden cue, a bus arrives, heading towards Bay Street. Even more miraculously it stops and we pay our two-dollar fares and sit separately wedged between commuters who, according to the first law of American transport economics, are sadly the ones who cannot afford a car.

Agnita says, "This is the first public bus I've seen. The overriding problem in getting anywhere outside the city for the car-deprived is in establishing how you do it. You can get around on foot, by bike, scooter, Segway, carriage, even helicopter, but try finding a bus. I think there might be a hidden conspiracy to stop visitors from escaping the city. I tried to get a bus to the Wormsloe Estate and asked maybe twelve people where the bus station was and got a succession of blank looks. Finally, I asked this dude who was getting out of his four-wheel drive where the Greyhound Buses went from and he said something like,

180

The repetitive rhythm of wooden building frontages in the Victorian District is broken down and made pleasurable through incidental detail that creates local familiarization and reinforces its essential character and identity.

"Er ... I think its left ... No, right ... No, left up the boulevard, but if you are going there, keep your head down.' I'm not exactly sure what he meant, but it sounded ominous."

We disembark at Broughton Street and walk to East Broad Street, and here it is. It looks like an unrestored shack, but was, according to the sign on the entrance, an ancient inn for seafarers, and claims to have been serving presumably pirated food since 1753. It must therefore house the oldest kitchen in the city, and boasts a "herb house" next door, which is even older. According to Terry, who has become our resident authority on local paranormal habitats, this is the most haunted building in Savannah.

Legend indicates the presence of a tunnel, now unfortunately sealed, leading from the basement to River Street. It is said that this once expedited the process of removing inebriated members of the inn's clientele to the keyside, where they were shanghaied and sold to sea captains as somewhat reluctant crew members. More credibly, it was likely used as a discreet conduit for smuggling barrels of rum into the city during the early prohibition period.

Ghostly apparitions of ancient seafarers are said to be occasionally observed in and around the premises, although, as Terry Fulbright helpfully points out, this has to be set against the fact that the contemporary observer knows little about ancient pirate dress or comportment. Miles chips in to say that as the inn was located on Oglethorpe's designated site for nurturing mulberry trees to support the ultimately unsuccessful silk industry, the ghostly presence of Jack Sparrow might well be a more benign reincarnated gardener.

Either way it encompasses fifteen dining rooms, and plays host to a community theater on weekends, with the waiters doubling as actors, and perhaps ghosts. We are shown to a table in a darkened corner of the Captain's Room, supposedly the most haunted room in the building. Conversation ebbs and flows interrupted by the arrival of our orders – bowls of crab soup, low country garlic shrimps, and crab cakes as a show of communal sharing. We order craft beers with the exception of Apolonia who insists on sampling a banana piña colada. A girl wanders by in a pirate outfit or it could just have been Dolce and Gabbana. She winks suggestively at Terry who turns a deep red and looks away.

Suddenly, a cold chill passes through the room, and all the candles on the table blow out. Terry immediately announces that this denotes a positive ghostly acknowledgement of paranormal pirate activity. Agnita coolly orders a box of matches and re-illuminates our plates, while announcing to adjoining diners that paranormal pirates are not going to prevent her seeing what she is eating. She earns a round of applause.

We do not linger and make a pact not to disclose to Mo where we have been.

Things outside are getting pretty gusty. Tree branches overhead are shuddering and creaking, with white-flecked ripples swirling across the choppy Savannah River. We wander down Liberty and then Bull Street, innocently joining the tail end of an all girl Bachelorette Segway Tour. We stop outside the Six Pence Pub, mainly to admire the authentic looking but redundant English telephone kiosk standing on the pavement.

The barman tells us that it was originally owned by a pair of legendary Londoners, Wally and Doris, but that was long ago. To encourage a more or less infinite consumption of alcohol, we learn that one can join an evening martini tour of the historic district, or a haunted pub crawl that promises convincing evidence of paranormal drinking activity. Terry Fulbright perks up at this point and orders a round of Chilly Mojitos. The remaining bachelorette party orders various, equally sticky concoctions and announces they are terminating their Segway tour at the Congress Street Social Club by the City Market, with its hidden promise of pool tables and dartboards.

A TV in the corner, largely ignored by the patrons, informs us that Hurricane Mathew is approaching Haiti and about to exert a chain of destruction from the Caribbean to the Carolinas, with Cuba and the Bahamas on its uncompromising path. More pertinently,

181

it is headed directly this way. Evacuation routes are already being posted in Chatham Country with a Hurricane Watch on when to get out of town, what to take, and where the public shelters are. Potential evacuees are being reminded that they cannot necessarily expect to board a bus, and must first register at the Civic Center. Pets are allowed, just as long as they have current vaccination certificates.

We look at each other with a certain degree of foreboding, but exit along with the bachelorettes, several of whom are exhibiting the aggregated symptoms of inebriation, marked by various degrees of difficulty in remounting their Segways. Some of the others of a more vigorous constitution make less than decent suggestions of possible future rendezvous and associated activities, while casting lascivious eyes over Miles and Terry. The latter are immediately tugged away by Agnita and Apolonia and redirected towards the opposite end of Bull Street. We deem it prudent to keep the Congress Street Social Club for another occasion and walk in a huddle through the sanctuary of Monterrey Square. The girls are still clinging to the arms of the recalcitrant pair to prevent sudden escape, as we march in military style across Gaston Street towards the home base destination.

We climb the front steps to Magnolia Hall and enter the living/breakfast room. Apolonia disappears and returns with a large bottle of Napa Valley Pinot Grigio.

Someone flicks the TV switch, and after what seems an endless advertising break we have a team of five election commentators attempting to unscramble the latest candidate polls, gesticulating and arguing loudly with each other. We break again and then it's back to a Trump rally.

Donald is claiming that the election is being rigged by corrupt media publishing completely false allegations of unwanted advances by Trump towards an assortment of ladies, and demeaning them with sexist language. Trump says, "Nobody has more respect for women than me."

Hilary is shown entering an anonymous stage in blue jacket and black pants, eyes wide, pointing ecstatically at someone in the front row, with a, "How wonderful and amazing to see you here," look.

Trump insists Hilary is on undisclosed stimulants and is challenging her to a drug test prior to their forthcoming final debate. He is making "Lock-Her-Up" the new rallying cry for his fired-up but increasingly nervous supporters. "Why don't we do that?" he says, with a serious expression.

Not even the Supreme Court is spared. Hilary references the liberal courts of the 1960s that would "Stand up to the powerful on behalf of our rights as Americans." Donald pledges to appoint conservatives "Who would interpret the Constitution the way the founders wanted it interpreted," presumably through telepathic communication with the said founders.

Mo and Martha B. enter. They have a suite on the ground floor and therefore assume a certain claim on the associated communal territory. They help themselves to what remains of the Pinot Grigio. Mo gazes at the screen aghast. His mouth opens. He catches the eye of Martha B. and quickly closes it again.

Trump is still thundering that mainstream politics is controlled by nefarious unseen forces. "There is nothing the political establishment will not do, no lie they won't tell, to hold their prestige and power at your expense, and that's what's been happening," he shouts.

"He's a master of tortured syntax," says Agnita. "I think Winston Churchill would have replied along the lines of, 'This is the sort of English up with which I will not put.'"

Mo bravely says, "I think I can explain this," and begins what sounds like a complicated but erudite clarification of the two fundamental political stances, explaining that they stem from the new age of globalization, integration of trade, capital, and migration flows. "These are all being played out," he says, "against a backdrop of China's explosive impact on the world's economic stage, Europe's regional economic integration, along with that of financial markets. The entry of a vast unskilled labor force has resulted in rising inequality in labor and capital incomes. It will all of course re-adjust over time. It relates to the political economy – as Robert Reich said, income inequality is the defining issue for the United States. Americans have increased productivity but the top one percent control forty-five percent of the nation's wealth. The top five percent control seventy percent. The three richest people in combination now own as much as the lowest earning half of the entire population. But free market ideas seem to be out of favor. Hilary has dismissed the Trans Pacific Partnership. Donald threatens protectionism. This scarcely makes us citizens of the world. Racial and ethnic wealth disparities are growing, and everyone is focusing on home markets. Total aggregate US household debt is now almost thirteen trillion dollars. Is it any wonder we have polarized politics?"

Martha B. continues, "It is unsurprising that there are deep structural tensions. We have a mix of populist conservatives, most of whom are working class and dependent on Social Security and Medicare who mistrust the federal government. We then have the small government conservatives who favor major cuts in tax and reductions in public spending. The third group contains the establishment conservatives who reflect the interests of corporate America. At least Hillary looks sincere."

"Well," says Jean-Paul, "I think it was Woody Allen who said that sincerity is the secret of success – if you can fake that you've got it made."

Nods of tentative agreement. Apolonia yawns. Terry says he has to be up early.

I leave the three couples, and wander out to the porch. Schlomo and Angel from Paris, Texas are seated in intimate proximity, having taken a carriage ride back from a prolonged evening of hip hop, punctuated by discussion over the latter's academic future. Angel is looking flushed and excited. It is now hitting midnight and I decide to retire to my third floor attic. On the second floor, as I ascend, the lights are dim so I might be mistaken in recognizing the shadow of Miles Styles knocking, furtively looking around, and then entering the boudoir of Agnita van der Kampen.

183

URBAN GROWTH AND SOCIAL CHALLENGES
IN THE MID-NINETEENTH CENTURY

New rail and river traffic continued to fuel commercial growth and investment in public infrastructure such as waterworks, sewerage, and gasworks, even though the city had little in the way of financial resources. To bring the city debt back to manageable proportions, an income tax was levied on all resident professionals, including rice and cotton brokers.

In the early 1840s the slope below the bluff was reinforced with masonry, securing the plateau from potential geotechnical problems but also providing a secure embankment for new warehouses designed by Charles B. Clusky, and supported by vaulted arches.

The Central of Georgia Railroad continued its ambitious program under a new President, Richard R. Cuyler, despite periodic natural disasters and epidemics, which delayed completion until 1843 when the route to Macon was opened to much optimistic celebration. Within two years a additional line to Atlanta had been completed, and feeder lines began to be connected with other ports from which steamers were then able to serve the northern cities. In the meantime a number of southern cities at the center of the cotton trade were linked by rail to Savannah.

More wards and squares were constructed towards Gaston Street, the final squares being Troup, Calhoun, and Whitefield in 1851. Forsyth Place served as a central recreation area that was later extended to form Forsyth Park – the largest public open space in Savannah.

As the recession began to lift, the web of new transport routes were at the heart of a booming trade in cotton and lumber between the hinterland and the port, so that almost forty percent of the nation's cotton was shipped from Savannah and Charleston. The cotton industry and the construction of the Central of Georgia Railroad consolidated the position of Savannah that had previously been overshadowed in terms of enterprise and wealth by Charleston. Laborers, both black and white, worked around the clock for six months of the year unloading cotton onto the drays pulled by teams of horses, that transferred goods to the wharves and warehouses. The removal of obstructions in the river, thanks to an appropriation approved by Congress, allowed large ships to sail directly to the wharves at high tide, facilitating a significant increase in tonnage and number of cargo vessels, so that exports began to exceed even those of Boston.

As more channels of communication were constructed, the more merchant wealth poured into the city. The rolling stock and carrying capacity continued to increase, and by 1860 the rail network covered 1,420 miles through an interconnection of routes that opened up direct links with Florida, Alabama, and Mississippi. Steamboat services linked Savannah with other ports, and it became the third largest port in America for the export of cotton. The Railroad was subsidized by the city and thirty-five acres of land for a new freight depot and passenger station were granted in the poorer western quarter of the city,

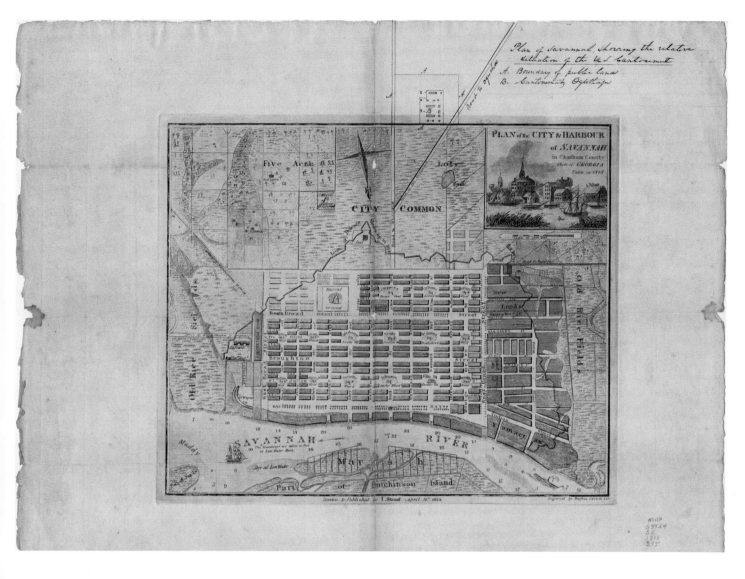

Plan of the City and Harbor of
Savannah, 1818.

broadly defined by Boundary Street, Hull Street, and Jones Street. A succession of talented engineer-builders constructed a number of elegant brick and cast iron buildings for the railroad including offices, warehouses, an engine room, and a roundhouse, some of which were recently adapted for reuse by SCAD.

New Industries and Exports

The city's role as a transport hub and major port attracted both investment and new immigrants, so that there was a major housing boom, which lasted until the 1860s. The west side of the city became almost overwhelmed by brickyards, sawmills, and foundries. On the wharves, steam powered cotton presses and rice mills operated on a twenty-four-hour basis, although much of the work in the city was seasonal, following the harvesting timetable for cotton and rice.

Timber was rafted into the city, so that new sawmills, steam mills, and wood manufacturers opened along the Savannah and Ogeechee Canal, and on the wharves of Fig Island and Hutchinson Island, with the largest on Musgrove Greek, which employed laborers on fourteen-hour shifts. Skilled workers and engineers were in short supply, but the buoyant economy encouraged more migrants from Europe and elsewhere. Shipbuilding, locomotive, and rail car construction also attracted machine shops and small manufacturing establishments, and renewed capital investment led to a high rate of industrial productivity.

In effect Savannah evolved an essential intermediary role as a reception and transshipment center for the flow of what was predominantly cotton, lumber, and rice, and which created the necessity for a wide range of services. By 1855, seven packing lines operated some sixty sailing vessels and steamers that linked Savannah with New York, Boston, Philadelphia, and New Orleans. The rise in exports gave rise to a commensurate increase in commission houses, built along the riverfront below the bluff. These premises, two- to six-stories high with ground-level warehouse accommodation, formed the basis of the city's commercial life, which revolved around the wharves, freight activities, and the steamers and schooners that transported cargoes to the north and south along the coast. Ten different banks operated in the city, along with fifty-nine insurance companies, providing sufficient capital for new start-up businesses. This was accompanied by a soaring value of land and considerable investment in new mansions and other property. Many of the older warehouses and mercantile houses designed by Charles B. Cluskey can be observed in their preserved and converted form along River Street and Factor's Walk.

Urban Growth

In the two decades from 1840 the city effectively doubled its population to around 22,000, with approximately one-third of these being slaves. Catholics arrived from Ireland, Jewish immigrants from Germany, and a smaller numbers of settlers from Britain and France, while there was an escalation in Protestant settlers who arrived via the northern cities to

Mercer-Williams House on Monterey Square. Completed in 1868 after the Civil War it was designed by John Norris for General Hugh Weedon Mercer. It was restored in 1969 by Jim Williams. The name of the square itself commemorators a United States victory in the war with Mexico. The square formed a central feature of the book and subsequent film *Midnight in the Garden of Good and Evil*, centered around the house.

seek their fortune in the south. This created an ethnically diverse and cosmopolitan population, with more than half the non-slave population being foreign-born. The Catholic Church grew in size mainly because of the influx of Irish workers, while Lutherans, Episcopalians, and German and Sephardic Jews from Europe also increased in numbers, church services being carried out in different languages. Walter J. Fraser recounts that by the middle of the century Savannah housed a Catholic cathedral and thirteen churches – two Presbyterian, two Methodist, three Episcopal, one Baptist, one Lutheran, and one Unitarian, together with two synagogues, while most of the black population attended the three African Baptist Churches. The latter not only provided a forum for black preachers, but for black leaders through an emphasis on equality and literacy that countered the ingrained position of dependence and subordination.

The open-air market was a meeting place as well as a site of commerce. Located in Ellis Square, it consisted of individual stalls beneath a pillared roof that housed permanent market traders and enslaved women who came from the countryside to hawk vegetables, fish, and eggs. Other goods for clandestine offering were the result of a discreet waterborne traffic in alcohol and stolen artifacts. People did not just shop, but met to use the public water pumps and to show off fashions amidst a cacophony of noise, hawkers, and strolling musicians, and shops that appropriated street space to store goods and slaughter animals.

Urban growth extended to the south from Liberty Street to Gaston Street and along Bull, Barnard, and Abercorn Streets. The number of wards grew to thirty-six by 1858,

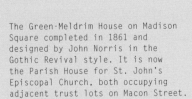

The Green-Meldrim House on Madison Square completed in 1861 and designed by John Norris in the Gothic Revival style. It is now the Parish House for St. John's Episcopal Church, both occupying adjacent trust lots on Macon Street.

constructed incrementally around twenty-four squares defined by more than 300 buildings. A line of commercial buildings facing East Bay Street was known as Stoddard's Upper Range named after its builder, and became the center of the thriving cotton trade. The United States Customhouse was constructed on Bay Street designed by John S. Norris in a neo-Classical style, indicating the prestige of the city and its importance as a port.

The same architect went on to design a large number of private brick-built residences in the form of mansions and townhouses in revivalist styles along the new streets and squares, surrounded by lush vegetation. Norris proved to be a versatile designer of large mansions for wealthy cotton brokers in Lafayette Square and Madison Square. What is now known as the Green-Meldrim House on West Macon Street was designed in a neo-Gothic style becoming the most expensive house in the city, and taking eleven years to construct. It now serves as the rectory of St. John's Episcopal Church on Bull Street, designed by Calvin Otis who also designed an Italianate mansion on Monterey Square alongside the monument to Count Pulaski. The Mercer house later gained some notoriety as the Mercer-Williams House – the setting for Midnight in the Garden of Good and Evil. The ornamented squares were shaded by lush vegetation, live oaks, magnolia, and chinaberry trees, although the thoroughfares remained in an unpaved and unhealthy condition. The squares stood out in contrast to the Yamacraw area to the west, which deteriorated further into unsanitary slum buildings amidst an otherwise vibrant collection of processing plants and factories.

Public Services

The two main political bodies were Whigs and the controlling Democratic Party. Both parties were represented by wealthy merchants and senior professionals, but these often dissolved into factional interests over fiscal matters. In June 1858, Mayor Richard Wayne died in office and was given a massive funeral after being re-elected five times since his original election in 1844. Despite being a slaveholder, 100 members of the First African Baptist Church sang at the gravesite.

Continued and necessary improvements to municipal infrastructure included the Savannah, Albany, and Gulf Railroad, for which the city was one of the major subscribers. This left Savannah with an indebtedness that could only be serviced by various low level taxes on such things as rentals from market stalls, although this was later extended to taxes on income and real estate, together with a value added tax on goods and services. Other improvements included a continuous dredging program on the Savannah River, a modern water supply system, an underground system of gas pipes to fuel new street lights, an extensive drainage system, and paved streets, all aimed at improving public health. Polluted water being identified as the frequent cause of illness, new reservoirs were built to the west of the Canal Basin where it was treated and fed to a distribution tank in Franklin Square.

Fire continued to be a constant threat, and new fire stations were built in Liberty Square, Washington Square, Pulaski Square, Lafayette Square, and Oglethorpe Avenue. A growing population and a high death rate from cholera, yellow fever, and malaria also brought a need for new burial grounds. These were established beyond the city limits and the old inner city cemeteries closed down. Separate reservations were made for white, black, and Jewish burials. Yellow fever in particular caused hundreds of deaths and became known for a time as "Savannah Sickness," which occurred in the hot and humid summers, and struck particularly at the white community who had little immunity. By the end of 1854, 1,049 people had died, most of them white. The epidemic created intense debate over its cause, with suggestions ranging from rotting rubbish in the streets to dredged mud from the Savannah River. It was not until the end of the nineteenth century that the medical world discovered that the disease was transmitted by mosquitoes.

Social and Economic Differences

Between 1850 and 1860 politics remained the domain of the privileged. Only 136 different representatives ran for 143 mayoral and aldermen posts, reflecting the restricted choice available for electors, but also the vested interests at stake.

The polarization of Savannah society continued to reflect an embedded difference of class and race. An editorial in the Savannah Georgian sanctimoniously announced that the institution of slavery was of great benefit to both races. The elite, which in many cases involved the descendants of early settlers, owned large tracts of land, personal property, and the slaves to go with them. By 1858 six percent of the population owned the majority of

190

Savannah's property along its most prominent streets and the majority of slaves. Groups or even families of slaves were not infrequently given as gifts for marriage, or were handed down from father to son. Intermarriage between old established families tended to assure the preservation of wealth and political connections. They formed a formidable and well-connected minority who nevertheless dominated business and political affairs, and through these the equally "incestual" social milieu of entertainments and exchanges. Clubs were available for many recreational pursuits including fishing, swimming, hunting for quail, snipe and duck, horse racing, cricket, sailing, and rowing regattas. These, together with various cultural bodies, catered for both bodily and intellectual pursuits, with the latter mainly associated in membership of the exclusive Savannah Club, which hosted readings and lectures by visiting writers. Wealthy families summered mainly in northern destinations such as New York, New Haven, and Rhode Island to avoid the heat.

During the 1850s there was a resurgence of interest in the arts. The Playhouse Theater on Chippewa Square was enlarged and attracted some of America's best-known actors and opera singers who in turn drew fashionable audiences. St. Andrew's Hall was erected by the St. Andrew's Society of Savannah, and a museum was built at the corner of Bull and Taylor Streets. The sons of the city's privileged class were sent to northern preparatory schools and graduated from the best universities, returning to become involved in business and political matters but also immersing themselves in the arts: founding libraries, publishing, and historical societies. The passing of time also witnessed parades and displays of weapons by groups such as the Volunteer Guards.

The Georgia Historical Society was founded in 1839 at the home of Israel Tefft and other eminent scholars, and housed a large library of books relating to the State of Georgia. Two years later, William Bacon Stevens delivered the oration to celebrate the founding of Georgia at the Unitarian Church, and later published his History of Georgia. This formed the precursor to a long series of debates and topics between the 250 members comprising educationalists, thinkers, and writers resident in the city who provided an intellectual counterpart to the grueling world of business and plantation life. Later members included George Wymberley Jones, doyen of the Wormsloe Plantation, and Andrew Low. Members gathered periodically in St. Julian Street and in private homes. Celebrated guest lecturers included the English writer William Makepeace Thackeray.

A cultural and somewhat puritanical divide existed between the more conservative upcountry Georgians who were cut off from the extravagant pleasures of Savannah, and the city residents. A more pertinent division of wealth emerged through ethnic and religious denominations, the well-connected Protestant and Jewish communities subscribing to the established traits of property ownership and slave subordination. Slave owners, and even dealers, apparently saw no disparity between their religious and occupational beliefs. By way of contrast, the generally impoverished Irish Catholics who made up almost twenty-five percent of the white population were widely viewed as destabilizing elements.

A Continually Stratified Society

The middle class constituted a special socio-economic sector of society, mainly consisting of migrants from northern cities, who worked in the commission houses or other businesses as clerks, bookkeepers, and in various building and shipping trades. They also owned or managed most of the retail establishments, many living in small apartments above their businesses. While they earned a reasonably good living, few became really wealthy, although some acquired sufficient holdings to own slaves who went on to learn the many artisan trades. Middle class whites were also vulnerable to insecurity through downturns in the economy or competition from newcomers and freed slaves, which perpetually threatened impoverishment or forced them to change their employment. They had little common ground with the wealthy of Savannah, which broadly comprised planters, bankers, merchants, and lawyer elites who gained political power and prominence.

Laborers on the bottom rung of white society were virtually on an economic par with freed slaves. Many of these were Irish males who arrived in large numbers from a problematic homeland, and found employment as common laborers or in the shadow economy, while women worked in factories and as household help. Only one in five households represented nuclear families. The city imported only around five percent of the value of commodities that it exported, pointing to the lack of a consistent consumer economy.

Some of the poorest people were destitute and most lived in the squalid and overcrowded wooden tenements of Oglethorpe Ward to the west of Broad Street and in the wards east of Habersham Street. The Irish gained an unfortunate reputation for unruly behavior, being informally categorized as either virtuous or vicious. However, the increasing ranks of Irish proved adapt at electioneering, and from 1849 the ranks of city aldermen began to reflect a strong Catholic representation.

The paucity of educational facilities for the poorer sections of the community, along with a commensurate lack of motivation, was a factor in economic disparity. Catholic and Episcopal churches ran free schools, and various public-spirited citizens—"Friends of Education"—promoted and partly sponsored two public schools for white children. By 1860 it was estimated that enrollment represented around forty percent of Savannah's white child population.

The Board of Health, together with a number of charitable organizations funded by wealthy and concerned bodies, sought to care for the physical needs of poor whites in dire need. The Bethesda Orphanage was reopened in 1855 in order to look after the large number of orphaned or abandoned children, in part to separate them from what was seen as the morally degrading conditions associated with the Savannah waterfront, but also to make them orderly and useful members of society. The white poor and sick were taken to the Poor House and Hospital, which were funded by businessmen and physicians, while the City Dispensary provided free medicine. Benevolent groups of women also provided accommodation in return for housekeeping with the intention of easing the path of poor females into domestic service, while church groups also provided boarding houses with strict rules as to conduct. In part, this acted to re-direct the public gaze and maintain the surface image of a wealthy and sophisticated society.

By mid-century, around 700 free blacks lived and worked throughout the city, although they had to register their place of residence on an annual basis, to have a white "guarantor" and to work on public projects for twenty days each year. The building boom enabled some slaves to find sufficient paid employment to free themselves. Some were skilled craftsmen or artisans such as carpenters, tailors, or bakers who owned property, paid city taxes, and occasionally owned slaves, while others competed for laboring jobs with poor whites. Free females worked primarily as cooks, nursemaids, and seamstresses. The luckier ones were bequeathed money or property from their previous owners, and set up businesses for themselves with a will to succeed. By 1860 there were also around 2,000 mulattoes in the city with white fathers, some of whom remained supportive and ensured a continued livelihood.

The number of black slaves in Savannah numbered around 7,700. This represented a reduction in the proportion of slaves in the city to around thirty-eight percent of the population. While many worked in plantations, an increasing number rented rooms and worked in the city, either in some form of domestic employment as cleaners, gardeners, and carriage drivers, or were hired out by owners to work in hotels, manufacturing establishments, or as laborers on the railroad in competition with poor whites. A larger number also profitably utilized their own spare time, and either produced goods to sell in the market or ran small businesses. In any event, money had to be remitted to their owners on a monthly basis. In these circumstances blacks and whites often worked side by side, and skilled workers competed for jobs as machinists, coopers, masons, carpenters, masons, and plasterers. Other forms of biracial association or fraternization were discouraged as this was thought to break down the ingrained divisions and thereby pose a threat to society. Most white townspeople continued to harbor the impression that the institution of slavery was morally just, and that protected slaves were more fortunate than free laborers. Several hundred free blacks, together with slaves, served with the ten black Savannah Fire Companies, acquired their uniform and marched in the firemen's annual parade.

Public disorder was, to a large extent, in the eye of the beholder. As "unlawful assemblage" of blacks resulted in the first place from the nervous reaction of white citizens and officials, arrests were frequently made for trivial reasons so that even obstructing a sidewalk could be interpreted as insubordination or a blatant disregard for a city ordinance. At the same time, owners of premises selling liquor to black people or to anyone on the Sabbath could technically be prosecuted. New ordinances that permitted heavy fines for illegal sale of alcohol accomplished little, partly it was said because of the indifference and collusion of the police themselves.

A Fugitive Slave Law passed by Congress could be used to return escaped slaves who fled to northern cities. Police were constantly on the lookout for runaway slaves, and even raided church gatherings if there was any mention of emancipation. Most prison inmates were convicted for crimes against property and for those lawbreakers who were convicted, the jail was itself dehumanizing. This, together with public disorder, was in many ways the downside of the prevailing economic boom, as increasing numbers of poor immigrants arrived in the city. In response to this the City Council increased the city watch and petitioned the United States Government to remit the Oglethorpe Barracks to the city for training. It also served as a headquarters for a new uniformed police force, which later became the model for other southern cities. The new chief of police, Joseph Bryan, was a principal slave trader, and authorized his charges to rigorously enforce the law. A martial spirit tended to pervade the city, through various types of military organization, including volunteer home guards and fire company militias at one end of the social spectrum, and the Georgia Hussars, Chatham Artillery, and Oglethorpe Light infantry at the other.

The recession that swept through the country in the late 1850s calmed the hectic economy but went on to create a severe depression followed by a crime wave. By this time, Savannah was the largest slave-trading city in Georgia. Slaves were held in pens and taken in handcuffs to the auction block while brokers bought and sold. A large slave auction of entire families held at the Ten Broeck racecourse in March 1859 attracted 200 prospective buyers. This focused wide attention on auction proceedings, which came about through the need to pay off the creditors of a dissolute and absentee Georgia plantation owner, Pierce Butler. The sale netted more than $300,000 or an average of $716 a person. A reporter for the New York Herald Tribune, Mortimer Neal Thomson was present, posing as a buyer, and wrote a report for the paper on March 9th setting out every stage of the humiliating process. It was reprinted in several other papers including England's Times, and excited wide condemnation and considerable antislavery sentiment in the North. At the same time, this increased secessionist sentiments in the South, fuelled in Savannah by ardent editorials in the Savannah Morning News.

The well-documented case of Thomas Simms, an enslaved bricklayer who, in February 1851 stowed away on a ship bound for Boston is remarkable, not so much because of the date, ten years before Civil War broke out, but because of the Fugitive Slave Act that was passed by Congress in 1850. Simms was seized on the streets of Boston by police officers and despite intervention by the Boston Vigilance Committee, the Massachusetts Supreme Court returned him to Savannah accompanied by Boston marshals, and he was imprisoned in the Chatham County jail. He was later sold to another owner in Mississippi. The intense publicity and controversy surrounding the case in the Northern States was undoubtedly an instrumental factor in the growing chasm between North and South, and set both sides to ponder the future of the Union. In 1857 a Supreme

Court ruling stated that a fugitive slave could not necessarily gain his or her freedom by travelling to a free state, so that from this time refugees from the South who fled to northern cities had to be discreet.

As late as 1858, a new schooner was commissioned in New York by a dissolute Savannah merchant and politician, Charles Lamar, for $25,000 and immediately sailed to the West coast of Africa, and brought back 600 hundred captives from the Congo River, later depositing them on Jekyll Island before federal authorities impounded the ship and charged its crew with piracy. Lamar was later brought to trial, but was freed, much to the anger of many northern political figures that shared abolitionist sentiments.

Increasingly volatile press coverage and a rising tide of anti-slavery propaganda from the North came together with the election in November 1860 of the first Republican President, Abraham Lincoln, an avowed abolitionist. The country was on a troubled path to Civil War.

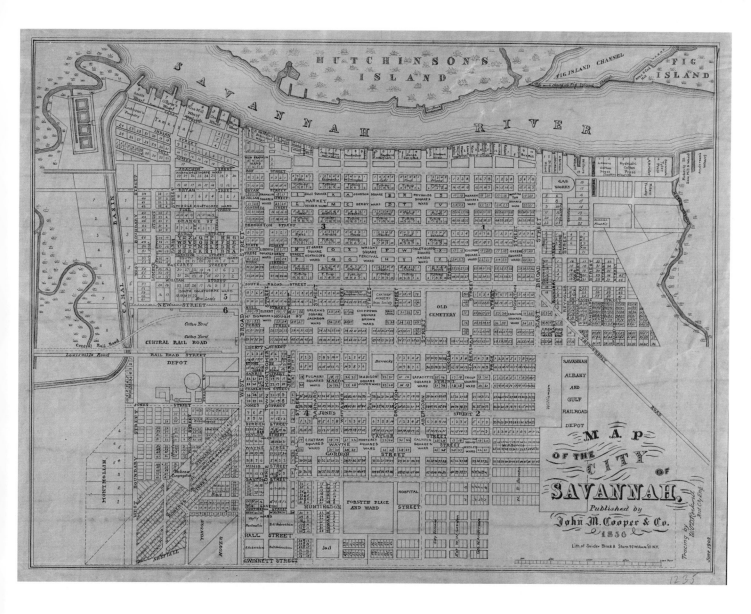

Map of the City of Savannah showing
the completed build-up of wards,
published by John M. Cooper & Co,
1856.

198

SAVANNAH AUTUMN 2016: DAY 5

Our group assembles in ones and twos the next morning. Two maids bring and then replenish pots of coffee, cereal, and plates of croissants and Danish pastries. Terry claims to have had his first full night's sleep since arriving. Apolonia looks on maternally and serves him pastries, neatly avoiding the three-inch pile of Terry's presentation notes. Agnita and Miles appear late and sit at opposite sides of the large circular table. Schlomo appears, biting into a large pastry and saying he is ravenous. Angel is nowhere to be seen.

We are gathered on the porch and leave together, wandering past Hodgson Hall, dedicated in 1876 as the permanent home for the Georgia Historical Society on Whitaker Street, defined by a row of palmetto trees, and with the oldest collection of archives in Georgia's history. Martha B. informs us it used to house the public library and now contains a veritable treasure trove of historical material.

At Poetter Hall we are confronted by a hurricane warning notice, although at present there is pale sunshine slanting through the clouds. Schlomo assures us, mistakenly as it turns out, that it will swerve away from the Atlantic coast and leave us basking once again in the mild, autumn weather.

Mo has, against our expectations, conjured up a little tour. The Savannah School of Art and Design can legitimately lay claim to the adaptive reuse and restoration of many heritage buildings, instilling an artistic sense of purpose and cohesion within the Landmark District. This morning we are being taken for a walk around some of these. Martha hands out photo-copied route maps. We depart from Poetter Hall, which serves as the admission center, and proceed to Alexander Hall, a conversion of a 1940s flour mill and now housing the painting department. Mo is pointing wildly here and there, "The beautifully proportioned Anderson Hall was an elementary school built in 1896 designed by Gottfried Norman; Bergen Hall was originally built in 1924 as a dry goods wholesalers; and Bradley Hall was constructed in 1906 as a US Marine hospital."

Mo tells us that the Clarence Thomas Center for Historic Preservation on East Broad Street was originally built as a Franciscan convent and orphanage, while the SCAD Studio built in 1839 once housed a gas showroom. The list seems to be endless, indicating a formidable role undertaken by an educational body for sustaining the historic area through design and conservation, which underscores its actual teaching curriculum and therefore its accommodation requirements.

Mo marches on and we file behind, cameras—or in most cases mobiles—clicking at countless conversions and new-build complexes for galleries, studios, libraries, ateliers, and centers for collaborative learning. Eckburg Hall was built in 1892 as an Elementary School on Henry Street, and its extension on Martin Luther King Boulevard was originally part of the Central of Georgia Railway complex dating back to 1887. Granite Hall was originally an Italianate-style mansion constructed in 1991, while Hamilton Hall was once a power station. We reach the end of our educational walk on Habersham Street, where SCAD's Moorish-looking Habersham Hall once served as the Chatham County Prison. Schlomo enquires if this is where they incarcerate intemperate guests, and I remind him that SCAD in Hong Kong is converted from a former Magistracy, and that they prudently retained the cells.

We file back to Poetter Hall for the late morning session. Coffee is again in abundance, and the talk is about an impending hurricane likely to hit the Atlantic coast. There is general agreement that any hurricane christened *Mathew* must be benign rather than belligerent, but is nevertheless coming directly this way. We are comforted by the fact that most major hurricanes have somehow managed to swerve away from this innocent corner of the Georgia coastline for decades, generally heading towards the low country of South Carolina. It is decided that we will in any event stay and ride out the storm.

Mo invites us to sit and Terry Fulbright simultaneously stands and clears his throat several times. Mo introduces the subject.

"This is really the counterpart to Agnita's presentation. There is of course an obvious correspondence between the city and the suburb. In America we can probably start from around the same historical period. Jon Teaford has in the past made the point that while the suburb is not necessarily *suburb*—ordinate to the central city—it is in many way *sub*versive to its traditional centripetal role. And we have some pretty weighty sprawl to contend with. It is in fact steeped in the politics of contestation and the rhetoric of opposing viewpoints. The characteristics of sprawl vary considerably. As Oliver Gillham has stated in *The Limitless City*, on one side are those bodies and individuals who support a necessary strategic opportunity to direct or redirect urban development trajectories through smart growth, from an environmental, urban design, and economic perspective. Pitted against this are those who argue that suburbia has proved both popular and cost effective in providing low density affordable housing over the years that best meets people's aspirations. To set the record reasonably straight we are now going to hear from Dr. Terence Fulbright."

201

FIFTH READING BY DR. TERENCE FULBRIGHT
THE ENIGMATIC FRONTIER: DECONSTRUCTING SUBURBIA

The first 19th-century city edge developments have been described by Dolores Hayden as "borderlands," which over the course of 200 years have become the dominant American cultural landscape. The supposed pastoral lifestyle is associated with the first urban fringe settlements of the 1820s that almost incidentally introduced residents to a daily commute to the industrial city. However, the prospect of an Arcadian sublime largely turned out for many to be something of a mirage. Suburbia began as a rural retreat for prosperous families from the congested urban quarters of the city, accessible only by horseback or private carriage, but evolved into an uncoordinated padding out of metropolitan regions in the late twentieth century. Less than sustainable subdivisions made up of model single-family houses have, over the past seventy years, been constructed at ever increasing distances from the central city. In the process, suburbia has ceded many of its historical associations with the city itself, and in the main has increasingly reflected few satisfactory aspects of urban life.

So how did this come about? What were the original catalysts for suburbia? The term has been in use for centuries, generally associated with settlements or even certain undesirable uses that were allocated to sites on the outer city limits. Perhaps the first committed professional disciple was Alexander Jackson Davis who produced a guide to rural residences in 1837 with designs that ranged from the neo-Classical to the more ostentatious Queen Anne, Greek revival, and neo-Gothic styles. He went on to put these designs into effect for the exclusive gated community of Llewellyn Park, some twelve miles by rail from New York City, and laid out over some 800 acres. This "picturesque" development was situated in rugged, mountainous topography, which was reconfigured to absorb on extensive arrangement of speculative villas for wealthy industrialists distributed within an exotic garden landscape of forest groves, waterfalls, and lakes. The impetus for country mansions around the growing cities elevated the status of owners and opened up new development trajectories. In Savannah, the plantation house probably served much the same purpose, but with the added reassurance of a productive hinterland.

Expanding rail connections opened up opportunities for larger suburban settlements in the countryside, including, in some cases, enormous mansion estates. For the most part, economic activity was confined to the city, but beltline railroads in the mid-to-late nineteenth century encouraged manufacturing industries to decentralize their operations in special suburbs.

Kenneth Jackson notes in *Crabgrass Frontier* that a milestone in suburban growth came with the end of the Civil War in 1865, which marked the beginning of large-scale private investment in railroads to link the main cities. The first genuine commuter railroad related to real-estate speculation was the New York and Flushing Railroad, bringing previously remote country areas within one hour of Manhattan. As early as 1849, there were more than 100 commuter trains every day serving Boston. Businessmen behind the Pennsylvania Railroad to Pittsburgh bought up farmland along the route and turned this into suburban developments. These set a fast paced precedent for smaller but expanding settlements to initiate railroads with the aim of assisting the development of trade and commerce, such as Savannah's Central of Georgia Railroad.

Olmsted and Vaux, the designers of Central Park, laid out a number of planned residential communities within parkland settings, such as Riverside west of Chicago, decorously integrated into the tranquil rural landscape on a 1,600-acre tract, and offering enticing opportunities for market gardening and self-sufficiency. Estates and houses were designed by well-known architects, such as Louis Sullivan and Frank Lloyd Wright. It was accompanied by one of the first restrictive covenants, which sought to establish overall consistency over lot sizes and building setbacks – a modest forerunner of New Urbanism's later emphasis on the design code. Arguably the most durable innovation was the notion of a social and economically separate entity from the city itself, perpetuated by rigid zoning for residential purposes. It has since been designated a National Historic Landmark.

From the 1870s the momentum towards more affordable subdivisions for modest middle class families in relatively close proximity to city centers was carried forward through streetcar suburbs. While their forms and layouts varied with location, it might be more accurate to call the initial layouts urban expansion areas, with new owners pursuing relief from overcrowded inner city tenements.

Frederick Jackson Turner, writing in the early 20th century, astutely describes the growth of industrial cities as the new frontier that would reshape society through the broadening of opportunities. However, he also cautioned, in what became known as the "frontier thesis," that the ability to acquire land across an unfolding frontier was inherent in the "character" of the United States, and that continuing economic change would make the city a place of constant transition, made up of migratory forces that would accelerate suburban expansion, and with it social segregation. This has proved to be not too wide of the mark – in fact, according to the Urban Land Institute, by 1965 the population of American suburbia had overtaken that of central cities.

The first "horse car suburbs" were reliant on carriages pulled along metal rails, so that subdivisions followed linear main street alignments with unpaved secondary streets to the rear. From the 1880s, electric trolleys boosted inner suburban development, doubling or even tripling metropolitan built-up areas. Transport operating companies began to blatantly engage in land speculation along designated routes with lots generally laid out in an expedient grid form. The companies successfully fought off attempts to bring either transport routes or zoning subdivisions under municipal control, although some housing was built by philanthropic organizations. This period marked the beginning of suburban real estate as a major business concern, with an emphasis on speculative house construction through standard designs and extravagant marketing campaigns for prospective purchasers, with properties offered on easy payment terms. However, purchasers often found that property taxes were necessary in order to obtain paved streets, infrastructure, and services.

The lucrative franchises associated with streetcar routes became subject to purchase and amalgamation, and by the turn of the twentieth century some 30,000 miles of urban railway had been electrified. Weekend leisure outings were encouraged by operating companies who invested in amusement attractions such as Coney Island in Brooklyn at the end of lines that radiated out of the central city. It was only one more step from there

203

204

Forsyth Park's cast iron fountain, installed in 1858 at its northern end. It was modelled on a feature displayed in the 1851 Crystal Palace Exhibition in London. The approach from the north is on a direct axis with Bull Street, helping the spatial integration of the park with the overall gridded framework of the Historical Area.

to the development of residential subdivisions in the newly accessible suburbs, linked directly by street cars to downtown business districts with a flat fare, tapping into a growing real estate market on the urban periphery.

Farmland was discreetly acquired along proposed new routes, and if owners held out then they were adroitly bypassed by the new road and trolley alignments. Development conditions for the new "streetcar suburbs" laid down rules concerning minimum residential size, type, and set-backs to ensure an exclusive up-market image, and in so doing introduced a manipulative use by speculators of public agencies for profitable private ends – something that was to mark future waves of suburban development. Affordable land supply was periodically made available by extending the radius of the streetcar alignment from the city, and new infrastructure continued to be publicly financed. This indirectly allowed politically connected land investors to raise development value and attract purchasers, thereby theoretically benefitting the local economy.

But the suburbs were not merely the outcome of new transport systems. In the early nineteenth century metropolitan growth was developing in different ways around and beyond the urban fringe. This tapped into a romantic ideal related to privacy and the rural landscape that perhaps revived the very forces that many immigrants had brought to the country – a family oriented and religiously inspired vision of refuge, stability, and even self-sufficiency. The rural ideal was reinforced by a growing literature critical of the

city, its polluting industry, deplorable overcrowding, and fearsome obstacles to progress. The suburb therefore held both a symbolic and cultural value, physically signified by the single-family dwelling but at a comfortable distance from its neighbors. Its virtues were spread throughout the aspiring middle class by the landscape architect Andrew Jackson Downing who prepared extensive portfolios of cottage designs – the forerunner of suburban developer blueprints. Pattern books introduced a range of styles, and house kits could be delivered for assembly by individuals or small contractors. Land owners produced large-scale layouts, and lots were then often auctioned off to secondary developers. This enabled many recent immigrants to become house owners in growing middle-class suburbs on the outer periphery.

An outward shift in industrial development created the foci for extended metropolitan regions. As land was annexed, privatized, and developed, so the political geography became more complicated. Businesses benefitted from metropolitan fragmentation and lower taxes. Residential suburbs first became the refuge of the elite on large sites, but were quickly followed by a wave of planned communities complete with highly restrictive covenants, unfortunately including scarcely disguised forms of racial zoning. However, the pace of metropolitan growth also led to social and economic change, and the stimulation of low income and working class suburbs.

The main catalyst was mass-production of the automobile. The Model T Ford put the price of a car within the affordability range of millions. Cities had to be virtually re-planned to accommodate motor vehicles, with many influential members of city development authorities, including property, development, and motor-related suppliers having a strong vested interest in advancing new road building and street widening. In 1910 there were around 460,000 automobiles on the nation's roads, but by 1920 this had increased to eight million and the writing was on the wall. This was not without some help from vested interests. The first tolled expressway, the Long Island Parkway, was constructed in 1911, dedicated to speed and separated from local traffic. This was the beginning of many such highways constructed over the next twenty years. The Federal Highway Act of 1916 facilitated funding for primary road construction and brought about a growth in construction activity. The new Bureau of Public Roads was established in 1921 to plan a network that would connect all cities with a population in excess of 50,000.

In 1922, General Motors, Phillips Petroleum, Firestone Tire and Rubber, and Standard Oil teamed up to quietly purchase the entire stock of America's electric streetcars and then scrap their operations in order to promote sales of automobiles. New auto suburbs were indirectly subsidized by local and federal road improvement programs with new interstate highways gradually forming a national route network. This was of course not all bad news – at least not at first.

Around the same time, a Division of Building and Housing was set up by the federal government in order to regulate construction through greater standardization. The new national building code was later accompanied by model zoning ordinances that were intended to rationalize land use and ensure effective service connections. Demonstration projects included the then radical layout ideas associated with Radburn, designed by Clarence Stein in 1928 in the form of a residential "superblock" as part of a unified layout pattern. This was oriented towards connective open space and separation of automobile and pedestrian traffic, which constituted a breakthrough in suburban planning.

Between 1920 and 1929 employment in America's downtown areas virtually tripled, accompanied by an unprecedented building boom. With automobile registrations rising by 150 percent, worsening commuter patterns led to growing congestion in cities and as suburbanization increased and city boundaries expanded, the differences between urban and rural became increasingly indistinct. However, during the same period, factory employment in central cities continued to decline, and the Great Depression, following the stock market crash in 1929, brought the development momentum to an abrupt halt.

After Herbert Hoover's presidential election victory, in 1929 he took steps to use federal investment in home ownership to combat the Depression, and three years later signed into law the Federal Home Loan Bank Act. The Federal Housing Administration was established to supply funds for new mortgages and offer advice on design and layout. This eventually led to the infamous "red-lining" of neighborhoods by the Home Owners Loan Corporation established under President Roosevelt, where loans were subject to specific conditions enabling them to be discreetly refused on racial grounds.

In the wake of the Depression, the primary emphasis was on job creation rather than public housing, and early efforts by the US Housing Authority to acquire land for residential purposes were successfully challenged as being unconstitutional. In fact it was at first legally deemed not to represent a public use at all. However, the 1937 Housing Act became the first legislation to be widely adopted by most states, partly as an economic stimulus, although the actual amount of public housing constructed was quite low in relation to the total market volume. The essential reason for this was the constitutional aspect – municipalities had to make a voluntary application for federal housing assistance and establish their own housing agency with the provision of tax exemptions. Underlying issues often came down to the protection of property values and slum clearance, so that the vast majority of completed low-income projects came to be located in the already poor ghettoes. Public housing remained as a federal commitment but the prevailing mindset suffered from a lack of coherent long-term social objectives, and a failure to overcome a "survival of the fittest" mentality that has tended to pervade the workability of most poverty assistance programs since that time.

Planning variations of Radburn followed in an adapted form as part of Roosevelt's town-building program during the 1940s, but failed to ensure a sufficiently robust translation of physical and social goals into fully integrated urban growth models at a time of post war industrial decentralization and suburban expansion.

The legacy of this lack of a guiding strategy in the face of market forces was to usher in a new federally assisted era of suburban development. It was one that created a long-term duality in housing policy, and arguably led to the expedient concept of private property having more importance than well-considered neighborhood design. Private developers catered for predominantly white, middle-class purchasers, who enjoyed significant tax and other subsidies. What became known as "tract mansions" increased in size, while disadvantaged families remained largely reliant on public housing elsewhere, reinforcing an already polarized society and leading to declining urban conditions in cities.

The culmination of World War II and the buoyant momentum of America's war industry coupled with the country's comparative insulation from the massive damage inflicted on Europe left the economy in a challenging situation, poised to exploit a euphoric post-war sentiment through new market initiatives and subsidies. The post-war period coincided with American economic dominance over global affairs, and mass consumption through private ownership was a crucial aspect in stimulating continued economic growth via construction and manufacturing. The outcome was affordable suburban developments made possible through generous federally orchestrated mortgages for suitable qualified applicants, including blue collar workers and returned servicemen and their families under the GI Bill. This was also buttressed by favorable tax treatment to homeowners.

In terms of the suburbanization process, we can belatedly recognize a lack of foresight, co-ordination and even responsibility for the far reaching consequences by the main protagonists – the planners of highways, the architects of sub-divisions, the developers and the mortgage operatives, with debt financed costs borne in large part by society whether by public investment in suburban infrastructure or through mitigation of environmental degradation. Even the immediate post-war President Harry Truman is reported to have warned against the consequences of an influential cabal of auto manufacturers, oil producers, road contractors, and house builders that formed a powerful and long lasting lobby for suburban development.

The suburban home might, by the 1950s, have become a private utopia for many, but few people at the time talked about model communities. Acquiring an affordable home outside the central city was as good as it got in the euphoria that marked Federal Housing and Veteran's Assistance programs, and home ownership was considered in itself a stabilizing influence on society in general. These not only provided development financing, but mortgage insurance for up to ninety percent of a house price up to 9,000 dollars allowed the mortgage provider to make periodic advances to the developer – probably the greatest incitement to entrepreneurship in the history of post-war construction.

The impact of rapid demographic change remained elusive in its connotation, however, being inevitably intertwined with the concept of middle-class betterment, security, and achievement of the American Dream. In the land of the free any bothersome preoccupations with civil rights, or even those relating to the future health of cities and metropolitan regions themselves, tended to be overlooked. Most mortgages were allocated to suburban situations as this was where the majority of houses were being constructed. The most extreme example of this was Levittown comprising some 17,000 tract houses on Long Island, New York, constructed through prefabrication and accessible only by car, to which the major automobile manufacturers duly responded with alacrity.

Suburban neighborhoods made up of virtually identical houses such as the Levittowns, lent themselves to kindly ridicule as with Malvina Reynolds's pointed ditty about "little boxes made of ticky tacky." For many new occupiers, this admittedly created a considerable improvement in their quality of life, and in the early 1950s made for a newly prosperous and comfortable lifestyle, reflected and broadcast in the popular culture of the time that made the American middle-class the envy of the world. One quarter of all existing housing in America was built in the decade between 1950 and 1960, to guidelines set out by the Federal Housing Administration. This was, unsurprisingly, countered by an equal and opposite effect in the denser and more depressed parts of older cities, excluded from guaranteed mortgages through discriminatory lending practices that were only made illegal under the Fair Housing Act of 1968.

Two pieces of legislation actively accelerated the pace of unplanned residential sprawl amidst a maze of administrative jurisdictions. The first influential but ultimately questionable legislation was the Interstate Highway Act of 1956, under the Eisenhower administration, on advice from a coterie of representatives from General Motors, the Teamsters Union, and the trucking industry. This effectively provided for the construction of over 42,000 miles of highways, partly to connect growing metropolitan areas. At the height of the Cold War, highway legislation was discreetly linked with national defense and the perceived need for interstate highways to facilitate rapid dispersal of people and resources in the case of an atomic attack – hence a policy of cleaving new expressways through cities, and shifting the movement of freight from trains to trucks. It ended up with "beltways" around the most prominent urban areas. The measure was subsidized with ninety percent federal financing at a cost of tens of billions of dollars. Its provisions facilitated private companies to exploit America's love affair with the automobile through the direct relationship between suburban real estate development, car manufacturers, trucking organizations, and the financial sector.

The second of these was the hidden federal subsidy that led to the accelerated depreciation of greenfield commercial property whereby costs could be written off in seven years. This was something that actively encouraged and facilitated short-life commercial real estate in the outer "greenfield" reaches of suburbia, but also inadvertently encouraged planned obsolescence as the foundation of the centerless commercial suburb with its "big box" typology. Accelerated depreciation created an extraordinary situation whereby realms of less than viable commercial structures were built in locations devoid of adequate population catchments, or even in many cases acceptable building construction, simply to exploit the significant tax write-offs on offer. After developers and loan organizations had directly benefitted from this, increasingly obsolescent buildings were then sold to a further generation of owners, or simply demolished. Accelerated depreciation was only struck down by the 1986 Tax Reform Act, but by then much of the damage had been done. It has been estimated that 4,000 malls were, even at the turn of the millennium, either empty or abandoned.

There is a long-held fable that the suburb not only represents the middle-class soul of America, through its questionable association with social mobility, but also represents a proven tendency for a high percentage of upper income groups to gravitate towards new housing on the outer periphery of metropolitan areas. Certainly as suburban housing got progressively larger in size and farther away from central cities, the more mobile and financially able families in older suburbs didn't just move out, they moved upwards and outwards, encouraged by federally supported tax deductions applied to mortgages – the so-called "mansion subsidy." Outside the cities, densely settled residential areas that had previously taken on the characteristics of bedroom suburbs began to attract office parks and land hungry industries.

In the 1970s Melvin Webber introduced us to the unsettling notion of the "non-place urban realm," which duly arrived with a force that catapulted suburbia into the Edge City, exhaustively researched by Joel Garreau. Over time, new building types emerged around freeway intersections – the big-box outlets, office nodes, and industrial parks that introduced a new spatial and economic dimension to the outer metropolitan area. Garreau details the process by which the malling of America became the mechanism through which to hone and elaborate the essential shopping core with commercial office developments as the embryo for new service employment nodes surrounded by housing subdivisions and tract homes. With more jobs came more people and more housing on the urban periphery, and the emergence of two or even multi-income family types. Workers began to commute between residential suburbs and commercial nodes in the "edge city," so that by the turn of the millennium metropolitan areas were becoming borderless territories, forged from an assumption of an infinite supply of greenfield land. Investment was drawn by low cost and readily available large sites, while also exploiting direct access to the highway network for import of raw materials, product distribution, and accessible sources of labor. This came to constitute a pattern of urbanization that was not merely "sprawl" in terms of sparse settlement but rather unstructured development, the result of countless independent decisions but with ineffective coordination and inadequate overall planning and urban design.

The result was an "Exurbia" that created a decentralized counter-force to the central city. This prioritized convenience over community, amenity over identity, and the "here and now" over longer-term sustainability. The Exurbs tended to morph into full-blown suburban business cores or new communities on the outer metropolitan fringe with close links to transport hubs, serving as major regional employment centers and represented by various spatial forms. A corollary to Exurbia is the "Edgeless Cities," which represent dispersed, low-density concentration of offices with no clear boundary definition. Variations on these—the abstractedly identified "Boomburbs" and "Metroburbs"—have stealthily developed in recent times almost by accident; the former evolving through constant annexation of adjoining land thereby conveying the negative epitomy of sprawl, while the latter tends to represent an accumulation of core business centers, exurban communities, and specialized subcenters. These are obviously difficult to adequately synthesize into a composite whole. The reality is that all these aspects collectively embody the political, physical, economic, and social dynamics of the contemporary metropolitan template with its intricate regional variations. Edward Soja refers to the bourgeoning peripheral urbanization as *exopolis* – the simulated city full of "non-city-ness" and the "nexus of contemporary life," but nevertheless countering and complementing the traditional city at the same time. Mike Davies on the other hand refers to the "fortified cells of affluence" and the commensurate disappearance of real democratic urban space.

In the process, the suburb's ties to the central city became ever more tenuous while at the same time the sanctity of previously rural hinterlands have become increasingly compromised. In many cases this has involved damage to natural ecosystems, overwhelming of drainage systems, impaired water quality, destruction of habitats, and substantial carbon emissions through markedly increased traffic and construction. Preservation of farmland is a significant factor when considering competition for land, and is clearly in a somewhat precarious situation within growing megapolitan regions, given the slow but gradual reduction in farmland across the nation by 340 acres for every 1,000 new residents from the overall 930 million acres in 1997. And this is before we get to aesthetic compromise, dispersion of employment nodes, and lack of practicable community structures. The explosion of suburban development has been so great that by the Millennium the Federal Census Bureau had to redefine and reclassify new and varied forms of contemporary urbanization and the indeterminate boundaries within metropolitan districts in terms of a new designation – Combined Statistical Areas.

The Bureau defines suburbia as being within the metropolitan area but outside the "central city." However, this creates an ambiguous situation, as in 2003 the Bureau replaced this category with "principal cities," seemingly seeking to reflect the individual political jurisdictions that enjoy independent tax authority, planning, and regulatory powers. This anomaly underscores the difficulties in reconciling policies for the common good, given the tenuous relationship between a diverse range of bodies with the legal authority to protect their own immediate self-interests. Peter Calthorpe has reminded us that we have to recognize a coalition of interests against integrated planning: developers who continue to apply an expedient and formulaic approach; existing residents who wish to preserve property values; and municipalities anticipating tax advantages regardless of their spatial implications.

211

The identity and legibility of Savannah's plan form is generated through a combination of intensive foci, point references, clear boundaries, and characteristic landmarks. This is extended through more ambiguous aspects of physical definition - expressive places of convergence, congregation, spontaneous exchange, and social ritual that all play a part in the empirical urban experience.

Suburbs are a physically integral part of the metropolis but they are products of different processes. There is also an elusive problem of perception, whereby suburbs tend to identify with the historic city or central hub in terms of its image and cultural state, while at the same time seeking to bolster their individual identity, power, and decision-making base. Metro planning must therefore not merely explore the legitimacy of much suburban development, but find the means to resolve its wasteful and despoiling delineation through patterns of assimilation, retrofitting, and densification typologies.

Suburbia now represents a highly differentiated mosaic of settlements that accommodate a large and ethnically diverse cross-section of contemporary Americana. It is fast becoming "Post-Suburbia" with increasing heterogeneous configurations of multi-cultural enclaves representative of the new geopolitical economy. Of course some aspects of suburbia are admirable – it is in fact difficult to condemn stereotypes to which a large part of the citizenry have willingly subscribed. However, many have also mortgaged their future to an unstable "non-place," and the sprawling metropolitan region is of deep concern. If, as some have claimed, suburbia is "the engine of the nation," then it is long past its worthiness certification. Effective metropolitan planning and the position of the central city is dependent on it.

The frailty of the fiscal apparatus that has underscored the suburban model, reliant as it is on a buoyant economy and continual purchasing power, was amply demonstrated by the subprime mortgage crisis of 2008. One million two hundred thousand residential properties were foreclosed, bringing to an end the unprecedented housing boon that had become transformed into a speculative bubble, exacerbated by a lack of transparency over markets and an archaic regulatory structure. The conditions that underpin this go back to past measures established in the post-war period, when the federal government insured mortgages, creating a market for trading them. In 1968 the Federal National Mortgage Association was established as a means of minimizing risk to lending institutions, effectively creating a considerable subsidy to lenders, as mortgage interest was tax deductible. Sub-prime mortgage bonds were bought by banks and then metaphorically sliced up, becoming securitized according to different risk ratings. The securities, backed by subprime loans were vastly overrated although investors initially received a high return from what seemed like respectable banking instruments. Meanwhile the high rates of mortgage interest that fed the stock was being paid on the basis of loans taken out by those who could least afford them. With risk being passed down the line, the bonds became increasingly synthetic. This in turn led to credit default swaps on the riskier tranches, which were packaged into new bonds.

In the end we only narrowly averted a global financial catastrophe with impacts that still linger in planning terms within weak metropolitan economies, with over-development having led to widespread abandonment of subdivisions, and extensive foreclosures across the property spectrum. The Residential Mortgage-Backed Securities Working Group set up by federal and state regulators in 2012 in the wake of this debacle has since reached multibillion dollar settlements with almost every major bank in America, diverting money into "consumer relief" made up of private nonprofit organizations. However, credit "scores" verified by banks through tax returns, have become a prime cause of economic polarization in society. Government control of agencies that guarantee most new mortgages might have even inadvertently widened the gap and increased discrimination.

Ultimately, an important issue here is the status of planned settlements in the regional or metropolitan hierarchy. The optimum population size for an independent neighborhood or township, the essential building block for planned metropolitan growth, must form a viable basis for relative self-containment in terms of coordinated social, commercial, and service amenities and the many other functions of daily life. If we take the minimum size of a satellite community as being around 10,000 persons, with an average suburban household size of 2.6 persons, this suggests a requirement of at least 4,000 housing units, taking into account the overall demographic mix – far more than most private suburban developments laid out simply as housing tracts or even most New

213

Urbanism developments. Housing alternatives must form part of metropolitan policy to create an equitable balance that caters for real need across the board without benefitting one socio-economic sector over another. We are not therefore talking about the coherent design of settlements in isolation as is the case with most new planned neighborhoods, but a planned regional framework of townships serviced by public transit, which must be sufficiently robust to accommodate fluctuating patterns of growth.

Neither the model American garden city in its original conceptual form, nor contemporary privately built evocations of small and predominantly middle-class communities, fit comfortably into the modern planning lexicon – precisely because the organizational parameters have fundamentally changed. We now need to ensure a sustainable balance between urban and rural so that both sides benefit.

Thank you all for your rapt attention, and for not interrupting.

We wander off for a lunch break in twos and fours. Brit excuses herself in order to polish her presentation. Apolonia suggests that Terry should wind down gradually and invites him for enchiladas and a tequila or three at an Irish bar called Houlihans on Abercorn Street. The rest of us follow languidly, across Liberty Street and East Broughton Street.

We arrive in Reynolds Square and some sheltered seating. Agnita who carries around her pocket guide informs us that the square was first named Lower New Square but renamed in honor of John Reynolds, Georgia's first Royal Governor who was recalled to London within three years of his arrival having largely mismanaged the city's finances. The branches of street trees are beginning to ripple on the light wind and the more intense leaf canopies in Reynolds Square ebb and flow above the bronze monument to John Wesley, who, for different reasons, also became disenchanted with the city. Agnita continues, "The square was the site of the first silk filament, an enterprise supported by the Savannah trustees. It was destroyed by fire in 1758 and replaced by a multi-purpose meeting and entertainment center – the site of a gala event in 1791 attended by George Washington. Under the next two royal governors, the Square and its new Council House became the political center of the city."

We buy sandwiches and soda at a nearby shop and sit facing the Georgian façade of the old Oliver Sturges House where the voyage of the S. S. Savannah, the first steamship to cross the Atlantic, was planned. On the other side of the square is a pretty building that advertises itself as *The Olde Pink House*. Two large flags—the Stars and Stripes and the Union Jack—flutter above the front porch. Schlomo and I wander inquisitively into the lobby of what is evidently now a tavern. Schlomo smiles ingratiatingly at the demurely attired receptionist and supplies a brief synopsis of our visiting status. She blinks smilingly back under long lashes and tells us, or more accurately Schlomo, that the mansion began life in 1771. It was the private home of James Habersham, one of three brothers who took a different path to their Loyalist father during the American Revolution and became notable patriots. Another brother, Joseph Hamilton, was later responsible for the arrest of the last of Georgia's Royal Governors, James Wright in 1775. It remained a residence until 1812 when it was converted to the Planter's Bank and later the Marine Bank, and served as the headquarters for the Union General during the Civil War occupation of Savannah. The lady receptionist whispers to us that the ghost of James Habersham still creeps around the Planter's Tavern in the dead of night, and is often seen wearing a gray colonial army uniform. I make a mental note to inform Terry Fulbright who has begun to take an unhealthy interest in the supernatural.

"Oh, and I should tell you," she says, "we have a resident pianist in the restaurant."

We take a peek inside and sure enough the pianist is in full flow.

They call her Hard Hearted Hannah,
The Vamp from Savannah,
The meanest gal in town;
Leather is tough, but Hannah's heart is tougher,
She's a gal who loves see men suffer!
To tease 'em, and thrill 'em, to torture and kill 'em,
Is her delight, they say ...

Schlomo whispers, "Hannah must have been some lady. It was written by three guys, whether from unfortunate experience or otherwise is unknown. On top of all that it is said her principle characteristics were that she looks flashy, acts brashy, talks trashy, and spends all your cashy. It dates back to 1924 and is kind of Savannah's national anthem. It has been recorded by just about everyone from Peggy Lee and Ella Fitzgerald to Nancy Sinatra."

The diners love it. We tiptoe out, thanking our gracious informant, and return to the others.

Agnita and Miles are in deep conversation about the whereabouts of Leopold's Ice Cream Parlor, a legendary establishment so renowned for its calorie extravagant products that long queues begin to form in the early morning. I offer to lead the way to East Broughton Street where it is located and was founded in 1919. The owner, Leopold Stratton, also acts as a Producer for Paramount Pictures so the shop is lined with autographed pictures and posters.

Agnita says that after only a sandwich she has accumulated sufficient space for a large tutti frutti – a pastel pink concoction filled with candied fruit. Miles chooses peppermint, while Schlomo selects an implausible but evidently verifiable Guinness flavor from the menu, and is disappointed to learn it is only served in March. I go for Ginger, supposedly grown right here in Savannah.

We sit at a window table as the queue trickles out of the shop down the street. Schlomo is silently fascinated by a conversation at the next table. A lady in outsize shorts and a flowery top is righteously arguing that she cannot bear to watch the presidential debates. "The system has failed middle-class voters," she says. "The white vote is broken, the inner cities are on edge, job prospects are dismal, and the state of education is being diminished."

"The only thing school children can do these days is operate a cellphone," her companion adds.

"Trump is a chump," says the first woman, a poetic remark that I see Schlomo is quietly inserting in his iPhone log. The first woman grudgingly concedes the comparison but says, "What's to choose between them? He'd cut taxes, she'd raise them; He'd replace Obama Care and she'd translate it into Hilary Care; she'd smooth talk the world's demagogues and he'd snarl at them; she'd wheel out her husband to flatter the masses and he'd show off Ivanka."

Her companion nods sadly. "Do you want another ice cream," she says.

We stand to leave. Schlomo, with an excess of charm, leans over the ladies and says, "Can I tell you how much I have enjoyed your valuable comments. You are true patriots." They look up at him blankly.

We wander back down Abercorn, taking a detour through the Colonial Park Cemetery along Liberty Street to Madison Square. Terry and Apolonia duly arrive a few minutes later, flushed of face and tanked with tequila, to use Schlomo's apt observation.

OPPOSITE PAGE
Mix of uses on Broughton Street,
Savannah's main commercial
thoroughfare.

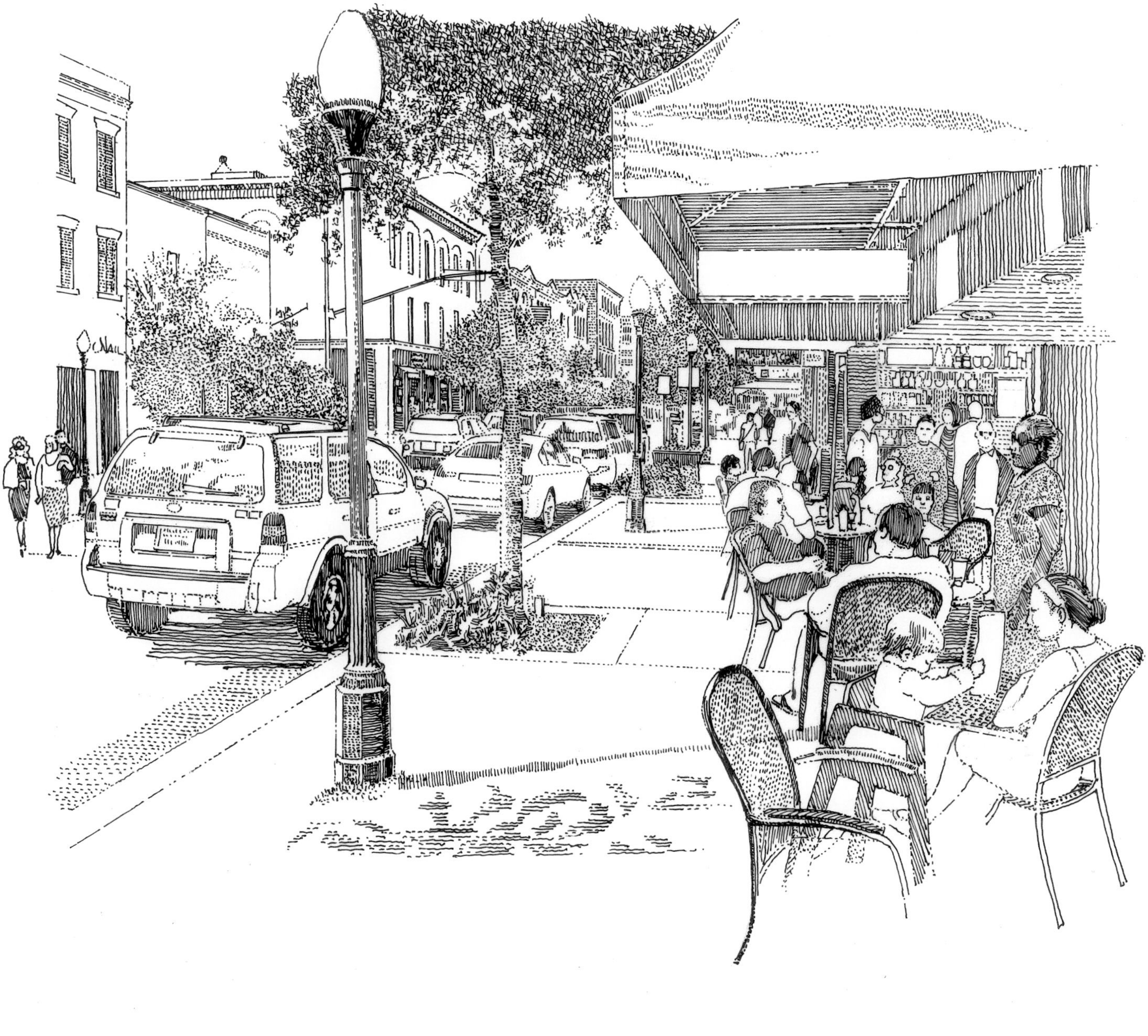

North-South Acrimony

CIVIL WAR AND ITS AFTERMATH

The issue of slavery was never simply a battle of morality between North and South. Conservative New York was less than supportive of Lincoln's policies, with race riots frequently convulsing the city. Democratic organizations promised poor whites that they would never have to compete with free blacks for jobs. In July 1860 a military company, the Blues from Savannah, had arrived in New York on the steamship Florida to meet their counterparts, conjoined by business and kinship ties. Largely made up of prominent businessmen, they carried out drills in full uniform, indulged in joint banquets, and together with their hosts toasted George Washington, Andrew Jackson, and other political leaders.

In the South, militias began to form, amid calls for dissolution of the Union. The Savannah City Council passed an ordinance forbidding the public gathering of black people and subsequently even attempted to secure legislation re-enslaving those freed. Vigilante groups focused not only on potential insurrectionists but on northern abolitionists, with early calls in some quarters for the dissolution of the Union. News of Lincoln's election fuelled more extremist rhetoric amidst calls for secession, while Georgia's first flag of southern independence was unfurled in front of the Nathanial Green Monument in Johnson Square to an applauding crowd, its design featuring a coiled rattlesnake, symbolic of fierceness and retaliation. Following this the city experienced a closing of ranks among all parties and white ethnic groups.

Georgia had supported a pro-slavery southern candidate in the presidential election, John C. Breckinridge, dividing the country along both geographical and ideological lines. What had until then reflected an acrimonious difference in attitude and policy, tinged with an increasingly virulent emphasis in the slave owning South against abolitionist sentiment, began to take on a more challenging and divisive tone. The "Declaration of Independence" itself, with its finely stated words on the equality of all men, was questioned as to its definition of "liberty" and precisely how this should be translated.

In the South the fear of insurrection, always near to the surface, erupted into accusations of northern high handedness and intrigue against the very social fabric of Southern society. The execution of John Brown, a northern abolitionist who had led a raid on the federal arsenal in October 1859 at Harper's Ferry, Virginia, as a means of arming slaves, was a further factor that aroused fiercely polarized reactions, one side accusing him of treason and inciting a slave insurrection, and the other calling for his canonization.

South Carolina seceded from the Union in December 1860, and on January 2nd 1861 three secessionists and slave owners were elected to the State Convention to decide on Georgia's fate. On the same day the State Governor, Joseph Brown, ordered the seizure of Fort Pulaski on Cockspur Island, and Fort Jackson, which controlled river access to the city. On January 19th delegates to the state convention voted to join South Carolina, Mississippi, Alabama, and Florida to secede from the Union – they were later joined by

Texas and Louisiana. New armored regiments were formed, celebrated in Savannah by a military parade, and all New York registered ships in the harbor were seized.

In February the Confederate States of America was announced, and the following month a new constitution was adopted under the Confederate Government with Jefferson Davis as president. Davis was a former Secretary for War and had a vision for a new Confederate States of America premised largely on the rights of white citizens, and therefore counterproductive to a sensible and peaceful settlement with the North. A key platform of the Confederate Constitution was the "natural and normal conditions of slavery as subordination to the superior race." This was an admission of the economic and social polarization that continued to exist in the South, and accomplished three fatal outcomes: first, it catapulted the Confederate South into a war they were not well prepared for with a volunteer army of just 17,000 in Georgia; second, it led to many wealthy white citizens shipping their possessions out of the cities ahead of an invasion; and third, it led inevitably to black defiance and solidarity in the face of vigilante groups such as the Savannah Rifles and the Rattlesnake Club. Some freed slaves sought protection from extremists by joining the Confederate side.

As a result of a Confederate attack on Fort Sumter in Charleston harbor, Abraham Lincoln began to assemble Union troops. One of the immediate problems for the Confederates was that of coordinating responsibility for mobilizing forces and city defense. In Savannah, various civilians with military or naval experience were appointed to positions of command, and new fortifications were constructed around the city. State troops also took over Oglethorpe Barracks that had long been used as a jail. A large group of teenage youths were organized as Savannah Cadets, while patriotic women were requested to assist with meeting the necessities of new recruits, including the manufacture of clothing, cartridges, and medical supplies. Shipbuilders, carpenters, and clothiers were awarded contracts for essential goods and services, although new works had to contend with rapidly declining tax revenues, and an appeal to banks to purchase state bonds. Other businessmen turned to speculation by ordering the import of necessary supplies and selling them at a vast profit. However, Union blockades along the coast were gradually reinforced to contain this. Banks sent gold and silver deposits out of Savannah, and merchants likewise moved unsold goods to safe locations by rail.

The various military companies that formed part of the First Georgia Volunteers were commanded by native-born sons of elite Savannah socialites, and many other professionals, tradesmen, and skilled workers joined the ranks. Other wealthy men formed their own companies. In early 1861 there were 14,000 troops stationed in the city, while groups of slaves were put to work on fortifications.

The war clearly held divergent connotations for different groups, and pastors delivered sermons from their pulpits, including the Southern Baptist Convention, embracing the war on religious grounds. The black community remained circumspect and cautious, however, anxious to avoid disloyalty but fervently anticipating hopes for freedom.

The first major battle between Confederate and Union forces was in July 1861 at Bull Run near Washington, D. C. resulted in heavy casualties on both sides from a lethal collection of rifles and field guns. It produced only an indecisive result, although the Confederate Colonel Francis Bartow and his adjutant John Branch were both killed. In November, a Union fleet invaded Hilton Head off South Carolina, and the bombardment and capture of Port Royal caused great consternation in Savannah. General Robert E. Lee was appointed to coordinate Confederate coastal defenses, and remained until the following February, building new batteries and overseeing additional obstructions in the Savannah River to prevent the passage of northern gunboats. New defenses were constructed on the landward side of the city, and a series of new forts built on its south-eastern flank. However, runaway slaves and river pilots headed to federal lines, providing valuable information about defensive fortifications and the local geography of the many rivers and creeks around Savannah. Other black church leaders publically supported Abraham Lincoln's Emancipation Proclamation.

A key breakthrough came with the amphibious landings by federal troops on Tybee Island in December where they erected gun batteries aimed at Fort Pulaski, just seven-teen miles from Savannah. The fort contained several hundred confederate soldiers. It had taken sixteen years to build and its massive walls contained over thirteen million bricks. It was considered impregnable. When asked to surrender the Fort, the comman-dant Colonel Charles Olmstead, spiritedly retorted that he was there to defend rather than surrender it. However, after constant mortar fire, the officers and men were forced to capitulate on April 10, 1862, allowing federal forces to control the mouth of the river and cut off access to blockage runners. Many affluent residents of Savannah began to send their families, possessions, and currency to safe havens in the interior. New security measures were put in place so that no one could enter or leave the city without a special pass. Massive inflation pushed prices beyond the reach of all but the most wealthy, and bread riots occurred in some of Georgia's cities.

Both equipment and food were also in short supply for the Confederacy troops, and for many volunteers and conscripted troops who became increasingly demoralized it appeared to be a "rich man's war, but a poor man's fight." As morale sagged further, desertions began to increase in large numbers, with the bounds of patriotism being limited by both suffering and the questionable merits of the cause itself. In April 1862, the Confederate Assembly called for the first military draft in American history, aiming to conscript all white men between eighteen and thirty-five years of age to three-year terms of service.

A makeshift stockade had to be constructed in Savannah to hold prisoners and was soon filled by more than 6,000 captured soldiers, while others were sent to Charleston. The vulnerable construction of the stockade located next to the Chatham County prison, and the poor conditions within it led to sickness and death, and several months later all prisoners were moved to a new stockade to the west of the city.

Guerrilla forces comprising escaped slaves operated from a colony at St. Simons on land left abandoned by some of the largest plantation owners. Their knowledge of the forests, marshes, and creeks was invaluable to Union troops. At the same time, raids were made on other plantation for foodstuffs, generating a necessary trade with Union seamen. The defenders of St. Simons went on to form the first all-black unit of the Union army. On January 1, 1863, President Lincoln made an "emancipation proclamation," which promised freedom from slavery, and at the same time authorized emancipated slaves to be incorporated into the armed services, formalizing a substantial recruitment effort.

During the year, various battles took countless lives at Fredericksburg, Vicksburg, and Stones River. Savannah battened down the hatches. The large number of military personnel in the city and the remaining prominent families created a ready audience for theatrical shows to benefit the Confederate cause, in the Savannah Theater, St. Andrew's Hall, and the Masonic Hall. Military displays also acted to generate funds, while many society wives contributed to groups such as the Soldiers' Relief Committee, the Georgia Relief and Hospital Society, and the Ladies Military Association.

In July 1863, 51,000 soldiers from both the Union and Confederate armies were injured or lost their lives at the battle of Gettysburg, which forced Robert E. Lee's troops to retreat into Virginia. By mid-1864 conditions in Savannah had deteriorated to the point where impoverished citizens had to steal food from stores. As the city lost its defense industries, many related jobs went with them. The Savannah City Council was forced to establish a "free market" that would distribute food to the poor. Other citizens brought bread, clothes, and other provisions to hand to the sick and emaciated Union prisoners. In the meantime, Lincoln concluded that an exchange of prisoners would be futile, as it could only prolong the bloodshed.

Surrender of the South

After Atlanta fell to General Sherman in November 1864 following a four-month campaign in the South, what remained in the city was burned. Sixty-two thousand Union troops marched south towards Savannah along with supply wagons, covering twenty miles a day and picking up both supporters and refugees en route anticipating a final battle. The army followed the line of the Central of Georgia Railroad, tearing up the tracks behind them and destroying the rolling stock, railroads, bridges, factories and rice mills as they passed through towns and villages. There was little resistance apart from a battle near Macon, which cost 1,500 lives.

The Savannah defenses were mounted on a narrow peninsula two miles to the west of the city, and on December 11th General Sherman's army enveloped the western and southern lines of defense. Sherman ordered an attack on Fort McAllister on December

13th, which was captured despite heavy casualties. The commander of Confederate forces rejected Sherman's request to surrender the city and moved his troops into South Carolina while an evacuation began. After their arrival in Savannah, Federal troops threw up entrenchments to prevent Confederates recapturing the city, controversially running these works through the Catholic Cemetery as a "military necessity." Many plantation workers saw their entire possessions disappear as Union forces swept through the area, foraging and pillaging all they could obtain, in particular stocks of staple food.

Finally, to protect Savannah from destruction, city officials led by the Mayor Richard Arnold surrendered the city and escorted the entry of Union troops to the City Exchange for a symbolic raising of the Stars and Stripes. The December re-election of Abraham Lincoln as President in a landslide vote ensured a massive Republican majority in Congress, and dashed the hopes of a peace plan on favorable terms to the South.

General Sherman entered the city on December 22, 1864 and established a residence in Pulaski House where prominent local personages arrived to pay their respects. There he wrote a telegram to President Lincoln, in effect presenting him with the keys to the city. Sherman allowed the city council "to continue to exercise their functions," and ordered all the essential local institutions to remain in service. The Historical Record states that at a public meeting in the Masonic Hall the following resolutions were adopted:

Whereas, by the fortunes of war and the surrender of the city by the civil authorities, the city of Savannah passes once more under the authority of the United States; and whereas, we believe that the interests of the city will be best subserved and promoted by a full and free expression of our views in relation to our represent condition; we, therefore, the People of Savannah in full meeting assembled do hereby resolve: That we accept the position, and in the language of the President of the Untied States, seek to have "peace by laying down our arms and submitting to the National authority under the Constitution, leaving all questions which remain to be adjusted by the peaceful means of legislation, conference and votes." Resolved, That laying aside all differences, and burying by-gones in the grave of the past, we will use our best endeavors once more to bring back the prosperity and commerce we once enjoyed. Resolved, that we do not put ourselves in the position of a conquered city, asking terms of a conqueror, but we claim the immunities and privileges contained in the Proclamation and Message of the President of the United States and in all the legislation of Congress in reference to a people situated as we are, and while we owe on our part a strict obedience to the laws of the Untied States, we ask the protection over our persons, lives and property recognized by these laws.

The southern peace commission rejected Lincoln's request for an unconditional surrender. However, on April 9th, Robert E. Lee surrendered his army of Northern Virginia to General Ulysses S. Grant. In all, more than one-quarter of Confederate soldiers lost their lives in the war, while others returned in battered spirits to an uncertain future. In the meantime, four black regiments of 2,300 soldiers arrived in Savannah, presenting a poetic finale to a longstanding confrontation. Savannah was left in a dilapidated state of neglect, and virtually cut off from the outside world as all rail connections had been destroyed, and the Savannah River obstructed. To make matters worse, in January 1865 an explosion at the city arsenal ignited a conflagration that destroyed 100 houses, further adding to the critical housing shortage. To preserve the city's operations, ward committees were set up headed by aldermen and established Confederate leaders.

Fundraising from sympathetic northern cities helped supply food that was in short supply, ostensibly to build a new unity but also to ensure a continuation of the profitable trade in Sea Island cotton. In mid-January Sherman issued a Special Field Order, setting aside the South Carolina and Georgia Sea Islands together with a wide band of coastline "for the settlement of the negroes now made free by the acts of war and the proclamation of the President of the United States." Sherman's essential proposal was to utilize unemployed black labor to help stabilize and re-build the city, and recruit freed slaves for army duty as full citizens. What became known as the "Sherman Reservation" was essentially a means of relocating women, children, and elderly blacks while the younger men were enlisted. A large group of black families moved to the Island of Skidaway and divided the old plantation land into 5,000 plots.

Several days later, on April 14, Abraham Lincoln was shot and killed by John Wilkes Booth. In the South there were some who considered this "righteous retribution," but a memorial service in Savannah was attended by 5,000 mourners with buildings and trees around Johnson Square draped in black.

The new President, Andrew Johnson, extended an amnesty to all Southerners with the proviso that they expressed loyalty to the United States and extended an approval of the various state governments, enabling a mutual transition to a new order. This brought about a new pattern of population movement: new arrivals from the north, animated by ambition, humanitarian intent, and moral righteousness; freed people who had been displaced from low country plantations tentatively trickling back while the original owners were arriving to claim their abandoned land; and black settlers beginning a migration to St. Catherine's Island and elsewhere in an exercise of self-sufficiency. To some it was a world gone into reverse – owners returning to find their houses occupied by former slaves; a resistance to labor in the wetlands; a new approach to self-determination; and a more robust approach to education. To underscore the situation, the Chatham County Colored Union League was established to pursue full citizenship and political rights.

As the mayor and aldermen resumed their political roles in the city in late 1865, Georgia's constitutional convention was charged by Congress to prepare the state for readmission to the Union. The members largely represented the established Whig conservatives, and at the state elections in November former Confederate officers and sympathizers were elected, reflecting the fact that blacks could not run for political office. The following month Savannah held municipal elections for the new civil government with much the same result. Many of the older fraternal and social societies, together with religious groups, acted to unite the community, although a number of militia groups that were technically outlawed survived by simply adjusting their operational titles.

Some previously prominent citizens managed to retain their property and businesses, and gradually prospered as the economy began to recover. However, many former low country planters were faced with estates that they could not work through lack of labor as freed slaves chose to live and work in the city or farm for themselves on plots frequently staked out on the plantations they had previously worked. Others used their military connections to embark on new political and commercial careers. By 1866 more than 40,000 freed people had left to settle on the Sherman Reservation, living mainly on subsistence farming. However, on January 10th it was announced that all black workers had to sign labor contracts, and the Freedmen's Bureau set about restoring the Reservation lands to their former owners. Planters then launched legal challenges to reclaim fertile rice production land in the Ogeechee district, which became the epicenter of the struggle for self-determination through a constant negotiation of employment rights and conditions. Former slaves were assisted in the legal challenges by northern educators and missionaries who moved into the area, opened schools, and conducted religious classes.

Control of Land and the Emerging Development Pattern

The control of land remained a major cause of unrest. In Savannah the inconsistency between the reversal of the Sherman Reservation Order and the fact that freed people should be granted compensation for improvements to land, stocks of cattle, and harvests they had produced, provoked violent resistance and uprisings. In some situations absentee owners, willing to re-work barren lands, engaged freedmen to oversee operations without interference, which was not too difficult to do as much of the old land labor was now mechanized.

By the mid-19th century, Savannah had grown to twenty-four wards, following the established configuration. The provision of a 1.7-acre civic square within each 10.5-acre ward facilitated a compact but walkable city, that grew not through expansion but through subdivision of lots, the original sixty-foot tything lots being divided into thirty-foot and twenty-foot lots. The ward system was developed as part of a regional land use system that included farms, estates such as Wormsloe and Beaulieu, agricultural villages, and fortified outposts that later became new development areas, connected to the city through new road systems which encouraged further settlement. Plantations were developed along the Savannah and Ogeechee Rivers and on the islands of Ossabaw, Wassaw, and Skidaway. The plan informed the condensed morphology of the city, and the modern-day street pattern closely follows the old alignments. The plan also influenced new architectural interpretations, being developed first for individual town houses and then for more condensed terraces.

Savannah's streetcar system developed much along the lines of other and larger American cities. It began in 1869 with the Savannah, Skidaway, and Seaboard Railway Company steam rail service, while operating horse drawn streetcars within the city. Urban development followed a north-south axis as it was constrained by low-lying land on the east and west. This led directly to the development of the Victorian District to the south of Forsyth Park. In general, lots resembled those in the heritage district, but as city limits expanded lots became larger and included commercial development. In 1870 the new Waring Ward was annexed by the city, forming part of the overall street grid framework. Other streetcar suburbs followed, filled with both freestanding and row houses.

The Republicans gained a substantial majority in the November 1866 election, and an act was passed on March 2nd 1887, to establish new state constitutions, which enfranchised black males through a division of the South into five districts under military command. Georgia, Florida, and Alabama were grouped within one district, and this ignited major rallies for various factions that combined both blacks and whites. Three-man registration boards were appointed for each senatorial district, and the process led to mass meetings and escalating tensions.

In December, the delegates met in Atlanta and the convention approved the enfranchisement of black men and a public school system for black and white children, but little in the way of land redistribution. However, optimism was rife that the revolutionary measurers approved would transform the social and political landscape of Georgia. The municipal elections planned for April 1868 generated rounds of outdoor rallies and meetings of different affiliations. A mass rally was held in Chippewa Square, and on voting day, April 20th, Republican candidates were elected both in Savannah and the outlying areas, although in the legislature whites drastically outnumbered blacks. This gave a strong impetus to new business, and more than 100 black organizations of all kinds. Included in these organizations was the Savannah Freemasons, one of many such fraternal bodies that sustained social and political bonds within the black community. New schools later received funds from the Peabody Trust and the American Missionary Association.

In March 1869 the Republican Ulysses S. Grant became President. Congress refused Georgia's election count charging fraud, and rejected the Fifteenth Amendment to the Constitution. In Savannah, blacks who were elected to office continued to be challenged in court with decisions made by the Chief Justice through an interpretation of the State law code.

In the Savannah elections for Mayor and Aldermen, held against a backdrop of labor issues that included strikes among black workers, the Conservatives swept the board, objections being raised to black voters who were said to be ineligible because of residency requirements. In December, the Reorganization Act returned the legislators expelled in September, and Aaron Bradley who took his seat in the state senate denounced an oppressive issue in Georgia whereby children of ten years were sent to work on chain gangs for minor offences.

The census carried out in the summer of 1870 had to designate individuals as "white," "black," or "mulatto." It painted a revealing picture of household configurations that frequently included core families together with elderly relatives, unmarried men, and single women, and liberated black families that tied freed people together. Black institution building was imperceptibly moving families out of poverty, often with the help of churches, missionary associations, and mutual aid societies. Many households took in boarders while in the poorer areas day laborers, seamen, and immigrant machine operators lived in the dilapidated tenements.

Black citizens also sought to assert their rights in campaigns against such things as the levy of a voter-registration tax and segregated street cars – an issue that was to become a cause célèbre almost 100 years later with the Montgomery Bus Boycott and the March on Selma, Alabama, which almost single handedly kick-started the American Civil Rights movement.

In counties outside the city, the large antebellum plantations continued to be broken up into smallholdings of three to ten acres for subsistence farming, while in lower Georgia the average size was reduced from 885 to 240 acres. In 1871 Savannah's port reached an all time record in terms of the nation's share of cotton shipped. In the rest of the city a vibrant underground economy continued to generate a fine balance between economic development and public order.

In early 1871 the Southern Claims Commission met to consider compensation for property losses including livestock and stockpiled food suffered during the war at the hands of Union troops, with an average claim of 357 dollars, mainly from former slaves who had supported the Union cause. The Commission provided an opportunity to shape the memory and provide a tangible record of events that were still raw in people's minds, underscored by the recent deaths and funerals of prominent Confederate military officers, including Robert E. Lee, and return of the remains of soldiers slain at Gettysburg.

The South in general remained in a state of tension, with vigilante groups and lynch mobs aiming their prejudices at groups they considered as social undesirables, leading to congressional hearings on the matter with a committee that took depositions from witnesses that included some of Savannah's leading figures. In the meantime, Senator Charles Sumner of Massachusetts proposed a Civil Rights Bill to Congress that would guarantee all citizens equal treatment and access to every institution including public transport. This well intended attempt to confront the segregation issue was voted down by the House of Representatives. The debate sparked a violent streetcar protest in Savannah over several nights and a case was put before the United States Commissioner in relation to violation of civil rights. The controversial ruling on August 4th was that Congress had not conferred the privilege of integrated transportation and that the state retained the prerogative to segregate facilities.

In 1875, the Civil Rights Act became law in the United States, but in 1876, the New

Sailing at 7pm
404

York Times reported that "blacks in Georgia were as far away from the ballot box as they were in the days of slavery." In the same year James Simms published a book, The First Colored Baptist Church in North America, which recounted the struggle for equality through a history of black control of churches led by ministers who formed a conduit for political leadership – a mantle that Dr. Martin Luther King was to assume in the 1960s.

In 1883 the Civil Rights Act was declared unconstitutional by the U. S. Supreme Court, in effect denying equality to black people and acting to again separate whites and blacks in schools and streetcars. Three years later, the former Confederate President Jefferson Davis visited Savannah to wide acclaim, and in a speech once again appeared to underscore secessionist sentiment and to justify the cause. The social division of labor continued much as before, although towards the end of the century a major portion of work on the plantations was carried out by new Irish and English immigrants and even Chinese labor, often with black overseers, workers performing seasonal employment. By this time rice production was much reduced, through a lack of workers willing to stand the unhealthy conditions. Sharecroppers, both black and white, worked under landowners or appointed supervisors, as this was almost the only way of life for landless farmers who were provided with housing, tools, and materials, and received a share of the crop.

Many workers were lured to cities in the north to work in industry and on the railroads.

The effective regeneration of the National Association for the Advancement of Colored People, founded in 1917, resulted in increased black voter registration in the post World War II period, and the election of reform minded officials. Civil Rights laws of 1964 and 1965 created a significant change in the South's racial climate, and helped usher in a "New South." The first fully integrated schools were introduced in 1963, the first Savannah member of the US Supreme Court in 1991, the first black mayor in 1993, and the first black majority city council in 1999. The South remains as more culturally conservative than the North, possibly reflecting a deliberate preservation of an antebellum-oriented visitor model. In common with many other parts of America, new values and social norms have become increasingly introduced through accelerated patterns of immigration.

A bronze group of figures representing a sculptural representation of an African-American freed family was designed by the sculptor Dorothy Spradley and completed in 2002. It sits on a site fronting the Savannah River, and acts to memorialize slavery while issuing a stark inscription as to its intent, actuality, and hope.

What remained intact throughout the Post-Civil War period has been the city's unique urban design of squares and elegant buildings, both public and private, which has continued to exert both a sensual and humanizing influence in the immediate post-war period. This became a significant factor in Savannah's slow rehabilitation and gradual recovery from immense human losses.

We are back at Poetter Hall.

Mo looks at his watch and stands up. "The last two presentations summarize where American urbanism is at this point in time, and the basic reasons why. As Agnita rightly states, our dilemma is that we are perhaps too much in love with the ability of the free market to provide the livable and sustainable urban environments that we are committed to deliver. Our cities and metro regions must now compete in the global market place, and we must make allowances for this. Our experience over the past 200 years suggests more rather than less interventionist controls but the problem is that these have been neither responsible nor visionary. The process seems to have taken over from any vision of the product. As Terrence has confirmed, the suburban model, compromised by expediency and diverted from metropolitan integration, is wasteful in almost every respect. We must now move on to our third tranche of thinking – the means to reshape, reconcile, and reconfigure the urban landscape. Brit Kris is going to get the ball rolling this afternoon."

Brit has changed from blue denim to a masculine, tailored pant-suit in dark gray which Schlomo whispers fits her far better than Hilary Clinton's sartorial choices. Jean-Paul who is sitting next to her is clearly thinking along similar lines, and smiles encouragingly.

SIXTH READING BY EVA BRIT KRIS
THE ELASTIC CITY: RESHAPING METROLAND

My presentation is essentially about the region, which will be the greatest driver of change over the next half century; and so it should be, but only if we get our collective heads together.

According to the latest Inventory of US Land Uses, excluding Alaska and Puerto Rico, there are 1.9 billion acres of total land area in America. Of this, 28.2 percent is forest cover; 26 percent grassland; 19.5 percent cropland; 13.0 percent special uses e.g. national parks and wildlife areas; 10.5 percent miscellaneous; and 2.8 percent urban. The latter is home to seventy-five percent of the total population of 328 million. However, stable patterns of land use at a national level can obscure different degrees of change at a regional and state level.

Lewis Mumford famously stated, "the metropolis should co-exist rather than compete with the region, as first among equals." This of course leaves open the political and economic changes that might be necessary in terms of public investment and organizational priorities to reshape the metropolitan region. With public support these measures might not necessarily be radical but must be matched by new processes of public empowerment, understanding, and direct citizen involvement in public policy and budget decision-making.

While the manufacturing industry opened up metropolitan growth, the decline of the industrial suburb and its dependent residential neighborhoods has been accompanied by a rise in the service economy, with more isolated but strategically located employment hubs accessible only by private transport. The twenty-first-century metropolitan reality is now a composite of highway infrastructure serving a diverse mosaic of housing, commercial, educational, and institutional developments and made up of central enclaves, suburbs, edge cities, and exurbs amidst a landscape of sprawl and environmental degradation.

The recession that began in 2008 had an impact that still lingers with malicious intent, but has in fact hesitantly achieved at least one outcome that has potentially significant consequences. In effect, it has not too gently put the brakes on a fifty-year program of suburban sprawl that has made us look more prudently at future modes of development. Let's examine the figures – in 1950 around seventy percent of the American population lived in 193 central cities located within 168 metropolitan areas. By the time of the 2010 census the situation was virtually reversed with sixty-eight percent of the population living in suburban communities within 383 metropolitan areas, along with the majority of employment opportunities. Eighty-three percent of the population now lives in metropolitan regions, with around one-third of these in mega regions, which contribute eighty-five percent of national economic output.

Now I want to discuss the trend towards metropolitan expansion – let's call it "Heading for Megalopolis."

The seminal work on the expanding metropolitan regions along the northeastern seaboard of the United States was Jean Gottman's *Megalopolis* published in 1961, which defined the term as what he called an "incubator of new urbanization" through its growing international relationships. His work is partly philosophical, in accepting continuous urban growth as being symbolic of human aspirations through history via migrations and consolidations of cultural and economic centers. Gottman was arguably the first geographer and urbanist to observe the decrease in the central function of large hub cities, but with commensurate specialization and rapid growth of the urban region through a new order of industrial and technological change. He also accurately perceived contemporary cultural preferences for the choice of suburbia as a pre-eminent residential location. "Megalopolis" has therefore been taken up as a term that reflects current trends in metropolitan expansion and integration. One of the characteristics of this, which we must consider a challenge, is the momentum needed to correlate urbanization with wider economic and environmental interests. That is to say, we must resolve the conflict between growth trends, the present freewheeling approaches to suburban development, the vested property interests involved, and official planning policies.

Gottman posed the question, "How large can cities grow ... and is there a limit?" The answer appears to be through the megapolitan assimilation of interdependent towns, cities, and metropolitan districts that form intricate networks of both national and international significance. Cities become defined in spatial terms by the degree to which they integrate different functions, with the most successful dominating adjoining territories that grow through a process of agglomeration, forming city regions. These informally establish hierarchical or polycentric forms that occur when one or more cities become dominant and others secondary, but where they continue to develop and group into larger conurbations through interdependencies. In recent times the growth of exurban and edge cities which are in themselves the indirect result of "interventionist" federal subsidies, have turned central place theory virtually upside down, with a high percentage of business activity increasingly dispersed in an extended way along growth corridors. It therefore seems logical to introduce a new metropolitan realm of government that might technically overlap with state jurisdictions but which might well be more effective in terms of achieving coordinated regional planning.

As a general rule, overall population densities are reduced through urban expansion, but the nature of megapolitan growth and its tendency to disperse this within and around nuclei and along connective development corridors blurs the distinction between urban and rural, and makes it necessary to examine their interrelationship. As Gottman observed, rivalry between competing large cities is one of the factors affecting growth and the economic forces that make up the incubators of change. But if these cities are located in relatively close proximity, the tendency to urbanize the intervening space is likely to consolidate their interdependence. The amount of urbanized territory in America has

The ordered composition of
heterogeneous building elements and
architecturally articulated street
blocks reflect an early version
of a design code that establishes
the volumetric components of city
space and encourages architecturally
responsive typologies.

increased dramatically since the mid-1980s, considerably disproportionate to the growth in population, illustrating the land extensive nature of new development and dispersed socio-economic patterns. As a result we can observe that the notion of "urban community" is being re-shaped, organized less through distinctive urban quarters and convenience, and more around vehicular accessibility.

According to the Urban Land Institute, suburban districts within the fifty largest metropolitan areas make up around eighty percent of their populations. At the same time, up to two-thirds of jobs are located in suburban situations, although there is evidence that this trend might be decelerating. Metropolitan development is therefore in a relatively dynamic state of growth and re-organization. Growth rates of office development in both the central city and suburbs from the 1990s show a close correlation, and multiple centers of economic activity have clear ramifications for the traditional relationship between the center and periphery, and its necessary connective tissue. Each activity center is essentially focused on an employment hub, and from around 1980 the employment mix has continued to change through economies of scale. A somewhat elusive aspect of the developing Megalopolis is the degree to which constant changes in interdependencies and transactional activities are giving rise to new and sometimes nebulous urban structures associated with developing cores, inner neighborhoods, and the expanding periphery, all of which are undergoing a metamorphosis.

This represents an emerging shift towards condensed growth corridors in response to evolving and integrative economic stimuli at a regional level, framed by the new knowledge and service economy. America is not alone in coming to terms with its new spatial order. This process has been happening in Europe for some time, functioning as overlapping metropolitan networks, and in Asia there is the Beijing-Nanjing-Tangshan megapolitan corridor in China, the Tokyo-Yokohama region in Japan, the Taipei-Kaohsiung corridor in Taiwan and the Seoul-Puson-Taejon region in South Korea. The American trend is therefore not an isolated one.

The National Census Bureau's Statistical Abstract states that around 230 million people live within 650,000 square miles of urban land – three times the urban population of 1950 but occupying some fifty times the amount of land at an average of 350 people per square mile. However, if we subtract all the uninhabitable wilderness and federally owned areas we find that around two thirds of the population lives at physical densities that are somewhat higher than in Western Europe. In fact, urban land is, by all accounts, on course to absorb a further ninety million immigrants by 2040 when the US population is projected to exceed 400 million. The majority are likely to be housed within emerging megaregions at a density of around 750 people per square mile. Two-thirds of the population will, in effect, live on around twelve percent of national territory.

So where do we go from here in terms of planning?

Clearly there has to be a coordination of governance at a regional level, which implies the

233

creation of a metropolitan regional body through smart growth legislation. An alternative is cooperative governance that unifies regional development, based perhaps somewhat optimistically on reconciling the interests of all subscribers towards mutual benefit.

Megapolitan areas comprise regional development structures with populations in excess of four million people and each includes at least one metropolitan conurbation in excess of one million people and probably several other smaller ones, with strong economic interdependence and cooperation reflected by overlapping commuting patterns. If we accept the trend towards Megapolitan growth with its accentuation on high technology and high-end manufacturing, it will be essential to reinforce its interface with the global trading economy. Certain specialized service industries form an obliging interdependence with the core city, while others are increasingly isolated and detached from energized sources of employment including a vulnerable manufacturing sector. Existing socio-economic trends demonstrate an increasing percentage of knowledge-based or "creative class" employment, which might suggest the need for a possible shift in regional planning emphasis towards facilitation and coordination of polycentric metropolitan forms, orchestration of the rural-urban continuum, and the establishment of firm and sustainable boundaries with regard to natural amenities and farming dependent counties.

A fundamental issue with respect to this is infrastructure – both new and upgraded. This means that high-speed rail and mass-transit systems must be viewed as necessary investments. The economic case for this is compelling. While interstate highways between metropolitan areas have transformed America's growth patterns and in particular its patterns of suburbanization, the expanding megapolitan scenario requires a re-emphasis on public transit systems. High-speed rail projects received a kick-start in 2009 as part of the American Renewal and Reinvestment Act, with plans to construct a national network integrating emerging megapolitan clusters based on analysis of various measures, including population size, spatial form, and economic activity to serve the evolving development pattern. It is therefore necessary to shore up undeveloped parts of the network and complete the missing sections.

Now it has been said that planning is one of the leading causes of statistics. However Arthur C. Nelson's fine-grained analysis of metropolitan growth in *Reshaping Metropolitan America* has identified some key market trends and a complexity of socioeconomic situations that are likely to reshape the housing market up to 2030 and perhaps beyond. These include stagnant median household incomes; significant loss of equity in home ownership due to the fall in house values; and restrictions on institutional support for leveraged mortgages.

Ethnic groups including African Americans, Asians, and Hispanics occupy around twenty-five percent of suburban populations, with a cross section of low, medium, and high income groups, and ethnic minority households represent by far the fastest growing population sector. Affirmative action has played a major role in increasing the percentage of the upwardly mobile black population in middle-class suburbs. According to the US Census Bureau forty percent of new immigrants now immediately settle in "gateway" suburban locations, but the traditional gateway cities still hold a majority of metropolitan area immigrant populations.

This is on top of other trends towards demographic diversity. At one end of the spectrum under the new information and service economy, small one- and two-income households are forging a return to the city as part of the "creative class" and occupying small rental properties, and among this sector there is a marked preference for "smart growth" over sprawl. At the other end, the Baby Boom generation is aging, and "empty nesters" and singletons make up around one quarter of the population bringing with them a requirement for some degree of "assisted living" facilities. Reduced household sizes will have a clear impact on the demand for smaller homes and space requirements, and therefore on the housing market as a whole.

The implications from this are that new residential and employment growth should be directed at existing urban areas and developing growth corridors, facilitating increased densities and a more resilient economic base through clustering of activities, with intensified regional nodes connected by public transit systems. Several aspects need to be considered holistically – the regenerative spatial implications, the evolving requirements of the post-industrial service economy, and the fragmented nature of political jurisdictions.

What we might gather from this is evidence of a latent demand for multiple and affordable urban housing options including "joined together" units; that is to say, terraced housing on relatively small lots such as apartments, condominiums, and multiplexes – much of it occurring through redevelopment and infill. In other words, we need to be looking at diversity of new housing products that allow users to maximize social and economic benefits. The challenge is, therefore, how to frame development scenarios, zoning, and urban design codes, that meet these changing market conditions.

In August 2016 the US Census Bureau reported that home ownership at 62.9 percent was the lowest in fifty-one years, having peaked at 69.2 percent in 2004. Lower occupancy rates, a rise in multigenerational and single-person households together with a substantial increase in the senior population sector indicate a need for smaller residential units and more urban rental accommodation.

Brit pauses at this point and beckons Jean-Paul Gournier. Jean-Paul stands up and begins to speak.

235

JEAN-PAUL

Brit has kindly allowed me, as a practicing urban designer, to interject something as we are both equally concerned, not just with the issues, but the means to generate sustainable urbanism. I would like to briefly talk about Development Trends and how to properly accommodate them.

MO

Says nothing but shifts uneasily in his chair and looks mildly perplexed.

JEAN-PAUL

Lee Rodney has identified the shifting notion of the "borderline" from its early colonial management function to its more precarious geopolitical role following the formation of the Department of Homeland Security in 2003. We could ask ourselves whether this is symbolic of a new protectionism not unrelated to a prevalent national discomfort with globalization. This might also relate to nostalgia for the sanctity of community rather than merely an impulsive counteraction to imagined external threat. In much the same way we applaud the prevalence of surveillance mechanisms in our urban territories as a means of coping with the War on Terror and to ease our elusive vulnerabilities that lie more in the field of imagination than fact.

We can observe certain specific trends from the 1970s onwards that have materially contributed to the metropolitan model. The ex-urban communities or "outer suburbs" centered around new industrial developments, together with campus-like business parks, have effectively underscored a transition from low-density suburbia to edge or satellite conglomerations with ready made interstate highways and even airport facilities on the doorstep. Development is characterized by a decentralized form but with solid urban attributes that tend to function as significant employment hubs with associated residential catchments.

Joel Garreau's famous definition was that for qualification as an Edge City, such developments must contain at least five million square feet of leasable office space; 600,000 square feet of retail space; have more jobs than bedrooms; have a high perception as a "place" in its own right; and have essentially been developed on a virgin site over no more than thirty years. Garreau identified several types of edge city that enjoy these commonalities, and range in size. In some cases, these entities house more commercial space than downtown central business districts and embrace large enclosed shopping malls with associated hotel rooms to support their commercial function. In addition to the agglomeration of commercial development in the edge city a more recent phenomenon is the dispersed grouping of "edgeless" office development nodes unrelated to forms of planned community and totally reliant on the automobile.

Garreau's perceptive analysis of emergent edge cities tunes us in to the self-indulgent nature of contemporary cityspace. Heidegger reminds us that a boundary is not merely where things stop but where things start. Are these development types a "new frontier" to something else, or are they rather a complementary appendage to what exists? Are they full of entrepreneurial pioneers in SUVs or do they simply cater for those looking for cost-effectiveness and convenience? And in what way is the Edge City opening up opportunities for repurposing the Central City? New types of business might be reshaping the new urbanism but so is globalization. The jury is still out on how, if at all, the smart age of information technology is refashioning the city, but it seems most likely that "edge" development will offset rather than replace downtown, reflecting the ever-changing geopolitical economy. Cities will still continue their traditional role as incubators of creative industry, if for no other reason than that eager young entrepreneurs want to live in them.

On average around one third of urban space as a whole is given over to non-residential uses. In projecting future needs there is a less-than specific trend towards teleworking, changes in average space requirements for workers, and e-commerce over retail space demand. An important aspect of this is the durability of non-residential fabric that has an average life span of around forty-five years, given the advances in communication technology and the appreciation of land value, which normally increases as building values depreciate. This suggests that certain types of non-residential stock such as unprofitable malls and some suburban office development along commercial corridors, often surrounded by vast parking areas, would be ripe for recycling or retooling over a much shorter life-span. Their locational and service attributes in combination with regeneration or replacement of obsolescent housing areas could be a catalyst in reshaping metropolitan areas over perhaps a twenty- to thirty-year period to meet new compact "livable city" criteria.

In fact, the majority of projected residential and non-residential requirements can technically be absorbed through consolidating new and rehabilitated uses and through transit-oriented developments built around pedestrian friendly neighborhoods. New and autonomous forms of urban mobility can only help matters. Infill and regeneration in some of the largest metropolitan areas is already a discernible trend, and creates opportunities to upgrade infrastructure and utility services with more integrated and "smart" capacity.

237

BRIT

This requires wide acceptance of an ambitious agenda for sustainable urbanism that spans all aspects of community design – physical, social, economic, environmental, and public health. A fundamental aspect is the need for change in the way in which land is managed and planning is regulated. An overall analysis based on surveys, mapping, and inventories set out by McHarg in *Design with Nature* is all it takes to identify areas most favorable for development and the most effective use of resources. However, the community needs to be convinced that this is the way to go, so planning discourse has to be both educational and persuasive. In particular, zoning must be redeployed in a responsive way, which could well require federal intervention through Metropolitan Planning Commissions. These have the ability to shape growth and development through comprehensive land use planning and zoning ordinances.

This brings us logically to regional strategy and the orchestration of an integrative network that establishes the context for growth but also appropriate levels of conservation, ecological protection, and broad scale linkage and continuity. Effective plan making at a neighborhood level needs a close measure of physical, but also social and economic fit within the metropolitan region. In the post-industrial period, the city and region must be considered as compatible elements with an emphasis on connectivity. Both planning and urban design are dependent on this inter-relationship.

JEAN-PAUL

We readily acknowledge the "hidden" federal subsidies of sprawl, but inefficient capital infrastructure is just as big an economic burden. If we examine the costs of roads, pavements, sewers, public open space, and water facilities, numerous studies have shown the savings that can be made on a per-unit basis by directing new development to consolidate existing urban and suburban centers rather than along traditional lines. However, an optimum density model and its resource efficiency for say a community of 50,000 people seemingly remains untested. At the heart of the cost debate is subsidy. During the post-war growth of suburbia, developers only paid for site infrastructure, while states, counties, and municipalities have been left to pay for the wider road and service networks as well as the institutional and community facilities, which must support the needs of new development areas. Such situations imply a need for increased levels of local tax, as outgoings in many cases exceed incoming revenue. Unfruitful competition amongst the constellation of local municipalities within the same metropolitan region has encouraged tax-producing uses such as shopping malls and business parks, whether or not they have a viable market catchment. This ultimately generates disparities between wealthy and poorer localities, and clearly represents a fiscal policy that is entirely questionable in terms of its wastefulness. The only sustainable solution is a single regional tax base at the metropolitan level that can share funds between localities, prevent unnecessary development, and provide for regional and local benefits such as transit systems.

Myron Orfield in *Metropolitics* advocates a need for more affordable housing at the metropolitan periphery and property tax-base sharing. It is anyway clear that regional development considerations must go hand-in-hand with preservation, rehabilitation, retro-fitting, and incremental re-building, recognizing the many dimensions of housing and community building.

BRIT

Government still sustains its massive subsidies for highway construction, reflecting a metropolitan planning model that is shaped by the motor vehicle and its accommodation. There are many self-interested parties involved, from departments of transportation, road builders, and oil interests. Fuel is extremely cheap compared to Europe and operating costs for private vehicles are low. Donald Shoup, a professor at UCLA has drawn out the relationship of land use to car space, and calculates that the actual cost of all parking spaces in America exceeds the value of all cars on the roads. Jeff Speck in *Walkable City* argues that parking costs are massively subsidized but also that they encourage excessive driving, increase energy use, and create traffic congestion before we even come to environmental quality and public health. The 3,000 metered parking places in Savannah might therefore provide some food for thought. Absurdly, zoning codes set out rigid rules for minimum parking provision, which lead to unnecessary over-supply, high costs, and physical wastelands. It has been estimated that there might be around half a billion empty parking spaces in America at any one time, and on-street parking requires an eighty-five percent occupancy of spaces in order to be considered efficient. Notwithstanding, the private car has, up to now, been central to the American lifestyle. Joel Garreau has drawn our attention to the 1990 US Census, which revealed that across America more households owned a car than owned a water heater.

We expect the term Smart City to provide for technological improvements, and improved connectivity is an important part of this. We are at the dawn of a new age for urban mobility through autonomous vehicles, which are likely to have substantial repercussions for improved road safety, convenience, and the potential for design of urban environments. There is additional evidence that in cities there is already a move from car ownership to shared usage, which will increase if driverless vehicles became generally accepted. Of all smart, urban hardware innovations it is changes in mobility that are likely to have the greatest impact on overall urban planning, design, and management if we are to achieve livable city ideals.

JEAN-PAUL

We need to consider Growth Management, although there is a need for pragmatism. It is important that metropolitan organizations have sufficient power to address smart and sustainable growth strategies and this can only be achieved through control over zoning at a regional level with an emphasis on mass-transit systems and green infrastructure. Regional planning must bring into play new organizational structures, aimed at achieving more streamlined and smart growth scenarios. In effect, land-use and transportation require planning coordination in order to overcome a situation that has for the most part moved us in an altogether different direction, where we experience a dichotomy

239

In the late nineteenth century developers began to construct terraces that formed a consistent part of the overall streetscape without compromising the overall plan. The sixty-foot-wide lots could accommodate three row houses in elegant and consistent styles, although some terraces could comprise up to three times that number.

between land as a resource to be properly harnessed, and land as a commodity for exploitation. Put simply we need to produce the right type of development in the right place for the right purpose, and there is some evidence that we are starting to move in the right direction.

BRIT

This is a continually contested area of planning, as it must balance a need to protect against development in certain areas, while promoting it in others. It essentially involves a sustainable means of equating growth with available infrastructure, along with a degree of consolidation through metrofitting at higher than existing densities to deal with development pressures in the face of what is often an inefficient use of land. The most direct way to do this is to impose an urban development boundary within which growth can be controlled, agricultural land safeguarded, and the rural landscape and its environmental resources protected. This implies that there should be no adverse impact on the tax base, nor should it detract from existing public interests. Higher urban densities backed up by containment policies and compact urban forms in turn lead to economic efficiencies and therefore increased resilience. Raising urban density thresholds and incorporating higher value developments in both downtown and edge locations also facilitate and sustain new economic sectors, particularly in service industry.

JEAN-PAUL

Several cities have aimed to preserve natural resources through designated priority funding areas which on approval are then subject to state sponsored housing and infrastructure programs. Portland, Oregon, with a relatively small population of around 600,000, has a history of enlightened public policies stemming from its parkway and pedestrian oriented plan, designed in 1904. In recent years the city has attempted to staunch uncontrolled growth through an "urban growth boundary," harnessing strong planning controls and working in tandem with the private sector under the auspices of the Portland Development Commission. At a wider level, cities that have invested in public transit, cycle paths, and a walkable urban street matrix have experienced a decrease in car ownership, or at the very least vehicle miles travelled, with a reduction in peak travel times. Statisticians have also shown a positive correlation between property values in the city and traffic-free urban environments.

BRIT

Other state funded initiatives include rehabilitation of historic neighborhoods, streetscape guidelines, brownfield revitalization programs, and purchase of farmland development rights to protect the rural legacy. The lesson to be learned from this is the need to build a consensus between ostensibly different groups – developers and environmentalists, corporations and social activists, neighborhood residents and social housing advocates, with a range of "demonstration" projects aimed at the public good.

JEAN-PAUL

To get an accurate picture of what has been happening in city and suburban regions it is necessary to look at the actual trends. We are technically able to extract demographic, economic, and social indicators from past census figures, and one person has done exactly that – David Rusk, an ex-mayor of Albuquerque, New Mexico. In large part this represents a "missing link" that has taken up so many words in the post-Edge City debate.

Cataloguing references on available census data and prevailing urban phenomena, Rusk uses the term "elasticity" as a means of measuring the ability of cities to expand their boundaries to "capture" a certain amount of suburban development. This extensive analysis indicates that the relative elasticity or inelasticity of a central city has a major impact on levels of population growth, income, and fiscal strength. It also underscores the divisive impact of concentrated poverty, and in particular its strong role in racial and ethic segregation, as public housing has been largely constructed in the poorer parts of cities, thereby perpetuating the problems associated with distressed neighborhoods. The US Department of Housing and Urban Development's Hope VI program is attempting to address this long-standing problem by providing grants to local housing authorities to replace seriously dilapidated developments with mixed-income projects.

BRIT

The United States Census Bureau describes a Metropolitan Statistical Area as comprising a central city together with other counties that have a significant interrelationship with the core city, which must have a population of at least 50,000 with well-integrated surrounding neighborhoods. Many metro regions now have more than one core, and the Census Bureau now recognizes 667 "principal" cities, although nine out of the twelve biggest cities have been reduced in terms of both size and density since 1950 through suburbanization. Many older cities have suffered from historical constraints and complacency in adapting to changing economic conditions, so that their inelasticity has trapped many disadvantaged people in a gradually deteriorating situation, both socially and economically. Rusk's analysis indicates that while in 2010 there were two and a half times more people living in urbanized areas than in 1950, they occupied five times as much land, with more than eighty percent of the additional population living in suburban locations.

JEAN-PAUL

The question then becomes why are some cities able to extend their city limits while others do not? The answer lies quite simply in the relationship between State and Municipal Government. Municipal boundaries are often set in stone or have made themselves annexation-proof, with city expansion resisted by self-interested but astute minority populations. In most cases this process has to be anyway approved by property and landowners who are often influenced by the basic costs associated with municipal service provision. In practice, as Rusk states, an elastic city allows for better planning through its enhanced tax base, which is the most frequent driver of municipal decision making. By comparison, inelastic regions are more fragmented, with a great number of suburban government bodies that tend to adopt conservative and often exclusionary planning and zoning policies to "safeguard" their communities.

In general, a number of large inelastic cities reached their maximum population levels during periods of high industrialization, and in some cases the loss of these jobs in the post-1970 period has had catastrophic consequences. Younger cities experienced increased job creation during this period, generating a higher educated workforce, with greater gains in median family income, which matched or exceeded suburban family incomes. Less government debt in turn generated more jobs in the new economy, making them attractive to new and skilled immigrants.

Rusk conducted an "elasticity" score of 137 cities within the 383 Metropolitan Statistical Areas after making certain justifiable exclusions, all with central city populations exceeding 100,000. The evidence points overwhelmingly to the fact that the regional economy rather than the city or suburb is the driving force behind economic growth and social balance. This is given even greater credence by locational priorities of the new "creative class," which drives new job location. It is worth noting that Savannah comes into the second highest category, capturing suburban growth and more than doubling its population with increased rates of household growth. Older areas with established morphologies and cultural traditions still possess intrinsic advantages and can offer certain "lifestyle" attractions, but to remain competitive development strategies must ensure reunification of city and suburb under the auspices of county-wide government in ways that protect all parties and ensure proper levels of service infrastructure, and tax base sharing to avoid fiscal disparities. Following the lead of the Sustainable Communities Partnership established in 2009, this then paves the way for more forceful initiatives towards inner-city areas.

BRIT

We need to look closely at the success or otherwise of urban policies in the recent past. The Office on Urban Policy set up in 2009 by the Obama Administration to focus on cohesive policies for metropolitan areas, represents a belated acknowledgement of the complex policy relationship between federal, local, and state bodies that evolved during the post-war period, where misdirected policies fractured the metropolitan growth model, and made it less than sustainable. The American Recovery and Reinvestment Act of 2013 has allocated funds for "smart city" initiatives, infrastructure, school districts, and other measures, including an under-funded neighborhood stabilization program aimed at preventing urban blight through "bottom-up planning" as the best means to confront and resolve localized problems and investments.

Arguably the next step is to ensure that the process becomes less top down and more pragmatic. But we must also remember that the best integrative intentions can be obscured and compromised if they are filtered down through layers of bureaucratic controls, restrictive covenants, and lobbying from special interest groups. We must therefore sometimes accept what is practicable and achievable rather than what might be most desirable.

America must discover where the future lies before setting out to actively accommodate it – and it will be megapolitan growth that will dominate the urban landscape. Planning is not merely about accommodating growth, but also about shaping it, and, in the process, maintaining an effective balance between the urban and the rural. As Edward Glaeser has stated, "if you love nature, stay away from it as far as possible, and live in the city."

That is all I have to say at this point.

243

Mo thanks Brit profusely, with a passing acknowledgement to Jean-Paul's unexpected but appreciated contribution. "Tomorrow we will conclude our presentations leaving one more day for us to draw together the strands of our deliberations, hopefully for publication. We must hold fast to this deadline, as my latest information is that Hurricane Mathew is now hurtling its way through the Caribbean aimed at Charleston and Savannah. Tomorrow might be the calm before the storm."

So here we are, returning once again to our lovely lodge. The late autumn afternoon is still warm but there is now a seeming change in the barometric pressure that we sense rather than feel. Blue-gray clouds flit across the sky above Forsyth Park and a light rain spatters across the fountain, competing with the spurts of water that cascade through the air from the mouths of the four stoic water nymphs. This fails to dampen the spirits of visitors who pose against the animated backcloth with smartphones and selfie-sticks poised and cameras clicking, positioned towards beaming faces.

Schlomo suggests that we likewise record our comparable and productive dialogue photographically – or digitally. Right on cue we are joined by Angel from Paris, Texas. She immediately reminds us that the fountain was modeled after a similar version in the Place de la Concorde that happens to be in Paris, France, a city whose geography has been lately explained to her by Schlomo. We line up against the decorative railing, arms around each other, tallest at the back, with Mo and Martha B. squatting uncomfortably in front. The fountain, like a large cake-stand gushes arcs of foamy water from its many orifices as we pass various photographic devices, one-by-one to Angel, who clearly has unparalleled experience at getting the best out of reluctant subject matter. "A bit closer together," she calls out. "Now say SEX." We all squeal with mock indignation but obligingly extend our frozen smiles and click, click, click she goes.

We walk slowly through the nearby fragrant garden for the blind, right by the Confederate monument, partly hidden by walls that capture the wonderful fragrance and scents from the plants that arouse the senses. "Blind visitors can read descriptions of the plants in Braille," says Martha B.

It is approaching Halloween, and we pass front porches filled with scary looking paraphernalia. Enterprising trick-or-treaters are capitalizing on growing public despair of each Presidential candidate by cleverly reproducing their most prominent and recognizable features on pumpkin lanterns. I enquire about this from the eight-year-old daughter of our housekeeper who replies "yes-they're called political pumpkins, or Trumpkins in the case of Donald." I reply that they might inadvertently strike terror in young children and old ladies. She admits that this might limit the normal gains to be made from trick or treating, but that they are going to only carry around the smiling ones, and leave the snarling and scowling ones on the porches. I note that an astute market analyst might be able to gauge the popularity of each candidate by carrying out an assessment of political pumpkins on this basis, particularly with regard to the ones that equate character with extravagant hairstyles.

At Magnolia Hall we assemble on the porch, where the ever-obliging housekeeper has already laid out a tray with tall cut glass flutes of California Cava, which sparkle and fizz as they catch the streetlight.

"I think I could get quite used to these academic hardships," says Jean-Paul. "Me too," says Apolonia. "Me three," adds Terry enigmatically.

"Hurricanes seem to come thick and fast in these parts," says Jean-Paul. "Georgia just dodged one exactly a year ago with Sub-tropical Storm Ana. Then there was Hurricane Sandy in 2012, which hit South Carolina between the eyes. The worst conditions are evidently to do with the post-hurricane floodwaters. There is insufficient maintenance of drainage systems in the low country so waters fail to disperse. Local governments are always short of money and resources. If the storm hits, Georgia will then face billions of dollars of expenditure to fix its devastated infrastructure, and will expect Uncle Sam to come to the rescue with a blank check.

"Georgia and South Carolina depend almost entirely on their gas tax to fund highway maintenance and they haven't raised this since the 1840s," says Mo, who evidently keeps tabs on these things.

Martha B. says, "The Republican controlled State Assemblies consistently shoot down efforts to obtain funds in order to patch up the roads, repair the bridges, secure the dams, and protect the drinking water, so it is Congress in the end who has to pay up.

Mo reiterates that this is just what and Brit Kris and Jean-Paul have been discussing – the need for more cohesive policies at a regional level, and this includes more tax base powers, however it is best achieved.

The group is in somber mood, but cheers up at Mo's suggestion of an evening walk to the City Market, and Brit's rapid assessment of its proximity to the Congress Street Social Club. There is a general feeling that this demands a certain low-key approach to apparel. Mo and Martha B. scurry away to see what suitable articles of proletarian evening wear might be found in their joint suitcase. Brit hastily changes back to denim, Agnita to what looks like a yellow boiler suit, and Apolonia chooses to remain in a dark blue kaftan. The male contingent choose to stay more or less as they are, although, Jean-Paul makes a brave concession by removing his tie. Schlomo pulls on a new white vest with "Keep Calm" spelled out in large blue letters.

Mo reappears in a brown suede jacket over an orange sweater, and is wearing a flat, cloth cap, which fails to stop his long hair sprouting wildly from each side. Martha B. has donned a red poncho and a blue and white beret. "Very patriotic indeed," murmurs Schlomo. We drink up and march outwards and northwards, Mo suggesting an alignment along Barnard Street through the various squares to West Congress Street, which despite the rising wind gives him a further opportunity to share his considerable store of knowledge.

245

Squares offer opportunities for passive activities and informal public rapport. Informal craft making in Chippewa Square.

"Chatham Square was laid out," says Mo, "in 1847 and named for William Pitt, the first Earl of Chatham, who famously sided with the colonists in their revolutionary struggle. John C. Calhoun, the US Secretary of State and Vice President had markedly different views on the English Bill of Rights than Pitt, but as a spokesman for the south he was appropriately honored by a named Square between Monterey and Whitfield. Gordon Row is an example of the flexibility inherent in the tything concept, where redevelopment produced a terrace of fifteen town houses within the five building lots, as a perfect example of building consolidation."

I am suddenly conscious of an unsubtle pairing off between our participants. Mo and Martha B. of course leading from the front, followed by Agnita and Miles, Brit and Jean-Paul, Apolonia and Terry, and trailed by Schlomo and Angel. My instinct is to join the first pair and learn more about the local geography from Mo, or join the last pair and break into what looks like an intense and private discussion. I decide to move up front. Suddenly, Mo and Martha B. are clutching at their headgear as a strong gust of hurricane induced wind races across Pulaski Square. Apolonia makes flapping motions with her arms to ensure that her kaftan does not morph into a parachute. Mo points us to the oldest building in the square – a three-story clapboard house constructed in 1839. It belonged to General Francis Bartow – Savannah's first Confederate hero who was killed at Bull Run.

An old man sits on a bench in Orleans Square turning strips of bamboo through a

City Market on West Julian Street occupies the original central market site in Savannah. Demolition of the old landmark structure in 1954 to make way for a parking garage heralded a new era of conservation and restoration in the City, and the establishment of the largest Urban National Historic Landmark District in America. A revitalized Ellis Square, reopened in 2010, replaced the garage with four levels of underground parking, and restored the historical connections between the square and surrounding buildings. Its regeneration covers four blocks of shopping, restaurant, and entertainment uses between Ellis Square and Franklin Square. The latter was substantially rebuilt in 1985, and is the site of one of the oldest African American Baptist Churches in America. The current building was constructed in 1859, and the Square is frequently used for concerts.

series of intricate twists and turns into ornamental shapes of an indeterminate nature. Mo purchases one and hands it to Martha B. who looks confused. Schlomo buys one and presents it to Angel who promptly kisses him on the cheek.

We continue through Telfair Square, its normal whispery enchantment now eclipsed and made angry by the gusting winds, which ruffle the bent tree branches in countless directions. Mo, now having to shout, tells us that the Square was first named Saint James Place after St. James Palace in London and renamed in 1883 after Edward Telfair, a Governor of Georgia who had died in 1807. His son Alexander built the Telfair Mansion designed by William Jay that was later donated to the city by Mary Telfair to become a public museum, the Telfair Academy of Arts and Sciences, opened in 1886. The site next door was later developed for the Trinity United Methodist Church, the first of its kind in Savannah.

A short walk farther and we are in Ellis Square – the original marketplace of Savannah. The square initially served as a gathering place for plantation produce and as a distribution center, where all members of society came together. In its original form the square was surrounded by houses belonging to some of the most well-known families including military, political, business, and professional leaders. The arched brick market building constructed in 1888 was a city landmark, and its unnecessary destruction in 1954 to be replaced by a parking garage marked the beginning of the Historic Savannah Foundation.

The city market, regenerated in 1985, is just to the West, around West St. Julian Street and Jefferson Street defining four blocks of cafes and shops facing busy courtyards. It is now in denial of the impending storm. Outside tables are full, served by scurrying waiters expertly navigating the many obstacles, balancing plates and glasses. A girl with a low top bends and puts a brown arm around the sculpted bronze shoulder of Johnny Mercer, while her companion takes a photograph.

Martha B. reminds us that Johnny Mercer was one of Savannah's most beloved native sons. He is equally referenced by the number of local establishments that honor their businesses with the prefix "Moon River," a song from the movie *Breakfast at Tiffany's* for which Mr. Mercer wrote the wistful lyrics to Henry Mancini's sweeping score. It is in fact a local river, although no one has actually measured whether it is "wider than a mile."

Mo observes that there was no original Moon River, but a large inlet known as the Back River on the outskirts of Savannah, around which a young Johnny no doubt picked huckleberries. It was astutely renamed by the Chatham County Commissioners in honor of the song and its nostalgic local undertones.

A candy shop is full to bursting point, a situation that extends to a good proportion of the customers. A sign says Pet Bakery, leaving open the question of whether the options include the baking of pets or the feeding of them.

A group of girls in white shorts, blue glittery tops and cowboy hats arrive in the square, balanced on each side of a wheeled contraption, which a sign tells us is a Slow Ride, Eco-friendly, Pedal-Powered Pub Crawl. They seem strangely familiar, yes, it is the same group as last night, legs working furiously. They stop and dismount, shrieking and squealing.

One has the temerity to hoist Mo's cap onto her mane of blonde hair. Martha B. hastily intervenes, thwacks at her soundly with a rolled umbrella and grabs back the cap. The girl runs off laughing uproariously to join her companions. Blinkered horses stand between the shafts of empty carriages and wait patiently for customers, jockeying for space with hop-on, hop-off trolleys.

We cross the road and confront a statuesque monument of six, full-size bronze figures standing precariously on a large podium, menacingly pointing rifles and bayonets at our group. The inscription informs us that it is dedicated to the volunteer settlers from Saint Domingue, now the island of Haiti, who fought on the Patriot side in the Revolutionary War during the Siege of Savannah in 1779. The drummer boy depicted in the ensemble represents Henri Christophe who later led the fight for Haitian independence, as recounted so enthrallingly by Miss Anriette on Tybee Island.

Ironically, the news is already filtering in of Haiti's tin-roof shacks being shredded by mercurial winds, crops decimated and a death toll in excess of 1,000 people. I remind myself sadly that for all the hopes and intentions, Haiti is now a helpless country, distorted by poverty and reliant on aid to counter a succession of disasters and embedded malfeasance.

In Franklin Square, people are sitting listening to a jazz quartet. We sit on a low wall, Mo beating out a timely rhythm with a long pencil reclaimed from the folds of his jacket. Brit and Jean-Paul are entranced by a lady clarinetist and sit close. I recall that Savannah has weathered many a disaster, minor and major, and offer up a silent plea that Hurricane Mathew replicates the passive itinerary of its saintly namesake.

We leave the square, passing the First African Baptist Church, with a congregation dating back to 1773 which Martha B. tells us was the first of its kind in North America, and that some 200 years later it hosted meetings of the Civil Rights Movement through rallies, meetings, and services.

Just around the corner from Yamacraw Village we locate the West Congress Street Social Club. It has a patio that in an adroit bit of marketing is advertised as being dog friendly. It advertises upcoming events that include the Aquaducks and the Train Wrecks, perhaps predictive outcomes of the forthcoming hurricane, the consequences of which the club intends to defy by staying open throughout.

Brit loudly announces hitherto unsuspected skills at pool, or what I am sure Wally and Doris from the Six Pence Pub would have called billiards, and announces she is willing to take on all challengers. Several hands go up, and Brit points to the first contender.

Miles and Terry discover the dartboards and request a set of darts at the bar, while announcing they are happy to take on suitably qualified opponents, indicating Schlomo and myself. Three of us with a combined background of whiling away the occasional evening in British drinking establishments that are never without a dartboard feel fully equipped for the challenge. Schlomo, not to be outdone, picks up and throws the first

dart, which sails over the heads of an adjoining huddle of drinkers, and embeds itself in the back of a thankfully vacant chair. The rest of us generously acknowledge that this is a performance unlikely to be repeated, only to be proved wrong with his two follow-up attempts. Agnita offers to replace my hapless teammate and throws a first-time attempt almost into the bull's eye followed up by another two throws only a little wider of the mark. Miles blinks in admiration.

In the meantime, Brit Kris has made a first break of seventy-two, and is wearing a smug smile of victory, striking a Wonder Woman pose, legs akimbo with her pool cue planted firmly on the floor between them. Her opponent sportingly submits in fear of further humiliation, and heads to the bar, returning with a tankard of craft beer to settle the agreed wager. Brit announces she is ready for a new challenge, but there are no immediate takers.

Schlomo and Angel are chatting to two of the passive cycling bachelorettes from the previous evening tavern crawl, who are busy preparing for stage two of the fun, and extracting somewhat questionable party gifts from a large bag – furry handcuffs, candy penises, edible undies, vibrators, travel-size inflatable dolls, and temporary tattoo transfers are placed on the table along with other playful toys. Some are difficult to identify with any degree of accuracy but are clearly essential for any respectable bachelorette party. Angel from Paris, Texas, oohs and aahs, eyes wide, and takes photographs for her Facebook page.

Schlomo says, "When you see the positively outrageous things people do to grab attention on Facebook, you just have to shake your head sadly and say, 'Now if only I'd thought of that.'"

Martha B. and Mo approach and are neatly deflected away from the table by Schlomo. They collectively peruse the menu and order up a selection of smoked wings, nachos, grilled cheese, and black beans, and a very promising honey bourbon BBQ.

Agnita and I are declared narrow winners of the darts match and we all sit at a long table, craft beers at the ready and a Cherry Coke for Angel. More bachelorettes arrive, just as Donald Trump and Hilary Clinton appear on a big screen interrupting an important baseball playoff game. Someone turns the volume down, which can only improve the tone of the dialogue. Hilary, in green pantsuit, is being hugged by husband Bill, Donald in a dark business-like suit and red tie has his arm around wife Melania prior to the final debate. There is a lot of hooting from the captive television audience and someone switches the channel back to Wrigley Field, where the Chicago Cubs are in the process of vanquishing the Cleveland Indians, having clinched the National League pennant.

The Savannah Craft Beer Fest, to which all the brewing companies subscribe, seems to have lingered long after Labor Day, and there are hundreds to choose from. Mo raises a bottle of something called "Swampy-Fox" ordered from an extensive menu and proposes a toast to the impending conclusion of our deliberations. Martha B. is holding a similar bottle rather self-consciously, with a label that says "Yoga Pants." Schlomo responds, hoisting two bottles of Bandicoot, evidently from the Moon River Brewing Company. The rest of us raise glasses of various substances and make joint expressions of agreement.

Terry says we might like to know that the Moon River Brewing Company now occupies the former City Hotel built in 1821. This building has the unenviable reputation as being the most haunted building in Savannah, which might go some way to explaining their product names. Terry's extensive research reveals that the property is haunted by the shadowy presence of someone killed in a dual, who was, perhaps not coincidentally, a heavy drinker.

We leave around 11 o'clock, some more reluctantly than others, and head back in the direction of Barnard Street and then south. A light rain is falling and the wind suddenly turns Martha B.'s umbrella inside out. We pass through Telfair Square with its fine set of sculptural figures that mark the Academy of Arts and Sciences, and the rain splattered Jepson Center for the Arts, and quicken our pace as the rain gets heavier. Across a deserted Pulaski and Chatham Squares and back to Magnolia, clothes soaked and hair dripping, in a generally happily intoxicated state of ribaldry. The housekeeper appears, gives us a stern look and retreats to the parlor. Brit and Agnita run up the stairs ostensibly to take hot showers, followed rapidly by Jean-Paul and Miles. Schlomo and Angel take up their seats on the porch. Martha B. heads into the kitchen to fix hot chocolate. I follow up the stairs and note Terry entering Apolonia's room hurriedly and discreetly holding a large fluffy white towel, illuminated by a low-lit, gilded candelabra.

I feel suddenly tired and switch on CNN in my room. Donald is insisting he intends to keep everyone in suspense as to whether he will accept the results of the impending election. Hilary says she now wants to concentrate on the issues. Another channel is hosting an assembled panel of election coverage journalists who largely share a leftist political ideology. One says, "It's time to send the sniffer dogs into the rubble to see if there's anything worth saving."

The sniffer dogs have apparently already commenced sniffing at the Justice Department and FBI who appear, following yet more Wikishock revelations, to be in a turmoil of indecision, disagreement, denial, or convenient misunderstanding.

Trump is in more attack dog mode, with toxic accusations urging those impatient voters who have already cast ballots for Hilary to promptly recall them.

Hilary is shown wearing a Chicago Cubs baseball cap.

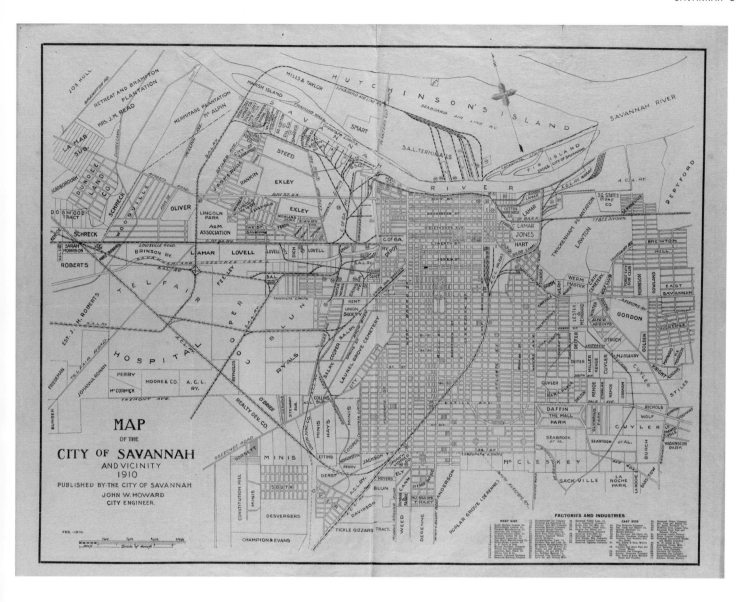

Map of the City of Savannah
and Vicinity, 1910.

The original U.S. Federal Building
on Wright Square, constructed in
1896 but partly converted three
years later to accommodate a post
office.

SAVANNAH AUTUMN 2016: DAY 6

We awake to find, from the morning news, that a State of Emergency has been declared. Georgia's busiest roads, including Interstate 95, are closing or being turned into one-way routes to help speed the likely exodus of people to safer places inland.

The first signs of strong winds and coastal flooding is forcing events to be cancelled, which according to the *Savannah Morning News* include auditions for *The Nutcracker*; the Annual Great Ogeechee Seafood Festival; the BBQ, Brews, and Bluegrass Festival; the Tybee Pirate Fest; and the Savannah Quill Writer's Convention. To make matters worse there is evidently a two-hour wait for pizza delivery. It is reported that residents are emptying stores, stocking up on generators, flashlights, and, most improbably, diet soda.

The local television station reports substantial damage on Tybee Island with storm surges seven-feet high. The roof of the historic Post Theater has been lifted off and all 3,000 residents have been evacuated. I offer up a silent prayer for the safety of Miss Anriette and her cottage.

Colleagues straggle into the breakfast room in ones and twos, some with clear hungover expressions that tend to inevitably follow a surplus intake of craft beer. Mo, however, welcomes every arrival with a wide smile and is being enigmatically described by Agnita, who is seated next to me, as "Bright eyed and bushy tailed."

"I have been considering the weather," he says. "It doesn't look good, but we cannot let a bit of wind and rain constrain our program. We are on a mission that we have to complete. While I understand that our hosts are moving students to safer ground, they have kindly made Poetter Hall available for our continued discussions."

I look doubtfully out of the window to see not yet mature trees and several individuals buckling under the fresh wind, and notice an umbrella flying through the shuddering tree canopies in Forsyth Park. Mo refuses to be bowed, and is now liaising with the poor housekeeper for a selection of raincoats, oilcloths, and any other available protective garments for our intrepid and hasty transfer to Poetter Hall.

We leave our warm and comfortable accommodation in a subdued fashion, skirting around the park and squares to avoid both the specter and consequences of falling trees. Agnes and Apolonia have rummaged in cupboards and astonishingly found rubber wellington boots, and are now splashing happily through the puddles and dislodging birdlife that has mistaken Forsyth Park for a Wetland Center. We arrive and disrobe in an almost deserted lobby, dripping rainwear creating little rivulets across the tiled floor. Martha B. strides to the kitchen in search of coffee, percolators, and cups.

We gaze out of the window towards Madison Square where the wind is hurling bits and pieces of vegetation as it heaves and whistles down Bull Street.

Mo decides to waste no time, but first he brushes water out of his long hair. He clears his throat and begins.

"Well, we have listened to the problems of the urban-suburban divide. Now how do we stitch together the two somewhat disparate sides of this apparent dilemma? It is implicit in all of this that to have a material impact on the underlying issues, we must extend our singular preoccupation with physical design and layout of privately orchestrated developments, and look for ways to resolve the underlying pressures, conflicts, and dichotomies that perpetuate the wider urban situation. A lack of consensus between participating parties, including end users, has reduced the power of architecture and planning alone to articulate the city building process or even to provoke an effective dialogue. At one end of the spectrum visionary expression has been replaced by sprawl and ostentation, while at the other the efficient 'big box' office parks, malls, and distribution centers are many steps removed from articulate urbanism, or even Robert Venturi's infamous 'decorated shed.'

"To look in more detail at how this divide might be reconciled, I am now passing the baton, so to speak, to Jean-Paul."

SEVENTH READING JEAN-PAUL GOURNIER
RECONCILING THE URBAN-SUBURBAN DIVIDE

Actually, this is not so much a *divide* as a *chasm*.

Anti-sprawl sentiment has coincided with a period where the sweeping process of federally backed urban redevelopment, highway construction, and mass production of housing, has for the most part diminished the ability of planning authorities to properly control and orchestrate production of the built environment. In the city, urban regeneration has given way to an ideology of urban management and regulation, and we can recognize a marked emphasis on the rationalization of urban space according to an agenda of order and efficiency rather than social, economic, and environmental engagement. At the same time, urban design has also lost much of its inventive spirit, particularly in relation to the private residential realm.

The Congress for the New Urbanism and the Center for Livable Communities, both dominated by architects, are the two bodies that have stepped into a public policy vacuum in bringing together urban thinkers from both the public and private sectors. The Congress and its associated charter are concerned with various scales of operation: building, block and street; and neighborhood, district and corridor. The Congress Charter comprises a mere twenty-seven statements that, put quite simply, underscore the social purpose of the urban environment and has indirectly led to a mutually workable alliance between the elusive potential of New Urbanism and the US Green Building Council. However, to make this merely an architectural debate is to miss the point. While strategic alliances have been assembled with federal agencies, in practice an urban design led coalition must establish its credentials as a vehicle that can effectively reconcile all development and regenerative imperatives. This demands an emphasis on process as well as product.

Much of the emphasis on community planning has in the past emanated from the work of Urban Design Assistance Teams established under the auspices of the American Institute of Architects. These do not necessarily have the ability to resolve complex social problems within communities, but embody the means to address urban regeneration at a grassroots level through workshops and charrettes at a time when cities are exhibiting the ingredients for strong economic and demographic change. The involvement of different stakeholders is accompanied by a wider recognition of preservation movements both to protect historical monuments and city memory. But this also requires a tied-together urbanism so that urban space has a positive and connecting function, just as it does in Savannah. What has come out of this process is a greater knowledge and concern for social justice, reflected in great part by a renewed design emphasis on the enclave, the street, and the urban place, and an equal environmental focus on pedestrian-friendly and energy efficient "green" environments.

There is, however, an important issue at stake. The more our urban environment is subject to the exigencies of purely market driven forces, the more our means of creating sustainable urbanism must be measured on the alter of authenticity. It might be argued that place identity is increasingly distinguished by commercial landmarks and associated imagery with central places embellished and animated in order to demarcate and respond to the behavioral patterns of consumers. At the same time we don't have to reinvent the principles of good urbanism. We can merely accept that it needs to allow for constant realms of adaptation through incremental and occasionally catalytic interventions in order to meet changing and possibly unpredictable circumstances to best possible effect.

Even healthy cities such as Savannah are in a constant process of revitalization, as they seek to preserve and reinforce their underlying attributes. We must accommodate change

258

Detached residential frontages in Savannah display a high degree of visual incident but also contribute to a coherent whole helping to enrich the physical qualities of street space.

to reflect the inherent dynamism of urban conurbations, not through totalizing solutions but through a responsive inventiveness in the face of impermanence. We must therefore learn, as Peter Calthorpe has pointed out, to respect the terms "contingent," "piecemeal," and "provisional." And we need to be inspired by the potential of an unselfconscious and spontaneous approach, not be inhibited by it. Design of the city will always be a work in progress. At the same time we must emphasize and elaborate cultural and historical aspects that are unique to urban places, and in the process perhaps generate a greater respect for the Vitruvian notion of firmness, commodity, and delight. We might not know precisely where we are headed, but will be better able to enjoy the ride and its repercussions.

New Urbanism might, in large part, be better termed a new "sub-urbanism" or a self-styled resurrection of an Old Urbanism – a return to the compact, mixed use, walkable and unpretentious neighborhoods that characterized Middle America. While this seems to have moved us imperceptibly towards traditional architectural forms, a need for greater densification and development coordination in the metropolitan area now places a significant emphasis on massing and relationships with the public realm rather than with external style that comes almost as a bonus. This is, only partly, a symptom related to the comfortable lure of convention and conformity. Much of it is based on a nostalgic attachment to the wholesome ingredients from another era that forged a correspondence with the American small town, seductively portrayed by artists such as Norman Rockwell, through a somewhat contrived but appealing evocation of a past and simpler age. Leo Marx in *The Machine in the Garden* underscores our not-so secret yearning for a pastoral ideal – something along the lines of Washington Irving's *Sleepy Hollow* where the cardinal image of American aspirations was a rural landscape. Literary behemoths such as Mark Twain, Henry Thoreau, Ernest Hemingway, and Robert Frost have all written versions of the pastoral. The notion of the bucolic ideal therefore runs deep in the American psyche. But in planning terms it might be said to be leading us, both literally and metaphorically, up the garden path.

The authentic small town model gained much of its credence through piecemeal development over time, with an economy far different from today where most residents, often over several generations, operated local businesses and worked within close proximity. It was in fact surprisingly self-contained, with a range of facilities, a main street, and a fine-grained matrix of local and secondary streets. It had local stores, places of entertainment, and institutions in which large numbers of people participated. If it was fortuitously located it had also access to a railway station. In physical terms, most of its residential buildings were individually constructed, according to a recognized palette of design and planning precedents, by experienced builders and craftsmen, creating a varied but consistent spatial and street pattern, and a subtle relationship between private and public realms. Above all there was a physical, economic, and social whole with an accepted set of inter-relationships.

If we compare this with the corporately inspired version prescribed by single developer clients, what we tend to get is a slick re-casting of purely physical criteria, that might be said to represent a "rediscovery" of these traditions. While this allows for a creditable reworking of conventional regulatory codes that might be technically aimed at producing more community-friendly layouts, it also tends to substitute for the many proven ingredients that make for real urbanity over time – the intricate subtlety and levels of difference that reflect genuinely diversified situations, multiplicities of ownerships, and the incidental accretions and adjustments that accrue naturally.

Let's take a look at the town of Celebration in Florida, as being representative of other, not dissimilar, New Urbanism projects such as Windsor in Florida, Kentlands in Maryland, Laguna West in California, and many more. We can only achieve so much through a "Pattern Book" approach, even with the participation of various prominent architects, but we should not dismiss it as merely a superficial collection of neo-traditional forms. The corporate entities behind these projects might well have exerted excessive aesthetic control even over such things as exterior colors, roof tiles, and styles of front porches, but they do illustrate a means of achieving consistent three-dimensional end states beyond the nebulous ordering capacity of zoning codes. We have to also accept that some degree of

Stairways act as intermediate elements between the street and private residential entrances and form a powerful design typology along prominent terraces, and embody the means to integrate soft planting.

civic commitment is necessary to ensure that urban design tools can produce acceptable levels of variety and diversity.

Michael Sorkin in *Variations on a Theme Park* discusses the "city of simulations" through an architecture that co-opts themed image as a means of marketing the less-than-authentic. Others have referred to the "analogous city" as real estate becomes dominated by large corporate retooling, offering a less than heterogeneous experience, and often accessed through skyways and elevated or submerged pedestrian networks that downplay not only the priority of environmental comfort, but the social realm of co-existence and incidental encounter.

Above all, if New Urbanism is to serve as an adequate antidote to urban sprawl it must reflect a more ambitious agenda. It must first extend its influence from the small, independent and privately orchestrated residential enclave, to the more indeterminate realm of large-scale urbanism at the township or even the city scale that can establish a level of "fit" with the wider planning process, and the large number of private and public participants that this entails. In actual fact, the notion of planning codes, design parameters, and typologies can only go so far in terms of transmitting values that all urban contributors and practitioners can subscribe to. We must also leave the built environment to be shaped in countless ways to accord with stakeholder-derived objectives. This suggests

261

a central role for the urban designer as an improviser rather than elaborator, and posits a more extensive and invigorating use of the design compendium. Peter Calthorpe's inspired notion of the "pedestrian pocket" can, for example, be insinuated within a pre-existing gridded framework based on a walkable catchment of residents and workers set around a central transit station. This suggests that we should work towards a more complex and transformative agenda based on an incremental and adaptive approach that seeks to accomplish a richer and more multi-layered identity.

Now we come to the interface with the vagaries of public policy. At a specific level of smart growth, the Charter of the Congress for the New Urbanism states, and I quote: *We advocate the restructuring of public policy and development practices to support the following principles: neighborhoods should be diverse in use and population; communities should be designed for the pedestrian and transit as well as the car; cities and towns should be shaped by physically defined and universally accessible public spaces and community institutions; and urban places should be framed by architecture and landscape design that celebrate local history, climate, ecology, and building practice.*

Good design is difficult if not impossible to define, and aesthetic matters cannot be readily set out in a building code, nor should they be. It perhaps depends on where we choose to draw the line. We cannot ignore the fact that most projects of a "neo-traditional" nature perpetuate a familiar style that appears to ring all the right bells for a certain sector of the buying public and control boards. It can also facilitate a measure of design variety through an overall interplay between similar architectural components. The more that the design code is open to interpretation and negotiation with developers, designers, and the community at large the more that consistent urban design character is likely to interact with other facets of urbanism. It is also more likely to respect the heterotopia and the inevitable urban indeterminacy and diversity of the city rather than predominate in a purely design sense.

In any event, design considerations and underlying organizational principles must form part of the development control system to ensure that the conception of the whole is of more importance than the individual parts, both to achieve design and layout cohesion, and to invoke a sense of belonging on the part of the community. This is arguably of even greater concern in older communities with established cultural values, where new patterns of urban design must establish a fit with historic preservation areas and heritage landmarks.

The question is how we can best inject into the development process the lightest of touches that respects and facilitates the engagement of citizens, that relates to the notion of city as organism, and that plugs into the latent synergy of the community. This suggests a kind of urban acupuncture as physical therapy for the city that restores and regenerates its complexity without suppressing its spirit. Much of New Urbanism, notwithstanding the importance of the transect and charrette, is directed towards architectural image, which doubtless has an authentic role to play at a civic level, but also exerts a compulsive overemphasis on the *design* over the *urban*, leading to fragmentation of our values. We need to work towards a more integral urbanism and we have the capacity to produce it, but the emphasis needs to be on responsive processes rather than totalizing products. Enhancing the quality of urban environment must reflect the needs of individuals but it should also enrich the wider needs of the community at large.

Communities don't just happen. They evolve and change for countless reasons, and are not something we can simply buy into without civic obligation. Furthermore, there is a misconception in placing an emphasis on an ideal image of community, over its intrinsic properties, which require a mix of housing, schools, shops, and different kinds of amenities in order to offer choice. The "urban villages" that make up large parts of America's oldest cities work because they have evolved distinctive characteristics, sometimes over a century or more, with embedded social and economic frames of reference that are far from exclusive. They still evolve and are open to change, addition, and attrition, even at the expense of physical coherence, and have come to represent what are often the most identifiable urban districts in terms of their physical representation.

Thomas A. Horan in *Digital Places* stresses that communities of interest must relate and intersect with communities of place. De-industrialization brings with it opportunities for

OPPOSITE PAGE
Subdivision of building lots facilitates the introduction of terraces of town houses with different widths. Variable-building heights and semi-basements within a restrictive design code creates a level of variety within a restrained organizational pattern.

both conversion and redevelopment, and this requires both public and private investment, together with innovative funding mechanisms. We might anticipate that this will extend present trends for urban revitalization, providing that socio-economic, environmental, educational, and housing conditions are satisfied, to foster opportunities across the entire community spectrum for an acceptable quality of life. This means that policies should not simply be restricted to downtown areas. Above all, planning at a regional level must engage with the community as a whole, and reverse the widening polarization between poor and middle-class economic groups and their inherent realms of segregation.

While superimposed controls are quite finite, unpredictable interactions and activities are infinite, often contradictory, and continually open to stimulation according

Individual stairways and bay windows create a distinctive and stylistic streetscape composition through elegant repetition on McDonough Row, completed in 1882.

to changing events and circumstances. This is what creates synergy. We do not have to design for it – it is simply sufficient to generate the appropriate urban conditions for it to happen naturally. For example, new live-work communities spawn the need for a range of integrative uses that can evolve and change according to different circumstances. Sophisticated information technology facilitates new connective mechanisms geared to choice and spontaneity rather than programed routine. These forms of empowerment have physical and economic implications that suggest a need for new hybrid and adaptive typologies – partly stable and partly transformative.

Now what are the roots of New Urbanism? I have asked Brit to inject some thoughts into this.

BRIT

The embryonic "New Urbanism," with its attendant promotion of concerns and credentials came about in the early 1980s, with the development of Seaside in Florida. New Urbanism is at the very least a well-articulated alternative to its sprawling suburban cousins. But firstly, it is scarcely new. The Duany / Plater–Zyberk template for Seaside is appropriately modified from Clarence Perry's original neighborhood concept apart from a little tweaking of the actual grain and a manicured nod to the rationalized traditional. It is in essence a more urbane and coordinated version of suburban Americana but primarily an architecturally precious one, designed for a single developer and marketed to a determinedly discerning and wealthy sector of the purchasing public. The jury is still out on whether the stimulating vocabulary of consistent but expressive architectural forms in ice cream pastel shades can be substantiated in terms of a model than fulfills the wider frame of urban objectives. Its design ideals, which achieve a balance of consistency and variety, might be said to resolve the elusive link between architecture and neighborhood design – not quite uniform but definitely part of the same design family. However, to utilize its exhilarating rationale for a small and privileged enclave, as a basis on which to pursue an entire urban theory that is applicable at the larger context, takes some persuasion.

The "traditional" reference applied to New Urbanism residential projects, in the main, is in the axial street plan and in the placement of built structures to define the development "grain." The key to its aesthetic value system orchestrated under the baton of a single developer is an overall unity in the use of architectural elements and massing that allows for a measure of diversity in their application through use of a design code. Architectural interpretation is caught on the horns of a dilemma between the clean lines and readily applicable styles, purloined and imaginatively adapted from a pre-existing vernacular typology, and the fact that all buildings must subscribe to the same design palette.

Its immediate relevance is that it has, quite admirably, re-introduced the concept of neighborhood design and spatial articulation into the lexicon of urban discussion and debate, through a reinvigorated assembly of familiar and appealing components. Nevertheless, it neatly sidesteps issues such as how larger urban entities grow and change in response to evolving and indeterminate socio-economic conditions that underscore the essence of responsive urbanism. A more applicable model at the city enclave level requires integrative planning, with particular regard to the cross-section of development entities that incorporate a wide social and economic mix at different scales within the regional context. This is not essentially a matter of normative order at every scale, but more about achieving a twenty-first-century agenda for planned communities at workable densities, involving a wide range of interested parties.

JEAN-PAUL

Urban "specialists" now come from a variety of professional disciplines – engineers, architects, land use planners, transport planners, landscape architects, and environmentalists. We must also contend with ever larger and more centralized government bodies that frequently operate as regimented policy silos. Thus there is a marked tendency to prioritize the maximum efficiency of individual processes, backed up by regulatory structures that often conflict, one with the other. We need urbanists who can bring all these interdependent aspects together, along with recognition of more open-ended and often ambiguous concerns such as political priorities, social issues, land use management, market economics, and affordability. Empathy with the subject is insufficient – we need skill and understanding to properly address the problems at every scale, but particularly at the regional level where there might be various layers of government controls and priorities. And now more than ever we need to actively reconcile the relationship of the built environment to ecological and resilient concerns.

There is a good case to be made that an urban design emphasis towards livability should focus equally on connective elements rather than merely on built fabric, as an uninterrupted "frame" around which to structure the overall ease and safety of pedestrian movement. This can also be extended by simultaneously addressing new and revitalized linkages and continuities. Certain types of connection can sometimes come about through group efforts. The High Line in New York City, abandoned as a freight rail structure in 1980 and given a new life as an elevated urban pedestrian connector, follows an engaging elevated course that incorporates contrasts in scale and user experience. Its exhilarating mix of passive spaces, urban texture, and varying surface treatment forms an altogether new form of public space connector. At the other end of the scale, the Rails-to-Trails Conservancy was founded in 1988 as a non-profit organization to revitalize abandoned railroad alignments and connect these into linear greenways, extending nature courses and habitat restoration initiatives within and through metro conurbations, capable of linkage with existing promenades, parks, and incidental spaces.

There is also a question as to the relationship between urbanism and density. While older neighborhoods can be tree-lined and walkable—in themselves, attractive attributes—a reasonable urban density is necessary to achieve a mix of uses that encourage both diversity and inclusionary environments. By the same token, however, density in itself does not guarantee urbanity, and whether we are building towns from scratch, or retrofitting existing ones, we have to balance the density issue with the nature of the community we are planning for.

New Urbanism has grown through common interests and informal cooperation between like-minded practitioners some of whom also happen to be active communicators. This has represented a re-focusing of values, drawing on the merits of traditional low-density neighborhoods, with a degree of variety and choice that appeal to the marketing motives of developer clients. In the process it has undoubtedly found a niche suburban market on sites of 300 to 1,000 acres for compact neighborhood developments, composed of a range of small town housing types including apartments, single-family houses, and retirement units with urban cores, civic, and retail space. However, the success of such developments still depends largely on the automobile and access to a nearby highway.

BRIT

An important legacy of the New Urbanism process is the pro-active role of the charrette as an interdisciplinary and iterative working forum with stakeholders, including local planning boards and investor representatives, multi-disciplinary professionals, and members of the community to evolve agreement on a layout's urban qualities and the components of a form-based code. The combination of charter and charrette effectively defines the approach, although the range of participants and duration of the process might fluctuate according to the complexity of the initiative. In any event it cuts through the constraining trinity of land-use zoning, finance, and local community objections. While the charter embodies and articulates the values of the mission, the charrette lies at its core. It is defined as "a collective planning process" that harnesses the talents and energies of all interested parties to create and support a feasible and, perhaps, a transformative plan while including for essential market and affordability criteria. In practice it brings together design, planning, building, and marketing, reshaping the neighborhood development approach through assembling a shared vision by capturing "consensus and compromise" through to actualization.

267

There is one major consideration however. Large urban quarters, subject to periodic change and regeneration, are rarely if ever built or redeveloped by one large developer, and the recipe for a consistent urban design language geared to a regenerated city enclave through codes and guidelines is elusive, particularly when these must represent complex and adaptive forms, together with a mix of end uses. We need to get to the real heart of the multi-dimensional problems that beset metropolitan planning with its awkward and often paralyzing interface between central city and suburbia. The charter of the 2009 New Urbanism Congress sensibly advocated the restructuring of public policy and development practices with regard to neighborhood design and place making, but falls somewhat short in coming to grips with the prevailing metropolitan landscape that requires essential injections of economic revitalization, high-density infill, and transit-oriented development. The elaborate and competitive setting in this situation is likely to be shaped as much by market forces and financial injection than by regulatory codes. It is therefore the context that must frame the approach and level of fit, rather than exalted master planners in the City Beautiful tradition. This accords more with the affinity between urban design and the complex forces of change that we encounter in the city.

JEAN-PAUL

We can recognize this in older city neighborhoods where the developing realm of streets and places was essentially incremental, and most buildings were designed and developed, either individually or in small groups, in accordance with a clear development framework and public realm. In these situations, both consistency and novelty are expressed through differences in lot width, vertical divisions, the rhythmic patterns of roofscape, fenestration, building material, color, and texture. Thomas D. Wilson lists various non-traditional facets of New Urbanism that are successfully resolved within the plan for Savannah. These relate to its multi-centric plan form that facilitates cellular growth; the hierarchy of street widths between interlocking wards; the creation of neighborhood identity; the siting of prominent civic buildings; traffic calming, introduced through the alignment of streets and their conjunction with squares; and the more elusive tendency of the plan to disincentivize exclusionary development through the concept of spatial equity together with the capacity for natural growth through incremental development.

I would now like to discuss how we can shape the Compact Neighborhood.

A key to neighborhood integration is to build in the capacity for variety and diversity at various levels along the street frontage with features that enliven the streetscape. In this case, the more participants the better, providing that they observe broad design parameters. Codes are not by any means architectural blueprints and can be open to interpretation by architects and volume builders through the introduction of a consistent place-making structure. Even small infill projects can provide effective design interfaces between the public and private realms. This is, in fact, precisely what we find in Savannah – the resilient notion of urban blocks that circumscribe streets or public places, with a mix of uses and residential types, and rear service lanes for utilities.

Current demographic trends suggest a need to maximize housing choice, which instills long-term benefits to the urban community in terms of convenience, flexibility and the process of ageing in place. An appropriate building typology should therefore encompass variants, including the integration of accessory units, positioned either within deep lots or by increasing lot-widths in consistent increments. This will, of its volition, propel diverse design interpretations. A further initiative is the "incremental growth" house starting with a simple design, which can be extended on deep but narrow lots according to future needs and resources. Joined-together buildings of whatever type or size increases the potential for urban definition, and increased population density. In turn, this maximizes development value and generates growing place identity through its embedded community values.

Many planning jurisdictions now call for an inclusionary policy for a given percentage of affordable housing. The planning challenge in designing and integrating this is firstly the need to offer a range of types and sizes together with "self-contained" phasing, and second a requirement to secure sufficient population density to support public facilities,

Street terraces are based on
consistent subdivisions of building
lots under the tything concept.
Periodic restoration offers a
controlled mix of historical
associations that can be appreciated
through patterns of shape and
texture establishing a visual
affinity with the wider qualities
of use.

a viable mix of uses and cost-effective public transport. In turn, this effectively translates into a commitment to make urban places work and ultimately acts to equate community values with property values.

This is precisely what we admire in the place-making components of Savannah. A sense of balance and composition that suppresses a tendency towards either homogeneity or heterogeneity, but contributes towards the characteristic unified "grain" of the city. Within this delicate relationship of urban parts, irregularities become enlivened points of interest rather than random assembly or something that upsets the overall equilibrium. The conclusion we might draw from this is that a clear, long-term planning framework, a detailed process of public consultation, and design parameters that embody adaptability and flexibility in their application through different development bodies are crucial in orchestrating the livable community, not merely its built environment but its social and economic properties, and its role in preservation, restoration, and place making.

This logically leads on to stylistic concerns. Style and massing are subjects central to urban design and we cannot dismiss these as belonging to a separate category of aesthetics. They are essentially concerned with the degree to which we can purposely subordinate the design of individual parts towards a more harmonious and complementary whole. They might also touch on the tangible differences between traditional and modernist modes of expression, and the overall design vocabulary that we judge to be most suitable at an enclave-building level. Clearly there must be something of a compromise between rationality and order associated with any development, and the need for aesthetic awareness and the intuitive perception of built form relating to cityscape. Cultural factors have a profound influence as do the particular environmental circumstances and the community appreciation of complexity, pattern, and harmonic relationships.

Builders of what we now term vernacular architecture and urban design were necessarily engaged with incremental additions or spontaneous infills on relatively standardized street lots. In the process they found a means to express an independence of the parts but nevertheless subscribed to the larger form creating what we can perhaps call a "rhyming urbanism" where individual elements combine in a way that exerts a balance between likeness and difference. It allows for individuality and even a sense of arbitrariness at the local level, and consistency in a more totalizing sense. We might put this down as appealing to an intuitive aesthetic value system that heightens and stimulates our interest. Post-modernism is to some extent a reflection of this – an attempt to humanize buildings and the wider urban environment through an elusive introduction of recognizable building elements that draw on familiar and even neo-classical forms, with occasional embellishments and ornamentation.

This has a certain visceral appeal to those who embrace the ideological and community values of a traditional street and neighborhood, although others might dismiss it as pastiche or even parody. The perpetual argument over style and massing is not easily resolved, but underscores an old dichotomy as to where creative architecture related to the individual building stops, and a more deliberately nuanced urban design and even a landscape based urbanism, responsive to a wider community clientele, takes over.

The architecture of community is of a similar dimension, revolving around building types that establish a designed relationship with both the public and private realms. In the tradition of Americana it evokes the internal-external functions such as porches, loggias, yards, and deep verandas, with a degree of restrained ornamentation and complexity that enhances their appreciation at a human scale. In meeting our latter-day environmental concerns the strong association of these elements with green building assists with the achievement of acceptable performance standards.

Juxtaposition of architectural elements creates diversity and contrast with spatial dimensions that heighten the visual experience of the street user.

Much of America's most enduring built heritage, in common with much European civic architecture, has a basis in neo-classicism stemming from the Greco-Roman tradition. This has not happened by chance. The *American Builder's Companion*, compiled in the early nineteenth century, provided a source book of details with a limited design vocabulary, which influenced generations of architects and contractors. In the process it helped to establish an intelligible mode of urban architecture that has to an extent been resurrected under a rationalized vernacular mantle, and has seeped its way into the mainstream design lexicon surreptitiously, endorsed by the Congress for the New Urbanism and rooted in many of its applications. Many of the stylistic influences have established the aesthetic and compositional basis for residential, civic, and ecclesiastical buildings, due, in no small part, to the structural ability of the materials employed such as wood, brick, and stone. This has generated a revived fashion for neo classical architecture where the assemblage of parts is akin to a compositional grammar, and has enabled an inherent sense of order through symmetrical and uniform proportions, articulated by both structural clarity and refinement that we can observe so well in Savannah. It also arguably forms the intellectual basis for much post-modern design.

Finally, I would like to examine the need for regulatory standards that embody a sympathetic relationship with the achievement of good urban design.

Clearly a "one size fits all" approach to zoning standards is undesirable, and accounts for some of the most wasteful characteristics of suburban layouts. As urban design practitioners have plaintively pointed out for some time, regulatory standards, in particular the overly dimensioned ones for residential-street sub-divisions, date back seventy years. If these are applied strictly in accordance with supposed "health and safety" measures, they can account for up to fifty percent of a new development area being given over to roads and other paved spaces. They have, over the years, been perpetuated largely because of their wholesale adoption for mortgage insurance purposes or as part of appraisal procedures for federal loans. Whatever the reasoning, this has had a debilitating impact on residential configurations at a range of densities.

A tested means to regulate urban design without excessively intruding on architectural interpretation is the New Urbanism "Form-based Code," and might be said to revive principles and practices associated with some of the oldest urban settlements in the United States, such as Savannah, that are rooted in tested patterns of growth, civic design, and diverse phases of regeneration. A prescription of block placement, maximum and minimum heights, configuration of entrances, and overall form can be enforced through purchase and lease conditions that help to establish a consistency of design interpretation together with overall street and place character. It can also be customized and applied to different urban density situations within a metro region. The challenge is to make this work at the more intense city scale in terms of revitalization, consolidation, and infill, which shifts the planning emphasis from a need to conform with inflexible regulatory requirements, to a positive process that promotes a dynamic vision at a desired scale and quality. This does not necessarily imply a reduction in control, but a reframing of it.

We must tread a delicate path in setting design codes that can both control and shape urban environment. In effect this requires an appropriate balance between building forms and massing that establish a relationship with the wider urban design of the district, the continuity of street frontages, and the design of the individual building. The aim is to establish what might be termed "palettes of possibilities," which strive to encourage an overall sense of order and consistency while allowing for a significant degree of variety and diversity. This requires a combination of design consistency tempered by flexibility in interpretation where the urban parts, however autonomous they might be, mesh together

Classical architectural
interpretations together with
decorative elements provide a mix
of contrast and complexity to the
street frontage.

quite seamlessly. However, in the process we must acknowledge that urban areas are not static – their component parts are in a continual state of change and adaptation.

The urban-rural transect associated with the New Urbanism approach establishes a basic ordering of elements from the rural periphery to the central core or street block level, drawing on planning theory that dates back to early city models that provided for an interconnected hierarchy of urban and rural settlement patterns. The more contemporary concept of the bio-region equally stresses the concept of mutual interdependency of all land uses that respect natural landscapes and ecologies. This must be seen as part of a design continuum that can be used to define and classify urban settlements according to the twenty-first-century imperatives of ecological fit, equity, technological parameters, and affordability.

The traditional city image represents for many an ideal urban state associated with authentic community character, long standing cultural associations and recognizable heritage. In an important sense our new ways of thinking about urbanism have penetrated and refashioned the skeptical and conservative world of real estate. It is superficially easy to purloin the down-home identity of Savannah in reincarnating an image that can be effectively marketed. Mellow character reflecting decades of slow growth, economic change, and the eclectic allure of adaptive reuse along with the intimate priorities of a supportive community, cannot simply be dematerialized and reproduced in an isolated homogenous context. The average small town evolved over many decades or

even centuries in response to changing circumstances and tribulations, and was constructed by a sequence of developers who produced a commendable consistency of detail. The economics and social landscape of contemporary development dictate that the new urban community has to be properly envisioned in planning and design terms, but with a sensible degree of flexibility in its detailed interpretation.

The New Urbanism ideal of streets and places needs to age in place and absorb the elusive patina of time, providing that the overall plan form, like Savannah's, is sufficiently robust.

Thank you.

The twin spires of the Cathedral of St. John the Baptist form a vertical landmark in the central city, rising above the surrounding streetscape.

Mo stands and proposes a vote of thanks to Jean-Paul. I add positive words of support as my presentation is next and our joint take on responsive urbanism is complementary. In the lobby there is a large notice. Tropical storm force winds of up to 150 miles per hour are being reported as the hurricane hugs the coast of Georgia. The State governor has ordered an evacuation of the entire Georgia coast, including Tybee Island and St. Simons Island. All residents of Chatham Country are being urged to evacuate to safe areas east of the Wilmington River. The American Red Cross has opened shelters across the State. Amtrack is suspending services, with trains and cruise lines being rerouted. Emergency food distribution assistance is being requested from the Homeland Security Agency.

Lunch is a potential problem, although no one seems unduly hungry. We discuss the options of returning to the nearby Six Pence Pub. Agnita wonders innocently if the impending hurricane might have reduced the queue at Leopolds. The dilemma is resolved by Martha B. who prudently produces a large bag of assorted sandwiches conjured up by Magnolia's resident housekeeper, modestly bypassing any need to obtain emergency relief from the Homeland Security Agency. Martha B. takes the opportunity to inform us that the Americans were not overly interested in initiating anything as peculiarly British as a sandwich until after the revolution, and that it was largely refined by immigrants who found untold ways of combining bread and meat. Thus America engineered such culinary staples as the hot turkey sandwich, roasted paninis, buffalo wings, sub sandwiches, sweet-onion chicken teriyakis, corned beef, BLTs, and Falafel. Schlomo adds that in Los Angeles he can order Elvis sandwiches, which comprise peanut butter, banana, and bacon. And that is before we get to the more than 100 imaginative varieties of hamburger. In turn, this has spawned countless publications, claiming inside knowledge of sure-fire diet regimes geared to stemming the accumulation of fat on the lower body.

After all this, what emerges from the various packages are only slightly less imaginative combinations of ham, roasted pork, salami, and Swiss cheese, prudently served with root beer and refills of coffee.

We chatter rather aimlessly to take our minds off the impending storm.

Martha murmurs, "Did you know the average American eats 200 sandwiches a year?"

Apolonia, who has a built-in capacity for less than useful snippets of information says, "It was of course the English who actually invented the sandwich almost coinciding with the founding of Savannah, although there was no evidence that these events were connected."

Schlomo breaks in to say that this was probably Britain's sole majestic contribution to the culinary arts.

Apolonia continues, "It is attributed most appropriately to the 4th Earl of Sandwich in what one can only describe as a sudden Eureka moment, reportedly to most easily assist his prolonged presence at the gaming tables. I am inclined to think, however, that he was simply getting disenchanted with having to put with Kedgeree every morning."

Martha says, "Well it took until 2006 for a Boston court to definitively rule that a sandwich had to include two slices of bread, which effectively ruled out use of the term 'sandwich shop' for purveyors of burritos and tortillas, but seemingly opened the gastronomic door to croque monsieurs, submarine concoctions, and Philly cheese steaks."

Terry says, "Ordering simple things in bars confuses me. I went into a place the other night promising Bar Food and asked for a sandwich. The barman said, 'We have pastrami, bacon, shredded pork, cajun chicken, shrimp, cheese, tomato, and fried egg smothered with a range of appetizing dairy products.' I said I would take the tomato. 'Sorry,' he said. 'We only serve the *stomach* buster – that's pastrami, bacon, shredded pork, cajun chicken, shrimp, cheese, tomato, and fried egg between two large loaves. We sell a lot during the World Series. We even have an audio jingle if you would like to listen to it.'"

Schlomo says, somewhat enigmatically, "If America was to become the only country to survive a nuclear holocaust we would still be able to get cheeseburgers but there might just be a surplus of televised ice hockey."

"Yes," answers Miles. "Bars can be alien territories for the unworldly. I talked to a fellow next to me at the Six Pence Pub. He had a scraggly beard and said he was a vet. I said I had a sister-in-law who was also a vet and was kept pretty busy during the lambing season in Yorkshire. The fellow gave me a funny look and said he had to leave and got on his Harley to go attend an Iraq War Veteran's Group meeting. I think they were still trying to get compensation for traumatic stress brought on by the failure to discover Baghdad's missing weapons of mass destruction."

The wind is rising outside, shrieking and howling as it rattles our rain lashed windows. Mo prudently suggests an early start, and gives a short introduction setting out my modest biography. I stand and commence.

EIGHTH READING

RESPONSIVE URBANISM: RECONFIGURING THE URBAN AND REGIONAL LANDSCAPE

Our respected professor Hooguahay has charged me with the somewhat thankless task of finishing off our presentations, partly because he has seen me taking a lot of notes and avoiding controversial issues.

I will try to bring together certain strands of discussion under the conveniently open-ended auspices of urban responsiveness, illustrated in part by some sketches of this wonderful city. And with responsiveness comes responsibility.

Responsive urbanism is quite simply about preserving natural resources, minimizing adverse land use impact, maximizing positive land use interactions, emphasizing public gain from planning decisions, promoting social equity, and, of course, not forgetting place-making. These principles can be applied to both policies and projects, and should have both individual and collective benefits. In this sense we can use the term "growth" as having a specific development direction that includes urban consolidation.

Of course that's really not so simple. We must first recognize the problems. Sprawl is everywhere across America, and for concerned urbanists there is a general consensus that it cannot remain unchallenged and unchecked. It is estimated that two million acres of farmland and natural terrain continue to be converted to suburban development every year in the United States, far and away the most profligate use of land in the developed world. The fundamental argument against suburbia is not that it has failed to provide countless millions of Americans with unprecedented levels of comfort and security, it is that there has been only marginal control and policy-coordination associated with the process to protect the public good.

278

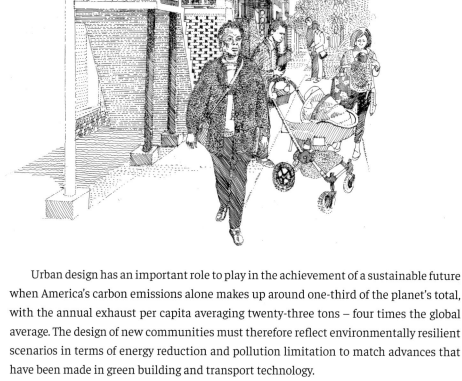

Raised entrance porches provide for
a consistent street edge. Strict
compositional geometry is alleviated
by a complex but consistent collage
of fragmentary elements, turning
streets into forms of urban
expression while reflecting the
underlying grain of the city.

OPPOSITE PAGE
Independent Presbyterian Church
on Bull Street creates a vertical
landmark, emphasizing the value of
trust lots for distinctive public
buildings.

Urban design has an important role to play in the achievement of a sustainable future when America's carbon emissions alone makes up around one-third of the planet's total, with the annual exhaust per capita averaging twenty-three tons – four times the global average. The design of new communities must therefore reflect environmentally resilient scenarios in terms of energy reduction and pollution limitation to match advances that have been made in green building and transport technology.

The impacts of environmental destruction are real, the consequences are severe, and the costs are various – to the natural habitats, to the quality of life, and to what is actually paid out in US dollars in a token attempt to correct matters. Costs fall either directly or indirectly on local taxpayers and the benefits to our urban and regional landscape are not altogether apparent. We need fiscal reforms to encourage the right sort of development

where we want to see it, and discourage it where we don't – development that is sustainable, livable, socially responsible, and affordable, particularly in terms of housing, a staple of economic development. In other words, we need responsible growth, or what Brian W. Blaesser has astutely termed "growth management with an attitude."

A fundamental dichotomy is that while suburban living is popular, sprawl and its associated problems are not. One represents the allure, the other an almost inadvertent but unwelcome outcome. Sprawl is the consequence of the way in which suburban development has been carried out, not the cause. It is ultimately the government's responsibility, in emphasizing the sanctity of our urbanization process, to ensure that the tail is not wagging the dog. The answer is not no-growth, but the need for political will to institute sensible regional planning and its necessary component initiatives of density, connectivity, environmental sustainability, and inclusionary zoning – in fact a mix of ingredients appropriate for small urban townships.

Post-war zoning has acted to reduce the range of uses within neighborhoods, while pre-existing street patterns, culs-de-sac, and lot divisions tend to constrain the capacity for physical change, preventing a greater degree of permeability and the ability to integrate new uses. Similarly, street design standards applicable across America emphasize vehicular access for all urban situations, and maximization of traffic flow for suburban conditions. In the latter case this has encouraged a mode of urbanization having little regard for environmental sustainability, walkability, or pedestrian connectivity. It is necessary to understand the precise consequences of continued sprawl and its possible remedies in the face of existing government mechanisms. We cannot retrace our steps, and issues of environmental protection, municipal taxation policy, traffic, transport, and overall land-use reconfiguration can only be addressed holistically at a regional scale.

Given the vested interests and organized resistance to any planning initiative that challenges or curtails property rights within many municipalities, controlled growth is no easy task, particularly when development values and large lot zoning might be at risk. A forceful approach is clearly dependent on government intervention in the regional planning process, particularly in the determination of land use regulation applied to existing settlements. This suggests that programs are best directed at consolidation and regeneration of areas with a consistent size and density, that integrate rather than isolate existing suburban settlements, and form part of regional growth corridors. These would aim to exploit opportunities stemming from such things as redundant malls, empty parking lots, leftover space, and underutilized infrastructure. However, whatever functions are introduced, they will need a solid catchment of users, which comes back to the question of density. There are two complementary sides to this – first is the importance of urban growth boundaries, and second is an essential focus on downtown improvement districts.

The urban design response to the challenges of a new and multi-facetted urbanism with a definite smart emphasis indicates that we have certainly turned an important corner. Smart growth is much to do with the effective transfer of information and ideas, and there should be no disconnect between tradition and innovation, and between an urbanism rooted in local conditions, and the avoidance of environmental degradation. Open space preservation is necessary to protect the environment and maintain its resources as part of the wider ecosystem. This includes wetlands, watersheds, forests, and habitat conservation. In this context, the US Department of Agriculture draws our attention to the fact that even farming and ranching have a considerable negative impact on biodiversity and that 788 million acres of land in America are simply devoted to livestock grazing.

Selected growth trajectories must be based on regional competitiveness, information, and communication infrastructure, effective public transport, human and social capital, conservation of natural resources, available housing options, and participation of citizens in decision making. One potential tool is a "transfer of development rights," not dissimilar to that used for conservation of important older buildings, where an allowable increase in floor area ratio can be transferred to an alternative site in order to retain the existing structure. This incentive-based procedure can also be used to preserve certain types of land in their natural state, while other sites can be amalgamated and consolidated for development as part of a planned growth strategy, which is itself dependent on agreed land resumption procedures and an equitable return to affected land owners. Its ultimate success of course is likely to be largely dependent on the dynamics of the real estate market.

We might look to Britain for something of a precedent. An appointed Urban Task Force published a manifesto in 1999 for an "urban renaissance" that addressed issues of density, integrated transport, patterns of employment, and sustainability. Its purpose was to recommend practical solutions to counteract urban decline, so it comprised a combination of initiatives to achieve mixed-use development, urban regeneration, social well-being, environmental responsibility, viable economic frameworks, and development densities sufficient to ensure the workability of public transport and other services. The starting point was to encourage the maximum use of brownfield land within urban growth boundaries. A basic presumption was that a well-designed urban environment can promote urban identity and development at an appropriate level of intensity, and that activity will shift towards places that have the right look and feel.

281

Within older downtown and inner suburbs having empty brownfield or underused sites, and with existing infrastructure able to sustain additional development, regeneration must be directed towards higher density, pedestrian friendly neighborhoods with a greater mix of uses. These areas offer a rich mix of existing urban conditions and historic places, often containing old wharf and industrial buildings that can be converted, some with historic preservation grants, that can leverage additional private funding directed at comprehensive upgrading, reintegration of housing, street-focused activity areas, new commercial operations, and related employment opportunities.

New and reinforced growth areas must also establish a viable catchment for regional transit systems. The Intermodal Surface Transportation Efficiency Act of 1991 allocated one quarter of federal transport funding to states and municipalities on the basis of their chosen priorities, be they roads, public transport, or cycle paths. It was linked partly with legislation intended to combat environmental impact. The Transport Equity Act of 1998 preserved these conditions and actually increased funding. Projects generally fall into two categories: local feeder systems that connect with wider regional networks and metropolitan rail initiatives, which have focused on light rail transit corridors, or combinations of rail and bus. These can increasingly assimilate the latest high capacity transit technology that allows flexibility for changes in routing systems, and can operate at a local or regional distribution level suitable for new or regenerated transit-oriented developments that function within a regional framework.

However, this all comes down to both efficiency and cost effectiveness. Commuting patterns are complex, with more trips now taking place between suburbs than between suburb and central city, and with home-based work having a potentially beneficial but somewhat indeterminate impact on road traffic. Both the dispersed location of edge city employment centers and big-box shopping malls with free parking continue to induce car travel as the easiest and most cost-effective option. In the face of this, metropolitan planners might well have to fall back on the infamous four T's – tolling, technology, tele-commuting, and transit.

To look on the positive side, in many ways the most high profile American cities might be said to be in better health than at any time in the past one hundred years. They appear to be coping well with the process and pace of urbanization together with the management of change in terms of ever increasing land value and its overall impact on urban form. Jonathan Barnett reminded us fifty years ago that while urban form was relatively unintentional, it was not accidental as it represented the collective outcome of the zoning and regulatory situation and the result of separate decisions by different bodies. To combat the worst excesses of this, Special Zoning Districts were introduced, pre-supposing the ability to impose some degree of design control and coordination. The question then becomes how far do we go in this regard.

The jury is still out on this but I think we can look to the Savannah plan for some indication of criteria for new development areas. First, we would have to formulate urban design parameters for such situations on a "carrot and stick" basis rather than strict controls, although I doubt if Oglethorpe would have put it in quite the same terms. This would be aimed at coordinating individual developments to achieve joint ends, so that the design and overall workability of the area in question adds up to more than the sum of its parts, in line with set objectives and mandatory requirements. These parameters would provide a design framework according to a conceptual approach to block form, massing, pedestrian circulation, connectivity, and necessary preservation along with landscape and ecological considerations, without necessarily prescribing particular architectural solutions. And there are so many things to take into account before we even start, for example local history, inherent building characteristics, density imperatives, and community priorities.

In this way, urban design does actually reflect public policy, but doesn't attempt to stifle creativity of interpretation. This effectively prioritizes the environment of the city as a whole and extracts public gain from private development over the course of time just as it has done under the Savannah plan, including its primary and residual spaces, and connective links. Savannah, for example, is about consistency, contextualism and high experiential quality. It was never about an overly architectural pursuit of the ideal city, where all the imponderables and unpredictabilities are smoothly ironed out into a polished finished product. We have, somewhat thankfully, put behind us the idea of the city as machine, as we are now hot on the trail of the ecological city and we need to take our stand as urbanists.

The nature and meaning of responsive urbanism must be guided by the development of a strong public realm. At the heart of this is the need for physical, social, and economic diversity as a springboard for creative urban thinking about the collective good. We can translate this into physical forms and places that will vary according to levels of intensity and size that reflect the overall community value system. This is rooted in older cultural traditions of successful urbanism in American cities to which we seem to be returning as part of twenty-first-century smart-city thinking. This constitutes a division in our planning approach to urban issues, and underscores the contrast between our idealized vision of what urban settlements should represent, and the miscellaneous cluster of independent forms that market forces present us with.

On top of that, there are countless aspects of planned environments that are pre-determined because of the exigencies of approval and expedient production processes, which conflict with the most direct means of achieving diversity without radical intervention. We can only achieve this through a process that opens up design possibilities so that we build an acceptable level of spontaneity into the development process. Building regulations are essentially to safeguard health and safety not to restrict design interpretation, but successfully articulated urban design will require carefully-crafted, form-based design codes, as put forward under the New Urbanism Charter. We arguably have to meet halfway on this – to accept sterile big box retailers, airports, and super highways, but to keep them at a respectful distance in exchange for stimulating and cosmopolitan urban environments.

There is a strong line of reasoning that public open space should represent the underlying and contextualizing aspect of responsive urban organization, establishing a set of distinct and cohesive relationships between the dominant natural elements within the region. These aspects form an interface between city, neighborhood, and hinterland: for example, river valleys, wooded spurs, and waterfronts, all of which express the ecological structure of the metropolitan region. Landscape planning policy needs to extend the influence of such features, providing an effective green framework for development and the ingredients for a fully integrated setting for buildings, circulation systems, and open space. Street planting creates a visual structure created by circulation systems which formalize the axial qualities of space, and link together recreational and amenity areas. A connective network of open squares can spatially define inner enclaves and reinforce visual cohesion and views along axial corridors, while structure planting defines important boulevards and urban fringe parks, emphasizing the continuity of the landscape linked to patterns of pedestrian movement. Within this framework we can promote different levels of diversity and development intensity in any form or scale we wish. Yes – it does sound eerily similar to Savannah.

Now I would like to turn our attention to the in's and out's of retrofit as this is the logical process that might help us take a firm step towards a more responsive urbanism. Much of suburbia represents something of an anomaly, in that even at second or third glance it is difficult to equate with rational environmental planning. At one and the same time it reflects the opportunist and exploitive nature of urban expansion that has taken place in America in the post-war period, and a refutation of its consequences.

City cores and suburbs present different but related geographies – the task is to make them more compatible and therefore more sustainable and resilient. Around eighty percent of the US population lives in metropolitan areas, but this paints a misleading picture, as a high percentage of housing lies within sprawling, low-density, suburban settlements. Average population densities have declined five-fold over the last century commensurate with the growth of suburban tracts. Land take has in fact accelerated at a much faster rate than population growth, with new development continuing to reinforce this trend. It is therefore necessary not merely to achieve a more workable pattern of urban design, but to reduce the per capita carbon footprint of suburbia, which is almost three times that of the city itself.

The challenge is to bring about new and transformative urban interpretations that help to resolve associated problems in the urban domain. These include provision of affordable housing and choice of tenure; new financing regimes; an increase in public transit options; an improved and shared public realm; and a means to introduce greater urban resilience. All of course easier said than done. This implies examining metropolitan regions as a whole using a range of performance and "quality of life" indicators, including governance, to map opportunity areas for intensification of underused land and redundant brownfield uses.

The suburb must now perform in ways that can address future needs rather than perpetuate past mistakes. Following the economic crisis in 2008, which brought a sudden halt to an excess of edge city development and underperforming retail centers, a number of municipalities have moved to revisit their regulatory apparatus and financing practices in order to tighten controls at a sub-regional level and consolidate wasteful suburban layouts. To a large extent this is dependent on a recalibration of land use zoning codes to ones that are based more on form and density. The focus must be broadly concerned with generating a more mixed-use urbanism, while respecting the ecological framework and reducing automobile dependency. This is a continuing process based on an inventive range of ways to intensify development capacity, and to make better use of existing infrastructure through improved connectivity, together with shared and integrated networks. The emphasis is therefore more geared to adaptation than redevelopment with an emphasis on cost-effective public transport, cycle-ways, and more user-friendly pedestrian systems. Procedures are now assisted by LEED tools for neighborhood planning introduced by the US Green Building Council and the Natural Resources Defense Council.

The subject of retrofit has been resolutely examined in terms of urban design solutions by Ellen Dunham-Jones and June Williamson. It involves a strategy of redirecting new growth into existing suburban areas while regenerating and transforming such ubiquitous real estate entities as low-density, residential sub-divisions, shopping malls, commercial strips, corporate campuses, and business and industrial parks into more cohesive urban entities. At the same time it is clearly desirable to retain some of their essential and beneficial characteristics through realms of innovation, consolidation, and creativity.

A new culture of compactness is dependent on connective channels of movement at a hierarchy of scales in the form of networks and matrices that extend from pedestrian links to mass-transit. These comprise streets, transport alignments, boulevards, promenades, and cycle tracks, some of which work in conjunction with each other and form the potential for new or reinforced activity nodes at prominent points of intersection. This essentially represents the mainstay of "smart growth" strategies that consolidate development trajectories and control congestion. In this way, urbanism becomes meaningful rather than simply purposeful. But it also provides something else – the ability to alleviate the repetitive blandness associated with high building intensity, by more loose-fit and low-energy insertions into the urban fabric that create flexible space and generate local identity and association.

Retrofitting has been gaining in terms of credibility, although its full fruition is likely to be long term. Its momentum has turned around the entrenched and simplistic zoning codes that have led to regimes of separation between urban functions and that have in turn led to piecemeal development and automobile dependency. It primarily acts to extend the process of adaptive reuse and infill, aimed at securing a more place-based urbanism at the enclave level as an appropriate response to changing demographics and the post-industrial economy. In this way, it embodies the potential capacity to incrementally re-orchestrate the urban form of the metropolitan region through a comprehensive and sustainable urban design approach as these regions continue to gradually morph into megapolitan ones.

Above all, this often painstaking process aims to re-orchestrate suburban entities of a certain size and type into compact, walkable, and mixed-use urban places that allow for population growth at densities that establish viable conditions for a mix of new and existing uses whose built form defines an active public realm, a main street with a diversity of uses, and feasible public transit options. In terms of meeting both market and sustainable objectives, retrofits must resolve some basic programmatic concerns, notably offering housing choice and affordability, access to jobs, and sufficient robustness so as to facilitate adaptation over the life span of buildings, with supporting networks of connectivity and use. These hold out the collective ability to energize the underlying urban structure, so that the larger the area concerned, the more infill is able to redirect the development pattern, integrate civic amenities, and increase pedestrian connectivity.

An important aspect of retrofit is physical revitalization of the public realm. This might include landscape and ecological repair strategies through pavement and planting strips; compact and user-friendly street-block sizes; well-defined public spaces; connective systems at an enclave or neighborhood scale for traffic, pedestrians, and cyclists; and both temporary and permanent urban design refits that support social and economic diversity. A fundamental initiative is to introduce a network of feeder transit infrastructure that enhances civic hubs. The challenge is to reduce fragmentation of uses and generate a critical mass of activity and density of development, which fosters pro-active approaches to mixed-use development orchestrated through stakeholder groups and public-private partnerships.

Regeneration will be a long and potentially complicated process that is likely to involve certain catalytic initiatives. As suburban areas become more diverse both in ethnic and demographic terms, growing populations can only be adequately absorbed and housed through densification, with a diversification of the overall housing stock together with a range of housing options and urban betterment initiatives. Residential retrofit might include side-yard or courtyard housing, townhouses, and other housing variants, all at different development densities just as it is in Savannah. This presents opportunities for purposeful infill to provide greater variety and choice within fine-grained layouts of compatible uses. While residential mix can vary within and between neighborhoods, the ways in which types are combined and higher density blocks inserted is part of the urban design challenge. Thus the ability to plan these areas comprehensively in a compositional as well as in a social and economic sense becomes a challenging part of the urban design process. Similarly, so-called "grayfield sites" that represent redundant or uneconomic uses in their existing locations, can be brought back to life by conversion to new uses, and the creation of a new urban grain obtained through higher-density infill. This has the additional advantage that higher real estate values increase the tax base which, at least technically, facilitates greater investment.

A significant factor that could work in favor of successful retrofitting is changing demographics, through the massive movement of diverse ethnic and minority groups to suburbs around the largest US cities in addition to a diversity of "lifestyle colonies." Inner-fringe suburbs are getting steadily denser, and this has created a continuing impetus towards social diversity and small business start-ups. At the same time, there is a substantial increase in one- and two-person households who are seeking different types of housing, including shared accommodation, small apartments, and even "accessory units" offered with a range of tenures. Retrofitting can therefore extend housing choice while zoning revisions that are now permitted in many cities can help to increase overall residential densities.

Retrofitting commercial cores requires something of a different process. The ubiquitous roadside "strip," which has become a feature of urban fringe suburbia, embodies a symbolic design language that might well have succeeded in developing garishness into a fine art, shaped by competition and invigorated by contrast and complexity, although rarely by design. The strip, in most cases, owes its form to century-old zoning districts that often followed streetcar alignments and gradually evolved commercial frontages along the most important traffic arteries, which provided direct highway access to forecourt parking. The horizontal layering of widely-spaced miscellaneous uses on deep lots, virtually inaccessible except by motor vehicle and massively uncomfortable for the pedestrian, has given rise to both functional and visual discord within the strip landscape. Transformation of this into a mixed-use focus with main street characteristics demands pre-conditions to which many participants must subscribe.

At the other end of the retail spectrum large specialist retail complexes on sites of up to 100 acres are dependent on wide rather than local area catchments. The Congress for the New Urbanism has provided examples of how commercial strips could be reconfigured into transit boulevards to better support mixed-use development and pedestrian comfort that both improves streetscape and enhances opportunities for upgrading of the adjoining development pattern to allow for greater commercial and residential densities, the effective integration of new urban places. Commercial retrofit therefore becomes the means to induce a transition from large, single-use complexes to more robust mixed-use development with active frontages based on a connective structure of vehicular-restricted thoroughfares as a means of evolving a street based urbanism.

Retail types must be associated with specific market catchments and standards. The amount of retail space in America exceeds twenty square feet per person, often in situations where commercial viability has been a secondary consideration to cheap land, short-term tax credits, and market saturation. This is unsustainable as to some extent obsolescence is built into the economic model from the very beginning. In this regard there is evidence that revitalized "downtowns" are in some cases outflanking regional shopping malls through their vitality, economic mix, and synergy between diverse uses.

The Urban Land Institute has suggested viable levels of downtown uses based on different population catchments within walking distance in order to generate viability, coupled with sufficient diversity to cultivate community identity and interaction. As urban densities increase, this then facilitates the integration of a wider band of uses that benefit from both tax-increment financing and visionary urban design. New regional megamalls or "lifestyle centers" can then continue to be advantageously located adjacent to outer highway interchanges.

Finally, at the heart of responsive urbanism is the way in which we deal with the Constitutional legalities. This essentially boils down to the tangled issue of "rights." The suburban hinterland has, from the 1950s, come to represent a zone of contestation. An obstinately recurring issue is the minefield of conflicts between what most of us see as the clear merits of smart growth, set against the protection of property rights guaranteed by the Fifth and Fourteenth Amendments to the Constitution, and their elusive legal interpretations that can undermine even the smartest planning scenarios. Normative judgments and political intervention to protect ambiguous constitutional aspects open up a Pandora's Box of precedents and priorities that raise questions over perceived freedom of action and the ability to meet fairly wide public interests over narrower private ones. We might acknowledge that the meek shall inherit the Earth, but this should not exclude them from obtaining planning permission for what to put on it.

The Fifth Amendment to the Constitution provides that private property is inviolate without proper compensation. This has somehow come to mean that owners have the right to do what they want with their property, and this opens up a can of worms when it comes to properly integrated planning scenarios. By comparison, Britain has an established and extremely elaborate government-controlled planning apparatus that relates policy making to both development and preservation, and where community value and public protection is ranked above individual interests. The planning tools to do this have been refined to the point where strict land use and building control mechanisms are adhered to without much acrimony, and there is popular support for public good over private benefit. This is backed up by the National Environmental Policy Act, which requires impact statements to set out all potential negative consequences of development.

The overwhelmingly privatized culture in the USA has, over the course of the twentieth century, reduced the effectiveness of regional planning structures, leaving an organizational vacuum. This has then been filled by an amalgam of community and business alliances, but with few shared values and even less resources to reconcile the disjunctures that emanate from unchecked opportunism. Even the implementation of an urban growth boundary supported by federal or state policies can be appealed on the basis of its specific intention to prevent or contain development. The US planning system is therefore characterized by close reference to the legal process, throwing open the door to ill-matched tussles between privately hired lawyers and disadvantaged local government bodies who are left to limply extract as many public benefits from private initiatives as possible.

The clear response is growth-management legislation, coupled with the designation and even acquisition of land by governmental environmental agencies that should be protected for conservation reasons. The notion of smart growth is not a euphemism but it has nevertheless become a catchphrase for both sustainable regional development and good neighborhood design. While these simple aspects might be dismissed as being too vague, there is wide agreement that the goals behind then serve the best interests of the community at large. However, to make this acceptable to all parties we must be concerned about fair treatment and if necessary make provisions for adequate compensation to landowners who might be negatively affected. In fact, most smart growth criteria easily pass the first hurdle of sound common sense, so there is an onus on us not to let legal loopholes stand in our way. In practice, we have to tighten controls within regional plans and procedures while keeping the door fully open to state and federal law. This really comes down to how we can best and most fairly deal with so-called property rights, and in the process make sense of policies that pertain to them.

Zoning is intended to form part of statutory land use classification and allocation in order to avoid undue interference in land matters, but here again we can identify opportunities for variance and amendment to what are often uniform zoning requirements. Jerold S. Kayden in *Smart Growth: Form and Consequences* identifies the Fourteenth Amendment's "Due Process" clause as posing complications with regard to property rights, which take planning into the shady areas of discretionary review and judgment. The issue then becomes one of fairness, so that both public policy and private rights are observed, uncertainty is minimized, and arbitrariness is negated. A central question is how far we can test the Constitution that was so eloquently composed but that came into force in 1789 subscribing to somewhat different circumstances. This sets out the rights and responsibilities of state governments and their relationship to the federal government, but it is notably the amendments, known as the Bill of Rights, that restrict what we might expect in terms of government protection. This poses an obvious dilemma in terms of the ability to restrict or redirect development on private land.

It is perhaps the same libertarians who, with an almost evangelical fervor, rush to the American Constitution for its somewhat elusive proclamation on individual rights and liberties, and who incidentally also claim that this sanctifies the right to bear arms, that has projected an insecurity and phobia into our collective psyche, and is at least partially responsible for our suburban obsession with the ingrained pathologies of safety and security. Be that as it may, the Fifth Amendment states that private property should not be taken for public use without just compensation, which seems fair enough justification to resume land for a public purpose. However, its Supreme Court interpretation is that conditions must reflect specific public interests endangered by any proposed development. This puts an ambiguous construction on public polices such as inclusionary zoning and broad environmental protection initiatives.

A clear problem here is the inevitable vagueness of many design goals set out for new communities themselves, whatever the admirable intentions. Terms such as *neotraditional, mixed use, livability, vitality, and diversity* form an important if elusive part of what we require or expect as the social, economic, and physical outcome of development over time. As urbanists we know instinctively what these imply, and how they can contribute to good urban environment. They form part of our planning and design vocabulary, and we acknowledge the benefits when we see and experience them. However, they are difficult to articulate in legally precise terms. This is made even more open ended when we are forced to concede that the built environments we hope to eventually attain must also be able to accommodate some flexibility in the interpretation of codes, with a purposeful degree of imprecision deliberately built in. In point of fact it is precisely this level of physical variance and spontaneity that we appreciate in our most successful older communities. The problem is that the level of indeterminacy implied can also be interpreted as a lack of clarity, and might come up against the legal "doctrine of vagueness" on which many planning appeals are based and, perhaps too, many succeed.

Smart growth relies to a large extent on discretionary controls, which encourage a synthesis of interests. The process is, therefore, not only somewhat open-ended in its procedural form, but potentially acrimonious in its outcome. In practice there is considerable leeway within the constitutional framework to embrace this, in large part through the need to contribute to positive environmental conservation and fiscal outcomes. We might expect that regional and local authorities could quite easily refine their regulatory instruments in ways that encourage smart growth while building in safeguards to prevent too much predetermination at the expense of landowners. The key is therefore to employ mechanisms that assist this process while at the same time resolving adverse impacts on constitutionally protected individual rights.

A central aspect of this, as outlined by Kayden, is the notion of private property and the Fifth Amendment's "Just Compensation" clause. While this clearly calls for compensation by Government to a private landowner in the case of land resumption for a public purpose that might permanently sterilize development prospects through its power of eminent domain, reasonable regulation over private land is generally considered a different matter. However, this would seem to leave the terms "economic viability of property" and "expectation from investment" somewhat open-ended, to be resolved through negotiation between all parties, or through recourse to a court ruling. There appears to be no set formula. This must be open to the construed legitimacy of the state's purpose and what it purports to achieve or what harm it seeks to prevent. In this sense there is something of an obligation on all sides to pursue acceptable forms of development that might, for example, be expedited through a simple transfer of development rights. In general we have to expect a good deal of sympathy in facilitating a legitimate smart growth agenda including much improved development patterns that are themselves being pursued by government, and in the process seek to balance public needs and private interests. If we don't achieve this then we will never get another Savannah.

A term called "tragedy of the commons" is occasionally cited in situations where private individuals or organizations act against the best interests of the wider community by depleting a public resource. It was based on an essay written by William Forster Lloyd in 1833 and perhaps gave birth to the following little ditty from Victorian times:

The law pursues both man or woman
Who steals the goose from off the common
But lets the bigger villain loose
Who steals the common from the goose

I end on this note of caution.

291

*

Mo stands up. "Thank you," he says. "And my gratitude to one and all. This concludes our presentations, but we have not finished yet. We must try to bring things together, and look to the future."

There is a look of general relief around the room, tempered by concern. As far as I can determine this is thankfully derived not from my delivery but by the storm that is doing more than just beating about the bush.

Hurricane Mathew seems to be nearing its height. We line up at the long windows, trying to see through the sheets of rain, now spiraling upwards and downwards in surges driven by the immense wind, generated through the heat and energy evaporated from the warm ocean water.

"The late hurricanes are the worst," says Mo as I am packing away my notes. "Just like your typhoons in Asia. What happens is that winds flow outward above the storm allowing the humid air below to rise. Interestingly enough, hurricanes used to be given women's names presumably on the basis of the latent dangers they might present to men. In 1979 the World Meteorological Organization belatedly discovered that men have as equally violent a temperament as most women, so they decided to alternate different sets of names. It's fortunate anyway that we now get advance warning from the National Hurricane Center, but this is not going to prevent their actual arrival. There is an important message to be derived from precisely what we have been discussing. Unless we introduce a proper means of land use control in and around our cities, we are in line for some disastrous repercussions. Our southern cities for example have little in terms of zoning, so much development has been built along river edges and floodplains with no levees in place. We live in a time of climatic change – sooner or later, but probably sooner, a hurricane will bring serious inundation with potentially severe consequences.

We hear rather than see the clanking, smashing, and uprooting that is going on in the hazy background, as unknown flying objects slam against walls and each other. The latest hurricane information is that we have at least another twenty-four hours before we see the sun again. Mo announces that our final roundup will now take place in Magnolia Hall tomorrow where we can spread out in comfort, albeit possibly hungry comfort.

The question now becomes how we get back there, or are we going to bed down here for the evening? What to do?

Brit says, "Let's make a run for it. Or, let's make a longer run for the West Congress Street Social Club." Schlomo, in iPhone contact with Angel from Paris, Texas who is tearfully crouched under a desk somewhere nearby, suggests we phone campus security. Jean-Paul wonders if we can settle ourselves with a better view of the storm. Mo who is always sensibly inclined towards the most direct approach to any problem is in touch with Savannah Fire and Emergency Services trying to hatch a discreet escape plan.

Mo of course succeeds, by assuming a bold air of authority. We seem to be the last to be evacuated so we have to turn lights out and secure locks before making a run to the doors of what looks like an armored truck. We dive in, pell-mell, ladies first, but needing a hand from the driver.

"Where to?" he asks.

"West Congress Street," says Brit.

"West Gordon Street," says Schlomo.

"Whitaker Street," says Mo, "and no stopping."

"I go via West Gordon to Whitaker Street," says the driver, and several minutes later, huddled against a wall next to Monterey Square, programmed with directions from Schlomo, is a bedraggled Angel. The doors open and she squeals and jumps inside.

So we arrive, just around the corner and more or less intact at Magnolia. Getting out is more difficult than getting in. The gate is locked and bolted so we have to surmount it, with Miles and Jean-Paul assisting everyone except Brit who hurdles it. Jackets billow out from the wind. One of Terry's knee ligaments gives way and he hops up the stairs supported heroically by Apolonia. Schlomo is hit on the forehead by a flying object that turns out to be a full bottle of craft beer, and catches it neatly before falling to the ground and passing out. We haul him up the stairs and lay him out in the hall. Angel and Martha B. rush to find first aid kit, and arrive back to find him sitting up and smiling in a slightly bewildered way, with a lump the size of a ping pong ball on his forehead and blood streaming down the side of his nose.

We walk, or in some cases limp, to the appropriate floors, driven upwards by the comforting thought of showers and fluffy towels.

It is two hours before I emerge, my clean drip-dry shirt still dripping slightly but drying rapidly from body heat.

Mo and Martha B. sit on easy chairs. Mo who has again raided the basement wine store is holding a large glass of something white. Agnita and Miles are sitting on a couch sharing the same *Interiors* magazine.

Martha B. is staring at the TV screen, most of which is taken up by Donald Trump who is wearing a cap with a slogan that says, "Let's Make America Great Again." The FBI's decision to reopen its email probe on Hilary is bringing out a hitherto unsuspected poetic vocabulary from Trump. He declares, "Hilary Clinton is corrosive to the soul of our nation, and must be stopped."

An aroused Hilary accuses Trump of stoking fear, disgracing US democracy, and insulting Americans.

Trump says, "This is a scandal bigger than Watergate. It is a disqualifying moment and it's everybody's deepest hope that justice at last will be beautifully delivered."

Hilary, not to be outdone, is telling a crowd in Dade City, Florida, "Who acts like this? I'll tell you who: a bully."

293

Mo absentmindedly switches channels. CBS is reporting evidence of what it calls the Trump Brand Blues. Occupancy and bookings at Trump hotels are down, and residents of Trump Tower have initiated a petition to change its name.

Hilary is shown arriving at a Jennifer Lopez "Support Clinton" gig in Florida. Hilary shouts, "We just heard Jennifer Lopez perform 'Lets Get Loud' – well I say let's get loud at the voting booth." To outshine Trump she is also wearing a baseball cap.

Brit walks in and says, "The trouble with politicians is that they will say anything, depending on which hat they are wearing.

Jean-Paul who is standing behind Martha B. retorts, "I've heard it said that politicians must have three hats – one to tip, one to throw into the ring, and one to pull a rabbit out of."

We all laugh, but continue to look worried. Martha B. turns off the TV and announces, "I think that's all I can take for the moment."

Our reliable and dutiful housekeeper is scrambling together what are probably the last remains of the store cupboard and deep freeze, and interesting aromas are beginning to penetrate the ground floor.

Terry enters limping, on the arm of Apolonia. Schlomo arrives at the same time with a large white bandage around the top of his head that dislodges his hair into an interesting vertical peak. He is supported by Angel from Paris, Texas, who has recovered from her hurricane ordeal and is reveling in her new role as nursemaid.

Schlomo says, "Wow, have you been watching CBS – the race for the number one position is just entering its final stage and its still unpredictable. Both sets of supporters are getting increasingly emotional: first one marginally ahead, then the other. Both trying their damnedest to satisfy the anxieties on each side, and the length of time it has taken to get a winner. It's going right down to the wire."

Apolonia exclaims, "Yes – that sums up the Presidential Election exactly."

Schlomo looks confused. "I wasn't talking about the election," he says. "I was talking about the Baseball World Series. It's tied three apiece."

"What interests me," intones Mo gravely, "is that the election is taking on the form of a referendum on the American way of life, just as we are discussing its urban values. Surveys seem to indicate an almost even split between a predominantly Democratic electorate who believe that the quality of life has got better over the last eight years, and a Republican electorate who believe it has got worse. It is not of course by any means as simple as that."

He continues, "Despite an almost total inability on the part of our candidates to address issues that are clearly of concern to a very divided nation, we must somehow try to equate social and economic frustrations with problems in achieving livable environments. It is not so much that certain groups are subject to exclusion of one form or another, although that might be the case in some situations. It is more that our supposedly 'free' system, in which we have traditionally placed so much faith and emphasis, has carried exploitation, irresponsibility, and short-termism to an unprecedented level. We have sacrificed community for an 'every person for him or herself' position. This is never more so than in our approach to urbanization and its many forces and directions. Dispiriting environments and stark inequality do more than polarize voting blocks, they deprive us of fundamental values. It is often said in America that small government is good government, and in the land of the free this tends to go down well. But let me tell you, we are now at a critical stage. I see that a new Gallop Poll reports an almost unprecedented low public trust in Government, and that fewer than three out of ten Americans feel they can rely on Government to do the right thing.

Martha B. interrupts, "There has been clear political realignments. At the heart of what we see now is an ideological confrontation between social liberal values and progressive ideas on one hand, and social conservative and economic liberal ideas on the other. The country is divided right down the middle. Who now interprets the vision of the founding fathers on equal liberties and rights?"

Apolonia inadvertently turns on the news again, or what turns out to be an extended commercial break.

"Nothing can stir up the viewing public more than the enterprising domination of the 200 or so American television channels by commercial interruptions that attempt to persuade us to forget what we have just been watching and concentrate on weighing up the pros and cons of unnecessary acquisitions," says Schlomo. "This is only barely alleviated by the fact that what they are interrupting are mainly less than compelling repeats of twenty-five-year-old sitcoms. The result is that it motivates an irresistible urge for continuous channel trawling, although on the positive side it does present ample opportunities to check for text messages."

Now we are back to the election candidates. Trump is saying, "America has lost 70,000 factories since China entered the Word Trade Organization. They come in. They take our jobs. They take our products. They make a fortune. And we owe them one and a half trillion dollars."

Later at another venue he exclaims, "I have a great relationship with China. I make a lot of money in China."

Mo snorts and says, "We don't just run a significant trade deficit with China, we run a deficit with the entire world. We haven't recorded a trade surplus since the 1970s."

I remark that Britain's own Prince Philip is said to have single-handedly coined the term *dontopedology* as the science of opening one's mouth and putting one's foot in it. Mo quotes Mark Twain to the effect that it is better to keep one's mouth shut and appear uninformed, rather than opening it and removing all doubt.

CNN is now announcing that both Trump and Clinton have placed full-page ads in the *Las Vegas Chinese Daily News*, one assumes as part of a flagrant and somewhat apologetic appeal to the minority voter.

"The real problem," comments Mo, "is that whoever the American voters elect, has the potential to inflict a less than positive future for the nation." When principles evaporate, both confidence and faith are punctured, and stability is put in jeopardy. With one candidate, we are presented with a continuation of a welfare and regulatory state, more entitlements and more income redistributions, coupled with what some might say was an unfortunate failure to distinguish between public office and a personal penchant for deleting possibly incriminating e-mails, while the average American citizen is subject to laws that are intended to protect against exactly this type of occurrence. With the other, we are subject to anxiety laden and hallucinatory claims and allegations that only survive in a fact-free cocoon. For the voter it represents a conundrum. For all the fine points in the Constitution about freedom of one kind or another, and government for and by the people, we must look carefully at how we protect this, because it is so open to abuse. Architects know that given the slightest opportunity, water can seep into any little crevice or wormhole, and weaken the entire structure, or worse. And in America, at the present time, we can sense and feel this weakening of established structures all around us."

Meanwhile, Trump is responding to a cheeky question about business practice, "I am a master of business ethics. I love business ethics."

"Business ethics is an oxymoron," says Schlomo. "It's like 'Military Intelligence.'"

"Or 'same difference,'" says Martha B. "Which rather sums up our contenders."

"Or airline food," says Mo cheerfully.

"Or responsible drinking," says Brit somberly.

"Good grief," says Terry, "and by the way, that's also an oxymoron. My grandfather used to say that when he read that alcohol was bad for you, he stopped reading."

A light supper is served on the large round table, and we lighten our consciences with bowls of clam chowder, although where the clams come from remains uncertain. The rain pounds down outside, clattering on the roof and drumming on the windows. More food arrives – chicken and sweet potatoes, shrimp and grits, and another two bottles of Chablis that Martha B. has managed to produce from somewhere.

Agnita says that her daily intake of stories from the *Wall Street Journal* reveals that the election is making people lose sleep. This leads to something called the "debate night effect," which unsurprisingly accelerates anxiety levels, and reduces cognitive performance the next day. She tells us that such information comes courtesy of an analysis of wearable devices that can evidently track this sort of thing, and is based on average sleep data from some ten million users nationwide.

"Presumably this doesn't account for the countless numbers of people who might be too afraid to get out of bed the next day," says Martha B.

"Perhaps, we should consider a return to the backroom patronage politics of Tammany Hall," says Jean-Paul. "I recall that Boss Tweed used to say he didn't care who did the electing, so long as he got to do the nominating."

"Well, what should the losing candidate do afterwards?" asks Brit.

"I think either of them could write children's books for the Under Fives," says Apolonia. "There is such an extensive cast of characters – children just love that so long as they leave out the bad language. I mean 'Crooked Hilary,' 'Little Marco,' and 'Lyin' Ted.' Could we have anything better than that?"

"Distorting Donald," says Martha B. immediately. "No, make that delusional."

"How about deplorable?" says Agnita.

"Given the current trend on Broadway, they could make the entire thing into a musical," retorts Brit.

"My husband Bill, Slinky Ivanka, Sleepy Jeb," says Agnita.

"Confused Comey," says Brit.

"Bruiser Bannon," says Terry.

"Pensive Pence," says Martha B.

"Who is that last one?" says Schlomo.

"And look at the supporting cast of pop stars," says Angel gleefully.

"I think that's enough innovative ideas for one day," says Mo. "We must get back on track tomorrow."

We bid each other goodnight, although, by the look of things, several of the couples will be bidding each other hello again quite shortly.

I mount the soft-carpeted stairs, contemplating the final morning ahead. If the storm clears we are due to depart in the late afternoon from Savannah/Hilton Head International Airport, surely one of the prettiest in the country, designed to achieve an antebellum fit with the City – an appropriate place to say our goodbyes. I will miss these people.

As is my new habit, I turn on the news prior to bed. A federal appeals court rules that Michigan has the right to prohibit voters from taking selfies when accompanied by their completed ballot forms – evidently one of the latest forms of political communication. This is being challenged by the American Civil Liberties Union, who states that this is a new form of political speech protected by the Constitution.

Both campaigns are shifting and reallocating their advertising dollars to reflect the unpredictability of the race in its final days.

The rhetoric is boiling over to match the scorched earth policy of the hurricane. Out on the campaign trail, Trump calls Hilary dark and divisive. Hilary calls Trump all noise and distraction. Trump is presenting a future where economic growth will guarantee a better future. Clinton sets out the necessity of redistributing a shrinking pumpkin pie.

I switch off the light wondering if this isn't perhaps a metaphor for what happens after polling day.

CITY EXPANSION AND THE TRICENTENNIAL PLAN

The onset of electric streetcars in 1890 stimulated city expansion in outlying areas, forming a ring of suburbs adjacent to the city, including the Thomas Square Streetcar Historic District, the Meadows, and Collinsville, increasing the urban population by ninety-three percent between 1890 and 1920. The Columbian Exposition of 1893 created a national momentum towards an attractive city environment and a vibrant public realm. Its influence prompted the eventual development of new residential "garden" districts in Savannah up to the 1930s, with new squares and crescents in Ardsley Park, Chatham Crescent, and Daffin Park. At the same time, new industrial development generated worker's communities such as Woodville and West Savannah.

By the 1920s the mobility offered through car ownership stimulated a second tier of suburban settlements with progressively larger lot sizes and separated uses. Its impact corresponded with similar situations across most American cities, with a greater privatization of space, larger commercial footprints, and buildings demolished to make room for new road space and vehicle parks. Savannah avoided the widespread demolition and resulting socio-economic polarization suffered by many larger cities, partly through its newly established Historic Savannah Foundation, and partly through the more sensitively informed use of urban renewal loans that were used to restore older parts of historic neighborhoods.

The growth rate of Savannah remained relatively consistent through the first half of the twentieth century, but accelerated rapidly from 1940 as a result of shipyard activity during World War II and thereafter as a result of national migration trends to southern states. By the 1950s, outer or "third ring" suburban developments and shopping malls began to develop, dependent on the private automobile, with subdivisions replacing the old ward system, creating a marked spatial distinction between the older city and its surrounding development patterns. However, the compact and user-friendly nature of the inner city itself and its high level of amenities has since created a greater emphasis on walking, cycling, and public transit, which reinforces the quality of urban living and sense of community. This also puts an onus on new planned developments to form part of a coordinated approach to urban expansion along similar lines, including more compact communities and reduced traffic generation. This requires continued respect for the well-established land use pattern while also reducing congestion, through traffic, and parking requirements. In 2004 the city purchased the River Street branch line from Norfolk Southern Railway, and new streetcar operations began in 2009, with other new lines planned as part of a multi-modal transportation model.

Savannah now has a diversified economy that to a large extent mirrors that of other east coast cities. The service, manufacturing, and government sectors account for around ninety-three percent of employment, with incomes well above the state average. Within

ISSUED FOR FREE DISTRIBUTION BY

SAVANNAH CHAMBER OF COMMERCE

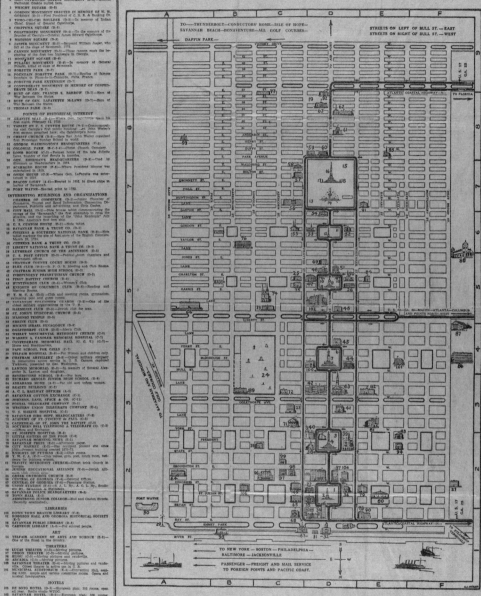

KEY TO MAP

HISTORICAL MONUMENTS AND SQUARES

1. JOHNSON SQUARE (D-2)
2. GEN. NATHANIEL GREENE MONUMENT (D-3)—General Nathaniel Greene buried here.
3. WRIGHT SQUARE (D-3)
4. GORDON MONUMENT ERECTED IN MEMORY OF W. W. GORDON (D-2)—First President of C. R. R. & Banking Co.
5. TOMO-CHI-CHI BOULDER (D-3)—In memory of Indian Chief, friend of General Oglethorpe.
6. CHIPPEWA SQUARE (D-4)
7. OGLETHORPE MONUMENT (D-4)—To the memory of the founder of Georgia—General James Edward Oglethorpe.
8. MADISON SQUARE (D-5)
9. JASPER MONUMENT (D-5)—Sergeant William Jasper, who fell at the siege of Savannah, 1779.
10. CANNON MONUMENT (D-3)—These cannon mark the beginning of the first two highways in Georgia.
11. MONTEREY SQUARE (D-6)
12. PULASKI MONUMENT (D-6)—In memory of General Pulaski, killed at siege of Savannah.
13. FOUNTAIN FORSYTH PARK (D-7)—Replica of famous fountain in Place-de-la-Concorde, Paris, France.
14. FORSYTH PARK (D-7)
16. FORSYTH PARK EXTENSION (D-7)
17. CONFEDERATE MONUMENT IN MEMORY OF CONFEDERATE DEAD (D-7)
18. BUST OF GEN. FRANCIS S. BARROW (D-7)—Hero of War Between the States.
19. BUST OF GEN. LAFAYETTE McLAWS (D-7)—Hero of War Between the States.
20. THOMAS PARK (D-9)

POINTS OF HISTORICAL INTEREST

21. GRANITE SEAT (D-1)—Where Gen. Oglethorpe spent his first night, February 12, 1733.
22. TABLET ON U. S. CUSTOM HOUSE (D-1)—Commemorating and Georgia's first public building—and John Wesley's first sermon preached here—Oglethorpe's home.
23. CHRIST CHURCH (D-2)—Here Rev. John Wesley organized first Protestant Sunday School in world.
24. GEORGE WASHINGTON'S HEADQUARTERS (C-5)
25. COLONIAL PARK (B-C-3-4)—Oldest Church Cemetery.
26. LOWE HOUSE (C-5)—Present home of the late Juliette Lowe, founder of Girl Scouts in America.
27. GEN. SHERMAN'S HEADQUARTERS (D-4)—Used by Sherman as Headquarters in 1864.
28. SCARBORO HOUSE (F-2)—Where President Monroe was entertained in 1819.
29. OWEN HOUSE (C-3)—Where Gen. LaFayette was entertained in 1825.
30. BEACON LIGHT (A-1)—Erected in 1852, to direct ships to harbor of Savannah.
31. FORT WAYNE—Erected prior to 1762.

INTERESTING BUILDINGS AND ORGANIZATIONS

32. CHAMBER OF COMMERCE (D-1)—Junior Chamber of Commerce, Tourist and Road Information, Convention Department, Publicity and Advertising, and Civic Center.
33. CITY HALL (D-1)—Note bronze tablet commemorating the voyage of the "Savannah," the first steamship to cross the Atlantic, and the launching of the "John Randolph" July 9, 1834. America's first iron ship.
34. U. S. CUSTOM HOUSE (D-1)—Note tablet.
35. SAVANNAH BANK & TRUST CO. (D-1)
36. CITIZENS & SOUTHERN NATIONAL BANK (D-2)—Note tablet marking the site of first store of the English Colonists, March 29, 1734.
37. CITIZENS BANK & TRUST CO. (D-2)
38. LIBERTY NATIONAL BANK & TRUST CO. (D-2)
39. LUTHERAN CHURCH OF THE ASCENSION (D-3)
40. U. S. POST OFFICE (D-3)—Federal court chambers and government offices.
41. CHATHAM COUNTY COURT HOUSE (D-3)
42. ELKS CLUB (D-3)—B. P. O. E. Meeting and Club Rooms
43. CHATHAM JUNIOR HIGH SCHOOL (D-3)
44. INDEPENDENT PRESBYTERIAN CHURCH (D-3)
45. FIRST BAPTIST CHURCH (D-4)
46. HUNTINGDON CLUB (D-4)—Women's Club
47. KNIGHTS OF COLUMBUS CLUB (D-5)—Reading and Meeting Rooms.
48. Y. M. C. A. (D-5)—Club and meeting rooms, gymnasium, swimming pool and game rooms.
49. SAVANNAH VOLUNTEER GUARDS (D-5)—One of the oldest military organizations in the U. S.
50. HARMONIE CLUB (D-5)—Jewish club for men.
51. ST. JOHN'S EPISCOPAL CHURCH (D-5)
52. MASONIC TEMPLE (D-5)
53. SHRINE CLUB (D-5)
54. MICKVE ISRAEL SYNAGOGUE (D-6)
55. OGLETHORPE CLUB (D-5)—Men's Club
56. WESLEY MONUMENTAL METHODIST CHURCH (C-6)
57. WARREN A. CANDLER MEMORIAL HOSPITAL (C-7)
58. CONFEDERATE MEMORIAL HALL (C, C, V.) (C-7)—Home and Headquarters.
59. PAPE SCHOOL FOR GIRLS (C-7)
60. TELFAIR HOSPITAL (D-8)—For Women and children only
61. CHATHAM ARTILLERY (D-8)—Oldest military company in continuous active service in U. S. Cannon captured Yorktown, presented by Gen. Washington.
62. LAWTON MEMORIAL (D-8)—In memory of General Alexander R. Lawton and daughter.
63. BENEDICTINE SCHOOL (D-8)—Boys school
64. RICHARD ARNOLD JUNIOR HIGH SCHOOL (D-6)
65. ABRAHAMS HOME (A-3)—For old and infirm women.
66. REALTY BUILDING (C-2)
67. A. C. L. RAILWAY OFFICES (A-2)
68. SAVANNAH COTTON EXCHANGE (C-1)
69. JOHNSON, LANE, SPACE & CO. (C-1)
70. POSTAL TELEGRAPH COMPANY (D-1)
71. WESTERN UNION TELEGRAPH COMPANY (D-1)
72. U. S. MARINE HOSPITAL (C-3)
73. SAVANNAH FIRE DEPT. HEADQUARTERS (C-3)
74. ACADEMY OF ST. VINCENT de PAUL (C-3)
75. CATHEDRAL OF ST. JOHN THE BAPTIST (C-4)
76. SOUTHERN BELL TELEPHONE & TELEGRAPH CO. (C-3)—Offices and Exchange
77. ST. JOSEPH'S HOSPITAL (B-6)
78. LITTLE SISTERS OF THE POOR (C-8)
79. SAVANNAH MORNING NEWS (C-3)
80. SAVANNAH PRESS (D-2)—Afternoon paper.
81. CITY MARKET (E-2)—Site occupied present site since 1763—Present building erected 1870-72.
82. KNIGHTS OF PYTHIAS (E-2)—Club rooms.
83. Y. W. C. A. (E-3)—Club rooms, gym, pool, lunch room, residence for business women.
84. TRINITY METHODIST CHURCH—Oldest brick church in Georgia
85. JEWISH EDUCATIONAL ALLIANCE (E-4)—Jewish Alliance club rooms also.
86. GREEK ORTHODOX CHURCH (E-5)
87. CENTRAL OF GEORGIA (F-4)—General Offices.
88. CENTRAL OF GEORGIA (F-4)—Passenger Station.
89. UNION STATION (F-4)—S. A. L. Ry., A. C. L. Ry., Southern Ry., Savannah & Statesboro.
90. SAVANNAH POLICE HEADQUARTERS (E-3)
91. TOWN HALL (E-1)
92. ARMSTRONG JUNIOR COLLEGE—Bull and Gaston Streets. (Recently established).

LIBRARIES

100. DOWN TOWN BRANCH LIBRARY (C-3)
101. HODGSON HALL AND GEORGIA HISTORICAL SOCIETY (E-7)
102. SAVANNAH PUBLIC LIBRARY (D-6)
103. CARNEGIE LIBRARY (A-4)—For colored people.

ART

104. TELFAIR ACADEMY OF ARTS AND SCIENCE (E-3)—One of the finest in the country.

THEATRES

105. LUCAS THEATER (C-3)—Moving picture.
106. ODEON THEATER (C-3)—Moving picture.
107. BIJOU (C-4)—Moving pictures and vaudeville.
108. ARCADIA (C-3)—Moving pictures.
109. SAVANNAH THEATER (D-4)—Moving pictures and vaudeville. Oldest theater in active use in U. S.
110. MUNICIPAL AUDITORIUM (E-4)—Convention Hall, seating 5,000. Ample and various committee rooms. Opera and musical headquarters.

HOTELS

111. DE SOTO HOTEL (D-5)—European plan; 300 rooms, open all year. Radio studio WTOC.
112. SAVANNAH HOTEL (C-2)—European plan; 300 rooms; radio in every room.
113. WHITNEY HOTEL (D-2)—European plan; 100 rooms; open all year.
114. JOHN WESLEY HOTEL (C-3)—European plan; 150 rooms, open all year.
115. SEAMEN'S BETHEL (B-3)—Home and club for seafaring men.
116. PULASKI HOTEL, 100 rooms (C-2)—Open year round.
117. OGLETHORPE HOTEL, 150 rooms, (C-2)—Open year round.
118. De REYNE APARTMENTS—Drayton and Liberty Streets. Fireproof. Furnished Apartments—Daily, Weekly, Monthly.

IF YOU HAVEN'T SEEN SAVANNAH
YOU HAVEN'T SEEN THE SOUTH

Savannah Chamber of
Commerce Map, 1930.

300

the County as a whole, tourism is a growing segment of the economy, with a major contributor being the Savannah College of Art and Design, which plays a significant role in the city. The main economic challenge, that echoes that of American cities as a whole, is to pursue the means to remain competitive in a changing world economy through a high standard of education, research, materials development, handling, and distribution. In this regard, Savannah can plan from a position of comparative strength, as the city has positioned itself at the forefront of effective planning and urban design. The Historic Landmark District, which has served as a successful model of urban regeneration, is now able to capitalize on the importance of environmental credentials in planning for new growth trajectories. This includes the establishment of the County as an employment and retail center and the establishment of a regional transportation authority as a critical component of this. A recognized challenge is the means to develop and regenerate through consolidation, encouraged by a shift in the tax base from buildings to land. The Georgia Brownfield Program assists potential developers by providing funds and expertise to return these sites to productive use.

The economic development vision is to provide for balanced economic growth that is conducive to knowledge-based business sectors; that is environmentally sensitive; that generates skilled job creation; and provides a tax base to support the community. This encourages the expansion of existing businesses as well as attracting new knowledge-based businesses. Mixed-use neighbourhoods with affordable housing are encouraged, with a diverse range of types. A notable aspect of this is the establishment of partnerships between government agencies, investors, developers, and lending institutions.

The protection of natural resources is an integral part of the plan, reflecting the city's social and economic values. These include habitat and tree protection ordinances, protection of surface waters and ground water resources, together with effective solid waste management programs. The preservation vision is to protect and enhance historically and culturally significant resources, including enhanced protection of wetland areas and nature reserves, and to maintain the city's comprehensive upgrading process that contributes so significantly to the quality of life of residents and as a tourist resource.

The Savannah Tricentennial Plan

Chatham County is the northernmost county on the Georgia Coast, situated between the Savannah and Ogeechee rivers. It comprises 522 square miles, and much of this comprises wetland, tidal creeks, and estuarine marshes so only one quarter is classed as development land. The City of Savannah serves as the economic, cultural, and government hub. The Savannah Municipality houses approximately half the total population of Chatham Country, which is projected to reach 334,000 by the end of the Tricentennial plan period. The Chatham County–Savannah Metropolitan Planning Commission adopted a comprehensive plan for long-term growth—a Tricentennial Plan, with a

A concert in Forsyth Park in front of the Confederate Monument and completed in 1879 to honor Confederate soldiers killed in the Civil War. It was constructed in Canada of Nova Scotia sandstone and Montreal limestone to ensure it did not contain Northern materials. Bronze busts of Confederate generals are displayed at the base.

planning horizon of 2033—the 300th anniversary of the founding of Savannah.

The plan follows a broad-based participation and advocacy process that sets out vision statements for land use, economic development, housing, historic resources, natural resources, and transportation. The land use vision is to provide a rational and consistent foundation for planning and zoning. This provides for expansion of downtown Savannah and its various neighborhoods in a way that reinforces historic development patterns and enhances their positive qualities. The concept of the public realm, embodied in the downtown squares, is extended to expansion areas through incentives to create public spaces and pedestrian-oriented places with maximum non-vehicular connectivity.

Savannah sets out three quality growth strategies. The first is the need to resolve the lack of consistency between the State-mandated comprehensive plans and the City and County zoning ordinances set in the early 1960s. The second is the need to expand areas of mixed-use development as part of planned suburban developments, based on the city's unarguable success in preserving its fine-grained mixed-use development patterns in the Landmark District. Outer suburban neighborhoods have fundamentally different characteristics however. The key is to limit uses to certain categories—single and multi-family housing, professional offices, neighborhood commercial, and such essential uses as medical and dental clinics—while excluding intensive CBD and highway dependent commercial uses that can be destructive to neighborhood development. The third is the need to preserve and enhance the public realm, in keeping with the integrity of the established planning model, and the open space and green elements that collectively account for more than thirty percent of the downtown area.

A lesson that has been learned in Savannah is that historic preservation and sensitive planning and regulatory policies can generate substantial economic benefits. The challenges associated with growth and development in Savannah echo some of the same issues faced by other city and metropolitan areas. In the downtown area, the guiding principles in developing the future land use plan according to the Metropolitan Planning Commission are the reinforcement of established mixed use areas; designation of downtown expansion areas, with compatible layout characteristics; promotion of infill residential and commercial development; designation of buffer areas to minimize land use and environmental conflicts; and the identification of expansion boundaries for growing commercial and institutional uses to serve surrounding districts. In outer areas the principles are associated with environmental protection of vulnerable water bodies; new mixed-use hubs and emerging development concentrations.

The historic district must contend with both expansion and inclusion, but brownfield and under-utilized sites must also be used to positively reinforce the compact character of the downtown area. At the same time, continued investment tends also to encourage gentrification that can cause displacement of both residents and businesses that are necessary to ensure a vibrant mix of uses and people. While adaptive re-use is generally to be encouraged, residential neighborhoods need to be protected from extensive conversions for commercial uses. Urban expansion requires urban planning parameters to be established to ensure an explicit continuity of streets, spaces, and places. Community Development Block Grants are managed by the city, and are intended to pro-actively address the problems of "brownfield" sites, which represent both vacant or underutilized areas occurring to the east and west of downtown Savannah, and "grayfield" sites, which represent outer ring underperforming commercial developments. The inner first and second tier suburbs display markedly different land use patterns, where older zoning ordinances have compromised development of cohesive urban layouts through the introduction of excessive lot sizes, and in the process have reduced site coverage and setbacks. There is a requirement for more affordable housing and mixed-use development, at an acceptable density, through consolidation of the urban street pattern. At the wider regional level, growth boundaries and related policies of community planning are necessary to ensure that the overall development is in line with the Comprehensive Plan in encouraging small, mixed use townships, conservation and urban design strategies.

Ninety-two percent of historic resources in the City of Savannah are residential structures, and the older housing stock provides both opportunities and advantages for rehabilitation in terms of maximizing use of the prevailing services and infrastructure. A listing on the National Register of Historic Places, is a prerequisite to obtain federal state tax incentives for rehabilitation. This places no restrictions on either the use or the disposition of property. The Georgia Historic Preservation Act of 1980 provides minimum standards and guidelines for local preservation ordinances, and the Certified Local Government Program facilitates eligibility for federal preservation grants and technical assistance. Long-term housing projections indicate a need for around 30,000 new housing units in Chatham County by 2030, of which around one third would be in the City of Savannah. The projected age distribution, as in other cities, indicates a marked increase in age cohorts above fifty-five years, and together with a projected increase in college students there is a need for more apartments rather than single-family homes. The best means to cater for affordable housing is to ensure a range of housing types in various locations and sizes, to ensure a diverse stock. This might require initiatives such as density bonus incentives to developers in order to induce the widest possible overall mix, or to facilitate "accessory units" in predominantly residential and mixed-used areas that have established walkable environments.

A cornerstone of the Comprehensive Plan for Savannah is that new residential developments must be subject to mandatory covenants governing what can be built within the community, acting to protect it from any future development that might have an adverse impact on its character. Neighborhoods with a historic zoning must allow for local design reviews of any alterations and new construction to ensure they meet established neighborhood design criteria. In 1990 the City entered into a Programmatic Agreement with the State Historic Preservation Office and the Advisory Council on Historic Preservation to conduct reviews for compliance with the Secretary of Interior's standards. This has enabled the City to assist in the rehabilitation of hundreds of affordable housing units. In these areas the need for standards and review mechanisms are essential. In addition the Historic Savannah Foundation continues to administer a revolving preservation fund to buy and resell endangered historic structures for rehabilitation.

SAVANNAH AUTUMN 2016: DAY 7

Morning brings us brighter news that the hurricane is moving steadily away, hopefully to some place more deserving. The sky is lighter, with a suggestion that despite the still falling rain, a struggling sun might find its way from behind the light clouds before the end of the day.

I begin to pack my clothes, and a few mementos: a selection of mounted photographs of the city, purchased on my first day from a weekend market stall on River Street; one or two books from the History Museum bookshop to join my already vast collection in Hong Kong; and a rolled up, antique engraving showing the early settlement of Savannah in all its budding glory.

Breakfast is a quiet affair. Agnita, bereft of her morning paper, is reading a book on house conversions, and tells me she is always looking at ideas for her colonial era cottage in New Haven. Miles is leaning over her shoulder enthusiastically pointing at something vaguely domestic, and nodding vigorously.

Brit and Jean-Paul are seated at the table eating a pile of fresh toast lathered with honey, engaged in a deep discussion on the various books on city form by Kevin Lynch, and leafing, with sticky fingers, through a book on townscape.

Apolonia is massaging Terry's knee.

Mo is writing another journal review, and Martha B. is catching up on emails between trips to the kitchen to clear used cups and utensils, and returning with fresh coffee and toast.

At precisely 9 am Mo takes a look out of the window, claps his hands for attention and says, "This is our final morning. This evening we depart to our various destinations. I appreciate everyone's thoughts, creative contributions, and critical thinking. This week has been a learning opportunity and it has got us well down the path that we promised. It is given to me to round up our discussion. Feel free to interrupt me at any time you think fit."

First, we have more or less got to grips with the Savannah planning model – how and why it existed; its sense of order and unity; and its organizational structure of wards and freeholdings, reflecting in the first place a social equity underscored by a clarity of intent. We can agree that this matched the ideological with the regularized physical structure that, as we have seen, can be expressed through egalitarian solutions as well as utopian ones. It can be used to reinforce power structures or underscore our need for community based solutions; to create a sense of composition but also aesthetic beauty; and to guide the orchestration of buildings and spaces, while facilitating versatile trajectories of leisure, recreation, and commerce. These surely represent compelling advantages in the design of new or reinforced settlements, marked by indeterminate patterns of growth and levels of unpredictability.

The attraction of Savannah is perhaps its historical uniqueness in terms of character – but also its consistency, vigor, and diverse dimensions. Instability is not wired in to the Savannah configuration and allure, but perhaps that is also illusory. The city has been remodelled and reconstituted over the years, but the plan has prevailed, forming an enduring permanence, constantly reinforced, refined, and reconciled with historical forces and events. It is, you see, the plan that endures – just as we can still perceive the invasive Roman footprint of 2,000 years ago in many modern European cities. But here we can experience it in three dimensions. Historical references abound, but the city is also about a continuity that still pays a silent tribute to the original homesteaders.

Savannah remains impregnated with the ancient associations and graceful values of the Antebellum South, but liberated from the monumentalities and stratifications that normally encode the subtle hierarchies of use. It is perhaps assisted in this through the blossoming educational and industrial economy now associated with the city together with the contemporary trappings of visitation. The city continues to represent, to an extent, the eighteenth-century European ideal of visual order with its predetermined emphasis on streets, squares, and public places. Its interstices provide for a timeless combinatory urbanism of city and landscape.

So, perhaps, a central question is whether the essential characteristics of the Savannah plan can be applied to contemporary settlements in our search for a more responsive and consolidated urbanism as we look to the future metropolitan model. The plan brings together the mutually supporting characteristics of formality and flexibility. It meets our criteria for a condensed pattern of urban growth and consolidation, providing an overall sense of composition necessary to bind together new development and retrofitted areas.

I seem to remember that Winston Churchill is said to have stated that American people will always do the right thing – but only after they have exhausted all other alternatives. Certainly in looking to the future we have to recall our past planning endeavors. We have had our successes and our innovations in the long history of American urbanization, but on the whole it is not such a convincing story. We can trace much of this back

Distinctive entrance conditions
create a strong street image
through a series of expressive
point references that interact with
passers-by who become participants
in the wider townscape experience.

to certain amendments to the Constitution that effectively compromised what should be the fundamental basis for effective planning and regulation by Government over the use of land to affect good stewardship in the face of private ownership. Now this is admittedly controversial and I will return to it shortly in dealing with the awkward issue of rights and legalities. In our examination of the post-revolutionary program of urbanization we have gone from one extreme of confident city building expansion in the early nineteenth century to a situation that cries out for intervention to get us back on the right track.

We can observe that planning in American city regions has changed its focus over the last century, from monocentric cores to decentralization and adaptation of the pre-existing urban landscape, and then to more totalizing solutions in response to the challenges presented by a growing population and the accommodation of the automobile. This

progression from idealism and imagination to expediency and exploitation is now subject to the more positive driving forces of livability and sustainability, but with a metropolitan and even megapolitan agenda. This can be regarded as a change in urban culture and ideological priorities, albeit a hesitant one. There are, however, strong indications in the early twenty-first century that we are seeing a return to the city, and a concern for a more integrative urbanism, with a policy-driven impetus towards urban consolidation. This is underscored by strident public demands for more responsive and participatory planning procedures, but with an equal emphasis on protection of the rural environment.

We might identify a further two forces – a normative plan-making approach aimed at more-or-less definitive outcomes, and an interventionist one based on regeneration and renewal. Attempts to reconcile these often contradictory forces through city and regional planning is one that is still unfolding and subject to multiple criteria broadly directed at the city, the neighborhood and the suburb. The conceptions of urbanism vary from an ordered and contextual process of plan making to a more incrementalist one of adaptation and adjustment. The first creates a master-planned vision for further development according to firm organizational principles while the second suggests a greater measure of public participation and self-organization. To sustain our complex, urban values we arguably need to facilitate a balance between the two. Underlying this is an elusive cultural conundrum that we must attempt to reconcile related to the achievement of both public benefit and private satisfaction – the one biased towards society gain, the other towards individual rights.

American cities in their most prolific development stages caught the wave of the European urban ideal, vested in the arts and crafts movement, and adorned themselves with beautification as a corollary to virtue. It produced a heady mix of rationality and romanticism so that the plan making process manifested itself in a high order of urban design, engineered towards a heroic purpose that went way beyond the merely functional. The demise of the City Beautiful, not coincidentally, was matched by urban intensification, industrialization, and the new borderlands: from landscape in the city to suburbia in the landscape, initiated largely through the linear street car alignments and with associated land subdivisions indirectly subsidized by publicly financed infrastructure.

309

In the early twentieth century, more-or-less at the point when America's largest cities were being rationalized through high-rise construction and new industrial development, they were subject to new realms of road building and rationalization of land holdings to accommodate the rapid increase in motor vehicles. Ideological discourse on the city was overwhelmed by a Modernist *avant garde* that put expedience above sentimentality, and found more than willing co-participants in their commercial clientele and city hall, both of which had agendas that called for efficiency, monumentality and mass production. Increasingly functional means of urban organization led to intensification of development nodes, but with an urban design of separation rather than cohesion. As central cities began to change, so did the approach to suburban development, given a considerable momentum after World War II through federally supported highway construction and tax incentives, the negative consequences of which were not immediately apparent.

In the process, and in all but a handful of cases, the role of the central city has been compromised, although in our major cities we can see encouraging signs of both cultural and creative industry regeneration. However, in the wider metropolitan regions, the pattern of land use is far from stable and has come to represent an *Exurbia* of sprawl, suburban business cores and edge conurbations representing a landscape of dispersion and frequent despoliation. As Albert Einstein said, "insanity is doing the same thing over and over again, and expecting different results."

The difficulties in reconciling what we have inherited with a coordinated approach to planning and urban design at the metropolitan level are immense, but not insuperable.

The challenge is to absorb different settlement types into a coordinated metropolitan planning model for both expansion and consolidation, with sets of networks and new modes of mobility that establish a coherent balance between the central city, its growth centers and development corridors. This must incorporate the spatial characteristics associated with revitalized city sectors within and around the core, together with established suburban communities and emerging decentralized urban edge typologies. But it must also respect and, if possible, resolve regional differences, social disparities, new economic trajectories, and localized issues such as political jurisdictions and agendas.

The Equality of Opportunity Project, a research study led by economists at Harvard and Berkeley, carried out in 2013, indicates that America has one of the lowest rates of upward mobility in the developed world. The massive growth in suburbia has acted to put the movement of jobs out of reach of many residents at a time when the job market itself is hollowing out. The conclusion is that the United States operates as a "collection of societies" with an inverse relationship between sprawl and intergenerational mobility.

We must attempt to define the specific consequences of sprawl even as we delve into the encouraging dimensions of smart growth, and there are a number of variables that we can measure including land-use mix, development density, activity centering, and street connectivity. We can also examine such things as public health indices and traffic safety according to characteristics of the built environment. Ultimately, we have to be concerned not merely with spatial patterns but with costs and benefits of sprawl as against compactness. Messrs Ewing and Hamidi in *Costs of Sprawl* have examined criteria that essentially relate to how we best live our day-to-day lives, and conclude that livability is overwhelmingly associated with compact and connected cities. From their indices of

sprawl, one of the most offending counties in America, somewhat ironically, is Oglethorpe County not too far away in Athens-Clarke, Georgia. Not too surprisingly, New York County, part of the NYC, New Jersey, Long Island Metropolitan Area, is the most compact.

311

Our initial presentations explained why things happened from a historical perspective. Our final presentations hold an important key, and we need to look at them together. The first is concerned with a reshaping of the Metropolitan Area through coordinated consolidation as we head towards a megapolitan model of growth; the second with how we reconcile the divide between urban and suburban growth and change; and the third towards a responsive urbanism. These all have in common the need for a controlled growth management approach. At the same time, some aspects of sprawl might well be acceptable, providing we can protect ecosystems and productive farmland.

It is quite fundamental to our current thinking that we adopt a measure of "elasticity" to support the capability of metropolitan regions and their central cities in order to set clear growth boundaries. We must relate inevitable population growth to a great many criteria including employment, fiscal robustness, and higher density neighborhoods. Cities vary in terms of their degree of elasticity, with older "metropolitan statistical areas" having insufficient authority over planning, environmental protection, and taxation. It is notably the younger cities that are, at least technically, better able to annex land and extend their areas of control.

The answer clearly lies in a more positive relationship between State and Municipal Government bodies allowing the more elastic cities to better orchestrate growth, enhance the tax base, and set development and planning policy at a reasonably comprehensive level. It has been established that the regional economy is the mainstay of economic growth, and that metropolitan areas with an effective integration of city and suburb are better able to absorb household formation and new job location. They also, not coincidentally, have less economic segregation and better ethnic and racial integration. This is at a time when cities are in the throes of responding to the locational priorities, and economic and cultural aspirations of a new creative and information-oriented class. It is true that city regions require fiscal stimulus but we also need smart initiatives to regenerate our existing cities, prevent blight, and better integrate public services, infrastructure, and new modes of transport.

So the next question is, how do we achieve a more responsive urbanism? There are many sides to this, and in recognition of the problems we face I can only reiterate what has already been stated – that our primary goals must be to preserve natural resources, to minimize adverse land use impact, to maximize positive land use interactions, emphasize planning gain, and ensure social equity.

So from all our discussion I would like to hear your brief views on how we take this forward in one way or another. Let us divide these views into two parts. First, what should our approach be assuming we are setting out some objective policies? I'm going to ask you all in turn.

We all stick our hands up like obedient children.

JEAN-PAUL

We must adopt a controlled growth approach. This is dependent on positive intervention in the regional planning process. We must build on cohesive policies, with ultimate authority resting with metropolitan rather than municipal government. Growth management means the establishment of firm boundaries to staunch uncontrolled growth and gradual social and economic deterioration.

AGNITA

Boost densities through incremental retrofit, with revitalization programs combining new and upgraded developments to avoid fragmented urbanization.

BRIT

Build consensus between all the many participants in the development process including public and private groups through stakeholder participation events.

TERRY

Develop a limited range of demonstration projects that explain and illustrate the scope of intentions, and to show exactly how "retrofit" can act to rectify and consolidate the worst excesses of suburbanization and better fit these areas within metropolitan growth corridors.

APOLONIA

Establish clear policies for smart growth in relation to the sanctity of private property rights. This is of critical importance, but also reflects concern over government intervention in a situation where public and private interests do not necessarily coincide. At the heart of this are two amendments to the American Constitution itself, but we must be able to reconcile public good over private interests to meet regional planning objectives and at the same time serve the best interests of the community. A shift towards growth corridors in response to various economic stimuli points to the need for regional bodies geared to the coordination of commercial, housing, and transit investment. This must be responsive to both technological and demographic trends, balancing regional growth with a resilient repurposing of the city.

MILES

Stemming from all this, our approach must be to ensure fair treatment to all parties so that, as we have underscored in the presentations, both public policy and private rights are observed, uncertainty minimized, and arbitrariness avoided.

SCHLOMO

313

We need a suitable definition of what constitutes the acceptable and achievable urban condition or conditions – what we might call the "urban life-world" as we head towards megalopolis. This must combine communal and new technological frames of reference with a large dose of ecological concern. The most profound urban design themes have not changed that much, and we are not dealing with static or visually comfortable situations but resilient ones. This suggests that our thinking should be focused on a new urban scale and new modes of transit. Most of us are now effectively living in the global city. This means balancing organizational efficiency with urban forms that are capable of infinite adjustment and extension.

ME

We must equate the legitimacy of the state's requirement for land use control with the "Just Compensation" clause in the Fifth Amendment. The power of eminent domain must also match expectation from investors, and the more we can clarify this as part of due process, the more we can properly meet the central purpose of urban design.

MO

The second part of our conclusion must relate to how we emphasize our smart urban design response, whereby we examine regional development potential through it's capacity for urban transformation into what we might term "consolidated development areas." This acknowledges that we must prioritize metropolitan growth trajectories that are able to resolve the negative characteristics of sprawl – the bigger and more consolidated the better. This brings us back to the lessons we can learn from Savannah assuming we can invoke the further potential of New Urbanism theory in contributing to livable townships. The model for this must be responsive to evolving residential requirements at appropriate densities, implemented by different private and public bodies in order to achieve a multi-layered identity and sufficient population catchment for the introduction of cost-effective public transit.

AGNITA

The direction must be to achieve a more integrative urbanism, with a strong public realm and a planning framework that can absorb levels of development at different intensities but which also reflects the wider community value system.

MILES

A connective network of spaces, just as in the case of Savannah, in the form of open squares as a means of formalizing the development framework, and defining enclaves while introducing "green" and passive recreational uses. The repetitive form of the grid, whether orthogonal or not, can establish an organizational and integrated setting for building groups and circulation, suitable for sequences of phasing.

TERRY

Spatial planning policy should seek to extend the influence of natural landscape features and native tree species through consolidated development areas, so as to provide a consistently green framework for urban design.

BRIT

We should attempt to integrate the notion of trust lots on which to erect essential community, cultural, and ecclesiastical buildings as a patterned sequence of accessible public uses that also act as urban landmarks. We must ensure consensus among all stakeholders, including government and investor representatives, through interdisciplinary charrettes. This should set the basis for innovative and well integrated forms of design and activity.

APOLONIA

New planning frameworks must be capable of transforming areas of sprawl into compact, walkable, and mixed-use, urban places, served by a hierarchy of complementary uses together with community focus. Retrofitting commercial strips must be based on viability, catchment, and potential reuse and integration at the urban scale within a more condensed and connective structure based on main streets and precincts.

SCHLOMO

We need to consider retrofitting in detail. This represents a means of properly directing new development and converting abandoned or uneconomic uses within suburban complexes in order to align growth patterns into urban townships at a variety of scales and densities. But let us not forget the heterotopia.

JEAN-PAUL

In shaping compact neighborhoods we can adhere to much of the New Urbanism agenda advocated under its Congress Charter, and extend this to various scales of operation at the building block, enclave, and district levels. The Charter advocates the restructuring of public policy and development practice, and we should recognize and identify new opportunities for its applications within the metropolitan landscape.

ME

To create a genuinely responsive framework for urban design that respects the inevitable consultations, processes, and procedures, we need to formulate form-based parameters for each case. These must establish organizational principles for a street and place oriented urbanism without prescribing detailed architectural solutions. We have to acknowledge the process of change and indeterminacy, and welcome diversity as part of a consolidated development area model.

315

MO

Well, such a model might well offer a realistic approach to a "garden city" metropolis. It is perhaps as much a social and environmental experiment as a physical planning one. While the original garden city vision represented a utopian dream of escape from urban squalor to the more egalitarian lifestyle of agriculture and artisanship, our ideas for the future city are somewhat different but similarly pioneering. They do have similar origins however. The first garden cities set out principles, which in turn informed the massive social housing programs that were to come. Similarly, American suburbia began as planned rural retreats from the crowded and polluted cities with the first "guides to rural residences" later giving rise to more modest versions of single-family homes on the urban outskirts, and later well beyond.

There was, however, one clear difference – while the British model was essentially a planned one, the American follow-through arose largely from privately sponsored streetcar suburbs. These later mushroomed into sprawling privately orchestrated exurbs, partly subsidized by single-minded federal programs, with little overall coordination and largely bereft of planning or design control. We are now trying to reconcile this situation with the growing patterns of urbanization that are giving rise to the new megalopolis. The contradictory forces at play are still unfolding and are broadly directed at the city, the suburb, and the neighborhood. If we are to properly coordinate this in terms of a more condensed and community oriented urbanism we need comprehensive planning action in line with purposeful land management.

As we have heard, much of this comes down to land value and control. The establishment of urban growth boundaries is a good start, as on one hand it circumscribes available development areas, while on the other it allows for this to protect areas of ecological, environmental, and rural recreational value in the form of green belts and eco-corridors.

Similarly, we cannot escape the next step – that of compulsory resumption or effective forms of land exchange to counteract the almost purely market-driven economics in relation to land, and its wasteful and unsustainable repercussions. This is of course a matter of degree. There is no real reason why land-use control cannot be put into the hands of a Government agency, as part of a consolidated growth model. It is admittedly contentious as we have pointed out – the market driven economics of land needs a conciliatory approach between government and landowners that must be carefully orchestrated. It must be based on maintaining use value, but in accordance with metropolitan planning priorities. It must also be based on fair compensation to all affected parties, as and when designated development areas proceed, possibly with private owners being granted stakes in a consolidated development area trust.

This posits development control under the auspices of a metropolitan agency and allows for both comprehensive planning and the integration of affordable housing. However, the main benefit is "certainty," which establishes opportunities for capturing land value and long-term stewardship that includes community infrastructure. Such a vision goes beyond the garden city to the livable city that aligns with other parallel consolidation and regeneration approaches, including renewal of brownfield sites. In this way, the promotion of new development plugs neatly into existing urban entities that already posses a diversity of place associations, existing infrastructure, and growth trajectories. The key term is "planned growth," positively targeted at a staged release of land for housing and other uses according to anticipated changes in demand.

Now I want to make a necessary point. Everyone has a political opinion – that is his or her right. It has been our fortune, or quite possibly our misfortune, to be gathered here during the final weeks of the presidential election. The Constitution is a wonderful document – make no mistake about it. Along with the First Amendment, Bill of Rights, and separation of power structures, we can recognize this as the foundation on which the land of the free has grown to maturity. It reflects the aspirations of society as a whole, poetically reflected in "The Star Spangled Banner." But, and it is a big but, its very freedoms are in need of greater consideration and definition, and perhaps our presidential election process has acted to reveal how our system can so easily be tested. The debates have become controlled largely through television channels, through sound bites, sloganeering, and insults, intended only to embarrass and denigrate. Whatever policies are there in the background, they have not been on display in the foreground.

Freedom requires constant monitoring to make sure it works in everyone's interests and that it does not constrain honest endeavor, or create chaos. We must ensure that it is not distorted, manipulated, and, perhaps, ultimately destroyed by artificiality or vested interests under its innocent cloak. But when the strings that bind it together start to loosen, or become subject to bogus interpretation, it needs to be attended to.

Several years ago we very nearly experienced a financial meltdown of the entire banking industry through the freewheeling practices of the shadow banking markets manipulated by predatory lenders who peddled subprime loans operating under an archaic regulatory structure. According to the then Secretary of the Treasury, Hank Paulson, it eventually took a decision by government to acquire preferred-equity stakes in a large number of financial institutions along with debt guarantees to cool down and eventually correct the escalating crisis. Structural imbalances still exist because of the difficulty in keeping pace with new and increasingly complex financial models in the multi-trillion-dollar economy. There is a need to mitigate risk, not transmit it.

Now, is there not something of a parallel here with our antiquated development control model, and the environment as a whole? Not the parts we thankfully protect by law such as National Parks, but the rest: the ecosystems, the cities, the suburbs, and the embryonic megapolitan corridors. There is a strong if not overwhelming argument that this is where individual freedoms stop and community interests come into play.

It might be said that the United States has a long-time, love-hate relationship with planning, reflecting a traditional wariness about government intervention, and perhaps also tied to the long-held view by many that land is simply a commodity to be traded. The sanctity of property rights coupled with an innate suspicion of authority is almost a religion, and defended as such. As a result, coordinated planning is subject to the indeterminate exigencies of land assembly, which is scarcely an adequate recipe for controlled urbanization.

We must remember that no one is trying to prevent development but to sensibly redirect it in order to best serve our metropolitan regions through sensible preservation and resource protection, together with place enhancement and everything that must accompany this in terms of land use control. It is inevitable that smart growth must on occasion deny the most immediate economic return, but in practice this often comes down merely to calming or diversifying expectation. We should not get into arguments over "essential" or "productive" use of land, outside the constraints associated with growth management that are set to define exactly this purpose. All this does not prevent legal appeals.

European urban environments that we admire so much and visit so frequently have not evolved their livable characteristics into modern times by accident. Firm controls are in place to constrain, protect, and direct development, all subject to prolonged consultation with stakeholders, and that includes the public at large.

The freedoms inherent in our Constitution have to be used with suitable restraint,

and the mechanisms that regulate these must be periodically evaluated to ensure they are realistically serving their intended purpose.

As urbanists we have to dispense with an overdose of theory and wrest back the planning and urban design system from property interests, lawyers, traffic engineers, and traditionally dominant economic forces on behalf of the community. It is, in passing, a message to our New Urbanism fraternity to look beyond small scale, self-contained, privately sponsored developments, albeit with the admirable intentions of replacing sprawl with improved neighborhood design, within its hierarchy of "transect zones" from the urban fringe to the urban core.

Joel Garreau posed the plaintive question, "if the future is out there, will we ever get good at it?" The 300-year-old Savannah provides us with a robust urban model, with a sound plan, and intricate fabric. There is much we can learn from this if we choose to do so.

And that is all I am going to say on the matter.

God bless, and Godspeed.

The typical Savannah street represents the most responsive of urban components, able to accommodate varied and overlapping elements that contribute to an overall sense of consistency tempered by difference.

And so we are standing on the front porch of Magnolia Hall in mid-afternoon. The hurricane has passed over, a lemon shaded sun hovers uncertainly in a hazy sky as we gaze out at a Forsyth Park swathed in piles of debris, tree branches collapsed full-tilt or lying horizontal on the grass along with the splintered remains of cracked stumps.

Mo and Martha B. are staying on for a few days to work on impending curriculums, and are smiling warmly and proffering hands and arms that extend from handshakes to bear hugs.

Mo promises us that he will edit our various presentations and privately asks if I can lend a hand, or two preferably. The intention is to publish these as a consolidated account of our collective thoughts and ideas.

Our individual flights to various US cities and beyond span several hours, but we have agreed to travel to the airport together. Angel from Paris, Texas comes along for the ride, and to ensure that Schlomo, who is still wearing his bandage, gets on the right plane.

The bond of comradeship is reinforced by promises to each other that we will keep in close touch, make prolonged visits to each other's home bases, and jointly entertain the possibility of follow-up seminars.

Thirty minutes later we arrive and disembark, struggling with cases, large and small, and holding on to shoulder satchels and handbags. Schlomo unloads a large rucksack, Jean-Paul a smart Samsonite suitcase. Most struggle with wheelie cases. We maneuver everything into the terminal, either pushing or pulling, check in individually, and meet in a coffee shop.

I note that communal banter is giving way to private intimacies and not a few self-conscious tears. I am pleased that my flight to New York's Kennedy Airport where I change for a fifteen-hour flight to Hong Kong is called first. I smile and wave goodbye. It has been a long week.

POSTSCRIPT

Mo has yet to find a publisher for our collective thoughts although several are said to be interested, and he hopes we might yet stimulate a bidding war. In the meantime he is attempting to negotiate serialisation in the *Harvard Review*, and is a keynote speaker at the next conference on The Importance of Team Spirit to be held in Bali, Indonesia.

Martha B. continues to stay within her circle of competence, supporting Mo dutifully, ensuring he does not bow to authority, and stoking his self-belief in invincibility up to a point that coincides with whether she agrees with him or not. On the side she edits a journal devoted to urban poetry and contributes generously to its content.

Dan Schlomo successfully persuaded Angel from Paris, Texas to take up a course of advanced photographic studies in downtown Los Angeles, by happy chance only a stone's throw from UCLA where she lives happily with Schlomo in a commune with four other couples. Her surprisingly artistic photographic output is subsidized by work as a cocktail waitress three nights a week at film parties held at the Disney Concert Hall. Schlomo, who has twice been married and divorced, likes to quote Samuel Johnson to the effect that their happy state represents the triumph of hope over experience. He is presently finishing a book on Zapp's Theory of Constructive Deconstruction, which predicts the instability of self-organizing workshops built around planning theory, although he has had certain problems finalizing the exact title. As a result he has obtained several large travel grants and is on the shortlist for tenure. A possible hurdle, however, is being under a threat of suspension for attempting to boost UCLA library attendance by surreptitiously replacing a shelf full of volumes dedicated to the Modern Movement with a complete set of Victoria's Secret catalogs.

Brit Kris moved from Boston to New York where she shares a roomy duplex in Tribeca with Jean-Paul Gournier. She teaches a course on Women in Planning at Parsons, occupies a corner space in Jean-Paul's office, and works on expanding the repertoire of his consultancy to include extremely extensive stakeholder charrettes, for which Jean-Paul is suitably impressed although not overwhelmingly appreciative. They continue to refine dual PowerPoint presentations and have become essential faculty members at New Urbanism conferences.

Miles Styles, after several months of Facebook correspondence, moved to New Haven and into Agnita van der Kampan's clapboard cottage, exchanging expertise on the European City for the History Department of a local school, despite ongoing doubts about the US public education system. Agnita continues to wear tight, two-piece suits and short skirts, to the grudging acknowledgement of the Wellesley College faculty, the admiration of students, and the constant delight of Miles, tempered only by an unforeseen transfer to maternity apparel several weeks ago. Agnita continues to develop geographic information computer models and flits between five screens in her university office and two in the cottage. Miles, who uses an iPad solely for emails as a reluctant concession to contemporary communication, is writing a book, *The Grid and the Cell* in longhand on foolscap paper.

Apolonia Karawice perceptively decided that Terry Fulbright needed some maternal care and affection. Having made a brief visit to his small apartment in Philadelphia she made the prompt decision that they would be more mutually comfortable at Cornell. Moreover, within a week she had, through her Faculty contacts, successfully transferred his five-year university exchange accordingly. Terry is now completing his post-doctoral research on the Metaphysical and Paranormal Dimensions of the American Suburb, and is taking a part-time course on Horse Whispering. Apolonia is largely engaged supervising groups of post-graduate students, occasionally distributing to them the fruits of her vegetable garden that she and Terry tend with both time and care.

For myself, I am back in Hong Kong, situated pretty well in the geographic center of Asia, where I have lived happily for forty years and from whence, notwithstanding the impact of the occasional typhoon swinging in from the South China Sea, I continue to research, ruminate, and write. When this begins to pale I go out onto the streets and attempt to illustrate my narratives. I am what some people like to call an Old China Hand, which, strictly speaking, gives me no right whatsoever to comment on American planning.

With the presidential election finally over, the best reality TV show fell back to earth, and proved the danger of relying too much on opinion polls. A victory for Donald Trump defied all the odds, shocked political and business elites, and initially, but only temporarily, sent financial markets and many neutral observers around the world into panic. In her concession speech, Hillary Clinton said she hoped Mr. Trump would be a successful president for all Americans and offered to work with her Republican rival despite being unfairly identified by half the voting population by the "crooked" epithet.

Having called for national unity, Trump declared that America will get along with all other nations and that while it was prudent to put America's interests first, it was necessary to deal fairly with everyone, something that several months later continues to be elusive in its intent.

House Speaker Paul Ryan stated that, "Trump heard a voice out in this country that no one else heard … He connected with people in ways that no one else did," although, mainly via Twitter.

Former president, Obama said he and Mr. Trump have had their differences, but that "the presidency is bigger than any of us."

ACKNOWLEDGEMENTS

The opportunity to delive into the intriguing history of Savannah arose from an invitation to undertake a short teaching stint at the Savannah College of Art and Design. I would like to firstly thank Robert Dickensheets, who at the time was Director of External Relations for facilitating my visit, and the many staff and students I was able to meet and talk with. During his long association with SCAD, Bob served as Professor of Historic Preservation which spanned the College's award-winning conservation and rehabilitation programme in Savannah, France and Hong Kong. I appreciated my discussions and exchange of ideas with Christian Sottile, SCAD Professor of Architecture and founder of the urban design and civic architecture practice Sottile and Sottile in Savannah; and who led design of the SCAD Museum of Art; Ryan Madson, Professor of Urban Design; and Professor Hsu-Jen Huang, Professor of Architecture. It was during these conversations and discussions that an extended framework for the book began to take shape. Tom Thompson, the Executive Director of the Metropolitan Planning Commission was a fountain of knowledge on current planning programmes in the city. I would also like to acknowledge the help and advice given by Kevin Klinkenberg, Head of the Savannah Development and Renewal Authority.

I was fortunate to be able to discuss the preservation process of Savannah, that has taken place over the last five decades, with Emma Adler, who with her late husband Lee Adler realized that Savannah's past was the key to its future, and helped to establish the Historic Savannah Foundation, effectively saving many of the city's finest buildings from the wrecking ball.

I would like to thank my long-time friends and colleagues at URBIS, in particular Alexander Duggie, Alan Macdonald, Sion Edwards, Craig Doubleday, Tim Osborne, David Morkel and Iris Hoi for their constant support. I am especially grateful to my assistant Lily Tam for her invaluable help in typing and co-ordinating manuscript drafts and her assistance with the editing process.

My great thanks and appreciation to Gordon Goff, Publisher and Managing Director of ORO Editions, and to Jake Anderson the Managing Editor for their encouragement and overwhelming efficiency in producing the book in almost record time.

I would also like to thank Mary Palmer Linnemann at the Hargrett Rare Book and Manuscript Library, University of Georgia for her help and advice in procuring historical maps of Savannah.

REFERENCES
AND SUGGESTED
READINGS

Seeking Savannah draws on many sources across a wide spectrum of thought and activity. A number of the publications on this list I have had on my shelves for twenty years or more, while others I have read and referenced during preparation of this publication. The list is, therefore, in large part a personal one. Certain critical lines of thought I have reconstituted and inserted into the mouths of my fictional characters during imagined philosophical deliberations, having emerged from my interpretation of many of these sources. I have highlighted a number of these for their authoritative insights on certain aspects of planning and design.

My knowledge of Savannah before my first visit was focused largely on the colonial city and its elegant and restrained design vocabulary rather than the evolution of the settlement. Walter J. Fraser's deft chronology and synthesis of events in *Savannah in the Old South* from 1733 until the mid-nineteenth century forms a fascinating and comprehensive account of historical developments set against a backdrop of unfolding political events, and I am happy to acknowledge a number of these valuable references. Thomas D. Wilson's *The Oglethorpe Plan* introduces a detailed perspective of the planning framework and its original intent, which reflected a social idealism towards building a model colony. For much of the background on slave conditions and inequalities in the approach to the Civil War and its aftermath, I am indebted to Jacqueline Jones's *Saving Savannah*. For the contemporary approach to planning I am grateful to the many sources in Savannah, and to the merits of the analysis contained in *The Comprehensive Plan for Savannah*, and the *Downtown Savannah Master Plan* produced by Chatham County-Savannah Metropolitan Planning Commission and the Savannah Development and Renewal Authority. These form clear statements of intention on how to both sustain and extend the best characteristics of the city. Chan Sieg's *The Squares* sets out a comprehensive description of Savannah's historic squares, with recourse to the Georgia Historical Society's archives. Also, I would like to acknowledge Lee and Emma Adler's *Savannah Renaissance*, which sets out an inspiring record of how the Historic District was saved from the forces of destruction in the 1950s, and I am grateful to my friend Bob Dickensheets who arranged a lunch with Emma who, from her prodigious memory, kindly set me straight on a number of facts.

The discourse on how and why Savannah came into being – ***Why Savannah*** and ***The Path to the Plan***, introduce sources that I have partly explored in my books on patterns of urbanization elsewhere, reflecting the important fact that Britain and other nations, with both trading and proselytizing intent, were not just exploring the Americas during the 16th, 17th, and 18th centuries, but were also on a strong colonizing course in Asia with a range of different outcomes. In North America there was an important emphasis on a form of colonial urbanization through re-settlement after the European Reformation, albeit with an underlying ideological agenda. But there was another important driver of change happening in Europe during this period – an intellectual and revolutionary philosophy that was aimed at achieving enlightenment and new forms of social equity. I have drawn on and referenced a number of publications that illuminate these aspects, including Peter Hall's *Cities and Civilization*; Robert Home's *Of Planting and Planning: The Making of British Colonial Cities*; Lewis Mumford's *The City in History* and Spiro Kostof's *The City Shaped and The City Assembled*

The merits of the Savannah Plan have been widely documented, but its inspirational design roots, centralized around the flexibility of the urban structure, remain open to speculation ranging widely from ancient city-building regimes, Renaissance designers, colonial precedents, and London's own rebuilding program, all of which were reportedly familiar to James Oglethorpe. This is referenced by histories of city form, some of them representing far-reaching utopian concepts.

The Heterotopia that infiltrates the City reflects theories that arose through the writings of Michael Foucault and Henry Lefebvre, usually in a translated form, which includes Foucault's *Politics, Philosophy, Culture: Interviews and Other Writings* edited by L. Kritzman. Its association with city development and urban design represents the counter-sites of "difference" that we now acknowledge as contributing sets of changing values within the community relating to aspects of exclusion and social balance. A further valuable reference is *Heterotopia and the City* edited by Michiel Dehaene and Lieven De Cauter. David Grahame Shane in *Recombinant Urbanism* has insightfully drawn on heterotopias as part of a detailed discussion on city modeling.

The discussions on American urbanism are inserted as a running dialogue interspersed within sections on the historical growth of Savannah. These sections present a counterpart to the single city through an examination of five aspects.

Planning the Promised Land examines the urban history of America from the mid-nineteenth century and draws out the conflicting influences that have created profound cultural impacts on planning directions up to the present time. I particularly commend *American Urban Form* by Sam Bass Warner and Andrew H. Whittemore; *America's Urban History* by Lisa Krissoff Boehm and Steven H. Covet; *The Evolution of American Urban History* by Howard P. Chudacoff, Judith Smith, and Peter C. Baldwin; and the incisive *New Urbanism and American Planning: The Conflict of Cultures* by Emily Talen.

The Enigmatic Frontier charts the growth of suburban development and the forces that brought this about. Kenneth Jackson's *Crabgrass Frontier*, Dolores Hayden's *Building Suburbia* and Robert Fishman's *Bourgeois Utopias* set out in great detail the reasons behind the growth of American suburbia. References include both historical texts on city expansion influences, the rapid growth in the post World War II period, and the rise of edge conurbations and sprawl that pose continuing problems for sustainable land use planning. *The Limitless City* by Oliver Gillham offers a comprehensive examination of the definition and origins of sprawl and many other aspects of the sprawl debate. Jamen Kunstler's *The Geography of Nowhere* is what first put me on the track of what was happening to America's "Human made Landscape." I must also applaud Joel Garreau for his notable research on Edge cities, and for some memorable asides, some of which I have freely quoted.

The Elastic City debates the problems and potential of reshaping the metropolitan and even the megapolitan regions through a more coordinated regional emphasis on growth and development trends that American is currently encountering. The profound transformation of America's metropolitan landscape is admirably set out in Arthur C. Nelson's *Reshaping Metropolitan America*. Some of the facts and figures came from the comprehensive volume *Megapolitan America: A New Vision for Understanding America's Metropolitan Geography* by Arthur C. Nelson and Robert E. Lang (American Planning Association, 2011). The evolution of megapolitan thinking emanates from Jean Gottman, and was taken up by Robert Yaro from the Regional Plan Associations as a term that reflects current trends in metropolitan integration. Jean Gottman's *Since Megalopolis* is a seminal work on America's expanding metropolitan regions. I am particularly appreciative of the insights on "elasticity" in terms of metropolitan area growth extensively researched by David Rusk and set out in *Cities without Suburbs*.

Reconciling the Urban-Suburban Divide in large part represents a discussion on the compact, mixed-use, and walkable city or township, of which Savannah is an exemplar model. I commend the publications of theory and practice of the New Urbanism set out by Andres Duany, Elizabeth Plater-Zyberk, and Jeff Speck in *Suburban Nation*, and by Congress for the New Urbanism principles; Jonathan Barnett's *Redesigning Cities*; and *The Fractured*

Metropolis; and the thoughtful publications by Peter Calthorpe, in particular, *The Regional City and Urbanism in the Age of Climate Change. Tomorrow's Cities, Tomorrow's Suburbs* by the American Planning Association poses the interesting question as to whether cities can became dominant again and whether it is possible to restore vibrant life to the suburbs.

Responsive Urbanism examines the scope to reconfigure the urban landscape through a range of existing and potential measures including smart growth, shaping neighborhoods, retrofitting strategies, and legal issues surrounding land development. *The New Urbanism Best Practice Guide* was an authoritative sourcebook, as was *Resilient Sustainable Cities* by Leonie J. Pearson, Peter W. Newtown, and Peter Roberts. Jonathan Barnett's *The Fractured Metropolis* sets out means to reshape the metropolitan region while restoring older cities. *Cities and Suburbs* by Bernadette Hanlon, John Rennie Short, and Thomas J. Vicinu sets out a systematic examination of new metropolitan realities in the US, also, Sonia A. Hirt's *Zoned in the USA*. For additional reading on retrofitting I commend *Retrofitting Suburbia*, by Ellen Dunham-James and June Williamson and the latter's publication *Designing Suburban Futures*. In covering the tangled issue of Constitutional legalities I am pleased to acknowledge the excellent chapters on "Smart Growth" and "The Constitution" by Brian W. Blaesser and Jerold S. Kayden respectively, in *Smart Growth: Form and Consequences* edited by Terry S. Szold and Armando Carbonell. These are both insightful and timely publications.

Because of the nature of the book as a discursive means of presentation, I have avoided actual references in the text unless a specific quote or line of thought can be attributed, but I would like to acknowledge the following that have served to provide authoritative and distinctive insights into particular aspects of the story I have set out. References are necessarily overlapping and are set out below by author in alphabetical order. If any omissions have occurred, the author will be pleased to correct them in future editions.

Abrahamson, Mark. *Urban Enclaves: Identity and Place in America.* (New York: St. Martin's Press, 1996).

Adler, Lee. *Historic Savannah.* Historic Savannah Foundation, 1968.

Alberti, Leone Battista. *Ten Books of Architecture.* (Landon, 1955 (De re aedificatoria), 1452).

Alexander, Christopher. *The Timeless Way of Building.* (Oxford University Press, 1979).

Arendt, et al. *Charter of the New Urbanism.* (McGraw Hill, 2000).

Bachelard, Gaston. *The Poetics of Space.* Trans., Maria Jolas. (Boston: Beacon Press, 1969).

Bacon, Edmund. *Design of Cities.* (London: Thames and Hudson, 1974).

Bailey, Anne J. and Walter J. Fraser Jr. Portraits of Conflict, A Photographic History of Georgia in the Civil War. (Fayetteville: University of Arkansas Press, 1997).

Bailey, Anne J. and Walter J. Fraser Jr. *Portraits of Conflict, A Photographic History of Georgia in the Civil War.* (Fayetteville: University of Arkansas Press, 1997).

Barnett, Jonathan. *Urban Design as Public Policy: Practical Methods for Improving Cities.* (McGraw Hill, 1974).

Barnett, Jonathan. *The Fractured Metropolis: Improving the New City, Restoring the Old City, Reshaping the Region.* (West View Press, 1996).

Barnett, Jonathan. "Social Equity and Metropolitan Growth," Ed. John C. Keene in *Planning for a New Century, The Regional Agenda.* (Island Press, 2000).

Barnett, Jonathan. *Redesigning Cities: Principles, Practice, Implementation.* (Planners Press, American Planning Association, 2003).

Bartley, Numan V. *The Creation of Modern Georgia.* (Athens: University of Georgia Press, 1990).

Beathey, Timothy, and Manning, Kristy. *The Ecology of Place: Planning for Environment, Economy and Community.* (Washington DC: Island Press, 1997).

Benjamin A. *The American Builder's Companion.* Reprint of the 1827 original. (Dover Publications, 1969).

Bentley I., Alcock A., Murrain P., McGlynn G., and Smith G. *Responsive Environments: A Manual for Designers.* (London: The Architectural Press, 1985).

Berger, Alan. *Drosscape Wasting Land in Urban America.* (Princeton Architectural Press, 2006).

Berlin, Ira. *Slaves without Masters: The Free Negro in the Antebellum South.* (New York: Vintage Press, 1976).

Besel. "Back to the Future: New Urbanism and the Rise of Neotraditionalism," eds. Karl and Andreescu Viviana in *Urban Planning.* (University Press of America, 2013).

Boehm, Lisa Krissoff, and Covey, Steven H. *America's Urban History.* (New York: Routledge, 2015).

Bogart, William T. *Don't Call it Sprawl: Metropolitan Structure in the Twenty-First Century.* (Cambridge University Press, 2006).

Boyer, Christine M. *Cyber Cities: Visual Perception in the Age of Electronic Communication.* (New York: Princeton Architectural Press, 1996).

Brownell, Blaine A., and David R. Goldfield eds. *The City in Southern History: The Growth of Urban Civilization in the South.* (Port Washington, NY: Kennikat Press, 1977).

Calthorpe, Peter. *The Next American Metropolis: Ecology, Community, and the American Dream.* (Princeton Architectural Press, 1993).

Calthorpe, Peter and Fulton, William. *The Regional City.* (Island Press, 2001).

Calthorpe, Peter and Lerup, Lars. *New Urbanism* (Michigan Debates on Urbanism, Volume II, Arts Press, 2005).

Calthorpe, Peter. *Urbanism in the Age of Climate Change.* (Washington DC: Island Press, 2011).

Carmona, Ed. *Explorations in Urban Design: An Urban Design Research Primer.* (Ashgate Publishing Limited, 2014).

Caro, Robert A. *The Power Broker: Robert Moses and the Fall of New York.* (New York: Alfred A. Knopf, 1974).

Castells, Manuel. *The Urban Question.* (London: Edward Arnold, 1977).

Chambers, Iain. *Border Dialogues: Journeys in Postmodernity.* (London: Routledge, 1990).

Chatham County-Savannah Comprehensive Plan. (Tricentennial Plan 1733–2033, April, 2005).

Chetty, R., Hendren, H., Kline, P., and Saez, E. *The Equality of Opportunity Project* (https://www.rc.fas. harvard.edu/the-equality-of-opportunity-project/)

Chudacoff, Howard P.; Smith, Judith; and Baldwin, Peter C. *The Evolution of American Urban History* (Pearson, 2015).

Coase R. H., *The Wealth of Nations* (15 Economic Inquiry 309, 1977).

Coleman, Kenneth. *A History of Georgia*, University of Georgia Press, 1991.

Downtown Savannah Master Plan: Preserving Our Past, Embracing Our Future. City of Savannah, Chatham County-Savannah Metropolitan Planning Commission, and Savannah Development and Renewal Authority, 2007.

Congress for the New Urbanism and The US Department of Housing and Urban Development. *Principles for Inner City Neighborhood Design, HOPE VI, and the New Urbanism.*

Cullingworth, Barry, and Caves, Roger W. *Planning in the USA: Policies, Issues and Processes* (Routledge, 2009).

Davis, Mike. *City of Quartz: Excavating the Future in Los Angeles.* (London, 1990).

Dehaene, Michiel, and De Cauter, Lieven, eds. *Heterotopia and the City: Public Space in a Postcivil Society.* (Routledge, 2008).

Design Manual for the Savannah Historic District. (The Chatham County – Savannah Metropolitan Planning Commission, 2011).

Comprehensive Plan for Savannah. (Chatham County Board of Commissioners and the Mayor and Aldermen of the City of Savannah, 2006).

Duany, Andres, Plater-Zyberk, Elizabeth, and Speck, Jeff. *Suburban Nation: The Rise of Sprawl and the Decline of the American Dream.* (New York: North Point, 2000).

Dunham-Jones, Ellen, and Williamson, June. *Retrofitting Suburbia: Urban Design Solutions for Redesigning Suburbs.* (John Wiley and Sons, 2009).

Eaton, Ruth. *Ideal Cities: Utopianism and the (Un) Built Environment.* (Thames and Hudson, 2002).

Ellin, Nan. *Integral Urbanism.* (Routledge, 2006).

Ewing, R., and Hamidi, S. *Costs of Sprawl.* (New York, Routledge, 2017).

330

Ferguson, Niall. *Empire: How Britain made the Modern World*. (Allen Lane, 2003).

Fishman, Robert. *Bourgeois Utopias: The Rise and Fall of Suburbia*. (New York: Basic Books, 1987).

Florida, Richard. *Cities and the Creative Class*. (New York: Routledge, 2005).

Foucault, Michael. "Of Other Spaces: Utopias and Heterotopias." In *Architecture Culture 1943–68*: ed. Joan Oakman. (Cambridge, MA: MIT Press, 1998).

Foucault, Michael. *Politics, Philosophy, Culture: Interviews and Other Writings*. Ed. L. Kritzman. (New York: Routledge, 1988).

Fraser Jr., Walter J. *Savannah in the Old South*. (The University of Georgia Press, 2003).

Gallay, Alan. *The Formation of a Planter Elite: Jonathan Bryan and the Southern Colonial Frontier*. (Athens: University of Georgia Press, 1989).

Gandelsonas, Mario. *X-Urbanism: Architecture and the American City*. (New York: Princeton Architectural Press, 1987).

Gans, Herbert. *The Levittowners: Ways of Life and Politics in a New Suburban Community*. (New York: Pantheon, 1967).

Garreau, Joel. *Edge City: Life on the New Frontier*. (Doubleday, 1991).

Gehl, Jan, and Gemzoe, Lars. *New City Spaces*. (The Danish Architectural Press, 2001).

Giedion, S. *Space, Time and Architecture*. (Harvard University Press).

Gillham, Oliver. *The Limitless City: A Primer on the Urban Sprawl Debate*. (Island Press, 2002).

Glaeser, Edward. *Triumph of the City: How our Greatest Invention Makes Us Richer, Smarter, Greener, Healthier and Happier*. (New York: Penguin, 2011).

Gore, A. *Our Choice: A Plan to Solve the Climate Crisis*. (Emmaus, PA: Rodale Books, 2009).

Gosling, David, and Gosling, Maria Christina. *The Evolution of American Urban Design: A Chronological Anthology*. (Chichester, UK: Wiley-Academy, 2003).

Gottmann, Jean, and Harper, Robert A. eds. *Since Megalopolis: The Urban Writings of Jean Gottmann*. (Baltimore: The John Hopkins University Press, 1990).

Gratz, Roberta Brandes. *The Living City: How America's Cities are being Revitalized by Thinking Small in a Big Way*. (Simon and Schuster, 1989).

Gratz, Roberta Brandes, and Mintz, Norman. *Cities Back from the Edge New Life for Downtown*. (John Wiley, 2000).

Hall, Peter. *Cities of Tomorrow: An Intellectual History of Urban Planning and Design in the Twentieth Century*. (Oxford Blackwell, 1988).

Hall, Peter. *Cities and Civilization*. (New York: Pantheon 1998).

Hanlon, B., Short, J. R., and Vicino, T. J. *Cities and Suburbs: New Metropolitan Realties in the U.S.* (New York: Routledge, 2010).

Harvey, David. *Social Justice and the City*. (London: Edward Arnold, 1973).

Harvey, David. *The Condition of Postmodernity: An Enquiry into the Origins of Cultural Change*. (Cambridge Mass: Basil Blackwell, 1989).

Hayden, Dolores. *The Power of Place*. (Cambridge: MIT Press, 1995).

Hayden, Dolores. *Building Suburbia: Green Fields and Urban Growth*. (New York: Pantheon Books, 2003).

Hegemann, Werner, and Peets, Elbert. *The American Vitruvius: An Architects' Handbook of Civic Art*. (New York: Princeton Architectural Press, 1988).

Hirt, Sonia A. *Zoned in the USA: The Origins and Implications of American Land-Use Regulation*. (Cornell University Press, 2014).

Home, Robert. *Of Planting and Planning: The Making of British Colonial Cities*. (London: E & FN Spon, 1977).

Horan, T. A. *Digital Places: Building Our City of Bits*. (Urban Land Institute, 2000).

Inman, Robert P., ed. *Making Cities Work: Proposals and Policies for Urban America*. (Princeton University Press, 2009).

Jackson, Kenneth T. *Crabgrass Frontier: The Suburbanization of the United States*. (Oxford University Press, 1985).

Jacobs, Jane. *The Death and Life of Great American Cities*. (New York: Modern Library Edition, 1993).

Jacobs, Jane. *Cities and the Wealth of Nations – Principles of Economic Life*. (New York: Random House, 1984).

Jencks, C. *Heteropolis*. (London: Academy Editions, 1973).

Jenks, Mike, Kozak, Daniel, and Takkanon, Pattaramen, eds. *World Cities and Urban Form: Fragmented, Polycentric, Sustainable?* (Routledge, 2008).

Jones, Jacqueline. *Saving Savannah: The City and the Civil War*. (New York: Alfred A. Knopf, 2008).

Katz, Peter. *The New Urbanism: Toward an Architecture of Community*. (McGraw-Hill, 1994).

Kennedy, Benjamin ed. *Muskets, Cannon Balls and Bombs: Nine Narratives of the Siege of Savannah in 1779*. (Savanna: Beehive Press, 1974).

Kostof, Spiro. *The City Shaped and 'The City Assembled.'* (Bulfinch Press, 1991).

Kunstler, James. *The Geography of Nowhere: The Rise and Decline of America's Man-Made Landscape*. (New York: Simon and Schuster, 1993).

Lane, Mills ed. *General Oglethorpe's Georgia: Colonial Letters, 1733–1743*. (Savanna: Beehive Press, 1993).

Lang, Robert E. *Edgeless Cities: Exploring the Elusive Metropolis*. (Brooklyn Press, 2002).

Lee and Adler, Emma. *Savannah Renaissance*. (Charleston: Wyrick and Company, 2003).

Lee, F. D., and Agnew, J. L. *Historical Record of the City of Savannah*, http://quod.lib.umich.edu/m/moa/AFJ9515.0001?rgn=main;view=fulltext

Lefebvre, Henri. *Writings on Cities*. (Oxford: Blackwall, 1996).

Lerski, Hanna H. *William Jay: Itinerant English Architect, 1792–1837*. (Lanham, MD: University Press of America, 1983).

Lofland, Lyn H. *The Public Realm: Exploring the City's Quintessential Social Territory*. (New York: Aldine de Gruyter, 1998).

Lucy, William H., and Phillips, David L. *Tomorrow's Cities, Tomorrow's Suburbs*. (The American Planning Associations, 2006).

Lynch, Kevin. *A Theory of Good City Form*. (MIT Press, 1981).

Lynch, Kevin. *What Time is This Place*. (Cambridge: MIT Press, 1972).

Marx, Leo. *The Machine in the Garden: Technology and the Pastoral Ideal in America.* (London: Oxford University Press, 1964).

McHarg, Ian. *Design with Nature.* (Doubleday, 1969).

Mitchell, W. B. *Classic Savannah.* (New Orleans: St. Martin Publishing Company, 1991).

Morris, A. E. J. *History of Urban Form: Before the Industrial Revolution.* (George Godwin Limited, 1979).

Muir, J. A *Thousand Mile Walk to the Gulf.* (Boston: The Riverside Press, 1916).

Mumford, Lewis. *The City in History: Its Origins, Its Transformations and its Prospects.* (Mariner Books, 1968).

Myers, Robert Mansion ed. *The Children of Pride: A True Story of Georgia and the Civil War.* (New Haven: Yale University Press, 1972).

Neal, Peter, ed. *Urban Villages and the Making of Communities.* (Spon Press, 2003).

Nelson, Arthur C., and Lang, Robert E. *Megapolitan America: A New Vision for Understanding America's Metropolitan Geography.* (American Planning Association, Planners Press, 2011).

Nelson, Arthur C. *Reshaping Metropolitan America: Development Trends and Opportunities to 2030.* (Island Press, 2012).

Newman, Oscar. *Defensible Space.* (New York: Macmillan, 1972).

Nye, David E. *American Technological Sublime.* (Cambridge, MA: MIT Press, 1994).

Oldenburg, Ray. *The Great Good Place.* (Paragon House, 1989).

Orfield, Myron. *Metropolitics: A Regional Agenda for Community and Stability.* (Cambridge, MA: Brookings Institutional Press, 1997).

Passell, Aaron. *Building the New Urbanism: Places, Professions, and Profits in the American Metropolitan Landscape.* (Routledge, 2013).

Paulson H. M. *On the Brink.* (Hachette Book Group, 2010).

Pearson, Leonie J., Newton, Peter W., and Roberts, Peter, eds. *Resilient Sustainable Cities: A Future.* (Routledge, 2014).

Pierce, Neal R., and Guskind, Robert. *Breakthroughs: Re-creating the American City.* (New Brunswick, SA: Transaction Publishers, 2013).

Porter, Douglas R. *Managing Growth in America's Communities.* (Island Press, 2008).

Puig, Arturo, Soria Y., ed. *Cerda: The five Bases of the General Theory of Urbanization.* (Electa, 1999).

Putnam, Robert. *Bowling Alone: The Collapse and Revival of American Community.* (Simon and Schuster, 2000).

Rodney L. *Looking Beyond Borderlines: North America's Frontier Imagination.* (New York: Routledge, 2017).

Ross, Benjamin. *Dead End: Suburban Sprawl and the Rebirth of American Urbanism.* (Oxford University Press, 2014).

Rowe, Colin, and Koetter, Fred. *Collage City.* (Cambridge, MA: MIT Press, 1978).

Rusk, David. *Cities without Suburbs.* (Washington DC: Woodrow Wilson Center Press, 2013).

Russell, Preston, and Hines, Barbara. *Savannah: A History of Her People Since 1733.* (Savannah: Frederic C Beil, 1992).

Ryan, Brent D. *Design After Decline: How America Rebuilds Shrinking Cities.* (Philadelphia: University of Pennsylvania Press, 2012).

Sassen, Saskia. *The Global City: New York, London, Tokyo.* (Princeton University Press, 1991).

Saunders, William S. "Sprawl and Suburbia." In a Harvard Design Magazine *Reader.* (Harvard University Graduate School of Design, 2005).

Scully, Vincent. *American Architecture and Urbanism.* (New York: Praeger, 1969).

Sennet, Richard. *The Uses of Disorder: Personal Identity and City Life.* (Faber and Faber, 1996).

Shane, David Grahame. *Recombinant Urbanism: Conceptual Modeling in Architecture, Urban Design, and City Theory.* (Wiley-Academy, 2005).

Shoup, D. *The High Cost of Free Parking.* (APA Planners Press, 2005).

Sieg, C. *The Squares.* (Norfolk: The Donning Company, 1996).

Sitte, Camillo. *The Birth of Modern City Planning.* Trans. by George R. Collins and Christiane Crasemann Colins. (New York: Rizzoli, 1986).

Smith, Derek. *Civil War Savannah.* (Savannah: Ferderic C. Beil, 1977).

Soja, Edward W. *Thirdspace: Journeys to Los Angeles and Other Real-and-Imagined Places.* (Blackwell, 1996).

Soja, Edward W. *Postmetropolis: Critical Studies of Cities and Regions.* (Blackwell, 2000).

Sorkin, Michael. *Variations on a Theme Park: The New American City and the End of Public Space.* (New York: Farrar, Straus and Giroux, 1992).

Spalding, Phinizy, and Harvey H. Jackson, eds. *Oglethorpe in Perspective: Georgia's Founder after Two Hundred Years.* (Tuscaloosa: University of Alabama Press, 1989).

Speck, Jeff. *Walkable City: How Downtown Can Save America, One Step at a Time.* (New York: Farrar, Straus and Giroux, 2012).

Stein, Clarence S. *Towards New Towns for America.* (MIT Press, 1956).

Steuteville, Robert, and Langdon, Philip. *New Urbanism Best Practices Guide.* (New Urban News Publications, 2009).

Szold, Terry S., and Carbonell, Armando. *Smart Growth: Form and Consequences.* (Lincoln Institute of Land Policy, 2002).

Tafuri, Manfredo. *Architecture and Utopia: Design and Capitalist Development.* (Cambridge, MA: MIT Press, 1988).

Talen, Emily. *New Urbanism and American Planning: The Conflict of Cultures.* (Routledge, 2005).

Taylor, William. *Cavalier & Yankee: The Old South and American National Character.* (Cambridge: Harvard University Press, 1979).

Toledano, Roulhac. *Savannah: Architectural and Cultural Treasures.* (New York: Wiley and Sons, 1997).

Turner, Frederick J. *The Frontier in American History.* (New York: H. Holt and Company, 1920).

Vance, James E. *This Scene of Man: The Role and Structure of the City in the Geography of Western Civilization.* (New York: Harper and Row, 1977).

Venturi, Robert. *Complexity and Contradiction in Architecture.* (London: Architectural Press, 1977).

Virilio, P. *The Lost Dimension and The Aesthetics of Disappearance.* Trans. by Daniel Mosherberg. (New York: Semiotext (E), 1991).

Warner, Sam Bass, and Whittemore, Andrew H. *American Urban Form: A Representative History.* (Cambridge, MA: MIT Press, 2012).

Webb, Michael. *The City Square.* (Thames and Hudson, 1990).

Whyte, William H. *The Exploding Metropolis.* (Garden City, NY: Doubleday, 1958).

Whyte, William H. *City: Rediscovering the Center.* (Doubleday, 1988).

Williamson, June. *Designing Suburban Futures: New Models from Build a Better Burb.* (Washington DC: Island Press, 2013).

Wilson, Thomas D. *The Oglethorpe Plan: Enlightenment Design in Savannah and Beyond.* (University of Virginia Press, 2012).

Zukin, Sharon. *Landscapes of Power.* (Berkeley and Los Angeles University of California Press, 1991).

Zukin, Sharon. *The Culture of Cities.* (Oxford: Blackwell, 1995).

Little Boxes: Malvina Reynolds, ©Omni Records 1962.

Hard Hearted Hannah (Publisher: ©Warner/Chappell Music Inc). Writers: Bob Bigelow, Charles Bates, Jack Yellen, and Milton Anger, 1924.

ORO Editions
Publishers of Architecture, Art, and Design
Gordon Goff: Publisher

www.oroeditions.com
info@oroeditions.com

Published by ORO Editions

Text by Peter Cookson Smith
Illustrations by Peter Cookson Smith unless otherwise noted
Book Design by Pablo Mandel
Managing Editor: Jake Anderson

10 9 8 7 6 5 4 3 2 1 First Edition

ISBN: 978-1-940743-71-4

Color Separations and Printing: ORO Group Ltd.
Printed in China.

ORO Editions makes a continuous effort to minimize the overall carbon footprint of its publications. As part of this goal, ORO Editions, in association with Global ReLeaf, arranges to plant trees to replace those used in the manufacturing of the paper produced for its books. Global ReLeaf is an international campaign run by American Forests, one of the world's oldest nonprofit conservation organizations. Global ReLeaf is American Forests' education and action program that helps individuals, organizations, agencies, and corporations improve the local and global environment by planting and caring for trees.